Biblical Interpretation

W. Randolph Tate

Biblical Interpretation

An Integrated Approach

THIRD EDITION

Biblical Interpretation: An Integrated Approach, 3d edition
1st edition © 1991
2d edition © 1997
3d edition © 2008
by Hendrickson Publishers, Inc.
P. O. Box 3473
Peabody, Massachusetts 01961-3473

ISBN 978-1-59856-080-0

Printed in the United States of America

First Printing — July 2008

Cover Art: Anonymous. Untitled 1920–1930. American Folk Art. Signed: Parkes. Oil on canvas. Ricco-Maresca Gallery, New York, N.Y.
Photo Credit: Ricco-Maresca Gallery / Art Resource, N.Y. Used with permission.

Library of Congress Cataloging-in-Publication Data

Tate, W. Randolph.
    Biblical interpretation : an integrated approach /
W. Randolph Tate.—3rd ed.
        p. cm.
    Includes bibliographical references and indexes.
    ISBN 978-1-59856-080-0 (alk. paper)
    1. Bible—Hermeneutics. I. Title.
    BS476.T375 2008
    220.601—dc22
                                        2008005391

Table of Contents

Unit II: The World Within the Text

Unit III: The World in Front of the Text

Unit IV: Integrating the Three Worlds

Appendixes: Synopses of Additional Interpretive Methods Employed by Scholars

Acknowledgments

I express special appreciation to Dr. Leon Golden of the Department of Humanities, the Florida State University for his catalytic role in the development of my interest in literary criticism. I also express gratitude to Evangel University for providing released time to pursue this project, to Dr. William Griffin, who was gracious enough to develop a program for the indexing, and to Dr. Mark House of Hendrickson Publishers for his editorial assistance in updating both the content and format for this new edition.

Preface to the Third Edition

Since the appearance of the 1997 revised edition of *Biblical Interpretation: An Integrated Approach,* the discipline of biblical studies has witnessed an explosion of critical praxes that have changed the face of hermeneutics so profoundly that a hermeneutics text without a discussion of these critical methodologies is severely limited in its vision. Over the last decade, biblical scholars have increasingly realized that interpretation always takes place within social locations that include interpretive methodologies which posture the reader before a text in particular ways by determining what kind of questions the reader asks of the text. Revisions that incorporate the developments in scholarship over the past decade are necessary for the book to have continuing relevance in the field of hermeneutics. For this reason, the third edition includes discussions of critical methodologies that I did not include in previous editions.

In response to students' and scholars' observations and recommendations, I have also made the following changes and additions:

1. Rather than placing descriptions (synopses) of critical methods exclusively in the last unit, I have included three of the most characteristic approaches pertaining to each of the three "worlds" of biblical interpretation at the end of each of the units where that world is discussed. Additional synopses related to each of the three worlds of interpretation can be found in the appendixes.

In this book I offer an approach to explicating texts that employs elements from a number of approaches from all three worlds: author, text, and reader. Since detailed treatment of these methods would make the book unwieldy as a text to be used in the classroom, I provide brief synopses that offer resources for further readings that reflect the current conditions of biblical hermeneutics. It has been my experience that most serious interpreters of texts are eclectic, either consciously or unconsciously borrowing insights and praxes from several interpretive methods. Although some interpreters focus on the text and its structures and strategies, they invariably find themselves employing historical data in their arguments. The intertextual critic is forced to know something about the literary past if he or she is to make sense of the literary allusions. Critics of the deconstructionist bent must also engage the past in order to understand the manner in which authors unconsciously inscribe marginalized elements of their cultures. They also must become knowledgeable of the history of interpretation. Rhetorical critics must examine the relationship between ideology and rhetorical structures. Feminist critics of all strands examine not only textual structures, but the language, institutions, and ideologies as they are reflected in the text in ways that marginalize segments of societies. Like deconstructionists, they also examine the history of interpretation. My point is that while we group the methods according to primary focus, readers should be aware that all critics find themselves working in all three worlds of author, text, and audience.

The fact is, however, that this is not a textbook on critical methodologies, but an introductory text on doing hermeneutics. I have not consciously adopted one single method, but think that an informed student of hermeneutics should be familiar with the options that the individual methods offer any interested reader. Once readers are familiar with the methods, they are free to borrow from each and combine insights as they see fit. I offer the synopses here to (a) introduce readers to the many doors of access that the methods present, (b) encourage interest in the methods and their potential roles in understanding texts more fully, and (c) assist the reader in recognizing the scope of biblical hermeneutics.

2. Given scholars' recognition of the constitutive role that readers and their presuppositions play in the interpretive enterprise, I have made some minor changes to ch. 8: What the Reader Brings to the Text.

3. I have added an index of subjects to make the book more user-friendly.

4. All of the above changes and additions, as well as new developments in the field of biblical interpretation, have necessitated an updated select bibliography.

Preface to the Revised Edition

I am more convinced than ever that the meaning of meaning is meaningless apart from the concept of intertextuality. By intertextuality I mean that human communication takes place within "con-texts." An author is a complex of "texts"—social, religious, linguistic, etc. An author can no more free herself from the influences of these "texts" than a zebra can remove its stripes. It is reasonable, therefore, to retain as an integral part of the discipline of hermeneutics the focus on researching the world of the author. More informed readers make better readers.

When we get right down to it, however, we read not authors, but texts. We interpret texts, not authors. Hermeneutics is first and foremost a discipline concerned with how readers assemble understandings of texts. This means that the primary focus of hermeneutics is the relationship between the enabling structures of a text and the activities of a reader. Consequently, a responsible hermeneutic will give a large portion of its attention to the strategies and structures of texts.

But like an author, a reader is also a complex of "texts." A reader can never stand outside these texts and examine a particular literary text from a position of Cartesian purity. Necessarily, then, hermeneutics has a third focus: that of the role of the reader. Readers read for a variety of purposes and under a variety of influences, and these purposes and influences are partially constitutive of understanding.

The focus of this revised edition has not changed. The focus on the three worlds remains intact. But I have attempted to place additional emphasis upon the relationship between text and reader by lengthening the discussion in ch. 7, "What Happens When We Read?"

A legitimate criticism has been that while talking about integrating the three worlds, I actually never did it. In response I have included an additional chapter on the Gospel of Mark in which I attempt to demonstrate the thesis that meaning really is the result of a conversation between a text and a reader, a conversation that is enhanced by attention to the world of the author.

A final word. Integrity demands that any hermeneutic should remain tentative. Indeed, included in any hermeneutic should be a place for conversation between those involved in the discipline. What I offer in this text is an approach that seems to work well for me and my students in our particular academic and religious contexts. I am, however, constantly in conversation with other approaches that differ sharply from the one offered here. I do not think that it is a healthy practice to engage in ideological warfare, but in a field of study where it is extremely difficult to define "the reader" and "the genre," we should always attempt to inhabit that shadowy space between the thinkable and the thing thought, always eschewing an either/or world in favor of an "and + and" one. This encourages conversation, and the very heart of hermeneutics is the conversation.

Preface

This is a book about interpretation, not a book of interpretations. It concerns the poetics of the discipline of hermeneutics. The book is not primarily prescriptive, but rather descriptive. In other words, I have not intentionally prescribed *a* hermeneutic, but I have offered a general description of the task of hermeneutics. Nonetheless, where there is thought there is also presupposition and thus an unavoidable prescriptive element. Presupposition is to thought as Sancho is to Don Quixote, a constant companion. First, therefore, I disclaim total objectivity as characterizing this work. To claim total objectivity for any activity communicated through the contextual and rhetorical nature of language is inexcusably presumptuous.

Second, as is to be expected of any introductory book, this work is not complete. Scholars have produced volumes on the various specialized areas of hermeneutics evidencing years of concentrated scholarly focus. In an introduction like this, limited treatment is necessarily the rule. It would be hoped, however, that this limited introduction to hermeneutics will have sufficient clarity and scope to hold the attention of its readers and be provocative enough to whet its readers' intellectual appetites.

Finally, I do not make the claim for definitiveness. A discipline as fluid as hermeneutics simply does not lend itself to this claim. Yet, those "who have ears to hear" will recognize that I have attempted to give audience to the range of interpretive voices presently jockeying for pole position. The implication is that all these voices deserve audience because they have valuable contributions to make to the discipline. Another implication is that hermeneutics cannot become a private exercise inseparably tied to systems of dogmas. Hermeneutics would become nothing more than individual hermeneutics of reduction. Part of hermeneutics is the art of conversation, a willingness to enter into a symposium of voices past and present. Hermeneutics in this sense becomes a hermeneutic of possibility, taking on the character of life itself, always adjusting itself to the fall of humankind into the solvency of time and history.

General

2d, 3d, 4th	second, third, fourth
B.C.E.	before the Common Era
C.E.	Common Era
ca.	circa
cf.	*confer,* compare
ch(s).	chapter(s)
e.g.	*exempli gratia,* for example
ed(s).	editor(s), edited by, edition(s)
et al.	*et alii,* and others
etc.	*et cetera,* and the rest
exp.	expanded
gen.	general
Gk.	Greek
i.e.	*id est,* that is
ibid.	*ibidem,* in the same place
KJV	King James Version of the Bible (Authorized Version)
lit.	literally
LXX	Septuagint (Greek translation of the Hebrew Bible)
NASB	New American Standard Bible
NIV	New International Version of the Bible
no.	number
NRSV	New Revised Standard Version of the Bible
NT	New Testament
OT	Old Testament
p(p).	page(s)
Pirqe 'Abot	The Sayings of the Fathers (Mishna)
repr.	reprinted
rev.	revised (by)
RSV	Revised Standard Version of the Bible
trans.	translator, translated by; transitive
v(v).	verse(s)
vol(s).	volume(s)

Resources

BDAG	W. Bauer, F. Danker, W. Arndt, and F. Gingrich, *A Greek-English Lexicon of the New Testament and Other Early Christian Literature*. 3d ed. 2000.
BTB	*Biblical Theology Bulletin*
ER	*Encyclopedia of Religion*
ExpT	*Expository Times*
Int	*Interpretation*
ISBE	*International Standard Bible Encyclopedia*
JAAR	*Journal of the American Academy of Religion*
JBL	*Journal of Biblical Literature*
JSOT	*Journal for the Study of the Old Testament*
JSOTSup	Journal for the Study of the Old Testament: Supplement Series
NTS	*New Testament Studies*
PMLA	*Publication of the Modern Language Association*
SBLMS	Society of Biblical Literature Monograph Series
TDNT	*Theological Dictionary of the New Testament*
VT	*Vetus Testamentum*

Biblical and Apocryphal Books

Gen	Genesis
Exod	Exodus
Lev	Leviticus
Num	Numbers
Deut	Deuteronomy
Judg	Judges
1–2 Sam	1–2 Samuel
1–2 Kgs	1–2 Kings
2 Chr	2 Chronicles
Esth	Esther
Ps(s)	Psalm(s)
Prov	Proverbs
Song	Song of Solomon
Isa	Isaiah
Jer	Jeremiah
Ezek	Ezekiel
Dan	Daniel

Hos	Hosea
Jon	Jonah
Mic	Micah
Nah	Nahum
Zech	Zechariah
Mal	Malachi
Bar	Baruch
Sir	Sirach
Wis	Wisdom of Solomon
Matt	Matthew
Rom	Romans
1–2 Cor	1–2 Corinthians
Gal	Galatians
Eph	Ephesians
Phil	Philippians
Col	Colossians
1 Thess	1 Thessalonians
1 Tim	1 Timothy
Phlm	Philemon
Heb	Hebrews
Jas	James
1–2 Pet	1–2 Peter
Rev	Revelation

Introduction

A JOURNEY INTO THREE WORLDS

Hermeneutics has traditionally been defined as the study of the locus of meaning and the principles of interpretation. Biblical hermeneutics, then, studies the locus of meaning and principles of biblical interpretation. Hermeneutics in the broad sense is bipolar: exegesis and interpretation. Exegesis is the process of examining a text to ascertain what its first readers would have understood it to mean. The varied set of activities which the hermeneut performs upon a text in order to make meaningful inferences is *exegesis*. Interpretation is the task of explaining or drawing out the implications of that understanding for contemporary readers and hearers. Thus, the transformation of these inferences into application or significance for the hermeneut's world is interpretation. Combine *exegesis* and *interpretation* with an examination of the hermeneut's presuppositional repertoire and we may speak of hermeneutics. The terms *hermeneutics* and *interpretation*, however, are often used interchangeably to refer to the process of determining the meaning and significance of a text. Through usage the term *interpretation* has become a comprehensive one. Not only does it refer to the applications inferred from exegesis, but it also refers to the entire process and poetics of hermeneutics. Since words mean what they mean through common usage, I use the terms *hermeneutics* and *interpretation* interchangeably, just as I do the two terms hermeneut and *interpreter.*

Carl Braaten sees hermeneutics as "the science of reflecting on how a word or an event in the past time and culture may be understood and become existentially meaningful in our present situation."[1] E. D. Hirsch Jr. assumes that hermeneutics involves explanation but is prefaced by understanding,[2] while Gadamer and Ricoeur argue that interpretation of texts does not exhaust the responsibility of the hermeneutical enterprise. Hermeneutics assumes the responsibility to move beyond the scientific

---

[1] Carl Braaten, *History and Hermeneutics* (Philadelphia: Fortress, 1966), 131.
[2] E. D. Hirsch Jr., "Objective Interpretation," *PMLA* 75 (1960): 463, 470–79.

explication of the text's language to the search for ultimate truth that is incarnate in the language of the text. According to Gadamer and Ricoeur, the search for ultimate reality through the language of the text is the most important task of hermeneutics. Duncan Ferguson defines hermeneutics simply as "the task of hearing what an ancient text has to say."[3]

The common ground shared by these and most other definitions of hermeneutics is literary meaning. Whether reference is to explanation, exegesis, or understanding, the construction of literary meaning is absolutely central to hermeneutics. But where exactly is meaning to be found, and how is it to be actualized? In present scholarship, there are three different groups of theories regarding the locus and actualization of meaning: *author-centered* (with attention directed to the world behind the text), *text-centered* (with the focus on the world within the text, or the textual world), and *reader-centered* (where the spotlight is trained upon the world in front of the text, or the reader's world). Since these three approaches are usually viewed as mutually exclusive in the articulation of meaning, and since one is often pitted against another, a brief canvas of each approach is not without value. (See ch. 9 for a more comprehensive discussion.)

Author-Centered Approaches to Meaning

Prior to the advent of New Criticism in the 1940s, hermeneutical interest converged on the author and the author's world. Meaning was assumed to lie in the author's intention, which was formulated in terms of the social, political, cultural, and ideological matrix of the author. Without an immersion into the author's world and the occasion which prompted the text, one could not attain meaning with any acceptable degree of plausibility. The text was seen as a shell with many layers. If the layers were appropriately peeled away, the scholar could discover the core and its original setting. This was the locus of meaning. The historical-critical method with its three attending criticisms—source, form, and redaction—pose important questions for interpreters. What circumstances prompted the author to write? What sources were used? What was the geographical location of the author and the ecclesiastical tradition of that location? What was the history of the text's devel-

---

[3] Hans Georg Gadamer, *Truth and Method* (New York: Seabury, 1975). Paul Ricoeur, *Essays on Biblical Interpretation* (ed. Lewis S. Mudge; Philadelphia: Fortress, 1980). Duncan Ferguson, *Biblical Hermeneutics: An Introduction* (Atlanta: John Knox, 1986), 6.

opment? Some of the more recent methods focus on the author's world as well as ask their own questions. What can we know about the psychological makeup of the author and how does this knowledge influence our understanding of the author's text? What were the social conventions and taboos of the author's world and how can we get at them? How were these social conventions and taboos reflected in rhetorical structures and strategies? These are the questions usually associated with social-scientific, socio-rhetorical, psychoanalytical, and tradition criticisms.

Several points argue against the purely historical approach and its locus of meaning. First, there is an inevitable gap between the originating moment in the author's mind and the cultural specificity of the author's language. In other words, can there ever be a complete guarantee that the author has successfully transferred authorial intention to the written page? Is the text a foolproof and undistorted mirror of the author's mind? These types of questions led Wimsatt and Beardsley to formulate their famous statement of the "intentional fallacy."[4] Second, with the inordinate amount of attention given to the world behind the text, the text itself has suffered from too little attention. Historical criticism has relentlessly sought to focus its illuminating searchlight upon the world behind the text, the real historical world within which a work of literature was given birth. The understanding (i.e., an understanding with any degree of plausibility) of the literary work hinges precariously upon a reconstruction of the work's historical milieu. It should be clear that the historical approach must ultimately lead to a view of the text as an artifact that can and must be understood by using the scientific tools of anthropology, archeology, and linguistics just as one would employ for any other artifact. But due to the historical method's exclusive focus on the world behind the text, the world within the text has been unduly neglected.

Text-Centered Approaches to Meaning

Since the 1950s a reversal in the way interpreters approach the text has occurred. With the modern emphasis on the autonomy of the text and the role of the reader in the production of meaning, scholars have dislodged the text from its historical mooring and set it adrift in a sea

---

[4] W. K. Wimsatt and Monroe Beardsley, "The Intentional Fallacy," in W. K. Wimsatt, *The Verbal Icon: Studies in the Meaning of Poetry* (Lexington: University of Kentucky Press, 1954), 3–18.

of relativity, where there are as many meanings of the text as there are waves of the sea. Rosenberg's assessment of the situation is extremely insightful. In his evaluation of David Gunn's belief in the text's autonomy, he observes that the political (and by implication, the historical, social and theological) dimensions of the text are made to be an incidental bonus in its unfolding as art, just as the historical investigations of the story made its artistic brilliance an incidental bonus in its unfolding as history. This persistent blind spot shared by the two disciplines (historical and literary criticisms)—the absence of a sense of necessary connection between the story's historical knowledge and its literary mode—is curious and interesting.[5]

Textual autonomy is the springboard for text-centered theories of meaning. This autonomy could not be stated more clearly than Abrams's claim that the author's "intention is irrelevant to the literary critic, because meaning and value reside within the text of the finished, free-standing, and public work of literature itself."[6] The renewed interest in the text itself instead of the world behind the text is the gift of what scholars today refer to as New Criticism and structuralism.

A text-centered approach is bittersweet. While it draws attention to the artistry of the text (New Criticism) and conventional literary codes (structuralism), the author (and to a great extent the reader) has been pronounced dead. But as I argue in unit I, although the meaning of a text may not be found in the author's world, at least our understanding of the text improves when we immerse ourselves in its history.[7]

Reader-Centered Approaches to Meaning

Different readers interpret a text differently. The various and complex reasons for this tautology will be the concern of unit III. The reasons are, however, associated with what might be called the reader's repertoire. The reader brings to the text a vast world of experience, presuppositions, methodologies, interests, and competencies. The reader must actualize the meaning that is only potential in the text. Most reader-oriented theories hold that a text means nothing until someone means something by it. More radical proponents of reader-response

---

[5] Joel Rosenberg, *King and Kin: Political Allegory in the Hebrew Bible* (Bloomington: Indiana University Press, 1986), 108.

[6] M. H. Abrams, *A Glossary of Literary Terms* (New York: Holt, Rinehart & Winston, 1981), 83.

[7] See Rosenberg, *King and Kin,* 106–8.

criticism go further to say that the reader creates the meaning of the text. Others, like Edgar V. McKnight, hold that meaning is produced by the mutual interaction between the text and reader.[8] According to this view, the text engages the reader as the reader engages the text. Meaning, then, is an invention by the reader in collaboration with the text rather than the intention of the author. The reader is constrained by the text, but is not divested of interests and presuppositions. The text is re-contextualized through the multicolored lenses of the reader. The fact is, however, that the hermeneutics of the world in front of the text involve more than the dialogic relationship between a reader and a text. In the last two decades scholars have introduced a number of issues that should be central to hermeneutics—the social location of both author and reader, the ideologies of authors and interpreters, the nature of language, the race, class, and gender of author and reader, the economics of author and reader, the textuality of history, and the historicity of texts to mention only a few.

An Integrated Approach to Meaning

To this point we have seen that author-centered approaches to meaning tend to neglect the world of the text and the world of the reader. Text-centered approaches, in claiming textual autonomy, downplay the boundaries imposed by the world of the author upon the text. Now we observe that reader-centered approaches generally find meaning in the interaction between the worlds of the text and the reader. The best we have here is the marriage of two worlds—the reader's and the text's or the author's and the text's. What I propose in this book is that meaning results from a conversation between the world of the text and the world of the reader, a conversation informed by the world of the author. Reverberations of the basic communication model are not accidental. Let me explain: In oral discourse, a speaker seeks to communicate some information to a hearer in such a way that it will be understandable. To accomplish this goal, the speaker makes primary use of language, a language which is generally shared by both parties. But there is another language which is also engaged, consisting of voice inflection, eye contact, physical gestures, etc. If for some reason the hearer fails to comprehend all or part of the message, the hearer can request the

---

[8] Edgar V. McKnight, *The Bible and the Reader* (Philadelphia: Fortress, 1985), 128.

speaker to repeat, elaborate, or modify the oral expression until the hearer's understanding matches the speaker's intent.

In written discourse, an *author* intends to convey meaning through the *text* to a *reader.* Enlisting vehicles such as sound, voice inflection, gestures, and oral dialogue, however, is not possible here. Consequently, the authors must arm themselves with a whole arsenal of literary devices through which they attempt to transfer the message in the intellect to the written page. These literary devices are the woof and warp by which the text communicates to the reader. Further, we may assume that the author has a particular type of reader or audience in mind, one at least familiar with the author's language and world. Otherwise, to speak of communication is absurd. The assumption here is that in the biblical texts, the subjective intention and discourse meaning overlap; that is, what the author intends and what the text says interact but are not identical. While the author is not available for questioning, some aspects of the author's world are. This assumption leaves sufficient room for the role of the reader in the production of meaning. Consequently, three realities converge: author's, text's, and reader's. We argue, therefore, that the locus of meaning is not to be found exclusively in either world or in a marriage of any two of the worlds, but in the interplay between all three worlds. Meaning resides in the conversation between the text and reader with the world behind the text informing that conversation. Interpretation is impaired when any world is given preeminence at the expense of neglecting the other two.

This model of communication sets the agenda for our discussion and for the basic structure of the book. Unit I is concerned with the world behind the text. Chapter 1 argues that the text is the result of an action performed by an author, and as such it is conditioned by the conventional codes that affect anything produced in that particular culture. This means not only that is it inseparably grounded in and influenced by that culture, but that it, in turn, influences its culture. I continue this argument in chs. 2 and 3 by discussing the indispensable adjunctive functions of grammatical, cultural, and ideological background studies within the discipline of hermeneutics.

Unit II deals with the world within the text. In ch. 4, I discuss the importance of genre and sub-genre. I define and illustrate several common sub-genres. Chapter 5 is limited to the broadest generic systems of the Hebrew Bible—narrative, poetry, and prophecy (apocalyptic is discussed in ch. 6). Chapter 6 presents an introduction to the generic systems of the New Testament, including gospel, letter, and apocalyptic. This unit argues that a plausible meaning is impossible without at least some competence in the literary systems of both the Hebrew Bible and New Testament literature.

If the discussion ceased at this point, this interpretive strategy might seem to place hermeneutics within parameters that would assure objective, definable, and communicable meaning. This is true as far as it goes, because as will be asserted in unit I, the text was birthed within a particular culture. I contend, therefore, that the text is an attempt to say something objective, definable, and communicable through conventions that reflect its culture. This recognizes, though, that interpretation has taken place over time, with each period influencing subsequent interpretations. In fact, any interpreter interprets a text over time. Time, however, is not static and neither are interpreters or their worlds. Both the interpreter and the interpreter's world are constantly caught up in the continual flux of what John Caputo calls internal time.[9] So any hermeneutical model must make allowances for a certain subjectivity, incompleteness, and open-endedness. Otherwise, how can we justify the ongoing, never-ending discipline of hermeneutics? Three chapters respond to this very question by addressing the role of the reader and the actual reading process. Thus unit III moves into the world in front of the text. In ch. 7, the reader is introduced to the dynamics of the reading process. The reader may come away with the notion that the process is so complex and has such a vast set of variables that meaning is ultimately unobtainable. However, if I have done my work well, the discussions in units I and II will have diminished this potential problem. In ch. 8, categories of presuppositions and preunderstandings are examined. These reader presuppositions are part of the reader's world and are just as constitutive of meaning as the presuppositions of the author. In unit IV, ch. 9 is a case study in Mark's Gospel, and ch. 10 summarizes the important issues in doing hermeneutics.

Since the category of methodological presuppositions is extensive, and since one's method dictates what questions will be put to the text, I have included at the end of each of the first three units a handful of synopses of critical methods that focus on the three worlds respectively. These synopses are illustrative of the manner in which methods govern how we appropriate texts. However, in the appendixes, I offer other synopses of critical methods that readers may find useful. Also in the appendixes, I offer additional synopses of methods that do not find a home in a single world, but seem to bleed into one or both of the other worlds.

---

[9] John Caputo, *Radical Hermeneutics: Repetition, Deconstruction, and the Hermeneutic Project* (Bloomington: Indiana University Press, 1987), 3–4.

THE WORLD BEHIND THE TEXT

WHY STUDY BACKGROUNDS? AN APOLOGY FOR HISTORICAL RESEARCH

Exegesis must never be swallowed up in application, but must always precede it. The exegetical questions must be answered before questions of application may be legitimately asked. In light of this, one of the cardinal rules of exegesis is that the interpreter must always approach and analyze a **text** in part or in whole within contexts: historical, cultural, geographical, ecclesiastical, ideological, and literary. **Exegesis** is the spadework for **interpretation**. Exegesis without interpretation is similar to discovering a cure for the common cold and then not publicizing it. Exegesis alone has no power to produce change—the goal of interpretation. It is a heart without a beat. Interpretation that is uninformed by exegesis, however, has no foundation, like the house built upon the sand. In his discussion of the relationship between the text and the world behind the text, Clarence Walhout rightly observes that this relationship "forbids us to conceive of texts as linguistic objects cut loose from their mooring in an actual world and allowed to drift in some detached sea of aesthetic autonomy."[1]

The goal of this chapter is singular: to demonstrate that the pursuit of **background studies** (i.e., exegesis) is an indispensable prerequisite for the explication of plausible **textual meaning**; that is, historical, cultural, generic, grammatical, ideological, and even geographical studies are prerequisites for a successful interpretation of a text. While it is true that texts exist and are valued independently of their originating circumstances, a knowledge of those originating circumstances will inevitably increase the appreciation of a text. In the past few years, interpretive methodologies have focused on the text and the reader rather than on the author. This swing of the pendulum has produced some

---

[1] Clarence Walhout, "Texts and Actions," in Roger Lundin, Anthony Thiselton, and Clarence Walhout, *The Responsibility of Hermeneutics* (Grand Rapids: Eerdmans, 1985), 56.

very healthy results, not least of which has been a renewed interest in the biblical texts and the role that the responses of readers play in the creation of meaning. However, this refocusing of attention has tempted some scholars to push the world within the text so far into the background that it becomes relatively unimportant in determining the meaning of a text. For example, Roland Barthes claims that "writing is not the communication of a message which starts from the author and proceeds to the reader; it is specifically the voice of reading itself; *in the text, only the reader speaks.*"[2] While Donald Keesey rejects the idea of *the* meaning of a text, his is a less radical view than that of Barthes:

> While we may agree that there is no complete, definitive, and absolutely correct interpretation of a poem, it does not necessarily follow that there are no better or worse interpretations, interpretations more or less complete, more or less accurate, more or less approximating a "best" reading.[3]

It is our contention that the most plausible interpretation or reading of a text cannot be realized apart from a consideration of the world that gave birth to the text. If we recognize that a text is a historical phenomenon in the sense that it originates at a specific time and place, under certain cultural, linguistic, political, and religious conditions, the validity of the above statement becomes more obvious. Literary works may communicate or at least address universal concepts, but they do so within cultural limits and by cultural conventions. A familiarity with these limits and conventions can be helpful in ascertaining from the text that which is universally applicable. Texts reflect their culture, and to read them apart from that culture is to invite a basic level of misunderstanding.

The reader may have noticed that I have consistently made reference to "the meaning of the text" and not to "the meaning of the author." This reference calls for some explanation, an explanation that will prevent an interpretive error. Most scholars today distinguish between authorial and textual meaning. Is the meaning of a literary work of art identical to what its creator meant in composing it? Without question an author purposes or intends to convey some message. Terry Eagleton observes that "every literary text is built out of a sense of its potential audience, includes an image of whom it is written *for:* every

---

[2] Roland Barthes, *S/Z* (trans. Richard Miller; New York: Hill & Wang, 1974).

[3] Donald Keesey, "General Introduction," in *Contexts for Criticism* (4th ed.; ed. Donald Keesey; Boston: McGraw Hill, 2003), 7.

work encodes within itself what Iser calls an 'implied reader,' intimates in its every gesture the kind of 'addressee' it anticipates."[4] Does the author successfully incarnate this intention within the text and communicate it to the audience? The answer to this question is rather complex.

From a phenomenological perspective, an author perceives an **object of consciousness** (the mental formulation of the text). This object is not synonymous with the text. The text is the concrete literary product of the author's object of consciousness. For example, I have a perception of what the book you are reading should be. The perception is not the book; the perception is the intellectual or conscious origin of the book. For every literary text there must be an originating moment when the author conceives of the literary object and perceives it to be a certain way. On the one hand, since perception takes place through time (diachronically), the object of consciousness undergoes a perpetual redefinition from moment to moment. On the other hand, this object of consciousness (regardless of the author's literary purpose) receives concrete expression at a particular time (synchronically) in the form of an inscription (i.e., the text). There is absolutely no way to guarantee a one-to-one correspondence between the ever-changing, **diachronic** object of consciousness and the permanent, **synchronic** linguistic representation of it. Indeed, it is probably futile to argue for a one-to-one correspondence between the original intentional object and the text, because there is no way to objectively demonstrate the truth for such a relationship. How is it possible to enter into the consciousness of another, especially when that consciousness is unavailable for questioning? Complete **authorial meaning** is unobtainable, since it is the product of the author's individual consciousness; textual meaning is the cultural specificity of the author's original object of consciousness. There is no way to determine definitively just how accurately the text represents the object of intention.

The **hermeneut** might argue, then, that the text exists as an autonomous object in no way dependent upon the authorial consciousness that gave birth to the text. But intentionality in this sense is not the same as what is usually referred to as authorial intent or purpose. The general reason for writing is to communicate. A logical assumption, consequently, might be that communication resides within the text itself. Nonetheless, we might reasonably inquire whether or to what extent the author was successful in communicating the intended message. Two disparate

---

[4] Terry Eagleton, *Literary Theory: An Introduction* (Minneapolis: University of Minnesota Press, 1983), 84.

assumptions are possible here: (1) the author was not entirely successful in communicating intent but did communicate a message; or (2) the
author was successful. In either case, it is presupposed that the author
communicated *some* message to an audience through the medium of the
written text. Since an author employs verbal symbols in communication, and since verbal symbols carry a wide semantic range of meaning, an author quite possibly (actually quite probably) communicates
much more meaning than was consciously purposed. This possibility
exists especially for writers who have unconsciously internalized symbols and concepts carrying unspoken, metaphorical usages that consequently have a tacit multivalence. By no stretch of the imagination may
we classify this unconscious communication as authorially intended,
but *it is in the text*. Therefore, a text does communicate; the author (consciously or unconsciously) communicates through the text, and the
way readers actualize this communication is the primary concern of
interpretation.

The above remarks bring us to the heart of the matter in this chapter: If the author's consciousness is private and ultimately inaccessible,
wherein lies the need for historical research? Why should the hermeneut
be concerned with the world behind the text? The answer is twofold.

First, an author perceives the object of consciousness (e.g., in literature, the object of consciousness is the text; in music, the symphony)
within the **context** of a particular historical moment. This perception
has its basis in all the various points of the author's culture and the author's unique assimilation of that culture; i.e., the original object of
consciousness is at the same time grasped by the individual within a
particular culture at a particular historical moment within that culture
and filtered through an individual psychology.

Second, the literary representation of the object of consciousness
has historical grounding. How can authors express themselves concretely apart from their contemporary matrix and their understanding
of it? Even Dadaism found significance within a preestablished system
of perception and reality. On a generic level, a literary text has meaning only upon the recognition that the author and reader share a body
of literary conventions. If the author seeks to transform or modify
these conventions, written discourse is possible only as far as the author
and reader share the knowledge of conventional norms. Regardless of
how much the author subverts conventional norms, understanding is
possible solely against the backdrop of the accepted norm. Subversion
is subversion only to the degree that the norms are transformed. The
world within the text is in the real world while being outside of it. We

define the world within the text exclusively in terms of the real world. Political satire, for instance, has no meaning apart from its contemporary political origin. Literature which makes a social statement loses its point if it is not interpreted within the light of those social issues being addressed. Therefore, we must approach the textual world in light of the real world in which it has its grounding. Without a sense of what the real world is like, it is impossible to imagine new ones. The same is also true for readers, even when the worlds presented to us are fictional ones. Clarence Walhout states this quite clearly:

> They [texts] become meaningful to us because we are able to compare their fictional worlds with the world that is already familiar to us. . . . We compare Huck Finn and Tom Sawyer to boys that we have known in actual life even though we have no doubt whatsoever which of the boys are fictional and which are actual.[5]

We can imagine new possibilities only against the backdrop of what we already know, of what in the real world is familiar to us. Outside of this relationship, communication is utterly impossible. The same can be said of an author. A text may be autonomous in relationship to the original intentional object, but the concretization of that object (the text) is conditioned by the real world of the author. How else does an individual communicate except through contemporary social, cultural, or literary conventions? For us to think that authors are not at least unconsciously marked in their thoughts and characters by their experiences in the real world is simply untenable. Behind every literary text, there lies a view of life, a view which has been conditioned by the author's real world. While an author may imagine a literary world with all sorts of new possibilities, the expression of such an imaginative world is impossible apart from the author's real world. An author can imagine a world and express it textually only through the real historical, cultural, literary, and ideological setting. For this reason, historical considerations are at once validated as an important adjunct to **hermeneutics**.

Since the text is historical in origin, having its birth within a complex of social, literary, linguistic, and ideological systems, certain limits are automatically placed upon the reader of the text. While these systems do not constitute meaning, they do serve as controls upon authorial literary expression. How does the author use or adapt available sources? What are the levels of tradition recognizable within the writings? Who is the author and under what circumstances did he or she write? What

---

[5] Walhout, "Texts and Actions," 59–60.

occasioned the writing and when? Because a text is historically conditioned, especially in its linguistic expression, these questions will continue to be appropriate. Consequently, any reading must be partially measured by the extent to which the reader shares the same worldview as the author. Louise Rosenblatt offers a similar view:

> I am even ready to say that in most readings we seek the belief that a process of communication is going on, that one is participating in something that reflects the author's intention. And especially if our experience has been vivid or stirring, we may wish to ascertain what manner of temperament, life-situation, social or intellectual or philosophic environment, gave rise to this work. Especially if it is a text of the past, we may wish to discover to what degree our experience differs from that of the author's contemporaries. All of the approaches of the literary historian become potentially relevant—textual study, semantic history, literary, biographical, and other types of history. All these may aid the reader to limit himself to the horizon of the author and his time.[6]

Biblical prophecy is an example. Frequently "historical" details are ripped from their linguistic contexts and then applied to some contemporary situation or event in the reader's age. We may read of a commentator's claims that "the north" and "the east" in the prophecy of Ezekiel refer to the Soviet Union and China respectively. Observations of this kind are independent of any interest in or consideration of the original historical significance of such references. Regardless of the hermeneut's religious tradition, interpretive methodology, or theological aims, there must be sufficient focus on the author's historical frame of reference. Attention to the author's historical circumstances supplies a valuable safeguard against arbitrary interpretations like the one above.

I am not suggesting that we substitute information *about* authors or their times for meaning. Meaning comes only through engaging the text. Historical knowledge of authors and their age enables readers to engage texts and to organize more plausibly the resulting experiences. Any non-aesthetic information (biographical, cultural, literary, religious, etc.) should be valued since it enhances the engagement experience. These areas of information about the originating world behind the text are heuristic adjuncts to the literary experience. In other words, understanding ancient texts requires a certain amount of historical spadework. McKnight rightly observes:

---

[6]Louise Rosenblatt, "The Quest for 'The Poem Itself,' " in *Contexts for Criticism* (3d ed.; ed. Donald Keesey; Mountain View, Calif.: Mayfield, 1987), 144.

There is no need for denial of the fact that certain states of affairs or developments operated in some sense as sources for biblical writings and that biblical writings now reflect those enabling conditions. But attention is to be paid to the realities behind the text (as far as they can be ascertained or imaged) in order to understand the text as a pattern of meaning that continues to have an effect on readers.[7]

While it is true that readers usually value a literary text independently of its originating contexts, a fundamental knowledge of these contexts will certainly increase one's appreciation and understanding of the text. The grounding of a text in its historical dimension is an important aspect of hermeneutics, because biblical texts (any text for that matter) reflect the enabling sources and originating conditions and circumstances. Consequently, the modern hermeneut should not shun the great bulk of information which those craftsmen of the **historical-critical method** have supplied. Speaking of the New Testament writings, Luke Johnson makes a similar observation:

> The NT came to birth among social structures and symbols different from our own. The writings are conditioned linguistically by that historical setting. Their linguistic code is not only alien but also only partially available to us. Precisely the "things that go without saying" are not available to us. Every responsible reading therefore demands historical adjustment. The writings are very much conditioned by the times and places of their origin, by the settings and intentions of their authors. The more we can reconstruct those settings and intentions, the better readers we are.[8]

For example, an understanding of the debate concerning ritual cleanness between the two prominent Jewish rabbinic schools of Jesus' day, the schools of Hillel and Shammai, is nothing less than essential to a plausible understanding of Matt 15:10–12. The historical reference places certain restrictions on the possibilities of interpretation.

Nevertheless, this is not to argue that meaning is the domain of historical studies, because meaning is a function of the textual world. But this does insist that knowledge (as far as it is possible) of the world behind the text illuminates the world within the text. For any single author, we may have little or no information about educational background, literary sources, or even personal religious convictions;

---

[7] Edgar V. McKnight, *Postmodern Use of the Bible: The Emergence of Reader-Oriented Criticism* (Nashville: Abingdon, 1988), 175.

[8] Luke T. Johnson, *The Writings of the New Testament: An Interpretation* (Philadelphia: Fortress, 1986), 6.

through historical research, however, we may discover a considerable amount of information about the educational systems of the author's time, the literary conventions in use, the political institutions under which the author lived, and the nature of orthodox and unorthodox religious views.

Summary

A text is the product of an author, and the author is a product of an age. Arguing for such a background study, Joel Rosenberg observes that because of an undercurrent of commentary by Shakespeare on contemporary political life and institutions, some Shakespearean scholars are sent to

> the English constitutional histories of Maitland and Elton as a way into *Henry IV*, or *Richard III* or even *Coriolanus* and *Julius Caesar*. This is not to suggest that a Tudor or Stuart audience needed to read such histories in order to understand their poet, only that some members of those audiences possessed the political and institutional sophistication required to make full sense of Shakespeare's political themes, and that such understanding was a principal ingredient of the literary delight they certainly experienced.[9]

This knowledge would have been readily available to many of the contemporary readers, but such is not the case for the modern one. The same is true for readers of the biblical texts. The author could assume a certain body of knowledge on the part of at least some of the contemporary readers, and much of this knowledge is accessible to modern readers only through historical research. Therefore, we should welcome any available background knowledge if it increases our ability to organize into a meaningful whole the various levels of materials that we encounter in the text. Hermeneutics should ideally result in the articulation of the most plausible meaning. But there can be no hermeneutical ideal without some measurably competent reading of the text. If background studies enhance our chances of attaining to the hermeneutical ideal, we should welcome such studies with open arms. These non-aesthetic studies should never become substitutes for the aesthetic experience of the text itself. They are precursors, not ends.

---

[9] Rosenberg, *King and Kin,* 108.

Background studies may be divided into two areas—**semantics** and **pragmatics**. Semantics is the study of the language of a text, while pragmatics is the study of the circumstances surrounding the individual linguistic expressions. Exegesis must give equal weight to both areas. Peter Cotterell and Max Turner suggest that semantics and pragmatics should be divided more conveniently into the categories of text, **co-text**, and context.[10] *Text* refers to the study of the actual words of the text; *co-text* is concerned with the relationships between words in sentences, paragraphs, and chapters; and *context* focuses on the historical and sociological setting of the text. The first two areas are the concern of semantics, while the latter is the domain of pragmatics. This observation by Cotterell and Turner is based upon their distinction between a sentence and an utterance. A sentence may occur repeatedly, while an utterance (which is the sentence within a particular *context*) can never occur more than once. Therefore, exegesis must be concerned with the explication of utterances, not sentences. This means that *pragmatics* must be an integral part of exegesis. When we begin to explore any text, we confront utterances instead of contextless sentences. When Paul wrote to the church at Corinth, he wrote within a particular context, a reconstruction of which yields a more informed reading of the text. In the remainder of unit I, I discuss the grammatical background (*text* and *co-text*) in ch. 2, and the *context* in ch. 3.

REVIEW & STUDY

Key Terms and Concepts

authorial meaning	historical-critical method
background studies	interpretation
context	object of consciousness
co-text	pragmatics
diachronic	semantics
exegesis	synchronic
hermeneut	text
hermeneutics	textual meaning

---

[10] Peter Cotterell and Max Turner, *Linguistics and Biblical Interpretation* (Downers Grove: InterVarsity, 1989), 15–19.

Study Questions

1. If an author's work unconsciously reflects his or her world, in what ways might a familiarity with that world assist in the interpretation of a text?

2. Which do you feel is the final source of meaning, the author or the text? Why?

3. What advantage does oral discourse have over written discourse?

4. How does the distinction between "sentence" and "utterance" suggest the need for exegesis?

5. In what way might background studies inform interpretation even when the author of a text is anonymous?

6. What is the difference between authorial intention and textual meaning?

7. In what way do background studies offer a "check" on interpretation?

Suggestions for Further Reading

Braaten, Carl. *History and Hermeneutics.* Philadelphia: Fortress, 1966.

Fee, Gordon D., and Douglas Stuart. *How to Read the Bible for All Its Worth.* 2d ed. Grand Rapids: Zondervan, 1993.

Freyne, Sean. *Galilee, Jesus, and the Gospels: Literary Approaches and Historical Investigation.* Philadelphia: Fortress, 1988.

Hayes, John, and Carl R. Holladay. *Biblical Exegesis: A Beginner's Handbook.* Atlanta: John Knox, 1987.

THE IMPORTANCE OF LANGUAGE:
THE GRAMMATICAL BACKGROUND

A fundamental truth: An author uses language in formulating a text. At the level of the text, the interpreter must give attention to the identification and description of details such as **phonology** (word sounds), **morphology** (word forms), **lexicology** (word meanings), and **syntax** (word relationships). Literature is the linguistic expression of a culture's entire **symbolic world**. The symbolic world refers to the infinite maze of interrelated customs, ideologies, religious expressions, and social relationships, within which a people finds its identity, its self-understanding, and its ultimate reason for being. We may reasonably assume, then, that if a culture's literature is the linguistic expression of this symbolic world, or at least the linguistic attempt to interpret the symbolic world, a study of that culture's linguistic expression—language in its many facets—should be an integral part of hermeneutics. We might also include more formal literary structures (such as genre, poetic subforms, and narrative subgenres) within this context, but these pertain more to the world projected by the text (discussed in unit II). Our primary interest here is with the grammatical elements of the language of the text. This is a primary level of hermeneutics, incomplete within itself, but an absolutely necessary precondition for the other contexts which we consider.

That the languages of the biblical texts are not those of the modern reader is an inescapable hermeneutical consideration when dealing with the referential function of language. The world within the text is projected on the most elementary level of words. These words combine to form sentences, sentences form units, units form sections, and sections form entire texts. Since writers communicate meaning through combinations of words, phrases, sentences, linguistic units, and concepts, these are important hermeneutical considerations.

The **grammatical context** is concerned with the original thought-world of the author as it is expressed through the language of the text.

The most basic level of this concern is the single word. The danger of overemphasizing the single word cannot be ignored. Nevertheless, while a text communicates its message through the relationships of its phrases, sentences, and larger lexical units, the hermeneut cannot neglect single words.

Often we encounter words within the biblical texts whose references seem foreign to us. This is true whether we are using the **original languages** or a **translation**. These words may carry technical, cultic, or figurative meanings unparalleled in our culture. The biblical authors could assume that the original readers would understand these special concepts without any accompanying explanation. Terms such as "kingdom of God" in the Synoptics, "justification" as used by Paul in Romans and Galatians, "covenant" in the Hebrew Scriptures and the New Testament, and "Logos" in the Gospel of John are examples.

To summarize, grammatical study is concerned with the analysis of the language of the text. An author combines words and phrases to express certain ideas. These words and phrases carry meaning simply because they are arranged into what we might call "sense units." The importance of grammatical considerations is that they increase the probability of the reader's recognition of these sense units. Below are (1) some basic guidelines to assist the beginning hermeneut in developing competence in grammatical studies, and (2) some examples of how to apply these guidelines.

Phonology

Word sounds can best be appreciated when pronounced in the original languages (Hebrew, Aramaic, and Greek) of the Bible. As in most languages, the biblical writers used a range of sound combinations for a variety of purposes. Experienced writers employ word sounds for emphasis, aesthetic and lyric expression, irony, or for didactic purposes. With stylistic devices, authors call the reader's attention to some aspect of their message. The writers of Hebrew poetry extensively used word sounds.

Alliteration

Alliteration is the practice of beginning a series of words or syllables with the same or similar sounds. Psalm 119 is an example in which each line in a series of eight begins with the same Hebrew letter. Bear in mind that Hebrew is read from right to left.

1.	אשרי תמימי דרך ההלכים בתורת יהוה
2.	אשרי נצרי עדתיו בכל לב ידרשוהו
	: : : : :
8.	את חקי אשמר אל תעזבני עד מאד
9.	במה יזכה נער את ארחו לשמר כדברך
10.	בכל לבי דרשתי אל תשגני ממצותיך
	: : : : :
16.	בחקתיא אשתעשע לא אשכח דברך
81.	כלתה לתשועתך נפשי לדברך יחלתי
82.	כלו עיני לאמרתך לאמר מתי תנחמני
	: : : : :
88.	כחסדך חיני ואשמרה עדות פיך
153.	ראה עניי וחלצני כי תורתך לא שכחתי
154.	ריבה ריבי וגאלני לאמרתך חיני
	: : : : :
160.	ראש דברך אמת ולעולם כל משפט צדקך

Assonance

Assonance takes advantage of the same or similar sounds (usually vowels) within words. A good example is the hymn in 1 Tim 3:16. A person who does not have a reading knowledge of Greek can still see that the first word in each line has the same final sound:

ἐφανερώθη ἐν σαρκί	*ephanerōthē en sarki*
ἐδικαιώθη ἐν πνεύματι	*edikaiōthē en pneumati*
ὤφθη ἀγγέλοις	*ōphthē angelois*
ἐκηρύχθη ἐν ἔθνεσιν	*ekērychthē en ethnesin*
ἐπιστεύθη ἐν κόσμῳ	*episteuthē en kosmō*
ἀνελήμφθη ἐν δόξῃ.	*anelēmphthē en doxē.*

Paronomasia

Paronomasia is a pun, a play on words that have the same or similar sounds but different meanings. In Amos 8:2, God asks, "What do you see?" to which Amos responds, "A basket of summer fruit." The expression "summer fruit" (*qayits*) sounds like the word for "end" (*qets*) in verse 2: "The end has come upon my people." The original readers would have appreciated the pun which is lost in translation. In 2 Cor 4:8

we see another illustration: *aporoumenoi all' ouk exaporoumenoi* ("Perplexed, but not driven to despair").

Onomatopoeia

Onomatopoeia involves using words whose sounds actually suggest the object or concept to which they are referring. For example, Richard Soulen suggests that "the Hebrew words *thohu wavohu* in Gen 1:2 suggest to the ear what the English translation communicates only conceptually: 'without form and void.'"[1] Such word sounds and their beauty of expression are usually lost in translation. When dealing with poetic passages especially, the ideal is to work with the original languages. If this is not possible, however, the student should consult several modern translations as some will capture the phonological qualities of the original languages.

Morphology

Morphology is the study of the forms of words. The languages of the Bible are highly inflected languages. By "inflected" we mean that a word changes in form depending upon tense, voice, mood, person, number, case, and gender. In Koiné Greek (the Greek of the New Testament) word order is much less significant than in an uninflected language like English. In English, the order is usually subject, verb, and direct object with prepositional phrases, adverbial clauses, and relative clauses occurring according to rules of syntax. In Greek, however, inflection is more crucial to meaning than word order.

Word forms influence meaning, and for this reason having the ability to recognize forms and their potential meanings is an essential part of interpretation. I may be able to ask a speaker of my language what is meant by an unusual statement or word or word form; the writers of the biblical texts, however, are not available for questioning. Therefore the best alternative is to equip ourselves with the knowledge necessary for recognizing forms and their possible meanings. For example, in 1 Cor 12:31 the word *zēloute* (translated as "strive for") may be either an indicative (a statement concerning a state of affairs) or an imperative (a command) in form. How is the interpreter to decide? Actually if

---

[1] Richard N. Soulen and R. Kendall Soulen, *Handbook of Biblical Criticism* (3d ed.; Louisville: Westminster John Knox, 2001), 125.

the interpreter is not aware that there are two possibilities, there will be no choice except that one made by the translator. The point is that the statement assumes a different meaning if it is translated as an indicative rather than an imperative.

Lexicology

While single words do not comprise the hermeneut's primary point of concentration, we often encounter words seemingly unclear in meaning but potentially having special significance for understanding a passage. A plausible explication of a larger passage may hinge upon the meaning of a word which appears vague to us. When such a word is understood in the way in which it would have been understood by the original author or audience, the entire larger unit may assume a sharper focus. In reference to word studies, Hayes and Holladay observe:

> we gradually broaden our understanding of the term, the passage itself and the other biblical writings in which it occurs. It is through this process of interrogation and analysis that we begin to increase our own understanding of the passage by actually re-entering and re-creating the thought-world of the author or text itself.[2]

Key Words or Phrases

Isolate key words or phrases. Readers frequently encounter words appearing to have technical, cultic, cultural, or theological significance. The biblical writers shared a conceptual world with their contemporaries. When they set about putting the message of faith into coherent systems, defining and articulating its unique character, their only recourse was to exploit familiar concepts. The concepts may have been redefined and reinterpreted, but their new interpretation has significance only against the backdrop of their original usage.

Reference Tools

Employ available reference tools to investigate the word or phrase. For the beginning student, there are basically three indispensable reference tools—Bible dictionaries and encyclopedias, lexicons or other word study books, and biblical **concordances**.

---

[2] Hayes and Holladay, *Biblical Exegesis,* 62.

Dictionaries and encyclopedias. These works offer the student an abundance of historical information on a variety of words and topics. For example, *The Zondervan Pictorial Encyclopedia of the Bible* (5 vols.; Grand Rapids, Zondervan, 1975) provides a fifteen-page discussion of the word "righteousness." The discussion is divided into topics such as "The meaning of the term linguistically," "Righteousness in the OT," "Righteousness in the NT," and "Righteousness in the modern world." Other useful dictionaries and encyclopedias include the one-volume *New Bible Dictionary* (*NBD*, Downer's Grove: InterVarsity, 1996), the multivolume *New Interpreter's Dictionary of the Bible* (Nashville: Abindgon, 2006), the *International Standard Bible Encyclopedia* (*ISBE*, 4 vols., Grand Rapids, Eerdmans, 1988), and the *Anchor Bible Dictionary* (*ABD*, New York: Doubleday, 1992). All of these works are accessible to students unable to work with the original languages of the biblical texts. Any of these works provide the student with valuable background material for words, phrases, and concepts.

A number of dictionaries and encyclopedias of literary, critical, and cultural theory also are available. Listed here are some of the most useful:

Cuddon, John Anthony. *The Penguin Dictionary of Literary Terms and Literary Theory.* 4th ed. London: Penguin, 2000.

Freedman, David Noel, ed. *The Anchor Bible Dictionary.* New York: Doubleday, 1992.

Hayes, John, ed. *Dictionary of Biblical Interpretation.* 2 vols. Nashville: Abingdon, 1999.

Macey, David. *The Penguin Dictionary of Critical Theory.* London: Penguin, 2000.

Makaryk, Irena R., ed. *Encyclopedia of Contemporary Literary Theory: Approaches, Scholars, Terms.* Buffalo: University of Toronto Press, 1993.

Payne, Michael, ed. *A Dictionary of Cultural and Critical Theory.* Cambridge, Mass.: Blackwell, 1996.

Word study books and lexicons. Word study books have a limited value for the student who does not know the biblical languages. When used with discrimination, they can supply useful information about specific words. These works can be single or multivolume. Generally the entries are arranged according to word families. The treatment may range from the earliest usage to the usage in the biblical text and beyond. Some of the better known word study works are:

Kohlenberger, John R., III, ed. *The Expanded Vine's Expository Dictionary of New Testament Words.* Minneapolis: Bethany House, 1984.

Renn, Stephen D. *Expository Dictionary of Bible Words: Word Studies for Key English Bible Words Based on the Hebrew and Greek Texts.* Peabody, Mass.: Hendrickson, 2005.

Robertson, A. T. *Word Pictures in the New Testament.* Nashville: B&H, 1973.

Vincent, Marvin. *Word Studies in the New Testament.* Peabody, Mass.: Hendrickson, 1985.

Wuest, Kenneth S. *Word Studies in the Greek New Testament.* Grand Rapids: Eerdmans, 1982.

Lexicons. **Lexicons** have a more limited use for students unable to work with the original languages. But for those students who are able to use them, lexicons provide a distinct advantage. A useful lexicon provides the student with etymologies, an identification and discussion of irregular grammatical forms, possible meanings, and the usage of a word within a given context. Analytical lexicons analyze (parse) the grammatical forms of the Hebrew and Greek texts. Theological lexicons provide advanced word studies on important Hebrew and Greek words. Below are separate listings for lexicons for the New Testament and Hebrew Bible.

Hebrew Lexicons:

Armstrong, Terry A., Douglas L. Busby, and Cyril F. Carr. *A Reader's Hebrew-English Lexicon of the Old Testament.* Grand Rapids: Zondervan, 1989.

Brown, F., S. Driver, and C. Briggs, eds. *A Hebrew and English Lexicon of the Old Testament.* Oxford: Clarendon, 1978.

Davidson, Benjamin. *The Analytical Hebrew and Chaldee Lexicon.* Grand Rapids: Zondervan, 1972. Repr., Peabody, Mass.: Hendrickson, 1981.

Einspahr, Bruce, compiler. *Index to Brown, Driver, and Briggs Hebrew Lexicon.* Chicago: Moody, 1976.

Gesenius, H. W. F. *Gesenius' Hebrew-Chaldee Lexicon to the Old Testament.* Grand Rapids: Baker, 1979.

Holladay, William L. *A Concise Hebrew and Aramaic Lexicon of the Old Testament.* Grand Rapids: Eerdmans, 1988.

Jenni, Ernst, and Claus Westermann. *Theological Lexicon of the Old Testament.* Peabody, Mass.: Hendrickson, 1997.

Koehler, Ludwig, Walter Baumgartner, and J. J. Stamm. *The Hebrew and Aramaic Lexicon of the Old Testament.* Translated and edited under the supervision of M. E. J. Richardson. 5 vols. Leiden: E. J. Brill, 1994–2000.

Greek Lexicons:

Berry, George Ricker. *A Dictionary of New Testament Greek Synonyms.* Grand Rapids: Zondervan, 1979.

———. *A New Greek-English Lexicon to the New Testament.* Chicago: Wilcox & Follett, 1944.

Bullinger, Ethelbert W. *A Critical Lexicon and Concordance to the English and Greek New Testaments.* London: Samuel Bagster & Sons, 1969.

Danker, Frederick W., Walter Bauer, William F. Arndt, and F. Wilbur Gingrich. *Greek-English Lexicon of the New Testament and Other Early Christian Literature.* 3d ed. Chicago: University of Chicago Press, 1999.

Liddell, Henry George, Robert Scott, and Henry Stuart Jones. *A Greek-English Lexicon.* 9th ed. with revised supplement. Oxford: Clarendon, 1996.

Louw, Johannes, P. Eugene A. Nida, Rondal B. Smith, and Karen A. Munson, eds. *Greek-English Lexicon of the New Testament Based on Semantic Domains.* 2d ed. New York: United Bible Societies, 1989.

Mounce, William D. *The Analytical Lexicon to the Greek New Testament.* Grand Rapids: Zondervan, 1993.

Perschbacher, Wesley J., ed. *The New Analytical Greek Lexicon.* Peabody, Mass.: Hendrickson, 1990.

Spicq, Ceslas. *Theological Lexicon of the New Testament.* Edited and translated by James D. Ernest. Peabody, Mass.: Hendrickson, 1994.

Thayer, Joseph Henry. *A Greek-English Lexicon of the New Testament.* Grand Rapids: Baker, 1977.

Wigram, George V. *The Analytical Greek Lexicon of the New Testament.* Peabody, Mass.: Hendrickson, 1983.

———. *The New Englishman's Greek Concordance and Lexicon.* Rev. ed. edited by Jay P. Green, Sr. Peabody, Mass.: Hendrickson, 1982.

Concordances. There are different types of concordances, but the most useful for those lacking the original languages are the analytical ones. These concordances allow the student to find the Hebrew or Greek word translated by the English word. This can assist the student in using the lexicons listed above when a knowledge of the biblical languages is absent. Listed here are some of the better Hebrew and Greek concordances:

Aland, Kurt. *Vollständige Konkordanz zum griechischen Neuen Testament: unter Zugrundelegung aller modernen kritischen Textausgaben und des Textus receptus.* New York: Walter De Gruyter, 1978.

Lisowsky, Gerhard. *Konkordanz zum hebräischen Alten Testament.* 3d. cor. ed. Deutsche Bibelgesellschaft, 1981.

Moulton, William, and A. S. Geden. *A Concordance to the Greek Testament According to the Texts of Westcott and Hort, Tischendorf and the English Revisers.* 5th rev. ed. New York: T&T Clark, 1997.

Lisowsky, Aland, and Moulton and Geden list passages where a term is used in a similar sense. The reason for this arrangement springs from a recognition that the same word may be used in a variety of ways with a variety of meanings. In other words, the semantic range of a word is not limited to one definition.

The most valuable concordances for those not acquainted with original languages are:

Strong, James. *Strong's Exhaustive Concordance of the Bible.* Peabody, Mass.: Hendrickson, 2007.

Wigram, George V. *The Englishman's Hebrew Concordance of the Old Testament.* Peabody, Mass.: Hendrickson, 1996.

———. *The Englishman's Greek Concordance.* Peabody, Mass.: Hendrickson, 1996.

Young, Robert. *Young's Analytical Concordance to the Bible.* Peabody, Mass.: Hendrickson, 1980.

A word of caution is needed here. While lexical tools are valuable for examining single words, there is a tendency for interpreters to "over-exegete" based on the information they contain. For example, if I wish to examine the meaning of a word, normally I need to know how the word was used at a particular time. If I consult **BDAG** or *TDNT*, I am presented in some cases with pages of information tracing the meaning of the word back over centuries. As I have already pointed out, languages are not static, and words change meanings over time. For this reason, the study of words should generally be *synchronic* and not *diachronic*.

A language has been compared with a river: take a cross-section here and the river can be described, or there and again it can be described, although the description will be different. If we see the length of the river as signifying time, then taking a cross-section at different points along the river, and comparing what is found, corresponds to *diachronic* linguistic study, while the examination of a single cross-section corresponds to *synchronic* study.[3]

For this reason, it is generally unacceptable to explain one writer's use of a word by that of another writer. It is also generally not wise to interpret an author's use of a word by that same author's use of the same word in a different text. Paul may not use the word *diakonos* (servant) in the same way that it is used in the Septuagint or in Matthew.[4] For further suggestions for concordances, consult David Bauer, *An Annotated Guide to Biblical Resources for Ministry* (Peabody, Mass.: Hendrickson, 2003).

Context

The range of meaning of a word or phrase is determined by its context. Word studies may supply a broad range of meaning for a word or phrase, i.e., ways it has been used in a variety of historical situations. This is helpful, of course, because an author often modifies the meaning of a word within a particular context; on the other hand, the author's modification may be set in relief by a knowledge of the word's historical uses. A word's range of meaning may aid in understanding its meaning within a particular context. For example, *mystērion* (mystery) was used in the mystery religions to refer to a body of knowledge that was available only to the adherents of the particular mystery. Paul, however, uses the word to refer to the "good news" and to the fact that God has extended his grace to Jews and Gentiles alike. The mystery, thus, is no longer a mystery! Words such as *sōtēr* (savior), *logos* (word, message), and *hamartia* (sin) also had long histories of secular usage but were modified within the context of Christianity. Christian writers employed the Koiné Greek of their time. They did not develop a new religious language exclusively for their purposes. They may have modified the vocabulary, but we must understand this modification against the current uses of the time.

Syntax

If the student remains at the level of analyzing single words and phrases and their historical contexts, not much will ever be accom-

---

[3] Cotterell and Turner, *Linguistics and Biblical Interpretation,* 25.

[4] For an excellent discussion of the potential misuses of word studies, see James Barr, *The Semantics of Biblical Language* (Oxford: Oxford University Press, 1961).

plished. A text is comprised of a series of sense units whose combination ideally results in a logical flow of thought or argument. For this reason, the interpreter must move beyond single words and phrases to sentences, sense units (usually paragraphs), larger lexical units, and finally to the text as a whole. For example, if I read the statement, "Santa is coming to town," the word "Santa" has meaning only in its relationship to the other words in the sentence. The sentence predicates something about "Santa." However, is "Santa" the slightly overweight bearer of gifts to children at Christmas? Or does "Santa" have some metaphorical or symbolic significance referring jokingly to some fat man in red with a long white beard? Is the force of the sentence a promise, an imperative, a concession (what linguists refer to as the elocutionary force of a sentence)? When is "Santa" coming to town? How will he arrive? These questions have answers only if we look beyond the sentence to the greater context of the sense unit and the text as a whole.

An effective method of ascertaining the logical flow of thought is to construct a **sentence flow** and/or a grammatical outline of a unit.[5] By identifying the coordinate and subordinate clauses, the student usually gains an initial sense of the thought flow. A grammatical outline will help the student identify adverbial clauses, prepositional phrases, relative clauses, infinitives, participial clauses, etc. and clarify their relationships with the main parts (subject, verb, direct object) of the various sentences. In constructing the sentence flow and grammatical diagram, the student will recognize associations not otherwise readily apparent. Also, figurative expressions, unusual grammatical constructions, and parenthetical excursions become recognizable.

Elements of syntax are best analyzed by working with the original languages, and a minimum competency in these languages should be a goal for any prospective Bible scholar. Until this goal is a reality, however, the student must combine two intermediate essentials: A mastery of English grammar and a rather literal translation of the Scriptures. This will allow the student to follow more correctly the thought flow of the text and will result in a more plausible interpretation.

Ideally, the student should move from one sense unit to another until the entire text has been covered. In this process, logical connectives such as premise and conclusion indicators should receive special

---

[5] For an excellent discussion of the sentence flow, see Gordon Fee, *New Testament Exegesis: A Handbook for Students and Pastors* (3d ed.; Philadelphia: Westminster, 2002).

attention. Words such as "therefore," "such that," "as a result," and "because," are red flags indicating a particular chain of thought or argument. Once the student has combed the entire text in this grammatical fashion, there will develop a tentative understanding of the central thrust of the text and the way in which the sense units are related to each other and to the whole. The following discussion of 1 Cor 13:8–12 illustrates the way a sense unit will be related to the larger context.

Paul's overarching reason for writing to the church at Corinth is to respond to a report of divisions which threatened the unity of the community (1:10–17).[6] Within this context Paul addresses the issue of spiritual matters in chs. 12–14. In ch. 12 he begins by stating, "Now concerning spiritual gifts, brothers and sisters, I do not want you to be uninformed" (12:1). The Greek word here for "spiritual gifts" is *pneumatikoi*. This word is different from the one normally used for spiritual gifts—*charismata*. Actually, *pneumatikoi* is better translated "spiritual matters" or "spiritual people." The translation "spiritual people" is one possibility. George Ladd writes: "In I Cor. 2:14–3:3, Paul describes three classes of people: *psychikos,* the natural man (2:14); *sarkikos,* the fleshly man (3:3); and the *pneumatikos,* the spiritual man (3:1). In this passage . . . the 'spiritual man' is the man whose life is ruled by the Holy Spirit."[7]

The option "spiritual matters," however, has much to commend it. Since the form of the substantive is genitive plural (*pneumatikōn*), the substantive may be neuter ("matters") or masculine ("people"). Add to this the neuter form (*ta pneumatika*) in 14:1, and the most plausible choice for translating *tōn pneumatikōn* is "spiritual matters." If we accept this translation, then the *charismata* are only part of Paul's interest, and perhaps not his primary one. Paul is concerned here with "spiritual matters," and his discussion of the *charismata* is significant only as *charismata* relate to his primary concern with "spiritual matters."

After Paul moves through his list of gifts, services, and kinds of workings, he metaphorically compares these gifts and their operations to the unity and function of the parts of the human body (1 Cor 12:12–26). His obvious purpose in this elaborate comparison is to show that, just as there are differences of function among the parts of the human body, there are likewise various charismatic functions within the body of Christ.

---

[6] See Johnson, *Writings of the New Testament,* 272–90.
[7] George E. Ladd, *A Theology of the New Testament* (Grand Rapids: Eerdmans, 1974), 473.

The human body is made up of parts, and with one part missing, the body is incomplete. Furthermore, if one member, say the eye, is given preeminence to the neglect of the other parts, the body would not long survive ("If the whole body were an eye, where would the hearing be? If the whole body were hearing, where would the sense of smell be? But as it is, God arranged the members in the body, each one of them, as he chose. If all were a single member, where would the body be?" [1 Cor 12:17–19]). The implication is obvious: If everyone within the community seeks after a gift because that gift is viewed as superior or impressive, then the unity of the charismatic body that God has ordained is jeopardized. Paul makes this explicit in 12:21–30, especially in verses 23b–25:

> And those members of the body that we think less honorable we clothe with greater honor, and our less respectable members are treated with greater respect; whereas our more respectable members do not need this. But God has so arranged the body, giving the greater honor to the inferior member, *that there may be no dissension within the body, but the members may have the same care for one another.* (emphasis added)

For a spiritually healthy body, all the members are necessary, regardless of their gifts. There is no hierarchy of the gifts on the basis of desirability. But how are we to understand Paul's statement in 12:31a ("But strive for the *greater* gifts")?

Based upon Paul's discussion in 1 Cor 12, we may be certain that the Corinthian believers were using what they considered to be the more desirable gifts as criteria for claiming spiritual maturity or elitism. Based upon our discussion above, we may also conclude that Paul goes out of his way to offer a corrective to this ranking of the *charismata*. Is it not then inconceivable that in his next breath Paul opts for just such a ranking by challenging these same readers to earnestly desire the "better" gifts? Certainly Paul is not suffering from doctrinal schizophrenia. The solution to this apparent dilemma is to be found in the word *zēloute* (1 Cor 12:31) translated as "earnestly desire" (imperative) in most versions of the New Testament (e.g., RSV, NIV, NASB). Grammatically we may translate this form of the verb in either of two ways: as a present tense indicative or a present tense imperative. I suggest that in the present context, the former is the better translation. This would then render the statement as an example of Pauline sarcasm. Paul is not bashful in using the literary device of sarcasm to get his point across (e.g., 1 Cor 4:10), and it would read: "you are striving for the better gifts. And I will show you a still more excellent (*hyperbolē*) way" (12:31). Paul thus proposes to the Corinthian believers the true measure of spiritual adulthood or maturity.

In 1 Cor 13:1–8a, Paul selects representative gifts (three from the list in ch. 12) and argues that they are for all practical purposes functionally insignificant when manifested outside the umbrella of love. Without the accompanying *agapē*, even generosity is functionally meaningless. In 13:4–8a, Paul describes love in lyrical prose form.

Then in 13:8b Paul again draws us to his original list by a second sampling: "But as for prophecies, they will come to an end (*katargē-thēsontai*); as for tongues, they will cease (*pausontai*); as for knowledge, it will come to an end (*katargēthēsetai*)." Note should be taken that Paul uses the same verb to describe the fate of both prophecies and knowledge. The root verb is *katargeō*, which usually means "to make invalid," "to make ineffective," "to nullify," or "to abolish" (e.g., Rom 3:3; 6:6; 1 Cor 1:28; Eph 2:15).[8] The verb *pauō* describes the fate of tongues and can be translated "to cease doing something," "stop (oneself)," or "cease" (e.g., Luke 8:24; Acts 20:1; Eph 1:16).[9]

In verses 9 and 10, Paul pursues two of the last three gifts even further: "For we know only in part (*ek merous*), and we prophesy only in part (*ek merous*); but when the complete comes, the partial (*to ek merous*) will come to an end (*katargēthēsetai*)." Two things should be clear at this point: First, Paul identifies the two gifts of prophecy and knowledge with that which is imperfect, and all three are described as being partial (*ek merous*); second, that which is imperfect suffers the identical fate of the two gifts—*katargēthēsetai*. Consequently, within this context, Paul argues that "that which is perfect" (*to teleion*) is set in juxtaposition to "that which is *ek merous*." But what is "that which is perfect"? Since *to teleion* is neuter in gender, we may rule out any reference to a person. Furthermore, since the New Testament canon was not even in its formative stage at this early period, we may also rule out the suggestion that *to teleion* refers to the canon. When used of things, the adjective *teleion* suggests completeness, or full measure (e.g., Rom 12:2; Jas 1:4a; 1 John 4:18).[10] The whole context is concerned with one thing—love. On the other hand, Paul's term for love (*agapē*) is feminine rather than neuter. Perhaps, then, Paul's "that which is perfect" refers to a state of completion or spiritual maturity whose hallmark is *agapē*.

This observation is supported by verses 11–13. In verse 11, Paul says that when he was a child (*nēpios*) he talked, thought, and reasoned as a

---

[8] Gerhard Delling, "καταργέω," *TDNT* 1:452–54.
[9] BDAG, "παύω."
[10] Ibid., 816–17.

child. This term *nēpios* occurs earlier in 1 Cor 3:1: "And so, brothers and sisters, I could not speak to you as spiritual (*pneumatikois*) people, but rather as people of the flesh (*sarkinois*), as infants (*nēpiois*) in Christ." Within this same context of 1 Cor 2:14–3:3 (referred to above), the worldly person (*sarkikos*) is in Christ, yet not a person of the Spirit (*pneumatikos*), for that one is only a child (*nēpios*). Ladd offers an excellent description of the *sarkikos*:

> [These are those] who are "fleshly" yet who are babes in Christ. They must therefore be "in the Spirit," yet they do not walk "according to the Spirit." Because they are babes in Christ, we must conclude that the Spirit of God dwells in them; yet the Holy Spirit does not exercise full control over their lives, and they are still walking "like men" (v. 3), manifesting the works of the flesh in jealousy and strife.[11]

In both 13:11 and 2:14–3:3, Paul is concerned with spiritual matters, not a literal child. After this reference to spiritual infancy, Paul claims that, when he became a man, he put childish things away. It is significant that the term Paul uses here for putting away is *katergēka*, a perfect form of the verb used in verses 8b and 10 in reference to the partials—prophecy and knowledge, and by implication the *charismata* inclusively.

Paul makes use of the metaphor of the mirror in 13:12 and offers a subsequent interpretation of the metaphor. Now in a state of spiritual infancy and immaturity, the Corinthians are using incompletes, partials (*ek merous*) by which to judge Christian maturity. Thus the Corinthians are misusing the charismata. Paul continues: "But then we will see face to face. Now I know only in part (*ek merous*); then I will know fully, even as I have been fully known." If the "now" refers to a state of spiritual childishness, we should expect the "then" to refer to that state of spiritual maturity or completeness marked by *agapē*—the "when that which is perfect comes." When Christians move into that state of spiritual maturity governed by love, with faith and hope running a close second, they will look upon fellow Christians through the clear glasses of love, rather than employing the incomplete gifts as the measuring rod of maturity.

The above discussion illustrates a hermeneutical paradox. Does the reader interpret the individual parts of a text in light of the whole or the whole in light of the individual parts? Once the student has analyzed the sense units and related them to each other, the sense of the whole may be ascertained. But then the student interprets each sense

---

[11] Ladd, *Theology of the New Testament,* 473.

unit in light of the sense of the whole, which has been delineated only in conjunction with the parts. This is the hermeneutical circle, and I know of no escape from it. Actually, as a hermeneut continues to study, sense units may be modified, and this may result in the modification of the interpretation of the entire text. This modified interpretation of the entire text precipitates a reexamination of many of the individual parts. So the hermeneutical circle is actually a hermeneutical spiral where, after each subsequent modification, the hermeneut moves to a different plane of understanding. In this sense, the spiral is infinite. **Grammatical analysis** does not make the student a master of the text. Grammatical analysis is only the starting point. But the serious hermeneut must address this point, for it is foundational for other areas of study.

Summary

While it may be claimed that the text is a verbal icon, it was first and foremost an icon within its original language. Recognizing this requires that the interpreter give appropriate attention to the identification and description of linguistic details such as phonology, morphology, lexicology, and syntax. Since a people's language encapsulates that people's symbolic world (a world reflected in the text), grammatical concerns are an indispensable part of hermeneutics. Grammatical emphases range from single words to the entire book.

Ideally a passage of the text should be interpreted within the structure of the whole, and the whole must be brought to bear upon the individual parts. The dilemma of determining which comes first is called the hermeneutical circle. Grammatical studies constitute the starting point for dealing with this circle. Tools such as concordances, lexicons, word study books, dictionaries, and encyclopedias are essential adjunctive tools in interpreting the grammar of the text.

REVIEW & STUDY

Key Terms and Concepts

BDAG	original languages
concordance	phonology
grammatical analysis	sentence flow

grammatical context	symbolic world
lexicology	syntax
lexicon	*TDNT*
morphology	translation

Study Questions

1. Do you feel that word studies constitute a part of exegesis? Why or why not?
2. In the Hebrew of Isa 17:12, the sound of the roaring of waves can be distinctly heard. Read this verse in the KJV, RSV, and NIV. Which do you think comes nearest to reproducing the sound of the roaring waves or the sound of a storm? Read Nah 3:1–3 in the NIV. What sensation do you experience?
3. Read the parable of the "Friend at Midnight" in Luke 11:5–8 (KJV). The word "importunity" in verse 8 occurs only here in the New Testament. In the NIV, it is translated "boldness" with a note that it means "persistence." Do a word study on this word using some of the tools discussed in this chapter to see if you agree with either of the above translations. If the word means something else, how does this affect your understanding of the entire parable?
4. Read the short epistle of 1 Peter. The section 2:11–4:11 is a call to acceptable conduct in a variety of settings, even during times of unjust suffering. In light of this context, how should we interpret 2:24b ("by his wounds you have been healed")?

Suggestions for Further Reading

Barr, James. *The Semantics of Biblical Language.* Oxford: Oxford University Press, 1961.

Cotterell, Peter, and Max Turner. *Linguistics and Biblical Interpretation.* Downers Grove: InterVarsity, 1989.

Fee, Gordon D. *New Testament Exegesis: A Handbook for Students and Pastors.* 3d ed. Philadelphia: Westminster, 2002.

Kennedy, George A. *New Testament Interpretation through Rhetorical Criticism.* Chapel Hill: University of North Carolina Press, 1984.

READING AND THE WORLD BEHIND THE TEXT: THE HISTORICAL AND IDEOLOGICAL BACKGROUNDS

Every text is created within some context. According to Paul Ricoeur, at least three developmental stages of a text must be considered in the interpretive process. First is the event, second the recording of the event in a text, and third the reading of the text.[1] Each stage is separated by a time gap. In the case of the biblical text, the gap between the recording of the event in the text and the reading of the text is centuries. During this time the text does not change, but languages and cultures do. The distinct possibility exists, therefore, that the interpreter will impose the understanding of his or her contemporary world upon that of the text. As will be seen in unit III, this imposition is inevitable; it need not, however, be wholesale. The most effective safeguard against a wholesale imposition of the interpreter's world upon the world within the text is the diligent study of the world that produced the text. Thus, what did it mean to be slapped on the face in an ancient Near Eastern culture? This knowledge is essential for interpreting Matt 5:39. Understanding the practice of purchasing fields and animals is significant for the interpretation of Luke 14:15–24. In the world of the New Testament, both reader and writer would have shared this common knowledge. The task of *pragmatics* (context studies such as historical and ideological ones) is to narrow the gap between the original readers and modern ones.

As the title of this chapter indicates, we will explore two major areas relating to background studies. The first area concentrates on general historical and cultural concerns and examines why a knowledge of these makes the difference between just a reading and an informed reading of

---

[1] See Paul Ricoeur, *The Conflict of Interpretation* (Evanston: Northwestern University Press, 1974).

a text. The second area of discussion focuses on the ideological contexts of both the Hebrew Bible and the New Testament. Since the second area may be less familiar to most readers, it necessarily will require more detail and attention.

Historical and Cultural Background

The preferred reading of any text is the one in which the interpreter establishes the most probable historical and cultural contexts. Simply put, the best reading of any text is informed by the interpreter's concern for date, place, originating circumstances, audience, and authorship of a text. Other cultural information, such as marriage practices, systems of taxation, architectural practices, home furnishings, implements of warfare, means of transportation, agricultural practices, geographical concerns, or political systems, may be the deciding factor between a more or less plausible reading. Why? Communication (whether written or oral) is colored by behavior patterns, which are themselves culturally grounded. Consequently, communication is not possible apart from the influences of culture. This means that the biblical authors communicate through their cultural filters, speaking to people within the same culture and to people who would understand the communication within the same cultural patterns. The biblical authors were not consciously communicating to readers in a twentieth-century Western culture. Therefore, since the biblical authors stood within a particular culture proclaiming a culturally conditioned message to a culturally identified audience, does it not seem logical that the modern hermeneut must, to as great a degree as possible, return to that world? Perhaps E. D. Hirsch is correct when he says, "the interpreter's primary task is to reproduce in himself the author's logic, his attitudes, his cultural givens, in short his world."[2] Mickelsen also supports this claim:

> The interpreter . . . stands in a modern culture, whether this be Western or another. He must understand the particular biblical culture which influenced the original source, message, and receptors. He must note both how it differs and how it resembles his own. Only then can he effectively communicate the message from one culture pattern to another.[3]

---

[2] E. D. Hirsch Jr., "Objective Interpretation," *PMLA* 75 (1960): 478.
[3] A. Berkeley Mickelsen, *Interpreting the Bible* (Grand Rapids: Eerdmans, 1963), 170.

Historical and socio-cultural research is not just an addendum to literary considerations, but it is both an intellectual and a practical necessity, because conscious or unconscious ignorance of the historical and cultural *Sitz im Leben* of a text most often results in vague and convoluted interpretation. This is usually the case when readers/interpreters remain prisoners of their own culture, imposing it upon the text, which is a product of another culture.

Historical and cultural information may be internal (information found within the text) or external (information found outside the text). While some texts virtually stand alone as far as background information is concerned, these are the exception. Most often the hermeneut must use both internal and external information in the reconstruction of the text's life situation. The internal information is primary, while external information serves a supportive and verifying role. Some examples of how historical and cultural reconstruction aid in interpretive plausibility should illustrate its importance.

Some Examples of Historical Background Studies

Example 1: Geenna

In Matt 5:22, we read, "But I say to you that if you are angry with a brother or sister, you will be liable to judgment; and if you insult a brother or sister, you will be liable to the council; and if you say, 'You fool,' you will be liable to the hell of fire." The word used here for "hell" is *geenna* and is found elsewhere in Matt 5:29, 30; 23:15, 33; and Jas 3:6. In the Authorized Version of the Bible the word "hell" also translates *hades*. While *hades* is consistently used to name the place of abode after death, *geenna* refers to a place of punishment usually associated with a perpetual fire. The Valley of Hinnom was the place where Ahaz sacrificed his sons and burned incense to idols. It also seems that prior to the Israelite conquest, this valley was a place of human sacrifice. Therefore, to later generations of Jews it represented a place of extreme abomination towards Yahweh. In fact, the site now called in Greek *geenna* became the place for dumping garbage that was consumed by a perpetual fire. As a result, whereas *geenna* originally referred metaphorically to the place of punishment after death, it eventually became a technical term for such a place. Since *geenna* was an actual physical place, it was ideal for this metaphorical application. The original readers or listeners would automatically make associations between *geenna* and the more abstract concept of a future place of punishment. Interpreters should keep this metaphorical character in mind when exegeting and applying any passage containing *geenna*.

Example 2: Revelation 3:14–21

In his book *The Letters to the Seven Churches of Asia in Their Local Settings*,[4] C. J. Hemer, in interpreting the following text from Rev 3:14–21, illustrates the importance of background information:

> And to the angel of the church in Laodicea write: The words of the Amen, the faithful and true witness, the origin of God's creation: I know your works; you are neither cold nor hot. I wish that you were either cold or hot. So, because you are lukewarm, and neither cold nor hot, I am about to spit you out of my mouth. For you say, "I am rich, I have prospered, and I need nothing." You do not realize that you are wretched, pitiable, poor, blind, and naked. Therefore I counsel you to buy from me gold refined by fire so that you may be rich; and white robes to clothe you and to keep the shame of your nakedness from being seen; and salve to anoint your eyes so that you may see. I reprove and discipline those whom I love. Be earnest, therefore, and repent. Listen! I am standing at the door, knocking; if you hear my voice and open the door, I will come in to you and eat with you, and you with me. To the one who conquers I will give a place with me on my throne, just as I myself conquered and sat down with my Father on his throne.

The church at Laodicea was famous for three things: its banking facilities, its textile industry, and its medical school—which produced Phrygian powder, an eye-salve. When Laodicea suffered almost total destruction by an earthquake around 60 C.E., assistance from Rome was refused, and the city was rebuilt from "her own resources." The prophetic utterance must be understood in the context of these facts, because the church had apparently assimilated the city's sense of pride and self-sufficiency in these things. Jesus then addresses the church in opposite terms; the church at Laodicea was actually poor, blind, and naked. They were in need of the spiritual correlates of those material things of which the Laodicean church was so proud.

In verses 15–16, we hear Jesus describing the Laodicean church as neither hot nor cold, but lukewarm. This passage has always been somewhat of a thorn in the flesh because theologians have not known

---

[4]C. J. Hemer, *The Letters to the Seven Churches of Asia in Their Local Settings* (JSOTSup 11; Sheffield: JSOT, 1986).

what to do with being coldly antagonistic towards Jesus. Through an interesting geographical study, however, Rudwick and Green[5] have suggested a promising interpretation: the church at Laodicea is being compared with the strengths and weakness of the city. Hierapolis was located within sight of Laodicea and was well-known for its hot calcium salt waters, which were prized for their healing properties. Also close to Laodicea was the city of Colossae, which was famous for its cold, refreshing stream. As the city of Laodicea outgrew its water supply, it was forced to pipe water in from a long distance through stone pipes. When the water arrived, it was warm and contained a sludgy deposit, making it almost undrinkable. While the hot water of Hierapolis healed and the cold water of Colossae refreshed, the Laodicean church brought neither spiritual healing nor refreshment. Like their water supply, the works of the Laodicean church were fit only to be spit out.

Example 3: Prophecy and the Exile

The prophetic writings offer another example of the importance of placing a text within its historical context. This context is both general and specific. The general context refers to developments in the Mediterranean world from the eighth to the fourth centuries B.C.E. Around 760 B.C.E. the nation of Israel was divided by civil war into two independent nations—Israel, the northern kingdom, and Judah, the southern kingdom. In 722 B.C.E. the northern kingdom of Israel fell to Assyria. Prior to this date, prophets such as Amos and Hosea preached to the northern kingdom, proclaiming its impending destruction and calling its people to repentance. The southern kingdom of Judah was defeated by Babylon in 587 B.C.E. The voices of the prophets Isaiah, Jeremiah, Joel, Micah, Nahum, Habakkuk, and Zephaniah can be heard pronouncing judgment upon Judah prior to this date. During the exile of Judah, the prophets Ezekiel, Haggai, Zechariah, and Malachi begin to announce Yahweh's future plans for his people.

The exile of Judah in 587 B.C.E. is the most critical historical event for interpreting the prophets because it has rendered a threefold division of prophecy—usually referred to as pre-exilic, exilic, and post-exilic. Each of these periods is characterized by a particular emphasis. The primary concern of pre-exilic prophecy was the announcement of impending judgment upon the nations of Israel and Judah. For instance,

---

[5] M. J. S. Rudwick and E. M. B. Green, "The Laodicean Lukewarmness," *ExpT* 69 (1957–58): 176–78.

in Isa 1–40 the primary thought is the destruction of a nation, and this dominates Isaiah's preaching from beginning to end. During the exilic period, because of the change of the historical situation, the message of wrath diminishes and the message of hope prevails. The return of the exiles and the establishment of a new state in the homeland become the chief themes of the exilic prophets. The prophets describe these events in miraculous terms. The actual circumstances of the return did not match the glory which the exilic prophets had anticipated, and the arrival of the exiles in Jerusalem was not greeted by any universal homage to Israel. So the disappointment of difficult times produced a problem with the eschatological hope of the exilic prophets. This gave way to a more patient anticipation of the coming day of Yahweh (which could obviously now not be seen as the return of the exiles), and the post-exilic prophets pushed it further into the future. An eschatological hope of the new Israel, with a new Jerusalem, blessed by the presence of Yahweh, became a prominent feature of post-exilic prophecy. The last of the canonical prophets still points toward the expectation of Yahweh's triumphant coming to his people. During this time highly imaginative language was used to describe the perfect age to come (e.g., Isa 65:17–25; Zech 14:1–9; Mal 4:1–6).

As might be expected, the events of the prophet's time influenced his message. Stuart rightly observes: "Unless you know these events and others within this era, . . . you probably will not be able to follow very well what the prophets are saying. God spoke in history and about history. To understand His Word we must know something of that history."[6]

Example 4: Philippians 3:2

When exegeting the New Testament epistles, it is desirable to know the author, place of writing, destination, and occasion for writing; moreover, the hermeneut must do additional historical research for small units or even for a sentence or word. An example of the latter is found in Phil 3:2: "Beware of the dogs, beware of the evil workers, beware of those who mutilate the flesh!" With biting sarcasm, Paul describes a group of opponents of the Philippian church. Three expressions describe metaphorically the opponents. Paul's choice of words reveals to whom he is referring and what they represent. He is speaking of only one group, the Judaizers, describing them in three ways.

---

[6] Fee and Stuart, *How to Read the Bible,* 157.

The first term Paul uses to describe the opponents is "dogs." This term must have had tremendous impact. First of all, being compared to a dog was insulting and dishonoring (1 Sam 17:43).[7] To be called a dead dog was the worst insult one could receive. It was considered a special judgment from God to be eaten by dogs in the street (1 Kgs 14:11; 16:4). Second, Deut 23:18 in the KJV forbids a person from bringing the "hire of a whore, or the price of a dog," into the sanctuary. Here, "dog" refers to a male prostitute (as the NRSV makes explicit). Therefore, to call a Jew a dog meant he was unfit for temple worship and thus excluded from the true worship of God. Third, the Jews felt they were superior to the Gentiles because they had the Torah. The Jews despised Gentiles and referred to them as dogs. Jesus refers to Gentiles outside the law as dogs in Mark 7:27–28. Fourth, Rev 22:15 speaks of dogs metaphorically as those outside of fellowship with the Lord when he sets up his final reign. Fifth, Paul's metaphor may also have brought thoughts of yelping animals (Judaizers) following him around and harassing him. Sixth, the possibility exists also that Paul may have been referring to Cynics along with Judaizers, because the word "cynic" comes from the same root as dog (*kyōn*). The founder of Cynic philosophy, Diogenes of Sinope, was called "the Dog" due to his impudence.

Any of these—Jews who want to prostitute the gospel, Gentiles, or Cynics—is a possibility. Due to the other descriptions of this group of opponents in the immediate context, however, the best choice here is that Paul wanted his readers to recall the male prostitute as referred to in the Old Testament.

The Ideological Context

As we mentioned above, writers can exercise no alternative but to express themselves in the conceptual and ideological categories of their own time. For authors to express themselves in a future ideological framework is impossible, while to express themselves in a conceptual milieu of the past would be anachronistic. A people's conceptual framework is especially evident in its religious and philosophical expressions, and these expressions most often are interrelated. An understanding of the ideological world which makes a text possible is essential to a critical reading of that text. This is not to suggest that an author is a prisoner of

---

[7] Otto Michel, "κύων," *TDNT* 3:1101.

a particular ideological world. An author may modify certain philosophical and religious concepts through reapplication or redefinition, but in order to appreciate the meaning resulting from such a modification, readers must understand the "normal" or accepted meaning or usage.

A literary work of art may transform the ideological structure of which it is a part, but it is still a part of that structure. People live their lives in accordance with societal roles in which ideas, values, and images tie them to particular social functions. Therefore, any literary expression bears the imprint of its historical epoch, and the most plausible reading is a critical one which takes into account this ideological imprint. Terry Eagleton underscores this point when he suggests that understanding literature "means understanding the total process of which it is a part."[8] He goes on to say:

> Literary works are not mysteriously inspired or explicable simply in terms of their author's psychology. They are forms of perception, particular ways of seeing the world; and as such they have a relation to that dominant way of seeing the world which is the "social mentality" or ideology of an age. That ideology, in turn, is the product of the concrete social relations into which men enter at a particular time and place. . . . To understand *King Lear, The Dunciad* or *Ulysses* is therefore to do more than interpret their symbolism, study their literary history and add footnotes about sociological facts which enter into them. It is first of all to understand the complex, indirect relations between those works and the ideological worlds they inhabit.[9]

Every writer has an individual psychology *and* is a product of society; every writer responds individually to a general history from a particular standpoint. But it is an individual response defined by a common ideological world. Furthermore, an author's current ideological world did not spring up overnight, but was formed over a period of time, having a continuity with its pre-history (i.e., each phase of a society's cultural development is influenced by previous phases). Consequently, to study the ideological world of a text one must have a wide vision. For example, to interpret the Genesis account of creation the interpreter must ask how that account relates to other earlier accounts within the Mediterranean world, for the society that produced the Genesis account was itself the product of a long history, a history which helped shape its ideological world. Ideally, the student of biblical literature should become acquainted

---

[8] Terry Eagleton, "Literature and History," in *Contexts for Criticism* (ed. Donald Keesey; 4th ed.; Boston: McGraw Hill, 2003), 421.

[9] Ibid.

with the history of literature, the history of religion, and the philosophy of religious texts.

Since there are numerous excellent works on the ideological worlds of both the Old and New Testaments,[10] we offer only an introductory treatment here in hope that we might convince the student of the indispensable nature of background studies.

The Ideological World of the Old Testament

The literature of the Old Testament has close and meaningful links to Mesopotamian, Canaanite, and Egyptian literature. Though there are differences between certain worldview elements, there are also similarities between the ideological worlds of the Hebrew authors and their counterparts. The literary productions of the Hebrew writers had as their sources the literary traditions and productions of the surrounding Near Eastern world, the most immediate contact being with Canaanite culture. The ideological elements within the Hebrew worldview were thus both continuous and non-continuous with those of their Near Eastern neighbors and ancestors. The ideological framework of the Hebrew authors is continuous in the sense that some formal literary practices and terminology are similar. The ideological framework is discontinuous because the Hebrew writers at various times consciously or unconsciously reshape literary materials or tradition in order to expound a differing ideological element within a worldview. As Jonas Greenfield observes: "The Hebrew writers have been called 'good students' of their Canaanite predecessors, but it is more accurate to designate them as active participants in a broader literary culture: they were participants and also innovators."[11] The links between the literary expressions of the respective ideologies go a long way in showing both the origins of biblical literature and its particular individuality. A **comparative study** of Mesopotamian, Canaanite, and Egyptian literature constitutes the best source

---

[10] For the New Testament, see Helmut Koester, *Introduction to the New Testament* (2 vols.; New York: Walter de Gruyter, 1982), vol. 1; and Everett Ferguson, *Backgrounds of Early Christianity* (2d ed.; Grand Rapids: Eerdmans, 1993). For the Old Testament, see David Damrosch, *The Narrative Covenant: Transformations of Genre in the Growth of Biblical Literature* (San Francisco: Harper & Row, 1987).

[11] Jonas C. Greenfield, "The Hebrew Bible and Canaanite Literature," in *The Literary Guide to the Bible* (ed. Robert Alter and Frank Kermode; Cambridge, Mass.: Harvard University Press, 1987), 560.

for discovering the literary norms from which and against which Hebrew literature developed.

David Damrosch offers a convincing argument for a comparative study of Hebrew literature and other ancient literature. He argues that at least Hebrew narrative "is the product of a rich mixture of direct use, thorough adaptation, and outright polemical rejection of earlier narrative practices."[12] Hebrew literature thus reveals a history of conscious generic adaptation, modification, and transformation; and these changes are significant for determining meaning. Damrosch outlines a process in Mesopotamian and Hebraic literary development in which there was a metamorphosis of genres over a period of time. During this process two or more literary genres were combined to form a new genre, which in turn reflected ideological peculiarities of the author's age. For example, poetic epic, characterized by an internal search for meaning within the brevity of life, was combined with historiography to produce a historicized mythology. Mirroring the *Gilgamesh Epic,* the Hebrew writers transformed this genre into historical prose narrative. Referring to this "cross-fertilization" of genres, Damrosch concludes:

> The origins of Hebrew historical prose can be traced in Mesopotamian literature of the second millennium, but not through a direct comparison of historical writings alone. Rather, the Bible's historical writing can best be understood as the result of a far-reaching transformation of earlier genres, resulting in a combination of many of the values, themes, and formal properties of historical chronicle with that of poetic epic. Scholars who have sharply separated epic from chronicle, and myth from history, have thus unduly restricted the Near Eastern evidence that can, and should, be used in assessing this movement, since the background to the confluence of epic and history can already be shown within Mesopotamian literature itself.[13]

Because innovation often grows out of a particular ideology, the student of the Old Testament should become acquainted with the ideological worlds of civilizations such as Mesopotamian, Egyptian, Hittite, and Canaanite. Below are some suggested sources that will familiarize the student with the ideological framework within which the Hebrew Bible was produced. For English translations of some of these texts see:

Breasted, J. H. *Ancient Records of Egypt.* 5 vols. Champaign, Il.: University of Illinois Press, 2001. Especially vols. 2 and 3.

---

[12] Damrosch, *Narrative Covenant,* 41.
[13] Ibid.

Coogan, Michael David, ed. & trans. *Stories from Ancient Canaan.* Philadelphia: Westminster, 1978.

Edgerton, William F., and John A. Wilson. *Historical Records of Rameses III.* Studies in Ancient Oriental Civilization 12. Chicago: University of Chicago Press, 1936.

Luckenbill, D. D. *Ancient Records of Assyria and Babylonia.* 2 vols. Chicago: University of Chicago Press, 1926–27.

Matthews, V., and D. Benjamin. *Old Testament Parallels: Laws and Stories from the Ancient Near East.* 3d ed. New York: Paulist, 2006.

O'Brien, Joan, and Wilfred Major. *In the Beginning: Creation Myths from Ancient Mesopotamia, Israel, and Greece.* Chico, Calif.: Scholar's Press, 1982.

Pritchard, James B., ed. *The Ancient Near East: An Anthology of Texts & Pictures.* 2 vols. Ewing, N.J.: California-Princeton Fulfillment Services, 1976.

Simons, J. *Handbook for the Study of Egyptian Topographical Lists Relating to Western Asia.* Leiden: E. J. Brill, 1937.

Sproul, Barbara C. *Primal Myths: Creating the World.* San Francisco: Harper & Row, 1979.

Thomas, D. W., ed. *Documents from Old Testament Times.* New York: Harper, 1958.

Ras Shamra Texts

These texts were discovered in 1929 in the ruins of ancient Ugarit, a Phoenician city on the Syrian coast. They are of utmost importance for understanding Canaanite culture and the ideological milieu within which Hebrew culture grew during the second millennium B.C.E. They also provide the modern hermeneut with a knowledge of the Canaanite pantheon along with the religious cult surrounding it.

Mari Tablets

Found in the palace archives at tell el-Hariri, a city of Mari on the Euphrates, these tablets aid in the reconstruction of the Amorite culture of the second millennium B.C.E., which is the period of the Old Testament patriarchs.

Amarna Tablets

These tablets come from El-Amarna in Egypt and are written in Akkadian. Most of these tablets are correspondences between the Egyptian court and the rulers of city-states in Syria, Phoenicia, and Palestine. Their usefulness lies in the insight they give into the social and political situations in Palestine during the first half of the fourteenth century B.C.E., which is the period just prior to the birth of the nation of Israel.

Royal Egyptian Inscriptions

These Egyptian reports of military campaigns and lists of conquered cities offer a glimpse of the social conditions in Syria-Palestine. They are of limited import, however, because the conquests to which these inscriptions refer were history by the time the Hebrews settled in Palestine.

Royal Assyrian Inscriptions

Valuable information concerning Israel's history is contained in these inscriptions. The practice of dating the beginning of a ruler's reign and certain natural phenomena (like a solar eclipse) is of great value in establishing the chronology of Assyrian Israelite rulers.

The Babylonian Chronicles

These historiographic texts from ancient Mesopotamia treat various kings from the Neo-Babylonian Dynasty (8th century B.C.E.) to the Seleucid period (3d century B.C.E.). These selective chronicles document the reigns of the various kings as well as notable military and cultic events.

Examples of Comparative Study

Perhaps some examples of the manner in which an author modifies or generally reacts to sources will demonstrate how crucial a comparative approach is to interpretation. A considerable amount of light can be shed on a text if it is interpreted against the backdrop of its written sources and/or its ideological framework. We will look at three such cases, from Job, Genesis, and the Prophets respectively.

Example 1: Job and the God El

The Ras Shamra texts portray El as the god who presides over the assembly of the gods and connect him with wisdom. El is also credited with two offspring, Yam (Sea) and Mot (Death). In Job 27, Job accuses God (El) of being unjust to him while blessing the wicked. Job 28 is a description of humankind's effort to uncover the earth's mineral wealth. Job says: "The sources of the rivers they probe; hidden things they bring to light" (v. 11). The source of the rivers is the dwelling place of El according to the Ras Shamra texts. Job asks, "But where shall wisdom be found? And where is the place of understanding?" (28:12). The Deep (Yam) responds: "It is not in me" (v. 14), followed by Death's (Mot) response: "We have heard a rumor of it with our ears" (v. 22). Job finally gives the answer in verse 23: "God understands the way to it, and he knows its place." It appears that Job's ancient source or tradition has already associated wisdom with El.[14]

Example 2: Genesis 1–11 and the Gilgamesh Epic

When a comparative study is made, differences in emphasis, deemphasis, exclusion, or combination of sources suggest specific interests, and as such they are clues to literary meaning. Our second example, involving a comparison of Gen 1–11 and the *Gilgamesh Epic*, illustrates this point. The *Gilgamesh Epic* and Gen 1–11 are both "the epic story of primordial times from the creation of human beings to the Flood."[15] In each story, four basic elements appear: the creation of the world, the creation of human beings, the Flood, and the establishment of the human order following the Flood. The *Gilgamesh Epic* moves towards a meditation on the limits of human culture, while the Genesis account of creation takes up the theme of separation between Yahweh and humans. Damrosch demonstrates how the opening section of Genesis transforms the older creation and flood stories in order to reflect on the nature of human culture. Every event in Gen 1–11 has a direct parallel in the *Gilgamesh Epic*.[16] Damrosch observes:

> Each of these parallels shows considerable differences as well as similarities (though the flood story shows a particularly close resemblance), and there is no need to suppose a direct dependence of Genesis on the *Gilgamesh Epic;* but it is evident that the two texts are parallel efforts, from roughly the same period, to rework the old mythic material of the creation and Flood. The many similarities between these texts, and their far-reaching differences both in form and theme will, I believe, suggest much

---

[14] For an excellent and somewhat detailed discussion of the relationship between certain Hebrew cosmological concepts and those found within the Ras Shamra texts, see Greenfield, "Hebrew Bible and Canaanite Literature," 545–60.

[15] Damrosch, *Narrative Covenant,* 91.

[16] Ibid., 118–35.

about the theological and literary forces at work in the early phase of the composition of biblical literature and will set the stage for a better understanding of the relations of the Yahwistic legendary material to the fully developed epic historiography of the story of King David.[17]

For example, the Genesis epic parallels the old Babylonian predecessors, where the story of creation, far from being the central point of the story, is merely a prologue to the flood story.

When we read the Genesis epic against the comparative backdrop of its earlier models, each similarity and subtle change becomes significant for meaning. Further, if these changes are due to ideological considerations, they may continue to be operative in other portions of the Hebrew Scriptures. The ideological lessons expressed in Gen 1–11 may be developed even further in the stories of the patriarchs and monarchs. If this is indeed the case, as Damrosch suggests,[18] then the development of the themes of separation, exile, and revolt are primary ideological concerns, and consequently thematic controls, throughout other portions of the Hebrew canon.

Example 3: The Prophets and Egyptian Wisdom Literature

Another area where a comparative study of ideological literature is essential is the association between the Egyptian wisdom literature and the ethical concerns found in the Hebrew prophets. Many consider the Hebrew prophets to have been the first to place moral concerns above cultic ritual in Israel. Moral behavior is the desire of God rather than sacrifice (Isa 1:11–17; Jer 6:20; 7:22; Mic 6:6–8; Amos 5:21–25). The same concept, however, is found in the Egyptian wisdom literature. In "The Teaching of Merikare" the following instruction is given to King Merikare:

> Make firm your place with uprightness and just dealing for it is on that which their hearts rely; more acceptable is a loaf (perhaps "character") of the upright than the ox of the wrongdoer.[19]

To summarize, the Old Testament writers were not working or living in a vacuum, but were sensitive to their culture and its traditions, as well the cultures around them. The writers imitated numerous alien

---

[17] Ibid., 120.

[18] Ibid.

[19] Moshe Weinfeld, "Ancient Near Eastern Patterns in Prophetic Literature," *VT* 27 (April 1977): 180.

types of speech and utilized them for their own purposes. They took over and adapted a wide range of traditions to make themselves clearly understandable to their audiences. They borrowed foreign and older traditions and adapted them to new situations, giving them fresh significance. A familiarity with these various traditions will put the reader in a more favorable position to offer the most plausible explication of a text or any portion of it. This is necessarily true because any adaptation, modification, or reapplication of any portion of a tradition is most accurately understood when the reader has some knowledge of the original tradition itself.

The Ideological World of the New Testament

The ideological world of the New Testament writings is especially that of first-century Judaism. But the symbols of first-century **Judaism** were transformed by the infusion of Greco-Roman culture. Consequently, it is more appropriate to speak of the ideological *worlds* of these writings. For this reason, the student of the Bible should have some background knowledge of the elements which constitute first-century Judaism and **Hellenism** and the ancient Mediterranean world. As Johnson observes, "the way humans organize themselves in the world depends little on biology and less on instinct but a great deal on humans' ideas about themselves and the world."[20] These ideas are most concretely expressed through a people's religious and philosophical productions. Since literary productions of a segment of a society are influenced by and have meaning in relationship to other literary productions within the larger society, students are better equipped to interpret the New Testament writings if they have a familiarity with the literature contemporary with the New Testament. Therefore, we will look briefly at what is meant by Hellenism, the philosophical and religious milieu of the Hellenistic period, the make-up of first-century Judaism, and comparative literature.

Hellenism

In 334 B.C.E., a young Alexander the Great set out to conquer the Persian Empire in the east. Traveling with him were poets, philosophers, and historians. He himself was a student of Aristotle and was

---

[20] Johnson, *Writings of the New Testament,* 12.

convinced that the Greek mode of life was unexcelled. Alexander's successors were generally of the same opinion and continued in the attempt to establish a Hellenistic world. For the most part, when Greek culture came into contact with oriental influences, the Greek element predominated; there was, however, a process of religious and philosophical interpenetration and mutual influence. This process of interpenetration of cultures in which the Greek element predominated is usually referred to as hellenization, while the period of such cultural confluence, beginning with Alexander the Great and continuing into the Roman imperial period, is referred to as the Hellenistic period. This does not mean that Hellenism ceased to be influential during the Roman imperial period. On the contrary, Hellenism continued to be effective throughout the Roman imperial period. By the first century B.C.E., a distinctively universal culture (an amalgamation of Greek and oriental) had emerged under the umbrella of a single political entity— Rome. Because Christianity had its birth during the Roman imperial period, we might rightly expect it to exhibit Hellenistic traits. Christianity was the heir of a hellenized Judaism. For the most part, the earliest Christians were people whose lives and thoughts were formed and molded by Hellenism. The earliest Christians used the **Septuagint** (the Greek translation of the Old Testament) as their Bible. This is significant when we recognize that religious and philosophical concepts are modified when writings are translated from one language to another.

Hellenism is characterized by **syncretism** (the mixture of worldviews and ideologies), especially in the area of philosophy and religion, where there is an obvious mixture of Greek and oriental elements. Even where local or territorial religious expressions remained the same in essence, these expressions appeared in Greek dress. The Septuagint is an example of this syncretism. The syncretistic tendency of hellenization resulted in a sort of universalization. When the local deities of the East came into contact with the Greek pantheon, the equating of these two was inevitable. This eventually led to the idea of the existence of a single divine power with multiple manifestations. But the sacrifice of local deities on the altar of universalism produced a view of the universe as one governed by chance and fate. This in turn resulted in a search for a more profound, individual religious experience. The universalization of Hellenism presented a universe where the individual had no control over his or her existence. A spirit of fatalism characterized the period.

When the ideal of individual citizen participation in the community was frustrated by the decline of the *polis,* the citizens lost their social identity. When the local deity became identical with other gods of other people (i.e., when individual religious experience gave way to religious universalism or monotheism), people lost their religious identity, and their lives became meaningless, governed by *tychē* (chance) and *heimarmenē* (fate). Since human life was predestined by these powers, humans had little or no control over their existence. In the wake of such losses, a need of individual salvation became paramount. This attitude characterizes the Hellenistic period, especially during the period of Roman rule when individual identity was expected to give way to the welfare of the state. As a result, both religious and philosophical expression in the Hellenistic period placed increased importance upon the individual and the salvation of the individual from the control of a universe governed by chance or fate. It was to this matter of individual salvation that all the philosophical and religious expressions spoke.

The Philosophical and Religious Milieu of the Hellenistic Period

Hellenistic Philosophies. Prior to the Hellenistic period, Greek philosophies were primarily concerned with creating a world in which there was some rational system of meaning—a universe governed by some ontological reality, against which everything has its meaning and significance. But when the universal ideal of the Hellenistic period failed, a sense of skepticism became prevalent. Therefore, the **Hellenistic philosophies**[21] (Stoicism, Epicureanism, Neopythagoreanism, and Neoplatonism) contained an element of skepticism.

Hellenistic philosophical schools were half religious and half philosophical. Members of such schools tended to live according to the teachings of their founding masters. The schools placed emphasis on ethics and offered their members a worldview and suggested practical ways for adherents to conduct themselves in everyday living. In a world where individuals were on their own, many were looking for such

---

[21] For information about the Hellenistic philosophies see Ferguson, *Backgrounds of Early Christianity,* 299–371; Koester, *Introduction to the New Testament,* 1:141–63; E. Bevan, "Hellenistic Popular Philosophy," in *The Hellenistic Age* (ed. J. B. Bury et al.; Cambridge: The University Press, 1923), 79–107; J. Dillon, *The Middle Platonists, 80 B.C. to A.D. 220* (Ithaca, N.Y.: Cornell University Press, 1977); P. Merlan, *From Platonism to Neoplatonism* (2d ed.; Hague: Nijhoff, 1960); R. D. Hicks, *Stoic and Epicurean* (New York: Russell & Russell, 1962); A. Malherbe, ed., *The Cynic Epistles* (Missoula: Scholars Press, 1977); and Wayne A. Meeks, *The Moral World of the First Christians* (Philadelphia: Westminster, 1986), 40–64.

guidance within a group of friends that would supply a sense of community. The Hellenistic philosophies spoke to the individual and his or her place in the universe. Paul Tillich offers the following insight:

> During this period when the skeptical mood permeated the ancient world, they wanted certainty above all; they demanded it in order to live. Their answer was that their great teachers, Plato, Aristotle, Zeno, Epicurus, Plotinus, were not merely thinkers or professors, but they were inspired men.[22]

Stories about the founders of these philosophical communities resemble accounts Christians related about their founder. For instance, Epicurus was called *sōtēr* (savior) by his followers. Commenting on this, Tillich goes on to say, "What does this mean? He was called *sōtēr* because he did the greatest thing anyone could do for his followers: he liberated them from anxiety."[23] The Hellenistic philosophies in one way or another offered freedom from the anxiety of the age by offering the individual a pattern of living that afforded at least a measure of control. These philosophical schools constitute one of the immediate sources for a great deal of early Christian thought. Therefore, a brief look at each is in order, but we must encourage students to take the time to plunge deeper into the philosophical and religious expressions of the Hellenistic age.

Stoicism. Stoicism was one of the most influential philosophical systems of the Hellenistic period. Founded in Athens by Zeno of Citium (332–260 B.C.E.), Stoicism acquired its name from the painted porch (Greek, *stoa*) in the Agora where its proponents taught. Stoicism was introduced in Rome (161 B.C.E.) by Panaetius who made Stoicism more practical. Seneca (ca. 4 B.C.E.–65 C.E.), a contemporary of Paul, did much to popularize the ethical teachings of Stoicism by his writings.

Resting on a religious basis, Stoicism made a strong appeal to the Roman character. For the Stoic, the universe itself was God, and the ultimate substance of the universe was a "fiery breath" or "spirit" which was distributed throughout in varying degrees.[24] This spirit was considered to be alive and rational, and in its manifestation as reason (*logos*) it introduced order into the world. Since humanity possessed in reason a particle of the divine breath, the individual was capable of entering

---

[22] Paul Tillich, *A History of Christian Thought* (New York: Simon & Schuster, 1968), 5.

[23] Ibid.

[24] Ralph P. Martin, *New Testament Foundations* (2 vols.; Grand Rapids: Eerdmans, 1978), 1:42.

into communion with the supreme reason. *Logos* refers to the reasonable structure indicated by a word, thus meaning the universal law of
reality. The *logos* is also the law which determines the movement of all
reality. According to the Stoics, the *logos* is in everything. (Compare
John's comment, "The true light, which enlightens everyone, was coming into the world" [John 1:9].) This idea of the *logos* is one of the
major influences of Stoicism upon early Christianity.[25]

The fundamental tenet of Stoicism is that virtue is the only good,
and vice the only evil. The wise person is not mastered by pain and
pleasure, wealth and poverty, or success and misfortune. Self-control
or contentment (*enkrateia*) is the hallmark of the wise person.

There are similarities between the teachings of the New Testament
and those of Stoicism. This is especially true of the writings of Paul.
Paul's Judaism was itself influenced by Hellenistic concepts and modes
of expression. Paul adapts the religious views of the Hebrew Bible and
Palestinian Judaism along with the style and views of Hellenistic popular philosophy.[26] Paul read a Greek Bible, which bore the impressions
of the Hellenistic society, wrote in Greek, and labored among Gentile
people.

We must understand that Paul was concerned about communicating to his contemporaries and would not have ignored the jargon of the
day or the meaning of established terms and concepts. Along with other
New Testament literature, Paul's writings took shape within and were
addressed primarily to the Hellenistic world. Consequently, we should
interpret them in terms of their meaning for that world.

Paul's ethical teaching is indebted to Hellenistic sources in a general
way. Scholars have pointed out the numerous Pauline phrases, metaphors,
and terms which were familiar in Stoicism. These include: metaphors of
life as warfare (2 Cor 10:3; 1 Thess 5:8) or as an athletic competition
(1 Cor 9:25); descriptions of God as "all in all" (1 Cor 15:28) and as the
one of, through, and to whom all things are (Rom 11:36); the term "your
duty" (Phlm 8); the concept of "spending" and "being spent" for others
(2 Cor 12:15); and disregard for the external circumstances of one's life
(2 Cor 6:8–10; Phil 4:11–12).[27] Phil 4:8 also contains clear Stoic influence. Paul commends two qualities in this verse that are not mentioned

---

[25] The discussion of *logos* is adapted from Tillich, *History of Christian
Thought*.

[26] Victor P. Furnish, *Theology and Ethics of Paul* (Nashville: Abingdon,
1968), 46.

[27] Ibid.

elsewhere in the New Testament: "pleasing" and "commendable." Other terms in this verse having a significant place in Stoic ethics are "excellence" and "worthy of praise."

The moral teachings of Seneca exhibit many parallels to the teachings of Jesus on the mount. Examples include Seneca's statements that "the mind, unless it is pure and holy, comprehends not God" and that "a man is a robber even before he stains his hands; for he is already armed to slay, and has the desire to spoil and to kill."[28] There are also echoes of the parable of the sower, of the mustard seed, and of the forgiven debtor.

Other New Testament writings also reflect Stoic concepts, such as John's Gospel and his portrayal of the *logos*. The metaphor that instructs the readers to "gird up the loins" of their minds (cf. 1 Pet 1:13, KJV) also appears in Seneca's writings as an instruction to let the mind stand ready.

The New Testament did enlist Stoic terminology and style. But its writers also altered Stoic patterns and used the major concepts with different meanings. Whether the concepts were modified or not, any reading and understanding of a text is enhanced by a familiarity with the text's ideological matrix.

Epicureanism. Epicureanism advocated the higher pleasures of the mind along with an emphasis on friendship and contentment. Like Paul, Epicurus was a father figure to his followers; he founded communities of followers and instructed these communities through letters. Unlike Paul, his birthday was celebrated annually, and his followers bestowed divine honors upon him.

It is through Lucretius (94–55 B.C.E.), though, that we have most of our knowledge about Epicureanism. According to Lucretius, nature is made up of matter and space, which he calls "the void." Matter is divisible, but it cannot be divided indefinitely because this would result in nothing. Eventually one arrives at the atom (Gk. "indivisible"). Atoms are the fundamental substance of everything in the universe. They can be neither created nor destroyed, but they can be arranged in different configurations.

Atoms and space constitute the universe, which is itself without limits. The physical world is comprised of atoms and exists and moves according to the dictates of law. As a result, nature is without purpose,

---

[28] See J. B. Lightfoot, *St. Paul's Epistle to the Philippians* (repr.; Peabody, Mass.: Hendrickson, 1993), 287–89.

having neither beginning nor end. If atoms—the building-blocks of the universe—are indestructible and non-creatable, then the world must be eternal.

Epicurus sought to deliver his followers from what he perceived to be the darkness of religion. He accomplished this through his materialistic approach to the universe. If the soul itself is a type of physical object composed of atoms, it will die when the body dies. Therefore, since the soul does not survive the death of the body, there is no future life of bliss or punishment to worry about now. This absence of any future life was intended to relieve the followers of any fear of punishment after death. If there is no future life to be concerned about, we should live with our attention directed squarely toward this life, of which the highest good is tranquility, the absence of agitation.

In the wake of the devaluating effects of the universalization of Hellenism, Epicurus succeeded in substituting a community or circle of close friends and associates for the loss of the sense of community so prevalent in Hellenism. Within this circle of friends, one finds the greatest pleasure of the soul. This idea of friendship is basic, for the individual is a stranger in the world. Each person needs friends who offer shelter and give pleasure.[29]

Some similarities between Epicureanism and the early Christian communities exist, but they seem to be only superficial. Yet, the Epicureans and Christians were responding to the same loss precipitated by Hellenism—the devaluation of the individual. The founding of a community where all were equal, whether slave, free, woman, or man, and where the community was insulated and separated from the world and bonded together by worship and reverence, is characteristic of both Epicureans and Christians. The following passage in 1 Thess 4:9–12 illustrates this point:

> Now concerning love of the brothers and sisters, you do not need to have anyone write to you, for you yourselves have been taught by God to love one another; and indeed you do love all the brothers and sisters throughout Macedonia. But we urge you, beloved, to do so more and more, to aspire to live quietly, to mind your own affairs, and to work with your hands, as we directed you, so that you may behave properly toward outsiders and be dependent on no one.

Paul is describing a quiet, separated life of tranquility. Gilbert Murray has suggested that the early Christian communities were patterned

---

[29] Ibid., 298–301.

after the Epicurean communities, even down to the use of the title
"friends" in John 15:15 and 3 John 15.[30]

Neopythagoreanism. In the first century B.C.E. there was a revival of the
ideas of Pythagoras. The Neopythagoreans were interested in astrol-
ogy and in the stellar space between God and the material world. This
space is inhabited by intermediary demons arranged in a descending
order. The Neopythagoreans also conceived of the material world as
evil, since it is so far removed from a transcendent god. This negative view
of the material world became one of the primary tenets of Gnosticism
and Neoplatonism.

The best known adherent of Neopythagoreanism is Apollonius of
Tyana, who is known through his biographer, Philostratus. Apparently
Apollonius lived during the first century C.E. Philostratus portrays him
as an itinerant teacher traveling to the major cities of the Roman Empire. He is a wise man with miraculous powers to heal the sick. He rejected marriage (at least for himself), was able to see into the past and
future, and taught a substitution of prayer and meditation for animal
sacrifice. The following parallels exist between Philostratus' account
of the life of Apollonius and that of Jesus:[31]

1. His miraculous birth
2. The gathering of a circle of disciples
3. Itinerant teaching
4. Collection of miracle stories (demon-possessed boy, lame man,
    blind man, paralytic)
5. Disappearance at his trial
6. The charge that Apollonius was a magician

The writings of earliest Christianity primarily took shape within
and were addressed to the Hellenistic world. Therefore, we must interpret them in terms of their meaning for that world. The hermeneut
should give due weight to the positive influence of Hellenistic philosophical thought upon these New Testament writings. But the influence of Hellenistic philosophical categories and ideas upon the New
Testament writers is not the only one. There was a veritable plethora of
interest in the oriental **mystery religions** during the Hellenistic period.

---

[30] Gilbert Murray, *Five Stages of Greek Religion* (Garden City: Doubleday,
1955), 204–5.

[31] See Ferguson, *Backgrounds of Early Christianity,* 361–63.

Any study of the New Testament must consider the influence of these religions or at least the conditions which gave rise to the unquestionably renewed religious sensitivity. There was also rabbinic influence upon both the form and content of the NT authors. But we must also underscore that the Jewish influence upon the New Testament writers was a Judaism that had been modified by Hellenism.

The Mystery Religions

During the Hellenistic period, there was a loss of confidence in the established gods/goddesses, religions, and philosophies. Many people sought help to live meaningful lives within an impersonal world. The classical gods of Greece were impersonal and capricious, state religions were irrelevant to the immediate needs of the common person, and emperor worship was a political tool rather than an intimate faith.[32] The time was ripe for the rise and success of the mystery religions.

The object of the mysteries was to secure salvation for people who were subject to moral and physical evil, dominated by destiny, and unable to free themselves from the corruption that beset the material side of nature.[33] By participating in mystery rites and dramas of the cult, the adherents believed that they could share in the life of their deity. The mysteries allowed the worshippers to commune with their god/goddess and to enjoy a better life, confident of immortality. The mysteries offered emotional release for the participants through rituals, communal meals, pageantry, ecstatic ceremonies, festivals, and in some cases orgiastic rites.[34]

Initiation usually involved purification of the initiate (*katharsis*), the assembling of the initiates for a ceremonial procession (*systasis*), the procession of the initiates (*mystae*) into the mystery's sacred precincts (*temenos*), and the encounter with the mystery's deity.[35] Following the initiation the initiate stood outside of a fate-dominated world and was reborn into the cult's deity.

Purification was symbolized through animal sacrifice, application of water and/or blood, eating sacred meals, or a combination of these.

---

[32] Merrill C. Tenney, *New Testament Times* (Grand Rapids: Eerdmans, 1975), 117.

[33] C. K. Barrett, *The New Testament Background: Selected Documents* (rev. ed.; San Francisco: Harper & Row, 1987), 120.

[34] Cyril Bailey, *Phases in the Religion of Ancient Rome* (Westport: Greenwood, 1972), 177.

[35] Ibid., 61–62.

Some of the mysteries included fasting, sacrifice, frenzied dancing and colorful processions, reenactments of the drama of their deity's wanderings, life, or entrance into immortality, orgiastic rites, and communal meals.

The gods of the mystery religions were originally fertility gods of agriculture, and the rites which initially secured crop and livestock productivity evolved into a personal religion. "In the myths of the mysteries, the deities are represented as wanderers whose journeys lead them from an existence of humanlike suffering to a transformed existence as celestial saviors."[36] Some myths were based upon a wife (or mother) who grieves for her lost husband (or child), and after a period of suffering, the lost family member is restored to the seeker—usually from the dead—and begins a new life.[37] The story of the wanderings, sufferings, and homecoming of the god or goddess offered the possibility that one's own suffering and wandering might come to an end through a personal soteriological relationship under the god's providential protection.

Although each mystery religion possessed its own rituals, symbolism, and interpretation of its rites, all of them shared several of the following common characteristics:

1. a firm organization to which all members were subject
2. membership through rites of initiation
3. participation in regular meetings in which sacramental ceremonies were celebrated
4. obligation to observe moral or ascetic precepts
5. mutual support of all members
6. obedience to the cult leader and the community of adherents
7. cultivation of secret traditions[38]

The mysteries became a primary institution in many hellenized cities prior to, during, and after the birth of Christianity.

When Paul and other New Testament writers penned their works, they employed many words, concepts, and categories that were current in the mysteries. Such concepts include divine instruction through dreams and visions, baptism, fasting, regeneration, rebirth, communion, heaven, hell, conquest of evil, the savior-god as the mediator between

---

[36] Luther Martin, *Hellenistic Religions* (New York: Oxford University Press, 1987), 59.

[37] Howard Clark Kee, Franklin W. Young, and Karlfried Froelich, *Understanding the New Testament* (4th ed.; Englewood Cliffs: Prentice-Hall, 1983), 33.

[38] Koester, *Introduction to the New Testament,* 1:198.

deity and the individual, and the shedding of blood. In Rev 12, there is reference to the woman and the dragon. Isis and Horus were also persecuted by a dragon named Typhon. The image in Rev 12 depicts a woman attired in royal clothes, clothed with power, and giving birth to a child. These symbols parallel Isis, her power, her birth, and persecution. Mithras was believed to have life-giving power: "You have rescued us, too, by shedding the blood that makes us immortal."[39] The evangelist Mark tells his readers that Jesus gave his blood for humanity's sins because he "came to give his life a ransom for many" (Mark 10:45). Mithras was both the mediator between good and evil, and the representative of deity on earth. In his struggle with the bull, Mithras portrays the human struggle of those in pursuit of good; and by slaying the bull for humanity's benefit, he brought life and victory over evil.

This mystery also held that the initiate should strive for perfect unity and freedom from sensuality. Adherents were to show perfect loyalty to their god and companionship toward their comrades. They were also to live a good life because they were giving the right service to god. The similarities between Mithraism and Christianity were so close that some of the early church fathers were amazed.[40] Yet, while some of the terminology and concepts were identical, the interpretations were often quite different. A case in point is the reinterpretation of the pivotal term in the mysteries—"mystery." In the ordinary sense of the word, mystery refers to knowledge that is withheld. According to the author of Ephesians, a mystery is truth revealed. In Eph 1:9, there is reference to the mystery, and in 3:6 it is defined. The mystery is that the Gentiles are also included in God's promises. Then the author goes on to say, "this grace was given to me . . . to make everyone see what is the plan of the mystery" (3:8–9). The mysteries sought to keep their rites secret from all but a select few. The writer of Ephesians took a term that was common to his audience and radically redefined it in order to declare the not-so-secret plan of God.

We emphasize again that the writers of the New Testament (or any document for that matter) could exercise no alternative but to express themselves in the ideological milieu of their times. To borrow terms and ideas from other religious, philosophical, or literary traditions and then reapply, modify, or redefine them is probably the surest way that writers

---

[39] Kurt Rudolph, "Mystery Religions," *ER* 7:236.

[40] George Gilmore, "Mithraism," in *The New Schaff-Herzog Encyclopedia of Religious Knowledge* (ed. Samuel Macaulty Jackson; Grand Rapids: Baker, 1977), 7:419.

can make themselves both heard and understood. The reason for this is that such terms and concepts already carry with them a range of meanings that the reader can then adjust when the terms and concepts are placed in a new contextual setting.

Judaism

Christianity was conceived at least partially in the womb of Judaism. But Judaism of the first century was anything but a monolithic religious tradition. There were numerous ideological threads running through it—Messianism, apocalypticism, legalism, Hellenism. Many times these threads were intertwined. To complicate matters, Judaism existed in two general forms—Palestinian Judaism and Judaism of the Greek Diaspora.

The historical trek that eventually produced first-century Judaism, or what some call Pharisaic Judaism, is long and complex. A reconstruction of that history should begin with the exile, proceed to the Persian period (538–332 B.C.E.), continue through the Greek period (332–167 B.C.E.) and the Maccabean period (167–63 B.C.E.), until finally it arrives at the Roman period (from 63 B.C.E.). But such a journey is not feasible for an introductory hermeneutics text. There are excellent New Testament introductions and texts on backgrounds which the hermeneutics student should consult, because there simply is no substitute for knowledge of the long and complicated history which spawned the Judaism of the first century. This is the Judaism that passed on a variety of ideological and pedagogical factors to early Christianity and its literary productions we call the New Testament. It was a Judaism that revolved around monotheism, national feasts, temple, synagogue, a sense of destiny, and most of all the Torah. What we do propose to do here is offer the student a brief introduction to the various parties within first-century Judaism having significance for New Testament interpretation.

The Pharisees. After the Maccabean revolt of 167 B.C.E., there were at least three courses which a person could follow: One could drop out of the mainstream of religious and political life into a private community; one could perpetually reinterpret his or her current religious tradition in the light of new circumstances; or a person could view the new circumstances apart from the religious tradition. The **Essenes** choose the first course, the **Pharisees** chose the second, and the **Sadducees** followed the last.[41]

---

[41] Ferguson, *Backgrounds of Early Christianity,* 480–85.

Although their power was limited primarily to their own fellowships, and their influence was concentrated upon the common people, the Pharisees were instrumental in giving Judaism its distinct character and definition after the fall of Jerusalem in 70 C.E. Judaism after this time was primarily Pharisaic Judaism.

The religious program of the Pharisees was supported by two primary underpinnings—the written Torah and the oral Torah. The Pharisees believed that the written Torah stood in constant need of interpretation and application to new and changing circumstances. They believed that God had given Moses both the written Torah and an oral one that interpreted and explained the written one. This oral Torah (interpretation) became as authoritative for the Pharisees as the written Torah. The interpretive applications which the Pharisees gave to the written Torah were as binding as the written Torah itself. Because of this openness to the interpretation of the Torah, the Pharisees were susceptible to doctrines that were unacceptable to the Sadducees (e.g., bodily resurrection, final judgment, and rewards and punishment after death).

Not usually recognized by the casual readers of the New Testament is the amazing amount of doctrinal agreement among the Pharisees and Jesus and the early Christians. A substantial amount of Jesus' ethical teaching is paralleled in the rabbinic writings. Even where there is disagreement, the meaning of Jesus' teaching or that of the early church must be understood in the light of the Pharisaic difference. For example, the practice of summarizing the Torah by the use of a few principles (Matt 22:36) was a rabbinic practice. Separation from the world meant to the Pharisee that the pious individual must avoid contact with those people who neglected the Torah (both written and oral); but for Jesus and the early Christians, separation from the world was a matter of attitude. When Jesus reinterprets the Torah in Matthew's Sermon on the Mount, he offers six antitheses whose premises are drawn from the written and oral Torah.

Another example where a comparison with rabbinic material is crucial for interpreting a remark by Jesus occurs in Matt 18:20: "For where two or three are gathered in my name, I am there among them." This is a reapplication of a rabbinic teaching that claims where two or three are together studying the Torah, God is with them (*Pirqe 'Abot* 3:2). As will be shown in unit II, Matthew is using this and similar sayings of Jesus to present Jesus as the personification of the Torah. Jesus also rejected the Pharisees' practice of giving priority to the oral tradition over the written Torah. As Ferguson observes, for Jesus, "The written word is authoritative, but the great fundamental principles therein take precedence and provide the standard by which it is to be interpreted and applied."[42] Jesus agreed with the Pharisees' desire to make the Torah applicable, but he disagreed with aspects of their methodology. This method of interpretation, **midrash**, was used extensively by the New Testament writers. Since we will discuss this in the next unit, suffice it here to say that in many instances a familiarity with this interpretive method is a definite plus for the modern interpreter.

The Sadducees. Whereas the Pharisees were connected with the synagogue, the Sadducees were affiliated with the temple. They were more open to hellenization and Roman rule than the other parties within Judaism. Acceptance of Roman rule ensured their power and influence. However, after the destruction of the temple and Jerusalem in 70 C.E., resulting in the loss of their seat of authority, the Sadducees never again exerted any influence upon Judaism.

As mentioned above, the Pharisees eventually accepted not only the books of Moses (Genesis–Deuteronomy) as authoritative, but also the Prophets and the Writings. They also placed the oral Torah on par with the written Torah. The Sadducees would have no part of this—accepting as authoritative only the written law of Moses (Pentateuch) and rejecting the authority of the Prophets, the Writings, and the oral Torah. Therefore, when Jesus responded to the Sadducees' questions concerning the resurrection (Matt 22:23–33), he answered them by appealing to a passage in the Pentateuch (Exod 3:6). The Sadducees' acceptance only of the Pentateuch as authoritative explains why Jesus did not quote a passage from a text which would have more clearly dealt with the resurrection (e.g., Dan 12:1–3, 13).[43]

The Essenes. The distinguishing characteristic of this group was their strict observance of the law. When Jonathan, a Hasmonean, became high priest in 161 B.C.E., the leader of the Essenes (referred to as the Teacher of Righteousness) along with his followers left Jerusalem and settled near the Dead Sea. This settlement was actually a community of scribes (legal experts) who, along with the Zadokite high priest, waited for the end of the age. During this interim period, the scribes of the community spent time interpreting the Scriptures, especially the Prophets, using a method called **pesher**. According to this method of interpretation, the Essenes interpreted prophecies as if their own circumstances were their fulfillment. The **Dead Sea Scrolls** produced by

---

[42] Ibid., 485.
[43] Ibid., 486.

the Qumran community give evidence of a group that lived according to a strict order of discipline. Activity within the community included a common meal, water baptism, copying of texts, and strict observance of the Sabbath. New members faced a three-year probationary period. The initiate was required to follow the strict habits, rules, and regulations. Furthermore, the newcomer was forbidden to share any information with outsiders as to the practices and beliefs of the sect. In regards to marriage, the majority of the Essenes did not marry. They saw women as selfish and unstable. Women, they felt, would cause their sect to become weak. If a man was bound to a woman, he was a slave and would not be a productive part of the sect. This sounds remotely like the Apostle Paul in 1 Cor 7.

Much like the early Christians, the Essenes felt they were living in the last days. They saw themselves as the righteous remnant of Israel. This is the main reason they withdrew into the wilderness of Judea—to prepare themselves for the coming events. They pictured their present world as coming to an end and wickedness being defeated; following this would be the inauguration of the kingdom of God. Naturally, their literature had a strong eschatological thrust.

One of the prominent features in Essene eschatology is a messianic hope. Hippolytus states that "all the Essenes were looking for the Messiah."[44] This messianic hope is evident in the form of three figures foretold in the Prophets: the prophet like Moses of Deut 18:15–19, the Davidic Messiah, and a great priest of Aaron's lineage.

There are many similarities between Essene literature and the New Testament, but nowhere in the New Testament is this similarity so prominent as in the Gospel of John. For example, John writes, "In the beginning was the Word, and the Word was with God, and the Word was God. He was in the beginning with God. All things came into being through him, and without him not one thing came into being" (John 1:1–3). The *Manual of Discipline,* which is part of the Qumran literature, states:

> From the God of knowledge exists all that is and will be . . . and by his knowledge everything has been brought into being. And everything that is, he established by his purpose; and apart from him, nothing is done (1QS 3.15 and 1QS 11.11).[45]

---

[44] J. E. H. Thompson, "Essenes," *ISBE* 1:997–1005, citing Hippolytus, *Refutation of Heresies.*

[45] Raymond E. Brown, "The Qumran Scrolls and the Johannine Gospel and Epistles," in *The Scrolls and the New Testament* (ed. Krister Stendahl; Westport: Greenwood, 1975), 186.

Other similarities between Essene writings and the Gospel of John include eschatological views, expectations regarding a messiah, and a strongly dualistic outlook (e.g., light vs. darkness, truth vs. error, death vs. life). Without question a study of the Qumran documents casts light upon numerous New Testament terms and concepts.

Other groups with which the interpreter should become familiar are the Zealots, the Herodians, and the Therapeutae. The customs and actions associated with these groups can illuminate a passage which might otherwise remain vague.

Comparative Literature

The writings of any period most often reflect ideas or forces shaping all aspects of a culture. As we have already argued, a knowledge of and a willingness to consult such literature in a comparative sense can greatly enhance a person's understanding of a particular text or a portion of it.

For English translations of some of these texts see:

Barrett, C. K. *The New Testament Background: Selected Documents.* 2d rev. ed. San Francisco: Harper & Row, 1987.

Cameron, Ron. *The Other Gospels: Non-canonical Gospel Texts.* Philadelphia: Westminster, 1982.

Cartlidge, David R., and David L. Dungan. *Documents for the Study of the Gospels.* Rev. and enl. ed. Minneapolis: Fortress, 1994.

Clark, G. H. *Selections from Hellenistic Philosophy.* 3d rev. ed. New York: Irvington, 1964.

Danby, H., trans. *The Mishnah.* London: Oxford University Press, 1964.

Dupont-Sommer, A. *The Essene Writings from Qumran.* Translated by G. Vermes. Cleveland: World, 1962.

Epstein, I., ed. Maurice Simon, trans. *Hebrew-English Edition of the Babylonian Talmud.* 35 vols. London: Soncino, 1960.

Ferguson, J. *Greek and Roman Religion: A Source Book.* Rev. ed. Park Ridge, N.J.: Noyes, 1980.

Hennecke, Edgar. *New Testament Apocrypha.* Edited by Wilhelm Schneemelcher. Eng. ed. edited by R. McL. Wilson. Louisville, Ky.: Westminster John Knox, 1991.

Josephus, Flavius. *The Works of Josephus.* Translated by William Whiston. Peabody, Mass.: Hendrickson, 1987.

Meyer, Marvin M., ed. and trans. *The Secret Teachings of Jesus: Four Gnostic Gospels.* New York: Random House, 1984.

Montefiore, Claude J., ed. and trans. *A Rabbinic Anthology*. New York: Schocken, 1974.

Neusner, Jacob, ed. *The Babylonian Talmud: A Translation and Commentary*. 22 vols. Peabody, Mass.: Hendrickson, 2005.

Philo Judaeus. *The Works of Philo*. Translated by C. D. Yonge. Peabody, Mass.: Hendrickson, 1993.

Richardson, Cyril C., ed. and trans. *Early Christian Fathers*. New York: Macmillan, 1970.

Vermes, G. *The Dead Sea Scrolls in English*. 3d ed. New York: Penguin, 1987.

Among the writings with which the student should become acquainted are the following:

The Writings of Josephus. **Flavius Josephus** is an important source for the history of the Jewish people during the first century C.E. His extant writings include four major works, the *Jewish War*, the *Jewish Antiquities*, *Against Apion*, and the *Life*. While Josephus' interpretations of historical events (some of which he himself witnessed) may be questionable, his writings constitute a valuable record of a turbulent period in Jewish history, a period which parallels the developing years of early Christianity.

Philo of Alexandria. A Jewish scholar during the first century C.E., **Philo of Alexandria** in Egypt attempted to reconcile the Greek rationality with the Hebrew Scriptures. Employing the Greek term *logos,* for instance, Philo identified the concept of Wisdom as the creative intermediary between God and the material universe. In his writings, Philo shows himself to be a product of Hellenism—an eclectic. In his fascination with numbers, Philo evidences the influence of the Pythagoreans; in his sense of human ignorance and evil, the Skeptics; in his idea of the body as the prison of the soul, the Platonists; and in his concern for freedom from passion, living according to nature, and *adiaphora* (indifferent things), the Stoics. Philo's conceptions of the Conscience as the internal judge, of the Spirit, of faith, of immortality, and other concepts are so similar to concepts in the New Testament epistles as to demand comparison. His allegorical method of interpreting the Hebrew Scriptures also serves as a model for New Testament writers such as the author of Hebrews, Matthew, and Paul.

The Dead Sea Scrolls. The Dead Sea Scrolls constitute a collection of writings used and preserved by an Essene community at Qumran. As well as copies of the Hebrew Scriptures, this collection also contains writings which were presumably composed by the Qumran community itself. Works such as the *War of the Sons of Light Against the Sons of Darkness* and the *Manual of Discipline* reveal a number of similarities between the Qumranians and early Christians (e.g., both groups felt that Israel had broken its covenant with Yahweh, both regarded themselves as the new Israel, both observed a communal meal of bread and wine, both advocated holding all things in common, both evidence a cosmic dualism).

Rabbinic Literature. Within Judaism there developed a need to interpret the Hebrew sacred writings in order to make them meaningful for different and new circumstances. This "tradition of the elders" (Mark 7:3) became known as the oral Torah and consisted of a body of legalistic interpretations which rabbis made over many centuries. These interpretations were eventually compiled and codified into the Mishnah around 200 C.E. The rabbinic method of interpretation called midrash is used by New Testament writers such as Matthew, Paul, and the author of Hebrews.

The Apostolic Fathers. Several writings (some of which may date prior to the canonical Catholic epistles) enjoyed a position of quasi-authority in early Christianity. These works offer valuable glimpses into the developing liturgy, episcopate, and worldview of a church on its way to becoming an institution. The writings normally designated "Apostolic Fathers" are the Didache, the Shepherd of Hermas, the epistles of Clement, the epistles of Ignatius, the epistle of Barnabas, the epistle of Polycarp to the Philippians, and the Martyrdom of Polycarp.

The New Testament Apocrypha. Early Christians produced an extensive corpus of writings which became known as **apocrypha**, either because they were thought to contain secret or hidden meanings or because the works remained hidden from ordinary Christians. Many of these writings have their origin in Gnosticism. Thus they were naturally shunned by orthodox Christianity. These works vary in genre—gospels, epistles, apocalypses, and acts. The value of these works for New Testament studies is that they offer insight into some of the concepts and teachings which orthodox Christianity had to battle in its struggle for identity and survival.

The Nag Hammadi Library. A collection of thirteen textual fragments discovered in 1945 near the city of Nag Hammadi, Egypt. Although originally written in Greek, these texts as we have them are composed of fifty-two treatises written in Coptic, an ancient Egyptian language. The text fragments date from the mid-fourth century C.E., but the treatises themselves are from the second century C.E. The texts include epistles, gospels, and apocalypses used by gnostic (see Gnosticism) Christians from the second to fourth century C.E. The Nag Hammadi texts were considered heretical by early orthodox Christianity. Although these texts improved the picture that scholars had of early Christian gnostics because these texts come out of gnostic communities, the picture is not complete. The reason for this incompleteness is that these texts do not set forth the gnostic system; a knowledge of the system seems to be taken for granted by the texts. Furthermore, the texts themselves are not entirely consistent in their worldview. Nonetheless, these texts do suggest that the Christian movement in the early centuries C.E. was anything but monolithic.[46] Other sources that will aid in interpretation include extant Hellenistic biographies, histories, and romances, Greek and Jewish epistolary writings, and the Old Testament Apocrypha.

In ch. 2, I referred to the idea of a people's symbolic world and to that people's practice of offering literary interpretations of experiences within that world. Literary productions look the way they do and say what they say because they interpret experiences within the symbols of the world that gives the text birth. For this reason, the interpreter must develop both an interest in and an acquaintance with the originating symbolic world. The religious experiences of the biblical writers necessitated that they reshape, modify, redefine (i.e., reinterpret) their symbolic worlds. An understanding of the way each writer accomplished this reinterpretation is greatly facilitated by a familiarity with the symbolic world.

Summary

A visit to the world behind the text is indispensable for the interpreter. Any literary work of art (at least any good literary work of art) will extend to the reader an open invitation to discover something about reality. By what is said *in* texts, there will be communicated something *through* texts. But the content of the text and its message are clothed in

---

[46] For an accessible translation and commentary on the Nag Hammadi Library, see James M. Robinson, ed., *The Nag Hammadi Library in English* (4th rev. ed.; Leiden: Brill, 1996).

the terms, ideas, symbols, concepts, and categories which are current in the author's world. If the interpreters do not give serious attention to that world *behind* the text, whatever they say about the world *within* the text—the literary context—will be less than it should be.

REVIEW & STUDY

Key Terms and Concepts

apocrypha	midrash
comparative study	mystery religions
Dead Sea Scrolls	pesher
Essenes	Pharisees
Flavius Josephus	Philo of Alexandria
Hellenism	Sadducees
Hellenistic philosophies	Septuagint
Judaism	*Sitz im leben*
logos	syncretism

Study Questions

1. Read the first paragraph in this chapter again. Draw a simple diagram illustrating the two gaps that are introduced. What do you consider to be the best way to lessen the size of these gaps?

2. Read the section in this chapter entitled "Historical and Cultural Background." Explain the following diagram:

3. In a New Testament introduction or some other source (e.g., Carolyn Osiek, *What Are They Saying about the Social Setting of the New Testament?* [New York: Paulist, 1984], pp. 73–83), read the section on the "household code." Then read Eph 5:21–6:9 and Col 3:18–4:1. How does an understanding of the social phenomenon of the structure of the household in the Greco-Roman world affect your interpretation of these passages?

4. Do you feel that the reading of a biblical text is enhanced by a fa-
    miliarity with other literature contemporary with the biblical text?
    Why or why not? Read the *Manual of Discipline* from a translation
    of the Dead Sea Scrolls and then read the Gospel of John. Make a
    list of similar terms, concepts, and views (e.g., the dualistic outlook
    in both).

Suggestions for Further Reading

Damrosch, David. *The Narrative Covenant: Transformations of Genre in
    the Growth of Biblical Literature.* San Francisco: Harper & Row,
    1987.

Ferguson, John. *Greek and Roman Religion: A Source Book.* Park Ridge,
    N.J.: Noyes, 1980.

Gager, John G. *Kingdom and Community: The Social World of Early
    Christianity.* Englewood Cliffs: Prentice-Hall, 1975.

Kennedy, George A. *Classical Rhetoric and Its Christian and Secular Tradi-
    tion from Ancient to Modern Times.* Chapel Hill: University of North
    Carolina Press, 1980.

Malina, Bruce J. *The New Testament World: Insights from Cultural Anthro-
    pology.* Atlanta: John Knox, 1981.

Meeks, Wayne. *The Moral World of the First Christians.* Philadelphia:
    Westminster, 1986.

Sanders, James A. *Canon and Community.* Philadelphia: Fortress, 1984.

Stambaugh, John, and David Balch. *The New Testament in Its Social En-
    vironment.* Philadelphia: Westminster, 1986.

Woude, A. S. van der, ed. *The World of the Old Testament.* Grand Rap-
    ids: Eerdmans, 1989.

ILLUSTRATIVE METHODS THAT FOCUS ON THE WORLD BEHIND THE TEXT

Every literary text is created by a communicating mind. The author seeks to communicate meaning to an audience. "Every utterance is an attempt to express something, an idea, a feeling, a set of facts, and is successful to the extent that it effectively communicates what it set out to communicate. A poem, then, would be good if it achieved what its author intended."[1] In author-centered criticism, the meaning of the text must be related to the mind which created it. If the author creates a text, then interpretation should concern itself with the relationship between the author and the text. The text is the effect, the author the cause. Author-centered criticism seeks to ascertain as much as possible about the mind and world of the author in order to determine what that mind communicates through the text. The better interpreters understand the creative mind, the better they will understand the creation of that mind.

Getting into the author's mind, however, is not easy. This holds especially true for ancient authors. If there is anything known at all about an ancient author, it is usually minimal. When the interpreter has other writings by the same author, these are examined to determine as much about the author as possible. In a sense, the author-centered critic seeks to create a profile of the author. In addition to examining other writings by the same author, author-centered critics also attempt to find out about the author's world. The assumption is that if an author is the product of his or her world, then the author's literary creation will reflect that world. The elements within the author's social, political, religious, and intellectual milieu are constitutive of meaning. Therefore, understanding the author's world makes for a fuller understanding of the text.

---

[1] Donald Keesey, "Historical Criticism I: Author as Context," in *Contexts for Criticism* (4th ed.; ed. Donald Keesey; Boston: McGraw Hill, 2003), 14.

Another important assumption of author-centered criticism is that history is periodic; that is, history can be divided into periods having relatively unique assumptions, values, and beliefs. This assumption permits the study of texts under headings such as "Renaissance," "Medieval," "Romantic," "Neo-Classical," or "Elizabethan." The best-equipped interpreter is knowledgeable of the assumptions, values, and beliefs characteristic of each period. Consequently, author-centered criticism has a historical focus. The historical focus supplies a check against overly anachronistic interpretations.

As we discuss text-centered and reader-centered theories, some of the shortcomings of author-centered criticism will come to light. We should, however, examine two of them here. First, historical periods are so complex and unpredictable that they produce complex and unpredictable individuals. While it seems commonplace that authors are affected by their contemporary conditions, obviously not every individual of a particular age is the same. Writers of literary texts can be quite extraordinary and unique individuals within their cultures. This uniqueness makes them stand out. Is it feasible, therefore, to assume that the individual mind is a microcosm of an interpreter's conception of a corporate mind? Second, always lying just beneath the surface is the interpreter's tendency to use the text to explain something about a culture or a period. When this happens, constructing a picture of a particular historical period becomes the end of interpretation.

Source Criticism

Source critics seek to identify earlier traditions and documents within a text. Since authors do not compose texts within literary vacuums, we should expect to find adaptations of earlier traditions for current purposes. It was argued previously that the recognitions of such sources may have a significant impact upon interpretation. The way in which an author adapts an earlier tradition or document may witness to the author's purpose.

Source criticism has enjoyed a long and venerable career in both Hebrew Bible and New Testament studies. Source-critical studies of the Hebrew Bible have focused upon the Pentateuch, and more recently have included other parts of the Hebrew Bible. For centuries the Mosaic authorship of the Pentateuch was generally accepted without much question. Gradually, however, scholars began to doubt whether everything in the Pentateuch could be from the hand of Moses. Under the influence of seventeenth-century rationalism, and because of passages which could not have been from Moses (e.g., the account of Moses' death [Deut 34:5–8], familiarity with the monarchy [Gen 36:31–39], and the phrase "until this day," which suggests that the passages containing it were written after the time of Moses [Gen 35:4 LXX and Deut 34:5–6]), many scholars further questioned Mosaic authorship of the Pentateuch. Based upon these passages and other discoveries such as historical inaccuracies, repetitions, and divergent writing styles, these scholars concluded that the Pentateuch was the product of an extended process of compilation.

In the second half of the nineteenth century, Julius Wellhausen and Abraham Kuenen popularized the view that the Pentateuch is comprised of four sources. Both Wellhausen and Kuenen detected a close relationship between the Pentateuch and the book of Joshua. They, therefore, spoke of the four-source hypothesis as relating to the Hexateuch. Later followers of Wellhausen claimed that the sources of the Hexateuch also formed the basis of the books through Kings.[2] All subsequent source-critical scholarship is deeply indebted to Wellhausen, and many scholars today feel that the four-source theory is still the best explanation for the composition of the Pentateuch.

The four-source hypothesis is really quite simple: The Pentateuch/Hexateuch is composed of four documents (designated J, E, P, and D) or parts of documents which are concerned with the same events. These documents were composed at different times by and for people with different concerns and purposes. Each source thus constitutes a layer within the Hexateuch, and each layer has its peculiar language, style, and theological viewpoint.[3] What follows is a summary of the characteristics of each source.

J (Yahwist)

The hand of the *Yahwist* is first detected in Gen 2:4b, where the divine name Yahweh appears. The Yahwist's depiction of God is simple, personal, and highly anthropomorphic. God walks, talks, forms with his hands, and experiments. God differs sharply from the transcendent

---

[2] A discussion of the various reactions and challenges to Wellhausen would take us too far afield here. For a concise and informative discussion of these challenges and alternatives, see A. S. van der Woude, *The World of the Old Testament* (Grand Rapids: Eerdmans, 1989), 166–205.

[3] Ibid., 188–90.

being in Gen 1:1–2:4a. Sections coming from the hand of the *Yahwist* include Gen 2:4b–4:26; 6:1–8; 11:1–9; 12:1–4a, 6–20.

E (Elohist)

This document favors the name *Elohim* for God and associates the divine name Yahweh with a revelation to Moses. The hand of the Elohist is found primarily in the patriarchal narratives. The Elohist depicts divine revelation as occurring through indirect means, such as dreams (Gen 20:3) or a divine messenger (Gen 21:17). The vocabulary of the Elohist is also distinctly different from that of the Yahwist (e.g., the reference to Mount Horeb instead of Mount Sinai). Elohistic passages include Gen 20:1–8; 21:8–34; 22:1–19.

P (Priestly Writer)

The Priestly document differs in many ways from the Yahwist and Elohist documents. The interests of the Priestly writer include cultic and priesthood stipulations, brief historical notations, the sacrificial system *after* Moses, minute details, and the calendaring of events. The style is formulaic and repetitious. God is depicted as a transcendent being, creating and arranging through fiat. The primary concern of the Priestly writer is God rather than human beings. The God of Gen 1 could never be characterized in the anthropomorphic terms of Gen 2–4. Included among the Priestly portions are Gen 1:1–2:4a; 5:1–27; 9:1–17; 11:10–27; 25:7–10.

D (Deuteronomist)

The bulk of Deuteronomy (chaps. 12–26) is the book of the law found in the temple during the reign of Josiah in the seventh century. The book has its own paraenetic style and vocabulary. Most scholars today, however, agree that Deuteronomy is the product of a complex process of compilation and contains much older material. Characteristic of Deuteronomy is the attention given to the Levites and the proclamation and interpretation of the laws it contains.[4] Some scholars today propose that Deuteronomy was composed in the courts of Hezekiah and Josiah, receiving its final form in the second half of the seventh

---

[4] Ibid., 190.

century B.C.E. at the hands of a circle of writers who produced the Deuteronomistic history.[5]

Although source criticism has been applied to all the writings of the New Testament, its primary focus has been upon the Synoptic Gospels. This focus is twofold: a concern for the relationship between two or more texts that suggests some kind of dependence, and the discovery of sources within a single text.

The nineteenth century witnessed a tremendous concern to uncover the history behind the Gospels. A great deal of energy was especially expended in the attempt to reconstruct the life of Jesus. For this reason, the Gospels were treated as sources for reconstructing history. If one Gospel were earlier than the others, then that one should be historically more reliable, for it would have been closer to the actual events. In the first quarter of the twentieth century, B. H. Streeter popularized in the English-speaking world a solution to the relationship between the Synoptic Gospels. His solution was a refinement of Holtzmann's (1832–1910) two-document hypothesis. This solution remains popular in source-critical studies today. Simply put, this hypothesis claims that Mark was the first Gospel and was a source for both Matthew and Luke. It also claims that Matthew and Luke made use of another, no longer extant, source which has come to be known as Q (from German *Quelle,* meaning "source"), and that Matthew and Luke each had sources, designated M and L respectively.

Recent scholarship has challenged the assumption that the Gospels can serve as sources for reconstructing the life of Jesus. Scholars generally recognize today that not only are the Gospels separated from the events they describe by at least a generation (Mark was composed around 70 C.E., and Matthew and Luke between 80 and 90 C.E.), but that the Gospels are theologically rather than historically motivated. We should also recognize that the two-document hypothesis has met with significant criticism. One older hypothesis (the Griesbach hypothesis) claims that Matthew and Luke were written before Mark, and Mark borrowed from Matthew and Luke, especially where Matthew and Luke agreed.

Source criticism is also concerned with identifying lost sources within the text. When they encounter a portion of a text thought to be uncharacteristic of the author's style, vocabulary, or ideology, source critics

---

[5] See Moshe Weinfeld, *Deuteronomy and the Deuteronomic School* (Oxford: Oxford University Press, 1972).

usually suspect that the author has drawn from a source. An example of this is John 21, where the Greek vocabulary differs significantly from that found in the rest of the Gospel (e.g., the use of *ischyein* rather than *dynasthai* and *exetazein* instead of *erōtan*). In Rom 3:25–26, we encounter the idea of God "overlooking" past sins. This seems to contradict (not only in vocabulary, but also in concept) what Paul has already claimed in Rom 1–2 (i.e., that God punishes all sin).[6] Some suspect the use of a source.

This brings us to a significant observation concerning source-critical studies: source criticism assumes that an author's usual or normal vocabulary, style, and ideology can be discovered. But can we sufficiently define an author's normal vocabulary, style, and ideology, and then use that definition as a canon by which to determine whether a passage is or is not the work of that author? Most source critics answer in the affirmative. Care should be taken, however, in assuming that an author cannot use vocabulary, style, and ideologies that seem to differ from those in other contexts. Even if an author incorporated earlier traditions or sources, this suggests that the writer recognized some agreement between his or her ideas and the source.

Resources

Habel, Norman. *Literary Criticism of the Old Testament*. Philadelphia: Fortress, 1971.

Tuckett, Christopher. *Reading the New Testament: Methods of Interpretation*. Philadelphia: Fortress, 1987.

Weinfeld, Moshe. *Deuteronomy and the Deuteronomic School*. Oxford: Oxford University Press, 1972.

Woude, A. S. van der, ed. *The World of the Old Testament*. Grand Rapids: Eerdmans, 1989.

Social-Scientific Criticism

Social-scientific criticism seeks to understand texts in their social, cultural, historical, and literary contexts in order to understand the social institutions, the cultural values, and the norms of a particular era. Social-scientific criticism of the Bible analyzes the social and cultural di-

---

[6] Christopher Tuckett, *Reading the New Testament: Methods of Interpretation* (Philadelphia: Fortress, 1987), 85.

mensions of a text by clarifying the differences between historical conditions and social institutions with respect to the biblical accounts thereby providing a clearer comprehension for the reading and use of the bible and biblical history.

Since the world of the modern reader is so far removed from the world of the biblical text, meaning cannot be adequately determined without consideration of social aspects. For example, the birth of Jesus should be examined within social, economic, political, and cultural contexts. If environment shapes attitudes, expectations, values, and beliefs, then knowledge gained from social-scientific criticism provides a more reliable understanding of the texts.

Whether one is speaking of interpreters, authors, or the group under investigation, all knowledge is socially conditioned.[7] Consequently, the method itself should distinguish and clarify differences between the social location (factors such as gender, age, class, roles, education, occupation, political and religious associations, language and cultural traditions, and location in place and time) of the interpreter, the author, and the object to be interpreted.[8] The problem for modern readers is that the Bible is a culturally conditioned book written in a different place and time and in a different social location. Only the original author and original hearer knew the totality of the conditions. The modern reader must be sensitive to the cultural diversity between Mediterranean cultures and Western culture.[9]

Social scientists look to modern Mediterranean cultures and use models that they assume have remained relatively unchanged for centuries in an attempt to make competent observations about the social data and dynamics of ancient Mediterranean cultures. In other words, social structures of contemporary Mediterranean cultures supply social scientists with information resembling ancient biblical societies.

To begin to understand religious acts, social-scientific criticism focuses on issues of self-identity, social organization, kinship systems, patrilineal descent, economic implications of marriage (both endogamous and exogamous), family, lineage, customs, economics, and political structures. By examining such issues, the social-scientific critic hopes to diminish the tendency of modern readers to project the structures of their own social

---

[7] John Elliott, *What Is Social-Scientific Criticism?* (Minneapolis: Fortress, 1993), 36.

[8] Bruce J. Malina, *The Social World of Jesus and the Gospels* (New York: Routledge, 1996), 37–38.

[9] Ibid., 25–27.

locations (individualism, progress, freedom, time, mobility, class structure, etc.) into the systems of both Israelite and early Christian cultures.[10]
The social-scientific study of the New Testament consists of four
approaches: the social description, the social history, the sociology of
knowledge, and the use of models from the social sciences. The social
description evaluates information gathered from New Testament literature and archaeology, i.e., art, coins, inscriptions, etc. It seeks information concerning the New Testament setting, which includes travel,
occupations, housing, money, economics, markets, clothes, food, etc.
The social history approach examines the social developments and
movements of the early Christians within the Greco-Roman world.
Sociology of knowledge looks at particular cultural groups and how
they organize and interpret experiences within society. Sociology tries
to reconstruct a group's worldview. Models from the social sciences involve the study of a number of similar cultures in order to create a grid
or model that allows anthropologists to map the "dynamics of a culture and to describe certain phenomena that occur in many cultures."[11]
These models examine issues such as rituals, kinship relations, purity-
pollution taboos, and economic systems. Those who practice this approach assume that the grid allows for a more objective examination
of a culture with less ethnocentrism. In other words, the grid allows
anthropologists to use a framework that differs from their own cultural
context. An example, according to Rhoades,[12] is that if social scientists
study the characteristics common to cultures that believe in demon
possession, they will be in a better position to examine the belief in
demon possession in first-century Israel and early Christianity.
    Obviously, the Bible is the product of individual members of faith
communities, and it consequently reflects the historical perspective
and cultural patterns of those communities. It is equally obvious that
modern readers interpret the Bible in terms of their own historical perspectives and cultural patterns. Social-scientific criticism attempts to
bridge the gap between these two truisms by providing methods that
explain what a text meant in its original historical and social contexts.
By applying the constructs provided by sociologists and social anthropologists, social-science critics employ cross-cultural models of human

---

[10] Gale A. Yee, ed., *Judges and Method: New Approaches in Biblical Studies*
(Minneapolis: Fortress, 1995), 45.

[11] David Rhoades, "Social Criticism: Crossing Boundaries," in *Mark and
Method: New Approaches in Biblical Studies* (ed. Janice Capel Anderson and Stephen D. Moore; Minneapolis: Fortress, 1992), 141.

[12] Ibid., 141–42.

interaction and methods of analyzing data regarding social organizations, politics, structures of authority, and social institutions. For example, social scientists have found that the Greco-Roman world was characterized by an intractable hierarchical structure that guaranteed a stable social order. The family was the microcosm of this structure with its tripartite relational organization founded on a pattern of dominance and subordination: parent/child, husband/wife, and master/servant. If the state was the structural macrocosm of the family and if the state's existence depended upon this family pattern, any deviation from the structure on the level of the family would have been viewed as a threat to the state's well-being. After experimenting with a new egalitarian structure, the church realized that such an experiment threatened its existence. Consequently, it adopted the pattern of dominance and subordination as its internal structure at both ecclesiastical and family levels. Based upon such an insight from social-scientific criticism, the interpretation and application of passages such as Eph 5:21–6:9, Col 3:18–4:1, and 1 Pet 2:13–3:8 take on new significance.

Resources

Brown, Raymond E., and John P. Meier. *Antioch and Rome: New Testament Cradles of Catholic Christianity.* New York: Paulist, 1983.

Elliott, John. *What Is Social-Scientific Criticism?* Minneapolis: Fortress, 1993.

Esler, Philip F. *The First Christians in Their Social World: Social-Scientific Approaches to New Testament Interpretation.* New York: Routledge, 1994.

Esler, Philip F., ed. *Modeling Early Christianity: Social-Scientific Studies of the New Testament in Its Context.* New York: Routledge, 1995.

Gager, John G. *Kingdom and Community: The Social World of Early Christianity.* Englewood Cliffs, N.J.: Prentice-Hall, 1975.

Gottwald, Norman K. *The Hebrew Bible: A Socio-Literary Introduction.* Philadelphia: Fortress, 1985.

Holmberg, Bengt. *Sociology and the New Testament: An Appraisal.* Minneapolis: Fortress, 1990.

Kendall, Diana, ed. *Race, Class, and Gender in a Diverse Society.* Boston: Allyn & Bacon, 1997.

Long, Burke O. "The Social World of Ancient Israel." *Int* 37 (1982): 243–55.

Malherbe, Abraham J. *Social Aspects of Early Christianity.* 2d ed. Philadelphia: Fortress, 1983.

Malina, Bruce J. *The New Testament World: Insights from Cultural Anthro-pology.* Atlanta: John Knox, 1981.

———. *The Social World of Jesus and the Gospels.* New York: Routledge, 1996.

May, David A. *Social-Scientific Criticism of the New Testament: A Bibliog-raphy.* 4 vols. Macon, Ga.: Mercer University Press, 1991.

Meeks, Wayne. *The First Urban Christians: The Social World of the Apostle Paul.* 2d ed. New Haven: Yale University Press, 2003.

Neyrey, Jerome H., ed. *The Social World of Luke-Acts: Models of Interpreta-tion.* Peabody, Mass.: Hendrickson, 1991.

Osiek, Carolyn. *What Are They Saying about the Social Setting of the New Testament?* New York: Paulist, 1984.

Rhoades, David. "Social Criticism: Crossing Boundaries." Pages 135–61 in *Mark and Method: New Approaches in Biblical Studies.* Edited by Janice Capel Anderson and Stephen D. Moore. Minneapolis: Fortress, 1992.

Rodd, Cyril S. "On Applying a Sociological Theory to Biblical Studies." *JSOT* 19 (1981): 95–106.

Rohrbaugh, Richard, ed. *The Social Sciences and New Testament Interpre-tation.* Peabody, Mass.: Hendrickson, 1996.

Tate, W. Randolph. *Interpreting the Bible: A Handbook of Terms and Methods.* Peabody, Mass.: Hendrickson, 2006.

Wilson, Robert R. *Sociological Approaches to the Old Testament.* Philadel-phia: Fortress, 1984.

Yee, Gale A., ed. *Judges and Method: New Approaches in Biblical Studies.* Minneapolis: Fortress, 1995.

Canonical Criticism

Unlike source criticism (which looks for the sources and traditions behind a text), form criticism (which seeks to identify the various forms within a text with their life-settings within the early communities), and redaction criticism (which finds meaning in the author's editorial activ-ity), canonical criticism[13] moves beyond the final redaction of a text to the point when the texts were accepted as canonical by believing com-

---

[13] The most notable works in the field of canonical criticism are San-ders, *Canon and Community;* Brevard Childs, *Introduction to the Old Testament as Scripture* (Philadelphia: Fortress, 1979); and idem, *The New Testament as Canon: An Introduction* (Philadelphia: Fortress, 1985).

munities. As Terence Keegan sees it, "What is most important is the text which is accepted by the Church as canonical. This canonically accepted text is the starting point of all biblical exegesis. This text is what the Church has taken into its life and what remains with the Church to the present day."[14] Canonical criticism is more concerned with the text as accepted by the believing communities than with what lies behind the text.

For canonical critics, the biblical texts are not merely sources for what lies behind the texts. Meaning in any final sense does not lie in the history behind the text or in the redactional activity of the author. The locus of meaning is the canonical text which was produced within and taken up into the life of the believing communities. For instance, the emphasis within Synoptic studies should not be what happened within the life of Jesus; emphasis rather should be upon the question of what the single text, say of Matthew, means.

In his treatment of the Hebrew Bible, Childs notes that the books of Ezra and Nehemiah do not cooperate well with the historical critic who attempts an accurate historical reconstruction of the period encompassed by the two books. Childs goes on to suggest that such attempts at historical reconstruction simply miss the point of interpretation. The focus should be upon what the canonical texts have to say as Scripture; that is, what do the texts of Ezra and Nehemiah say in their present individual arrangements and why were these texts, as they are, taken into the believing community as inspired texts? Exegetical concern is not primarily centered on what lies behind the text, but on the text itself. Also important within canonical criticism is the situation of the reader. Readers produce meaning within their present situations. This idea of reader-produced meaning, however, holds true only for members of the believing community.

Now I should explain the word, "primarily," in the last paragraph. Canonical critics are concerned with historical studies pertaining to the biblical texts. As Keegan points out, canonical critics perform historical studies but they do not read the biblical text historically.[15] Canonical critics study the historical processes of canonization. A text is composed, copied, re-copied, transmitted to subsequent generations, and finally canonized. This process is significant for how the church in every generation should understand and interpret a text. This interest

---

[14] Terence J. Keegan, *Interpreting the Bible: A Popular Introduction to Biblical Hermeneutics* (New York: Paulist, 1985), 30.

[15] Ibid., 137.

in the canonical process results in two interrelated activities in canonical criticism: (1) the examination of the process by which the biblical texts in a final, stable form were accepted as canonical; and (2) based upon this process, the development of a hermeneutic for the interpretation of these texts within the church today. What follows is a brief discussion of some key observations made by canonical critics concerning the canonical process and some resultant interpretive suggestions.

The canonization process of the biblical canon was always in a state of flux. During this process, what might be termed an orthodox idea of what constituted a sacred piece of writing simply did not exist. The Sadducees, Pharisees, and Essenes all recognized and used varying collections of books. In the process of the canonization of the New Testament books, various Christian communities regarded different collections as authoritative.

In order for a book to be finally accepted into the canon, it had to have a universal quality; it had to be able to speak to the changing situations within the life of the believing community in every age. Flexibility of application was a prerequisite for canonization. The needs of the community and the ability of a writing to speak to those needs resulted in its being selected while others, not able to do this, were rejected. After the canon stabilized, believing communities continued to adapt and reapply the canonized books to the communities' needs.

At every stage of the canonical process, believing communities applied the writings to their own situations. This took place through adaptation, expansion, and interpretation. Believing communities sought to understand the writings through resignification. Modern hermeneuts should study the process of resignification throughout the canonical process in order to produce guidelines for the interpretive process today. To some extent, the interpretive processes extrapolated from the canonical process itself should be used as interpretive guides in today's interpretation and resignification of the biblical texts.

The believing communities adopted and adapted entire texts, not partial ones. Entire texts were resignified so as to speak to the needs of the believing communities. Consequently, canonical criticism advocates a hermeneutic which considers the text as a unified whole. This focus does not mean that canonical critics are uninterested in historical-critical studies. Indeed, canonical critics employ source, form, and redaction criticism, albeit with an ulterior motive. They are interested in source criticism because it is important to ascertain the ways in which the sources were resignified; they are interested in form criticism because knowing the *Sitz im Leben* is helpful for understanding how a community shaped and used the form; and they are interested in redaction criticism to the extent that it offers insights into the manner in which writers in the communities reinterpreted and reapplied their sources.

Since the early believing communities resignified the texts, a plurality of meanings is suggested for the texts. Canonical critics do not advocate interpretive license; on the contrary, they insist that their hermeneutics derive from the interpretive activities observable in the stages of the canonical process. Multiple meanings are possible, but only insofar as they flow from the hermeneutics of resignification.

Resources

Childs, Brevard. *Introduction to the Old Testament as Scripture*. Philadelphia: Fortress, 1979.

———. The *New Testament as Canon: An Introduction*. Philadelphia: Fortress, 1985.

Keegan, Terence J. *Interpreting the Bible: A Popular Introduction to Biblical Hermeneutics*. New York: Paulist, 1985.

Sanders, James. *Canon and Community*. Philadelphia: Fortress, 1984.

Unit
II

THE WORLD WITHIN THE TEXT

THE BIBLE AS LITERATURE AND LITERARY FORMS

When a hermeneutic includes in part or whole the text as a locus of meaning, the hermeneutic is literary in nature. Central to our integrated approach is the text as a literary creation. The mainspring of any literary approach is the view that the Bible is literature; thus, the Bible as literature is *the* basic presupposition for literary criticism. But, as McKnight questions, "are the nature and content of the Bible consistent with a literary approach or orientation? Is the Bible as sacred scripture compromised by a literary approach?"[1] McKnight thinks not, and I concur. While God might be the author of sacred poetry and narrative, he used the verse and prose forms native to Hebrew and Hellenistic cultures. While the Bible may be part of God's revelation and self-disclosure to humanity, it is a revelation expressed in human language. In one sense the authors of the biblical texts employ the finiteness of written discourse to say something about an infinite God. Further, the written discourse is a special case of language—literary. By literary I mean creative and imaginative language, language adorned with artistic devices that transform and intensify ordinary language or everyday speech. This literary quality requires interpretation, and of central importance in interpretation are the concepts of **genre** and **sub-genre**.

The natural languages of the biblical texts, Hebrew, Aramaic, and Greek, are governed by grammatical, syntactical, and lexical codes. Literature also uses secondary languages called literary languages. These languages also have codes. These literary languages with their codes enable a reader to move beyond what the text *says* in its **natural language** to what the text is *about*. This distinction is the mimetic character of literature. In other words, literature has a referential quality and a **mimetic quality**. The referential quality is the relationship between the language of the text and the world projected by that language. The

---

[1] McKnight, *Postmodern Use of the Bible,* 168.

mimetic quality is the relationship between the real world and the world within the text. On the one hand, by means of the **referential quality of literature**, an author is able to use language to create the world within the text. This world may or may not be similar to the real world of the author (e.g., science fiction). In this textual world, words refer to objects which may or may not be recognizable in the real world. The referential quality enables the world within the text to have a story line and plot. On the other hand, the mimetic function enables the author to challenge the reader to discover some truth, message, or insight to which the textual world points. The following chart should make the distinction between the referential quality and mimetic quality more clear.

LANGUAGE

⟵ Referential quality

TEXTUAL WORLD

⟵ Mimetic quality

REAL WORLD

TRUTH, MESSAGE, INSIGHT

Any hermeneutic that takes the text seriously must give attention to both of these qualities. Traditionally, the field of hermeneutics (primarily the historical-critical and historical-grammatical approaches) has demonstrated a remarkable tenacity in its unwillingness to place as much importance upon the mimetic function of biblical literature as upon the referential function. Characteristic of this hermeneutic has been the persistent tendency to divert attention away from the text itself to the world which produced the text. This tendency has perpetuated an attitude towards the biblical texts which views them as distorted historical records at best and poor substitutes for more veritable originals at worst. One has only to recall the hypothetical Aramaic original for Matthew's Gospel, the sayings source "Q" used by Luke and Matthew, and the original documents from which Genesis was redacted. Recent literary approaches have come a long way in demonstrating that the biblical texts in their final forms are works of tremendous literary power and aesthetic quality. These approaches have not only shown that the biblical texts employ the syntactical, grammatical, and linguistic codes of the natural languages in creatively pleasing ways; they have also succeeded in spotlighting the Bible's equally creative use of the literary languages of the different genres and sub-genres. These may include a whole range of literary devices, such as style, point of view, characterization, plot, thematic organization, and dynamics of reticence. Hermeneutics can no longer be content only with the historical-critical attempts at a reconstruction of the original document, oral traditions, and *Sitz im Leben*. Nor can it be completely satisfied with the historical-grammatical method's parsing of the natural languages. While each of these approaches offers valuable heuristic background information often indispensable for interpretation (as we saw in unit I), hermeneutics must be equally, if not more, concerned with parsing the literary languages of a document's generic systems. Meaning is conveyed through both the natural and literary languages. Grammatical content cannot be separated from the **form** through which it is communicated. Inattention to genre ultimately precipitates an inattention to meaning. This means that a consideration of genre is an absolute must for hermeneutics.

We are constantly faced with the necessity of distinguishing between literary genres. Within a single week many students will read a short story, a poem, a tragic play, labels on food containers, a newspaper, a letter, a telephone directory, or a recipe. All of these "forms" communicate differently and represent different literary types or genres. When a reader approaches a text, a conscious or unconscious identification of genre is made. Even the casual reader knows that a poem must be read and interpreted differently from a recipe. John Hayes and Carl R. Holladay describe the issue as follows:

> The required effort and means necessary for the exegesis and interpretation of texts thus vary greatly, depending upon the nature of the texts and their relationship to normal communication. Some texts merely need to be read to be understood. Others require very detailed analysis. Some use normal, everyday language, grammar, and sentence structure. Others use a very specialized vocabulary, involved grammatical and sentence structure and distinctive forms of expression. Some texts employ symbolic and metaphoric language. Others seek to employ language and words so as to limit severely the range of meaning and the potential to persuade. Others seek to merely inform. Some texts are produced to entertain. Others seek to produce some particular response and action.[2]

---

[2] Hayes and Holladay, *Biblical Exegesis,* 7.

There is an intimate relationship and interconnectedness between form and **content**. Hermeneutics must concern itself not only with the content, but also with the form of the text. This concern entails understanding the conventions of the generic systems. This is true because different genres involve different literary codes and conventions. Perhaps a couple of illustrations will clarify this. In most cultures, unspoken rules govern what is worn and when it is worn. Rules of dress dictate that a person should not wear a ski suit to a formal wedding. Also, within a given society, rules or principles dictate family relationships. On the basis of these rules, persons within a particular social group will relate to other members of the group, making decisions such as whom they can or cannot marry.

Similarly, in language, rules of grammatical construction and syntax govern the way we group words or symbols. This ensures communication. Furthermore, rules govern or identify literary genres and subgenres. Consequently, we read different genres with different expectations and interpret them differently by recognizing the relationship between what is said (content) and how it is said (genre, form). Different kinds of genres are capable of different kinds of meaning and offer different kinds of information to a reader. Knowing the genre of a text or the sub-genre of a literary unit allows us to know what types of questions can sensibly be asked of the material.[3]

The most plausible understanding of a text and its subsequent explication is best actualized when the reader has an adequate grasp of the literary genres and sub-genres by which the author operates. Robert Alter puts it well:

> A coherent reading of any art work, whatever the medium, requires some detailed awareness of the grid of conventions upon which, and against which, the individual work operates. . . . Through our awareness of convention we can recognize significant or simply pleasing patterns of repetition, symmetry, contrast; we can discriminate between the verisimilar and the fabulous, pick up directional clues in a narrative and see what is innovative and what is deliberately traditional at each nexus of the artistic creation.[4]

Biblical texts are not simply conglomerates of disjointed and unsophisticated religious tradition, but carefully crafted works of great artistic accomplishment which we should study as unified wholes.

---

[3] Ibid., 83.

[4] Robert Alter, *The Art of Biblical Narrative* (New York: Basic Books, 1981), 47.

In the Bible, poetry has its own set of codes centered in the concept of parallelism, in which "the poet makes a statement and arouses expectation. To meet that expectation, the poet goes back to the beginning and says the same thing or follows a line of thought parallel to that already laid down."[5] Like narrative in general, biblical narrative utilizes plot; in plot, events are arranged so that the action is a unified whole. The fodder for narrative consists of characters, settings, and conflicts. Embedded within the two Hebrew genres of poetry and narrative are literary forms (which we will call sub-genres) such as **simile, metaphor, symbol, personification, hyperbole,** type-scenes, archetypes, fables, miracle stories, pronouncement stories, riddles, speeches, and prophetic utterances.

By creatively blending and arranging these sub-genres through the medium of the natural language, the author superimposes a **literary language** (or languages) upon the natural one. Consequently, literary meaning surpasses that conveyed by the codes of the natural language. Literary meaning results from an interaction of the codes of the natural language and the literary ones. I will have more to say about this in unit III, where we consider the dynamics of reading.

In the remainder of this chapter I examine literary sub-genres that are present in virtually all literary traditions. While some of the sub-genres in the Hebrew Bible are quite strange to those who have been nurtured in the Western literary traditions, the reader should find the following common forms familiar. The final two chapters of this unit concentrate on the major genres and sub-genres of the Hebrew Bible and New Testament respectively.

Common Literary Sub-Genres

Hyperbole

Briefly defined, hyperbole is deliberate exaggeration for effect. An example is 1 Kgs 1:40: "And all the people went up after him, playing flutes and rejoicing greatly, so that the ground shook with the sound" (NIV). Did the ground actually shake? That's not the point! The point is that the rejoicing was extremely great. Another well-known example is Yahweh's promise to Abraham that his descendants would be "as numerous as the stars of heaven and as the sand that is on the seashore"

---

[5] McKnight, *Postmodern Use of the Bible,* 135.

(Gen 22:17). The New Testament also contains many examples. For instance: "If your right eye causes you to sin, tear it out and throw it away" (Matt 5:29a).

Euphemism

When authors make use of **euphemism**, they substitute a less direct or less distasteful word or phrase for a more direct or shocking one. A euphemism is in one sense the opposite of hyperbole; i.e., euphemism is intentional understatement.[6] Modern translators of the Bible usually supply equivalent euphemisms for the target language. In the third chapter of Judges, Eglon's guards hesitate to enter the king's chambers because they think that he "covereth his feet" (KJV), euphemistically referring to a bowel movement. The translators of the NIV supply an equivalent euphemism with "He must be relieving himself." In Leviticus, the phrase "uncover the nakedness" (Lev 18:6–8, etc.) is a euphemism for sexual relations, including incest. Mickelsen suggests that there is an intrinsic delicacy involved in the use of euphemism which modern translators should imitate.[7]

Metaphor

John Gabel defines metaphor simply as "a word that is literal in the contexts within which it is usually found and is taken out of those contexts and used in a context of some other kind."[8] In Ps 119:105 the psalmist says that God's word is "a lamp to my feet." Taken at face value, this statement is false; i.e., obviously a word cannot really be a lamp. Nevertheless, in another sense it is true, for God's word and a lamp to light one's path are similar. These two concepts share an area of commonality or intersection: They both give guidance, keep one from stumbling, and dispel darkness. Ordinarily a metaphor illuminates, clarifies, or completes an abstract idea by replacing it with something observable, familiar, concrete. The effect of the metaphor may vary according to how much commonality there is between the abstract idea and the object.

---

[6] See Mickelsen, *Interpreting the Bible,* 192.
[7] Ibid.
[8] John Gabel and Charles Wheeler, *The Bible as Literature: An Introduction* (New York: Oxford University Press, 1986), 47.

Simile

A simile compares two objects, actions, or ideas by using words such as "like" and "as." The meaning of a simile is the comparison itself. In most instances, the two objects of the simile are familiar within the experiences of the audience. Some property of the second half of the simile serves to illuminate an aspect of the first half. When Job says, "A mortal . . . comes up like a flower and withers" (14:1–2a), he is comparing the brevity of a person's earthly existence to that of the field flower. The author is obviously not concerned with other properties of the flower such as color, fragrance, or shape. The comparison is direct and clear within the context. When the suitor in the Song of Solomon says that his beloved's "hair is like a flock of goats descending from Mount Gilead" (Song 4:1), he is not hinting that she should wash her hair. Apparently there is something about the scene of a flock of goats descending down a mountain that recalled the texture or flowing smoothness of his beloved's hair. The reader obviously should not attempt to burden the comparison with other elements such as the smell of a flock of goats or the height of the mountain. When a simile occurs, the reader should question why the author employs the particular simile at this place and how the simile elucidates the concept being presented.

Symbolism

When a concrete object which is found as the referent in a metaphor is displaced and used independently of the metaphorical context while retaining its metaphorical meaning or significance, it is a symbol. We are all familiar with the way in which objects such as the cross and the blood of the Christ have become symbols in Christian soteriology. In the Bible, objects (e.g., sheep, goat, lamb, lion, certain numbers, a race, or a fight) often stand alone to symbolize a more abstract idea or person.

Allegory

When a metaphor or symbol is extended in order to establish a relationship between the two objects in a systematic manner, the result is **allegory**. The metaphor or symbol splits several times into its component parts, and these parts then assume a one-to-one correspondence. For example, the story of Hosea's marriage in Hos 2 is an allegory of God's relationship to Israel as a nation. Hosea is commanded by Yahweh to take a wife, who is then unfaithful. This becomes an allegory of the family. Gabel describes it as follows: "Speaking to Hosea as his son, Yahweh, the husband, accuses Israel, the wife, of infidelity because she has deserted him and lavished her care on the pagan gods, her lovers."[9] A rather good example is Matt 22:1–14, the allegory of the wedding feast.

Formal Level (Referent)	Actual Level (Meaning)
King	God
Son	Jesus
Feast	Banquet
Servants	Apostles
Invited guests	The nation of Israel
Those accepting invitation	Church (converts)
Wedding garments	Righteousness
Excluded guests	Those found unworthy

Obviously the meaning of the allegory lies on the actual level and not on the formal. A note of warning is appropriate at this point: The act of writing allegory is not synonymous with the act of reading allegorically. To interpret a biblical passage allegorically when it is not allegory is simply to misinterpret. A sterling example of this error is an allegorical interpretation of the Song of Solomon (a series of love poems describing a relationship between lovers) as a representative of the relationship between Christ and the church.

Personification

In this device an inanimate object or group of persons assume the properties of a single human being. Examples include the personification of wisdom, evil, death, and the nation Israel: "Wisdom cries out in the street; in the squares she raises her voice" (Prov 1:20); "Abaddon and Death say, 'We have heard a rumor of it with our ears'" (Job 28:22); "when Israel was a child, I loved him" (Hos 11:1a). In each of these examples, a concept (wisdom, destruction and death) or a nation (Israel) assumes some property of a human being.

Apostrophe

An **apostrophe** is an address (usually of the exclamatory type) to an object or person. The object or person addressed is normally absent.

---

[9] Ibid., 29.

As if thinking out loud, the speaker is addressing someone or something present in thought only.[10] Jesus' lament over Jerusalem is an
apostrophe: "Jerusalem, Jerusalem, the city that kills the prophets and
stones those who are sent to it! How often have I desired to gather your
children together as a hen gathers her brood under her wings, and you
were not willing!" (Matt 23:37). We find a combination of personification and apostrophe in the liturgical Ps 24: "Lift up your heads, O
gates! and be lifted up, O ancient doors! that the King of glory may
come in" (v. 7). As the ark of the covenant is brought to the house prepared for it on Mount Zion, the gates are personified and called upon
(apostrophe) to open. In verse 8, the personified gates respond with
"who is the King of glory?" This type of fine line between personification and apostrophe is commonplace. The two forms are distinct at
two points. First, personification always ascribes to an inanimate object
some human trait, while apostrophe may refer to a human being; and
second, apostrophe will normally involve an exclamatory address, which
is not necessarily the case in personification.

Synecdoche

The practice of using a part to refer to a whole or vice-versa is
called **synecdoche**. When John says that "God so loved the world"
(John 3:16), his reference is not to the created world as a whole but only
to human beings. In this synecdoche, the whole stands for the part. An
example of the reverse is Matt 10:38: "And whoever does not take up
the cross and follow me is not worthy of me." "Cross" here stands in
for a whole range of self-sacrificial acts.

Metonymy

When two objects are so commonly associated with each other
that the use of one may imply or even substitute for the other, the result
is **metonymy**. For example, in the statement "the pen is mightier than
the sword," pen and sword are metonyms for the power of the written
word and military power respectively. This type of substitution is common within most literary traditions. Paul states: "For it is we who are
the circumcision" (Phil 3:3). Most readers know that circumcision was
the outward covenantal sign that identified Israel as the chosen people
of God. Paul enlists this concept in a new context to suggest that Christians are now the people of God. Paul thus substitutes circumcision for

---

[10] Mickelsen, *Interpreting the Bible,* 142.

the people of God. Luke informs us that, while walking with the two disciples on the road to Emmaus, Jesus instructed his two companions, "beginning with Moses and all the prophets" (Luke 24:27). Moses here is a reference to the Torah, the first five books of the Hebrew Scriptures, and the Prophets refer to the second division of the Hebrew Scriptures.

Satire

An excellent definition of **satire** is given by Leland Ryken:

Satire is the exposing, through ridicule or rebuke, of human vice or folly. It becomes literary when the controlling purpose of attack is combined with a literary method such as story, description or metaphor. Satire can appear in any literary genre (such as lyric, narrative, or drama) and can be either a minor part of a work or the main point of an entire work. Although satire usually has one main object of attack, satiric works often make a number of jabs in various directions, a feature that can be called "satiric ripples." It is a convention of satire that satirists feel free to exaggerate, overstate, and oversimplify to make their satiric point. Satire is a subversive form. It assaults the deep structures of our thinking and aims to make us uncomfortable. It questions the status quo and unsettles people's tendency to think that their behavior is basically good.[11]

Irony

In dramatic **irony**, the reader, though not the characters, always has a superior vantage point from which all the truth of a situation is known. This contrast between the reader's complete perception and the character's partial one generates irony. An example is the story of Ehud in Judg 3. After returning from the site of the oracle, Ehud informs the Moabite king, Eglon, that he has a word from the Lord for him. The king supposes that the word is the one received from the oracle, but the reader knows that the word is really the double-edged dagger concealed beneath Ehud's coat.

One of the most gripping instances of dramatic irony in the Bible is the book of Job. The reader overhears the conversation and bargain between God and "the adversary," but Job does not. If not given this insight, the reader might assume that Job is being unjustly punished

---

[11]Leland Ryken, *Words of Delight: A Literary Introduction to the Bible* (Grand Rapids: Baker, 1987), 329.

rather than tested. If Job had the same perception as the readers, there would be no irony. Job's ignorance of the situation and the reader's privileged knowledge are both required for the irony.

Irony also exists when a person says one thing and means the opposite or something different. For example, when Paul tells his Corinthian audience that "we [the apostles] are fools for the sake of Christ, but you are wise in Christ" (1 Cor 4:10), he is not offering a compliment; he means for his statement to be an accusation. Especially sharp irony like this is usually called sarcasm.

Archetypes

Within literature as a whole, characters, symbols, and themes seem to recur with regularity. For instance, the theme "from rags to riches," the character of the sassy servant in comedy, or the symbol of the gathering storm are familiar to most readers. One author suggests that archetypes "carry the same or very similar meanings for a large portion of mankind and appeal to what is most elemental in human experience."[12] Since archetypes are symbols or images shared by all, their potential for communication is almost infinite. When we encounter an **archetype** in literature, we are immediately faced with a whole body of meaning which the author does not need to explain. Archetypes such as the autumn of the year, the valley, the fox, the snake, birth, a smoothly flowing stream, a lamb, a rose, musical harmony, and the vulture communicate meaning without explanation. Phrases such as "Israel has played the harlot" or "tell that fox Herod" employ the archetype. These phrases need no explanation because the archetype immediately suggests and organizes the meaning. Archetypes are master images around which meaning is organized.

The Bible is the great storehouse of master images for literature in the Western world. An appreciation of literature outside the Bible is enhanced by a familiarity with the archetypes within the Bible. The primary reason for archetypal studies, however, is that the biblical texts themselves are saturated with these master images. As one author suggests, readers of the Bible can discover as much truth by tracing a master image through the Bible as by tracing some abstract idea.[13]

---

[12] Leland Ryken, *The Literature of the Bible* (Grand Rapids: Zondervan, 1974), 22.

[13] Ryken, *Words of Delight,* 29.

Summary

The ability to recognize the above sub-genres enhances a reader's appreciation for the literary artistry of literature. The absence of this ability heightens the risk of misrepresentation of the text's message. This is true whether the text is by Chaucer or the author of Job. However, as stated above, these sub-genres form only part of the structure of a text. A concentration on these sub-genres alone results in the neglect of the dynamics of the greater macrostructure as a unified whole. The interpretation of a text is exactly that—the interpretation of the whole and not just the stringing together of the interpretations of disjoined individual units. A narrative, a poem, a gospel, an apocalypse, or an epistle is a single generic whole, and each must be approached with full knowledge of its characteristic conventions and dynamics.

REVIEW & STUDY

Key Terms and Concepts

allegory	metonymy
apostrophe	mimetic quality
archetype	natural language
content	personification
euphemism	referential quality of literature
form	satire
genre	simile
hyperbole	sub-genre
irony	symbol
literary language	synecdoche
metaphor	

Study Questions

1. Read the prayer of Habakkuk in 3:1–19 and identify at least one occurrence of each of the following:

    a. Metaphor
    b. Simile

c. Personification

d. Irony

e. An imaginative reference to an event in Israel's history.

2. Read Luke 24:13–35. Briefly recount the story (what is said *in* the short pericope, i.e., the referential quality of the passage). Now based upon the language and progression of the content of the passage, give an account of what you think the passage is about (what is said *through* the story, i.e., the mimetic quality of the pericope).

3. The Song of Solomon has often been interpreted as an allegory in which the main characters are Christ and the church. Read the first four chapters of the Song and explain why you do or do not agree with such an interpretation.

4. If the authors of the biblical texts employ literary devices common to most secular literary traditions, what do you see as some of the implications of this for the interpretation and truth quality of the Bible?

Suggestions for Further Reading

Alter, Robert, and Frank Kermode. *The Literary Guide to the Bible.* Cambridge, Mass.: Harvard University Press, 1987.

Caird, G. B. *The Language and Imagery of the Bible.* Philadelphia: Westminster, 1980.

Gabel, John, and Charles Wheeler. *The Bible as Literature: An Introduction.* New York: Oxford University Press, 1986.

Mickelsen, A. Berkeley. *Interpreting the Bible.* Grand Rapids: Eerdmans, 1987.

Ryken, Leland. *Words of Delight: A Literary Introduction to the Bible.* Grand Rapids: Baker, 1987.

———. *Words of Life: A Literary Introduction to the New Testament.* Grand Rapids: Baker, 1986.

HOW THE HEBREW BIBLE COMMUNICATES AS LITERATURE

The Hebrew Bible is generally thought to contain two major genres— narrative and poetry—and a variety of sub-genres. Since Hebrew prophecy contains both narrative and poetic sections, we will treat prophecy in this chapter as a distinct genre having its own characteristic sub-genres. The Psalms and wisdom literature may also be treated as major genres. Since they employ the dynamics of Hebrew verse, however, I will approach them here as unique sub-genres of Hebrew verse.

Hebrew Narrative

Anyone familiar with the literary category of narrative recalls its typical features: narrative voice and time, **plot, setting, characterization, point of view**, and style. The suggestion that parts of the Hebrew Bible can be read in much the same way as other narratives (e.g., a novel or short story) may strike many modern readers as strange or at least surprising. A summary of the features of narrative plus examples from both biblical and secular sources will introduce those unfamiliar with narrative to its basic concepts. We will then study how these basic concepts are actualized in Hebrew narrative. Finally, no discussion of Hebrew narrative would be complete without at least a cursory glance at some of the unique sub-genres and their distinct characteristics.

Narrative Voice and Time

Before the actual poetics (the method of writing) of biblical narrative are discussed, a brief explanation of **narratology** (the principles of the study of narrative) will set a solid footing. Although there are several theories of narrative, they all have a basic structure in common:

An individual living in and conditioned by a real-life situation sets about writing a story (see the diagram below). Once this decision is made, the individual becomes someone different; as author, the individual assumes a different identity from his or her real identity, because the purpose and perspective are focused in a particular direction, toward a single literary objective—to convey a message to an audience or reader. The result is that in the process of writing, the **real author** becomes an **implied author**. The self who writes is somehow different from the self who thinks. For all practical purposes the implied author is the one whom the reader constructs from the text itself. For example, the only things we know about the author of Job are what we know from the text—his view of God and humanity; what, for him, constitutes true integrity; and his opinion of death. We know nothing of his everyday life, except what the writer chooses to reveal through the text. The author allows the reader access to only a limited area of his or her intellectual world.

Corresponding to the real author is the **real reader** (to be discussed at length in unit III), who is likewise conditioned by a range of variables—social, economical, political, ecclesiastical, doctrinal, methodological, and philosophical. This real reader or audience of the text may have been the original readers, readers during the Protestant Reformation, or those in an introductory literature class last week. There is also an **implied reader** who is the counterpart to the "implied author." The implied reader is the reader or audience presupposed by the narrative, the reader (or type of reader) whom the author has in mind during the process of composition. What type of readers did the author of the Joseph narrative (Gen 37–48) have in mind? What assumptions did the author make concerning the readers' background, level of knowledge about Joseph, or relationship to the author? Obviously, the answers to such questions lie within the text itself (although a knowledge of the cultural, ideological, historical world of the author can be extremely helpful here). The extent to which the real reader identifies with this "implied reader" usually determines the plausibility of a particular reading of the text. Some theories also postulate an "ideal reader" who is the persona the author actually creates or formulates during composition. The ideal reader is the hypothetical person with whom the author is in dialogue.

The next complementary duet consists of **narrator** and **narratee**. The narrator is the voice through which the author tells the story. The narratee is the person to whom the narrator is telling the story. The narratee may or may not be a character in the narrative. For example, the narratee in the Gospel of Luke is Theophilus, while in the book of Revelation, the narratee is actually made up of seven churches. I will have more to say about the narrator in the discussion on perspective.

The final pair of concepts consists of the **real world** and the **story world**. First, we need to distinguish between **historical narrative** and **mimetic narrative**. Historical narrative as understood in the modern sense endeavors to present an account of real historical events, persons, and places in their chronological order. Some events, persons, and places will be excluded, but those that are included must be presented in their proper sequence. The historian's ideological bias may dictate what information is included in the narrative and the amount of attention an event may warrant. Nonetheless, the modern understanding of historical narrative is characterized by a sense of "history for history's sake." It is not the modern historian's primary function to present the audience with a universal truth. Historians generally do not utilize formal narrative strategies such as plot, characterization, setting, **conflict, complication**, and **resolution** or artistic forms (e.g., personification, metaphor, allegory, archetypes). Modern historical narrative is expected to be as scientifically objective as possible. Its language is intended to be denotative with the historian avoiding the connotative language characteristic of mimetic narrative. Generally, historical narrative seeks to present things as they were, unlike mimetic narrative that seeks to present things as they might possibly be.

Based upon the recognition that art is more similar to philosophy because it addresses universals (i.e., art illuminates some universal human condition), Aristotle claims that art (including literary art) is superior to history. The same, at least in Aristotle's mind, cannot be said of history for it deals with what happened, as opposed to what happens. Mimetic narrative is story. It may be historical without being history in the modern sense. I call it "storicized" history. Mimetic narrative transcends history, for what is found in narrative is a redescription of reality, the creation of a literary world or a textual world that reaches beyond itself and beyond its historical milieu. Through a definable and well-structured artistry, it offers to guide the reader into the discovery of some universal truth.

The book of Judges is an example of mimetic narrative. Anyone who reads Judges more than once recognizes a recurring pattern: Israel sins against Yahweh; Yahweh causes Israel to suffer oppression at the hands of one of its enemies; Israel cries out to God for help; God raises up an individual to deliver and judge Israel; and Israel enjoys a time of peace. The cycle then begins over again. All the action in Judges revolves around this structural paradigm. The reader soon recognizes that Yahweh chooses the most unlikely candidates to be judges: Ehud is a southpaw, which in Hebrew culture was considered abnormal; Deborah is a woman; Barak is a procrastinator; Gideon is the youngest son of a poor farmer; Jephthah is a social outcast and a bandit; and Samson is what Kenneth Gros Louis calls the "county fair strong man."[1] Yet through these most unlikely candidates (or perhaps in spite of them) Yahweh constantly demonstrates his patient love towards Israel. The author has actually taken independent, autonomous stories from Israel's past, paradigmatically woven them together, and successfully communicated a truth through the whole.

Some scholars argue that by weaving these separate narratives together in this fashion, the author demonstrates the ineffectiveness of a theocracy and thus intends the work to serve as an apology for the monarchy. Whatever the case, the author has taken events from the life of Israel (i.e., events perceived to be from the real historical world of the nation), arranged them according to a particular order predetermined by a particular political or theological interest, and thereby created a world within the text. This is history at the service of mimesis, and it demonstrates the difference between historical and mimetic narrative. The author of a narrative (or of history for that matter) cannot include every minute detail of the real world in the narrative. Authors must be selective, including some things and excluding others. When we consider that the material included is itself represented in terms of generic conventions, the result is reality reshaped, tailored, redefined from the author's perspective.

---

[1] Kenneth R. R. Gros Louis with James Ackerman and Thayer S. Warshaw, *Literary Interpretations of Biblical Narratives* (Vol. 1, Nashville: Abingdon Press, 1974), 158.

The real world is the actual world in which the author lived when the text was written. The real world refers to the author's world with its patterns of behavior, social institutions, and ideological, economic, religious, and ethical structures. The story world is the world found only in the text. Framed by the beginning and ending of the text, it is a creation of an author who selects and arranges events in a complex structure. The arrangement of events and the characterization of individuals within the story do not correlate exactly with historical chronology nor with the real world persona. Events, characters, and places in the story world acquire their meaning and significance from the world created by the author. For example, in the Gospel of Matthew, Jesus is defined and given significance only within the world of Matthew's text. The meaning of what Jesus says or does in Matthew must be ascertained from the story world of Matthew, not by recourse to the author's real world. The story world is not a mirror of the real world with the author as the quicksilver behind the glass. Through artistic forms and strategies, the story world assumes its own reality, a reality that is capable of communicating its own truths.

This is something similar to a painter capturing only a moment of a landscape in his or her memory and then subsequently presenting that moment on canvas through the mediums of line, perspective, vanishing point, color, tone, geometrical shapes, and so on. The painting is not the material reality of the landscape, but an interpretation. The painting assumes its own identity. Where should we look for the meaning of the painting? Is it in the natural landscape which served as the pre-image? Does it lie in the viewer of the painting? Or is it in the painting itself? The answer is actually, "in all three." If we could view the landscape or some portion of it again, this might shed light upon the painter's interpretation, but can we ever recapture the identical landscape, the same cloud patterns, air currents, and singing birds? Obviously not! Consequently, to some extent the painting becomes its own source of meaning. At least the potential meaning is in the painting waiting for a viewer to actualize it. A similar case exists for narrative: An author structures a world in the text (story world). This story world is not synonymous with the real worlds of the author or reader. Meaning resides in the mimetic relationship between the story world and the real world. What is said *in* the story world is different from what is said *through* the story world.

An example from Judges again illustrates this difference: What is said *in* the story of Jephthah is quite distinct from what is said *through* it. In this narrative (Judg 11), we find (among other things) that Jephthah, whose mother was a prostitute, has been exiled from his people. But because of Jephthah's reputation as an able fighter, the men of Gilead seek his help when they find themselves in trouble with the Ammonites. Jephthah agrees (after some negotiation) to become Gilead's leader. After some interesting diplomacy, Jephthah requests help from Yahweh, vowing to sacrifice the first thing which comes out the door of his house if Yahweh will ensure victory. As we might expect, Jephthah is victorious, but upon his return home, the first to greet him from the door of his house is his daughter. Jephthah does fulfill his vow after his daughter bewails her virginity for two months. Basically, this is what is said *in* the story. But as interesting as the narrative is, what lesson or moral is the author offering the reader *through* the story? What application does the author expect from the reader? What truth about God, life, or humanity does the author suggest by the narrative? Perhaps in combination with the story of Samson (who also has taken a vow but broken it) our author is offering some instruction on the appropriateness or inappropriateness of making vows. As this example shows, meaning resides in the extra-textual reality to which the story world points.

One of the most insightful descriptions of the basic concepts in narratology is that by Gérard Genette in his work *Narrative Discourse*.[2] Genette names three main elements in narrative: **récit**, which is the actual order of events presented in the text (the plot); **histoire**, which is the sequence in which those events actually occurred as ascertained from the text (the story); and *narration,* which is the actual act of narrating itself. This means that the chronology of the actual events within the story may differ from the sequence of their presentation. One need think only of the effective use of flashback to see the distinction. For example, in Jon 4:2a we discover that Jonah prayed to Yahweh, "O LORD! Is not this what I said while I was still in my own country? That is why I fled to Tarshish at the beginning." Here is the narration of an event which occurred *after* God's initial commission in 1:2 and *before* Jonah's flight in 1:3. It is an account of a conversation which Jonah had with Yahweh several episodes back. In other words, the *récit* does not correspond to the *histoire*. Another example is the story of Micaiah and Ahab in 1 Kgs 22. After Micaiah is led before Ahab and Jehoshaphat, he relates an event (a vision) which had occurred prior to this meeting: "I saw the LORD sitting on his throne, with all the host of heaven standing beside him to the right and to the left of him. And the LORD said, 'Who will entice Ahab, so that he may go up and fall at Ramoth-gilead?'" (1 Kgs 22:19–20).

---

[2] Oxford: Oxford University Press, 1980

Again *récit* and *histoire* differ. Genette also offers five analytical categories for narrative. (1) **Order** describes the time-order of the story. It may operate by anticipation, flashback, or discordances between story and plot. The two examples above illustrate flashback. Anticipation is also found in the Micaiah episode. Micaiah, in flashback, anticipates in 1 Kgs 22:17 (the defeat of Ahab's army and Ahab's death) that which actually happens in 22:29–38. Here we have a combination of flashback and anticipation. (2) **Duration** concerns the way in which the narrative handles episodes. Episodes may be expanded, summarized, or elided. In Gen 37:36, the author describes Joseph being sold into slavery: "Meanwhile the Midianites had sold him in Egypt to Potiphar, one of Pharaoh's officials, the captain of the guard." This is summary; the author offers no details of the transaction. Two summaries of episodes flank an expanded episode in Gen 39:10–23. Preceding the seduction episode (vv. 11–20), we read: "and although she [Potiphar's wife] spoke to Joseph *day after day,* he would not consent to lie beside her or to be with her" (v. 10); and after the seduction episode, the author presents an equally brief account of Joseph's tenure in prison: "he remained there in prison. But the LORD was with Joseph and showed him steadfast love; he gave him favor in the sight of the chief jailer" (vv. 20b–21). The way in which God actually blesses Joseph in prison is described in great detail for 63 verses! (3) **Frequency** is concerned with the relationship between an episode and its narration. An event may happen once in the story and be narrated once, happen once and be narrated more than once (that Joseph was sold to the Midianites and taken to Egypt and sold there is told three times [Gen 37:28; 37:36; and 39:1]); happen more than once and be narrated more than once (two obvious examples are Abraham's attempt to pass Sarah off as his sister [Gen 12:10–20 and 20:1–17] and the dual account of creation in Gen 1 and 2); or happen more than once and be narrated only once. (In Jer 44, the Jews in Egypt tell Jeremiah that they have been burning incense to the "queen of heaven" and that their fathers, kings, and officials in the towns of Judah had been doing so *repeatedly;* yet the practice is narrated only here in the Old Testament.)

Genette's last two categories are **mood** and **voice**. I briefly mention them here because I address these issues at some length in the discussion of characterization, point of view, plot, and setting in Hebrew narrative. (4) **Mood** divides into the sub-categories of distance and perspective. Distance is the relationship between the narration and its own materials. Is the story told or represented, and is it narrated in direct, indirect, or free direct speech? Perspective is what is usually referred to as point of view. The narrator may be elevated above the characters in the story by being privy to more knowledge than the characters, the characters may be elevated above the narrator in a similar fashion, or the narrator and character(s) may be even-handed in their knowledge. The narrator may be "omniscient" outside the action of the story or within the action of the story. One example of the former is the narrator of the book of Job, while an instance of the latter is the narrator in Joseph Conrad's *Heart of Darkness,* where the narrator is actually a character in the action. Narration may proceed from the author's perspective, from a character's perspective, or from the perspective of various characters. (5) **Voice** concerns the act of narrating itself. What kind of narrator and narratee are implied? A narrator may recount the action as it actually unfolds, before it happens, or after the fact. The narrator may be absent from the narrative, inside the narrative in the first person, the principal character in the narrative, or a combination of these. For example, in Ford Madox Ford's *The Good Soldier,* the narrator is recounting a series of experiences of which he himself was one of the principal characters, while at the same time attempting to make sense of the events in the present. The distinctions in Genette's work highlight the difference between narration (the act of narrating) and narrative (what is actually narrated).[3]

On the one hand, Hebrew narrative is similar in many respects to narrative in general. On the other hand, it has some interesting and unique differences. Meir Sternberg has offered a compelling argument for one of the key characteristics of Hebrew narrative.[4] According to Sternberg the author of Hebrew narrative translated certain doctrinal views into literary correlatives. The doctrinal view of the omniscience of God is reflected in the standard literary use of the omniscient narrator (although there are exceptions, e.g., the books of Ezra and Nehemiah). Just as Yahweh knows all truth, but does not reveal its totality to humanity, so the omniscient narrator does not make the reader privy to all the truth of a narrative world. Human beings stumble and grope their way through life, learning through trial and error, reflection, and retrial. In a similar fashion, readers make their way through a text. The narrator tells the truth, but not the whole truth. As a result, "gaps of indeterminacy" (places in the narrative where some pertinent information is

---

[3] Gérard Genette, *Narrative Discourse: An Essay in Method* (trans. Jane E. Lewin; Ithica: Cornell University Press, 1980), 25–32.

[4] Meir Sternberg, *The Poetics of Biblical Narrative* (Bloomington: Indiana University Press, 1985), 157–58.

missing) are created in the text which the reader must fill. As the reader
moves through the text, information is encountered which generates
inferences. As the reading progresses, however, the text offers additional information (e.g., information concerning time, motive, cause,
effect) which requires the reader to reread the text, adjusting the previous inferences. Another product of these intentional gaps is the raising of "narrative interest": suspense, surprise, and curiosity. This idea
is discussed in more detail in unit III. Other translations of doctrinal
views into literary correlates include:

> the doctrine of free will into complex characterization, . . . human re-
> strictedness into studies in ambiguity, omnipotence and providence into
> well-made plots, control of history into cyclical and analogical design
> imposed upon recalcitrant matter, and the demand to infer from past to
> present into ordeal by interpretation.[5]

With this background to narratology, we are in a better position to examine the poetics of Hebrew narrative. We proceed by discussing in
turn the concepts of plot, setting, characterization, point of view, and
repetition.

Plot

Aristotle describes plot as action having a beginning, middle, and
end. Some type of conflict occurs at the beginning of the narrative, is
complicated in various ways through the middle, and is finally resolved
at the end. The basic plot, therefore, has a three-part structure: conflict,
complication, and resolution (*dénouement*). In the Joseph narrative, the
conflict arises between Joseph and his brothers when the brothers perceive that their father Jacob loves Joseph more than them (Gen 37:1–4).
This conflict is complicated by Joseph's dreams, by the brothers' plot
to kill Joseph, and by the brothers' selling Joseph into slavery. There is
no resolution until Joseph's final revelation to his brothers in Egypt.
The Joseph narrative, however, actually has multiple conflicts (Joseph/
brothers, Jacob/sons, Joseph's dreams/the fulfillment of the dreams).
Each of these conflicts is complicated throughout the story and is finally resolved at the end.

In the tragic plot, the **protagonist** makes a miscalculation due to a
bit of missing information. At some point in the action, the protagonist
discovers this missing bit of information, a discovery which propels the

---

[5] Ibid., 157.

protagonist into a state of misery. Again, the Jephthah story offers a prime example. Jephthah promises to offer as a burnt offering to God the first thing coming out of his house if God will grant victory. Due to the layout of the common home (it would have a type of fenced yard around it where the animals were kept) Jephthah assumed that he would be greeted by livestock. It was a perfectly logical assumption. Little did he know that he would be greeted by his only child, a daughter. The discovery of the missing information propels Jephthah from a state of happiness to a state of misery ("When he saw her, he tore his clothes, and said, 'Alas, my daughter! You have brought me very low; you have become the cause of great trouble to me. For I have opened my mouth to the LORD, and I cannot take back my vow' " [Judg 11:35]).

Setting

Setting is also a vital aspect of narrative. The setting provides the physical background for the action in the narrative. The setting of an event is usually crucial for interpreting a narrative unit. For example, David's encounter with Bathsheba takes place in the capital city of Jerusalem, a place where the king would not normally be during time of war. The Matthean account of Jesus' discourse on the law takes place on a mountain. This setting is not incidental when the reader discovers that Matthew is identifying Jesus (who reinterprets Torah) with Moses who received Torah on Mount Sinai.

Biblical narrative usually exhibits a special relationship between the action, the characters involved in the action, and the setting.[6] The setting in Hebrew narrative serves an aesthetic purpose, creating a distinct atmosphere. The setting may accomplish this through symbolic significance, such as the pit and prison scenes in the Joseph narrative and the pastoral scene in Gen 18:1–8. In this latter example, Abraham spots three travelers while he is sitting at the entrance of his tent in the heat of the day. In accordance with proper Mediterranean hospitality, Abraham goes out of his way to persuade the strangers to visit: "Do not pass by your servant. Let a *little* water be brought, and wash your feet, and rest yourselves under the *tree*. Let me bring a little bread, that you may refresh yourselves, and after that you may pass on" (Gen 18:3–5, emphasis added). At this point, Abraham seems to behave quite nonchalantly. But his actions when he leaves to get a little water and some food testify to the contrary: "And Abraham *hastened* into the tent

---

[6] See Ryken, *Words of Delight,* 54–62.

to Sarah, and said, 'Make ready quickly *three measures* of choice flour, *knead* it, and *make* cakes.' Abraham ran to the herd, and took a calf, *tender and good*, and gave it to the servant, who *hastened* to prepare it. Then he took *curds and milk and the calf* that he had *prepared, and set it before them;* and he stood by them *under the tree* while they ate" (Gen 18:6–8, emphasis added). Two features about this setting are important: its pastoral tranquility (trees, shade, tent) and its accompanying hospitality. Abraham's hospitality complements the pastoral tranquility. The result of the action is a blessing pronounced upon Sarah.

This example illustrates a conflict in Hebrew narrative—the conflict between the historical, aesthetic, and ideological purposes.[7] In some instances of setting, the historical purpose predominates and gives a verity and vividness to the narrative. For example, notice the physical precision of Gen 12:4–9:

> So Abram went, as the LORD had told him; and Lot went with him. Abram was *seventy-five* years old when he departed from Haran. . . . When they had come to the land of Canaan, Abram passed through the land to the *place at Shechem, to the oak of Moreh.* . . . From there he moved on to *the hill country on the east of Bethel,* and pitched his tent, with Bethel on the west and Ai on the east; and there he built an altar to the LORD and invoked the name of the LORD. And Abram journeyed on by stages toward *the Negeb.* (emphasis added)

At other times the ideological purpose will predominate in settings, like in the pastoral scene above. The aesthetic purpose can also be seen in this pastoral setting, in the contrast between the country and city life. In reality, however, these three purposes usually occur in combination within an elaborate interconnectedness resulting in an enjoyable reading experience.

Characterization

Adele Berlin identifies three kinds of characters in Hebrew narrative: Full-fledged, the type, and the agent.[8] The *full-fledged* character is multi-dimensional and complex, manifesting a range of character traits. This character confronts the reader with psychological, emotional, and spiritual complexities. David's wife Michal is a full-fledged character.

---

[7] See Sternberg, *Poetics of Biblical Narrative,* 44–56.
[8] Adele Berlin, *Poetics and Interpretation of Biblical Narrative* (Sheffield: Almond, 1983), 23–32.

The author goes to great lengths in presenting her as a woman with her own emotions and opinions.

A single character trait distinguishes the *type*. Such a type is Laban. From the first time we meet him in Gen 24, we are struck by his distinguishing materialism. In Gen 24:28–31, the author hints at this trait:

> Then the girl ran and told her mother's household about these things. Rebekah had a brother whose name was Laban; and Laban ran out to the man, to the spring. *As soon as he had seen the nose-ring, and the bracelets on his sister's arms, and when he heard the words of his sister Rebekah, "Thus the man spoke to me,"* he went to the man; and there he was, standing by the camels at the spring. He said, "Come in, O blessed of the LORD. Why do you stand outside when I have prepared the house and a place for the camels?" (emphasis added)

Laban's materialistic motivation is sustained in 24:47–51 and in his dealings with Jacob in Gen 29.

The *agent* type of character is nothing more than a functionary which the author uses to fill out the narrative. This character is usually not characterized at all, but simply serves the purpose of providing the necessary characters for a story. Depending upon the narrative and the purpose of the narrative, however, a single character's role may change. A full-fledged character may thus become an agent or a type in another narrative. What are the techniques of characterization in Hebrew narrative? To this repertoire of poetics we now turn.

Description. Hebrew narrative is rather sparse in its descriptive details. Some descriptive details are present, but only in the service of the plot. For example, the information that Eglon in Judges is fat leads the reader to see Eglon as the fatted calf for the slaughter. The uprightness and blamelessness of Job heightens Job's tragic loss. Bathsheba's beauty partly anticipates David's actions. But beyond general descriptions (e.g., the ruddiness of David, the height of Saul, the handsomeness of Absalom, the beauty of Sarah), Hebrew narrative gives precious little specific detail. Physical concretization of characters is simply not present in Hebrew narrative. The reader must gain insight into character differently than one would in most modern novels. It seems, therefore, that Hebrew narrative is less interested in presenting the appearance of a character than in guiding the reader into a discovery of what kind of a person the character is. This observation leads us to look at the other methods in the author's repertoire.

Interiorization. When the narrator supplies the reader with windows into the mental or emotional state of a character, the reader views the action (or a portion of it) through the eyes of the character. The author effects this interiorization in two ways. First, the narrator may comment on a character's thought or opinion. We become privy to the thoughts of a character, but the thoughts are expressed in the words of the narrator: "So Noah *knew* that the waters had subsided from the earth" (Gen 8:11b). Even God himself is not exempt: "God heard their groaning, and God *remembered* his covenant with Abraham, Isaac, and Jacob. God looked upon the Israelites, and God *took notice* of them" (Exod 2:24, 25). This type of interiorization is called external interiorization. Second, the narrator makes extensive use of direct quotes of a character's thoughts. This is **interior monologue:** "Then Moses was afraid and thought, 'Surely the thing is known'" (Exod 2:14); "Then Moses said, 'I must turn aside and look at this great sight, and see why the bush is not burned up'" (Exod 3:3). These windows into a character's thoughts enable the reader to make judgments about a character's emotion and motivation. These judgments in turn help the reader fill out the character, to know what kind of a person he or she might be.

Direct dialogue. Direct speech is the preferred method in Hebrew narrative for sustaining the action within the plot. **Direct dialogue** conveys the internal psychological and ideological dimensions of a character and is much more dramatic than exterior narration. The direct speech of Samson in Judg 14–16 illustrates the point. After returning from Timnah, Samson says to his parents, "I saw a Philistine woman at Timnah; now *get her for me* as my wife" (14:2). Although he is discouraged from taking a foreign wife, Samson replies, *"Get her for me,* because she pleases me" (14:3b). The sharp, demanding tone of this speech reveals Samson's character, a character marked by a sense of immediate, thoughtless gratification. Even in his remarks to God, Samson exhibits this same tone of ingratitude: "By then he was very thirsty, and he called on the LORD, saying, 'You have granted this great victory by the hand of your servant. Am I now to die of thirst, and fall into the hands of the uncircumcised?'" (Judg 15:18). Gratification and revenge mark Samson's character as seen through his direct speeches. Nothing changes at his death, for even here revenge is his motivation: "Lord GOD, remember me and strengthen me only this once, O God, so that with this one act of *revenge I may pay back the Philistines for my two eyes*" (Judg 16:28).

Actions. While in Hebrew narrative direct speech and actions are usually combined, actions can be narrated without speech. These speechless accounts of actions highlight character. They tend to serve as unannounced commentary on a character's speech. We already know from Laban's past record that he is adept at deception. Therefore, when we hear Jacob's proposal to Laban in Gen 30:30–33 and Laban's response in 30:34, we suspect that we are in store for yet another ruse:

> "For you had little before I came, and it has increased abundantly; and the LORD has blessed you wherever I turned. But now when shall I provide for my own household also?" He said, "What shall I give you?" Jacob said, "You shall not give me anything; if you will do this for me, I will again feed your flock and keep it: let me pass through all your flock today, removing from it every speckled and spotted sheep and every black lamb, and the spotted and speckled among the goats; and such shall be my wages. So my honesty will answer for me later, when you come to look into my wages with you. Every one that is not speckled and spotted among the goats and black among the lambs, if found with me, shall be counted stolen." Laban said, "Good! Let it be as you have said."

Sure enough, Laban does not disappoint us. His action is exactly opposite of his speech:

> But that day Laban removed the male goats that were striped and spotted, and all the female goats that were speckled and spotted, every one that had white on it, and every lamb that was black, and put them in charge of his sons; and he set a distance of three days' journey between himself and Jacob, while Jacob was pasturing the rest of Laban's flock (Gen 30:35–36).

But we also know that Jacob will not take a back seat to Laban when it comes to ingenuity and originality in trickery. So we are not entirely surprised at Jacob's response to Laban's ploy, but we are at least entertained by his creativity!

> Then Jacob took fresh rods of poplar and almond and plane, and peeled white streaks in them, exposing the white of the rods. He set the rods that he had peeled in front of the flocks in the troughs, that is, the watering places, where the flocks came to drink. And since they bred when they came to drink, the flocks bred in front of the rods, and so the flocks produced young that were striped, speckled, and spotted. Jacob separated the lambs, and set the faces of the flocks toward the striped and the completely black animals in the flock of Laban; and he put his own droves apart, and did not put them with Laban's flock. Whenever the stronger of the flock were breeding, Jacob laid the rods in the troughs before the eyes of the flock, that they might breed among the rods, but for the feebler of the flock he did not lay them there; so the feebler were Laban's, and the stronger Jacob's. Thus the man grew exceedingly rich, and had large flocks, and male and female slaves, and camels and donkeys. (Gen 30:37–43)

Contrast. By placing characters in juxtaposition, an author highlights character traits, especially those traits which appear to be incongruent to a character's social status. For instance, Adele Berlin describes how the author in 1 Sam 18–20 successfully, yet subtly, contrasts character traits in Michal and Jonathan.[9] The reader is struck with the incongruity. Jonathan displays characteristics usually identified as feminine, while Michal exhibits definite masculine traits. The relationship between Michal and David is marked by purely pragmatic considerations and "the feelings of love and tenderness that David might have been expected to have for Michal are all reserved for Jonathan."[10]

Even at their final parting, David cries, "I am distressed for you, my brother Jonathan; greatly beloved were you to me; your love to me was wonderful, passing the love of women" (2 Sam 1:26). I am not suggesting any sexual orientation here, but only that this contrast underscores elements in the personalities of Michal and Jonathan (and certainly David also). Michal is consistently portrayed as physical and aggressive, while Jonathan is usually depicted as accomplishing his deeds through carefully placed words. Also, Michal never gave birth to a child, the ultimate Hebraic sign of femininity.[11]

The story of Deborah and Barak is another example of character contrast (Judg 4–5). Deborah is always decisive. She sizes up a situation and then without delay acts. She says to Barak, "The LORD, the God of Israel, commands you: 'Go, take position at Mount Tabor, bringing ten thousand from the tribe of Naphtali and the tribe of Zebulun'" (Judg 4:6). But Barak hesitates: "If you will go with me, I will go; but if you will not go with me, I will not go" (Judg 4:8). At once Deborah recognizes his hesitation, rebukes him, and then goes with him. Later, once again Barak does not move until Deborah commands him: "Up! For this is the day on which the LORD has given Sisera into your hand. The LORD is indeed going out before you" (Judg 4:14a). Without a doubt, each character's personality is heightened by contrast.

Characterization by contrast is a creative and intriguing literary device, highly developed in Hebrew narrative. The reader is encouraged to watch for this device and to allow it to enhance the reading of Hebrew narrative.

---

[9] Ibid., 24–25.
[10] Ibid., 25.
[11] Ibid.

Point of View

Point of view or perspective is actually inseparable from characterization. But because of its complexity and centrality in Hebrew narrative, we need to examine it independently of characterization.

Like narrative in general, Hebrew narrative discloses only what the author desires. The author can elaborate or condense. Also, like most narrative, Hebrew narrative employs several voices or vehicles for narration; the author may present information through the voice and eyes of the omniscient narrator or any one of several characters within the narrative. The consequence of multiple narrative voices is multiple points of view. The multi-perspectival quality of Hebrew narrative affords a depth and fullness, for the narrative is presented from alternating perspectives, shifting from narrator to character to character.

The David and Bathsheba passage in 2 Sam 11 is a case in point. The passage begins with background information by the narrator: "In the spring of the year, the time when kings go out to battle, David sent Joab with his officers and all Israel with him. . . . But David remained at Jerusalem" (v. 1). In the next verse, readers are given the opportunity to see what David sees: "he saw from the roof a woman bathing; the woman was very beautiful." The third perspective is that of a messenger: "This is Bathsheba daughter of Eliam, the wife of Uriah the Hittite" (v. 3). In the remaining verses of the chapter, the author shuttles the reader from one character's perspective to another's—David's, Uriah's, Joab's, the messenger's, and Bathsheba's. The author even gives us Joab's perception of David's perspective. The last statement in the passage ("But the thing that David had done displeased the LORD" [v. 27b]) is the voice of the narrator. This statement is an example of what is called "breaking frame." The narrator turns away from the action and directly addresses the audience. In so doing, the narrator offers an evaluation of the story. Thus, the narrator gives the reader his or her conceptual point of view.

This shift from one point of view to another may result not only in different perspectives, but also in disparate ones. The result may be either irony or ambiguity. We have already seen in the story of Job that the reader may possess knowledge that the characters do not. We as readers know why Job is suffering, while the characters have other perspectives. The result is irony. The reader finds two disparate perspectives in the Joseph narrative. When Joseph's brothers return to their father with the blood-drenched coat, Jacob cries out, "Joseph is without doubt torn to pieces." But the readers and the brothers know differently. There is also an ambiguity in this narrative centering around

Reuben. In ch. 37, as the narrator shuttles back and forth between the perspectives of the brothers in general and Reuben in particular, some unresolved questions arise. We are told in verses 21–22 that Reuben suggests that the brothers throw Joseph into a cistern with the clear intention of later returning to rescue him: "Reuben said (this to) . . . rescue him out of their hand *and restore him to his father*" (v. 22). The "brothers" later pull Joseph from the cistern and sell him to the Ishmaelites (vv. 25–28). But then we discover that Reuben must not have been with the brothers when this occurred: "When Reuben returned to the pit and saw that Joseph was not in the pit, he tore his clothes. He returned to his brothers, and said, 'The boy is gone; and I, where can I turn?'" (vv. 29–30). Where was Reuben when the brothers sold Joseph? Do the brothers tell him of their actions? We do not know. The narrator has left us with some unanswered questions. When later we discover that Joseph had pleaded with his brothers for his life (42:21), Reuben replies, "Did I not tell you not to wrong the boy? But you would not listen" (v. 22a, b). Is this Reuben's first knowledge of their crime? The narrator sustains this ambiguity which centers around Reuben.

Generally in Hebrew narrative, the reader and characters are evenhanded in their knowledge. There are also instances, however, when the reader is privy to knowledge not available to characters. Such is the case with the story of Jacob mentioned above. This type of perspective is called *reader-elevated.* At the same time, although rare in Hebrew narrative, there are instances where a character may know more than the reader. An instance of this is in the Joseph narrative where the reader finds out about Joseph's reaction to being thrown into the cistern, a knowledge which the brothers had all along. This type of perspective is called *character-elevated.*

Style

Many scholars feel that if the stylistic uniqueness of Hebrew narrative could be captured in one word, it would be repetition. This is true for both the number of occurrences of repetition and the number of different types of repetitive devices. The majority of the sub-genres of Hebrew narrative are actually no more than forms of repetition. This proclivity toward repetition takes on vital importance for literary considerations in light of the Hebrew Bible's further tendency to suspend or limit description. The different types of repetition are deliberate narrative techniques. An ability to recognize these sub-genres of repetition enhances our understanding and appreciation of the art of Hebrew narrative. Below is a brief discussion of some of the more common repetitive sub-genres.

Leitwort. Sometimes an author may exploit the range of meaning of a word-root by repeating different forms of the root within a pericope or across several units. This technique, called *Leitwort*, may provide thematic cohesion or thematic emphasis within a unit of Scripture. Actually the individual context of a passage dictates the function of a *Leitwort*. An example is the twenty-one repetitions of the root for "to bless" in Gen 27:1–45. The first eleven chapters of Genesis contain a theme that is traceable throughout the remainder of the Hebrew Bible. This theme is the separation between humankind and God. This theme of separation is reflected at the level of the family, especially in the patriarchal (Gen 12–50) and monarchial (1 and 2 Sam, 1 and 2 Kgs) narratives. The Hebrews, like other social groups, established social conventions to safeguard family cohesion. One of these conventions was the father's practice of passing on to the eldest son the family inheritance and paternal blessing. When Jacob steals Esau's blessing in the Gen 27 story, the established social convention has the opposite effect. Instead of safeguarding the family cohesion, it is actually the source of family division and separation. Through the repetitive use of the word "to bless," the author draws the reader's attention to the convention and its reverse effect.

Key Phrases or Sentences. Hebrew authors repeat certain phrases or sentences in order to establish thematic unity in larger sections. These repeated phrases or sentences have a formulaic air about them. An example is the sentence "In those days there was no king in Israel; all the people did what was right in their own eyes." This occurs in full or part in Judg 17:6; 18:1; 19:1; and 21:25. The author emphasizes the theme of social anarchy by this repetition.

Motif. A **motif** is the recurrence within a narrative of some object, image, or action. Examples are stones in the Jacob narrative, water in the Moses story, or fire in the Samson story. Motifs may give thematic unity or coherence to a narrative, or they may carry symbolic significance (e.g., the stones in the Jacob story symbolize the hard realities of life with which he constantly wrestles, as opposed to the dream world of his son Joseph).

Themes. Certain **themes** occur with regularity in Hebrew narrative. Three such themes are the barren wife (Gen 11; 16; 20; 25; and 30), disobedience and rebellion in the wilderness stories (Ex 16:27–36; 32:1–35; Num 11:1–9; 12:1–16; 14:1–12; 16:1–50; 25:1–9), and the reversal of primogeniture (Gen 21; 25; 27; 37; 42; and 48). Themes tend to organize meaning according to patterns that the author invites the reader to discover. These themes also indicate elements of the author's worldview. For example, by repeatedly using the reversal of the rule of primogeniture, an author may be suggesting that God is not bound by human social conventions, but is free to circumvent these when the occasion calls for it.

Repetition of Sequences. This is a repetition of an activity, usually three times or three times plus a fourth with an intensification from one to the next occurrence. Examples include the three actions of Saul's messengers, Balaam's three failures to give directions to the ass, and the catastrophes in Job's story.

Chiastic Patterns. Words or events inversely repeated in order to shape episodes, speeches, or entire cycles of stories are termed **chiastic patterns** (chiasm). An example is Num 11:11–15:

A First question: Why has God mistreated Moses? ("Why have you treated your servant so badly?")

B Second question: What has Moses done to deserve an undue *burden*? ("Why have I not found favor in your sight, that you lay the burden of all this people on me?")

C Third question: Why should Moses *carry* these people as a nurse carries a baby? ("Did I give birth to them, that you should say to me, 'Carry them in your bosom, as a nurse carries a suckling child,' to the land that you promised on oath to their ancestors?")

D Fourth question: How can Moses supply food? ("Where am I to get meat to give to all this people?")

D' Response to fourth question: ("For they come weeping to me and say, 'Give us meat to eat!'")

C' Response to third question: ("I am not able to *carry* all this people alone")

B' Response to second question: ("for they are too heavy for me")

A' Response to first question: ("If this is the way you are going to *treat* me, put me to death at once")

Type scenes. This literary device is similar to themes, but differs slightly. George W. Savran defines **type scenes** as the repetition of "conventions of speech and behavior in analogous situations, such as betrothal scenes (Gen 24:10–61; 29:1–20; Exod 2:15b–21) and annunciation stories (Gen 18:1–15; Judg 13; 1 Sam 1; 2 Kgs 4:8–37)."[12] To this list of type scenes, one might add the trial in the wilderness, revival of the dead child, and the hero's journey from his homeland to a foreign country.

Each of these type scenes has its own basic literary structure. The betrothal and annunciation scenes are two helpful illustrations. In the betrothal type scene, a prospective bridegroom or his representative journeys to a foreign land where he encounters a young woman or women at a well. Either the man or the woman draws water from the well. After this initial meeting, the woman (or women) hurries home to share the news of the stranger's arrival. A betrothal is then finalized, often after the stranger has shared a meal with the woman's family. This is the pattern followed in the servant's search for a wife for Isaac in Gen 24.

The betrothal scene—all others as well—may be innovatively refashioned depending upon the author's purpose. For instance, in the Jacob narrative, the hero first meets shepherds at the well (Gen 29:1–8), and only later does Rachel approach the well (Gen 29:9). Not only does Jacob draw the water, but he must remove an obstacle (a stone) from the mouth of the well. This obstacle adumbrates the obstacle (fourteen years of labor) which he must overcome before he is given Rachel as his wife.

In the Samson story, the hero journeys to a foreign country, leading the reader to expect a betrothal scene. But neither drawing of water from a well nor a meal of hospitality follows. This foreshadows Samson's characteristic penchant for disregarding accepted protocol.

An interesting New Testament application of this type scene occurs in the Gospel of John (4:1–42). Jesus travels from Judea to Sychar in Samaria. While Jesus is resting at Jacob's well, a woman comes to draw water. A conversation ensues and the woman subsequently runs into the town and announces what the stranger at the well has told her. This prompts the whole town's exodus to the well, which finally results in the conversion of many of the Samaritans. Because of John the Baptist's remark in 3:29 ("He who has the bride is the bridegroom. The

---

[12] George W. Savran, *Telling and Retelling: Quotation in Biblical Narrative* (Bloomington: Indiana University Press, 1988), 7.

friend of the bridegroom, who stands and hears him, rejoices greatly at the bridegroom's voice"), the reader must inquire about John's purpose in using this type scene, especially since there is no mention of a hospitality meal.

The annunciation type scene also follows a well-established pattern. Usually a barren or aged woman receives a promise (normally from a messenger of Yahweh or a prophet) of a miraculous birth of a child. Ordinarily this child of miraculous birth is to be used by God in some significant way. Sometimes the story is complicated by the presence of another wife or concubine who is quite fertile. The births of Isaac, Samson, Samuel, the Shunammite woman's son, and Jesus are examples. As stated earlier, each type scene may have its own innovative refashioning. The scene involving the Shunammite woman in 2 Kgs 4 is complicated by the death of the child of miraculous birth. To further complicate and add suspense to the scene, the author has Elisha attempt to revive the child four times before he is successful. By reporting an event through a well-known sub-genre, an author immediately attracts the interest of the readers. Readers familiar with the sub-genre expect standard elements within it. When the author modifies these elements or simply omits them, the readers are supposed to ask why.

Quotations. The Old Testament authors show a distinct fondness for direct speech instead of third-person "telling." Through this technique the author establishes attitudes, motivations, and personalities; the writer thus forms a character by using the character's own words instead of simply describing the character in detail. Within this technique of direct speech, the author records instances where one character quotes another. A quote is said to be verifiable if the original speech is retrievable. In this case the original speech and its subsequent quotation can be compared. If the original speech is not available, then the quotation is unverifiable. When the reader is able to verify a quotation, some variations on the original may be observed: abbreviating, expanding, or paraphrasing. The differences between the original and the quote establish a character's motive or personality. An insightful illustration of this is found in Gen 42. Verses 18–20b contain Joseph's ultimatum to his brothers:

> Do this and you will live, for I fear God: if you are honest men, let one of your brothers stay here where you are imprisoned. The rest of you shall go and carry grain for the famine of your households, and bring

your youngest brother to me. Thus your words will be verified, and you shall not die.

When the brothers report this to Jacob, the message changes:

> By this I shall know that you are honest men: leave one of your brothers with me, take grain for the famine of your households, and go your way. Bring your youngest brother to me, and I shall know that you are not spies but honest men. Then I will release your brother to you, and you may trade in the land (vv. 33–34).

The quotation of Joseph's speech is significantly different in several ways from its original. First, the brothers twice refer to their being honest men. Second, Joseph does not promise that he will give the brother back, but only that they will not die. Third, the brothers' addition of "then I will release your brother to you" is ambiguous; which brother do they want Jacob to assume is to be returned; the hostage or their youngest brother? Or does the reader know that "the brother" is none other than Joseph himself? Either this is a ploy by the brothers to soften the effect on Jacob or another attempt to deceive him. Judging from their behavior after they return to Egypt, the former is more likely the case. And last, the brothers put yet another promise in the mouth of Joseph—the promise that they will be allowed to move freely about the land. This misquote by the brothers reveals something about their character. They reformulate Joseph's ultimatum in a more positive light for the benefit of their aging father. This reformulation is additional evidence for the reader (not Joseph, since he is out of the picture here) that the brothers have indeed changed in their attitudes concerning their father.

It is interesting that when Yahweh himself quotes someone, each instance is a verbatim repetition of the verifiable original. This circumstance is determined by the author's view of the absolute consistency and truthfulness of Yahweh's character.

Since these repetitive techniques rarely occur in isolation, but are interwoven in a variety of ways, Hebrew narrative is rich in aesthetic quality. Plausible interpretations are virtually unobtainable if the interpreter is unwilling or unable to give appropriate attention to the details of these literary forms and sub-genres. To plumb the depths of meaning in Hebrew narrative, the reader should be willing to "first gain a better understanding of each of these individual genres in their distinctiveness and interrelationships in the narrative."[13]

---

[13] Ibid.

Intratextual Dynamics

The reader may be asking at this juncture if there is really a homo-geneity of literary practice within such a heterogeneous work as the Hebrew Bible. Can the reader really expect so much commonality or agreement in form within a volume of literary works that span over nine centuries? Yes and no. There is both continuity and discontinuity. There is continuity due to the constant dialogue which later literary compositions hold with earlier ones. This dialogue is present at a vari-ety of levels. First, there is the practice of recasting and reapplying ear-lier texts to later situations. This is especially true of the prophetic texts. Second, there are numerous instances of one author consciously offering a critique or even a parody of an earlier text or literary type. For example, the author of Ecclesiastes seems to challenge the idea of linear, progressive history found in earlier works like Genesis. This same author also questions the conventional view of wisdom. LaSor states it well:

> In a word, he sought to use traditional tools of wisdom to refute and revise its traditional conclusions. Like Job, he protested the easy gen-eralizations with which his fellow teachers taught their pupils to be suc-cessful. They had oversimplified life and its rules so as to mislead and frustrate their followers. Their observations seemed superficial and their counsel thin in a world beset by injustice, toil, and death.[14]

Finally, there is the common practice of **allusion**, where one au-thor (perhaps sometimes unconsciously) frames a story or an episode like one written much earlier. For example, by constructing an analogy between the stories of Ruth and Abraham, the author of Ruth portrays Ruth as a matriarch of the Davidic line. Without going into great detail here, suffice it say that the reader needs only to compare a couple of texts (one concerning Ruth and the other Abraham) to see the begin-ning of the analogy: Boaz says to Ruth: "All that you have done for your mother-in-law since the death of your husband has been fully told me, and how you *left your father and mother and your native land and came to a people that you did not know before*" (Ruth 2:11, emphasis added). Com-pare God's word to Abraham: "Go from your country and your kindred and *your father's house to the land that I will show you*" (Gen 12:1, empha-sis added). The regularity of allusions like this is persuasive evidence that the writers were at home in texts written hundreds of years earlier.

---

[14] William LaSor, David Hubbard, and Frederic Bush, *Old Testament Survey* (Grand Rapids: Eerdmans, 1982), 589.

This is possible because the texts are all part of the same religious tradition, sharing common literary as well as worldview elements.

The "no" part of the answer to the above question derives from the evolutionary nature of the Hebrew Bible. The so-called golden age of Hebrew narrative is pre-exilic. This period includes the books from Genesis through Kings. By the time of the post-exilic period, new patterns of narrative expression emerge. The "classical" period of Hebrew narrative exhibits the narrative structure outlined above. Throughout the post-exilic period, however, there is a range of narrative styles (though still similar in many ways, especially in the use of common sub-genres). For example, the more historical texts of Ezra, Nehemiah, and Chronicles do not employ the omniscient narrator, but personal, first-person accounts. Further, if one moves from a text like Genesis into Jonah or Esther, the differences are striking. Many of the familiar characteristics of Hebrew narrative are replaced in Jonah and Esther by elements of farce, comedy, and detail. Examples of comic farce include the dimensions of Nineveh in Jonah and the one-year perfumed bath of the virgins in the story of Esther.

Obviously there is a dialectic of a sort in the narrative literature of the Hebrew Bible between the generic structure and the evolution of time. But it is a safe wager to concentrate on the explication of Hebrew narratology. These are texts in which the narrative worlds were formulated by authors with different purposes and perspectives. But they are also texts whose narrative worlds were created in an active, dynamic, and conscious dialogue with earlier texts. So, while there is discontinuity within the corpus of the Hebrew writings, the literary continuity is weighty enough to justify similar narrative analysis of the canon.[15]

As one part of the sacred canon of Christianity, the Hebrew Bible holds for many people a special place in revealed truth. For this reason, many well-meaning Christians wave red flags when descriptive terms such as "story world," "narrative world," "artistic creativity," or "literary archetypes" are mentioned. In more Fundamentalistic circles, there has been a persistent, unconscious misperception in the "correlation of the truth-falsity distinction with the history-fiction distinction."[16] Elements regarded as historically verifiable are understood as truth, and mimetic or imaginative elements as false. The basic problem concerns

---

[15] See Robert Alter and Frank Kermode, "Introduction to the Old Testament," in *Literary Guide to the Bible* (ed. Robert Alter and Frank Kermode; Cambridge, Mass.: Harvard University Press, 1987).

[16] Lundin, Thiselton and Walhout, *Responsibility of Hermeneutics,* 74.

the confusion between truth and **truth value**. Is it possible for a mimetic text whose content was never intended to be historically accurate to communicate truth? If the answer is *yes*, then the text has truth value. An author communicates truth by creating a mimetic relationship between the world within the text and the real world, even though the state of affairs depicted in the text is not historically verifiable. So a mimetic text asserts some truth by telling a story; it conveys truth about the real world. Authors of mimetic texts generally are not interested in communicating propositional truth, but literary truth. Mimetic narrative is not instructional in the same way as a lecture in history. Hebrew narrative contains history, but it is not historical narrative; it is mimetic narrative. It uses gaps, perspective, characterization, patterned repetition, setting, plot, and a host of other literary devices to communicate its message. All this engages the reader. The reader cannot stand outside the text, but becomes a participant, filling out the work, making connections between textual segments, evaluating new perspectives, and reevaluating previous ones in light of new information. The reader of modern history may remain outside, simply absorbing the facts. But in mimetic narrative, the author challenges (indeed requires) the reader to actualize the meaning latent in the text.

A rather extended example illustrates that claim. After David carries through his plans to have Uriah killed in battle and to marry Bathsheba, Nathan, the prophet, confronts him with a story in 2 Sam 12:1–4. David is appalled by what he perceives to be a real (historical) life event and proclaims, "As the LORD lives, the man who has done this deserves to die; he shall restore the lamb fourfold, because he did this thing, and because he had no pity" (vv. 5–6). Having taken the story as a description of an actual theft of a lamb, David passes sentence upon the perpetrator of such a despicable act, making reference to the laws of property protection in Exod 22:1: "When someone steals an ox or a sheep, and slaughters it or sells it, the thief shall pay five oxen for an ox, and *four sheep for a sheep*." What David does not realize is that he is passing sentence upon himself. What the reader must determine is whether the sentence was carried out or not. Did David pay back with four lambs? The child born to Bathsheba dies on the seventh day after birth. That this child is the firstborn male, coupled with the significance of the seventh day in the sacrificial system (cf. Num 29), hints that for the narrator the first of the four required payments has been made.

If there is any doubt that the narrator is carefully and creatively presenting the fulfillment of David's announced sentence, one need only read further of the account of Amnon's death. Two years after

Amnon's rape of his sister, Absalom has Amnon killed at Baal Hazor, where the sheepshearers are gathered: "Then Absalom commanded his servants, 'Watch when Amnon's heart is merry with wine, and when I say to you, "Strike Amnon," then kill him' " (2 Sam 13:28). The word used here for "strike" (*nākāh*) is the same one Nathan uses in reference to Uriah's death. The hiphil form of the verb here and the reference to the sheepshearers have strong lamb and sacrificial overtones. This knowledge should be enough to spur the reader to anticipate the sacrifice of a third son (lamb). This expectancy is fulfilled in the person of Absalom. The author prepares the reader in 14:25–26 with a bit of information which seems to interrupt the flow of the narrative:

> Now in all Israel there was no one to be praised so much for his beauty as Absalom; from the sole of his foot to the crown of his head there was no blemish in him. When he cut the hair of his head (for at the end of every year he used to cut it; when it was heavy on him, he cut it), he weighed the hair of his head, two hundred shekels by the king's weight.

The lamb imagery here is unmistakable. Like the sacrificial lamb, Absalom is perfect, without blemish. He also "sheared" his head when his hair became too long (like a lamb would be sheared when the wool became too long) and would weigh the hair. We are then told that the weight of the hair was about 200 shekels (five pounds). So just as a lamb was sheared and its wool weighed for sale, Absalom (the perfect lamb) sheared his hair and then weighed it.

Having picked up the pattern thus far, the reader should now anticipate that the narrator will shortly offer an account of Absalom's death, and that the death will be clothed in lamb and/or sacrificial imagery. The expected account takes place in 2 Sam 18:9–15. A couple of significant references almost leap out at the reader here. First, Absalom's mule runs under the "thick branches" of a large oak, and Absalom is left hanging in the tree by his hair (v. 9). And second, after Joab upbraids a soldier for not killing Absalom, the soldier replies, "I would not raise my hand against the king's son" (v. 12a). Both references are distinctly reminiscent of the language concerning Abraham's sacrifice of his son Isaac in Gen 22 and the subsequent intervention of Yahweh's messenger in providing a sacrificial ram in Isaac's place. Absalom's entanglement in the oak branches recalls the language of Gen 22:13, where "Abraham looked up and saw a ram, caught in a thicket by its horns. Abraham went and took the ram and offered it up as a burnt offering instead of his son." Even the specific language of the later narrative conjures up images of the former, in that the use the Hebrew word *s'ôbek* ("thick branches") in 2 Sam 18:9 is similar in sound and construction to the word *sĕbak* ("thicket") used in Gen 22:13. The soldier's refusal to *raise his hand* against Absalom echoes the language of Gen 22:10, where Abraham "*reached out his hand* and took the knife to kill his son" (emphasis added). In the death of Absalom, the third lamb has been slain in payment.

The fourth and final payment is David's son, Adonijah. Fearing Solomon, Adonijah fled into the tabernacle and "went to grasp the horns of the altar" (1 Kgs 1:50). Once again the description has obvious sacrificial imagery (cf. Lev 4:7, 18; 8:15; Ps 118:27). As the reader should expect by now, after a short reprieve, Adonijah is slain (1 Kgs 2:25).

Now the author of this extended narrative could have simply informed the readers that David sinned and that he paid with the death of four sons. This would have taken about two sentences. But that would have made for dull reading. The author desired to construct a narrative in such a way that, given just enough hints, foreshadowing, and gaps, the readers might discover these facts on their own. The author has created the possibility that a reader can discover a mimetic relationship between the narrative and a truth in the real world. That truth may be that Yahweh is faithful to his law in judgment as well as in blessing. Yet the author does not offer this truth propositionally, but mimetically. So what we have here is history in the service of mimesis. If we accept this distinction between history and mimesis and do not impose demands of historical verisimilitude upon texts that were never intended to be objective history in the modern sense, most troublesome issues, such as chronological and logical contradictions, simply evaporate. As modern readers of the Hebrew narratives, we should allow the narratives to speak truth as narratives.

Hebrew Poetry

Poetry in general is highly structured and compact, and **Hebrew poetry** is no exception. Hebrew poetry utilizes figurative, metaphorical language and is especially characterized by thought parallelism. The following examples illustrate the way thought is paralleled in Hebrew poetry.

As the deer longs for flowing streams, so my soul longs for you, O God. (Ps 42:1)

O that my vexation were weighed, and all my calamity laid in the balances! (Job 6:2)

Your cheeks are like halves of a pomegranate behind your veil. (Song 4:3b)

Besides sharing figurative language, these texts evidence other note-worthy traits. Each example contains two parts, which Alter calls "vers-ets."[17] Furthermore, the second verset seems to be related in some way to the first verset. In the second example, "vexation" and "calamity" are related as are "weighed" and "laid in the balances." Scholars have traditionally referred to this relationship between the versets of a line in Hebrew poetry as **parallelism of thought**. Parallelism of thought gener-ally consists of three types: synonymy, antithesis, and synthesis. In syn-onymous parallelism the second verset restates in a different way the thought of the first verset:

he washes his garments in wine
and his robe in the blood of grapes. (Gen 49:11b)

Antithetical parallelism expresses in the second verset the same idea as in the first but in a negative manner:

A wise child makes a glad father,
but a foolish child is a mother's grief. (Prov 10:1b)

In synthetic parallelism, the second verset complements the first by clarification or explanation:

So I will send a fire on the wall of Gaza,
fire that shall devour its strongholds. (Amos 1:7)

The consuming of the fortresses is the result of the fire upon the walls.
    But there is something more going on in most Hebrew poetic paral-lelism than simply static synonymy, antithesis, or synthesis. There is movement from verset to verset. For example:

Wine is a mocker,
Strong drink a brawler. (Prov 20:1a)

"Wine" has been intensified in the second verset with "strong drink," and "mocker" has been heightened to "brawler." Clearly, words spo-ken in mockery are not as strong as the physical actions of the "brawler." There has been a focusing through *intensification*.[18] It should

---

[17] See Robert Alter, *The Art of Biblical Poetry* (New York: Basic, 1985).
[18] Ibid., 27–61.

be added that this focusing or intensification is quite common in the occurrences of graded numbers which follow the pattern of x, x + 1:

Once God has spoken; twice have I heard this. (Ps 62:11a)

we will raise against them seven shepherds,
and eight installed as rulers. (Mic 5:5b)

Another type of movement between versets occurs in Amos 8:10a:

I will turn your feasts into mourning,
and all your songs into lamentation.

In this line, "all your songs" is a specific element within the larger event of "feasts" as is "lamentation" of "mourning." This type of focusing is what Alter calls focusing through *specification*.[19] Most instances of antithetical and synthetic parallelism are actually variations on the above types of focusing. Alter offers yet another type of movement within a line of verse—movement from *cause to effect:*

I call upon the LORD, who is worthy to be praised,
so I shall be saved from my enemies. (Ps 18:3)

The relation between these two versets is obviously one of cause ("call") and effect ("saved").[20] On the one hand, the importance of at least an elementary acquaintance with the structures and dynamics of Hebrew verse cannot be overemphasized. This emphasis becomes at once justified when the reader recognizes how much of the Hebrew Bible (Wisdom literature, prophecy, Psalms, and poetic sections within narrative books) is Hebrew verse.

On the other hand, as intriguing and essential as the dynamics of parallelism are, to concentrate attention only here will result in neglecting another essential quality of Hebrew poetry. Above I described poetry as heightened language. By this I mean that poetry (especially Hebrew poetry) is the language of imagery and the picturesque. It confronts the reader with word pictures, concrete images. Narrative examines a concept by telling a story through the instruments of plot, characters in action, and setting, having as its basic unit the scene; but the poet examines the same concept by drawing a verbal picture and asking the reader to pause long enough to form a mental picture. The warp and woof of the poet's art are metaphor and simile. These are similar in

---

[19] Ibid., 35.
[20] Ibid., 33.

form and operation. Whereas a simile says that one object or concept is "like" another ("your teeth are like a flock of shorn ewes," Song 4:2a), the metaphor claims that one object "is" another ("A garden locked is my sister, my bride," Song 4:12a). Through this use of metaphor and simile (along with other forms such as personification, hyperbole, apostrophe), the poet pictures reality and challenges the reader's imagination. Leland Ryken offers the following advice:

> The prevalence of images in poetry requires us to read poetry with what psychologists call the right side of the brain. This is our mental capacity to think in pictures. We first need to experience poetry with our senses and then become analytic in determining the connotations and logic of the images in their context in a poem.[21]

This brings us to a crucial point: The metaphorical nature of most Hebrew poetry requires the reader to experience an effect on one level (the literal level of the metaphor) and then to transfer that experience to another level. The reader must first pause long enough to allow the metaphor or simile to construct the literal picture before too quickly rushing on to the second level of meaning where logical associations are made between the bifocaled levels of the metaphor or simile.[22] Simply put, two things must occur when reading poetry—seeing and thinking.[23]

Seeing occurs on the literal level of the image while thinking takes place when we trace the associations and meanings between the literal and interpretive levels. How does the hermeneut actualize this movement between the literal level of imaging and the level of interpretation? One of the best articulations of this process (which I summarize below) is by Ryken.[24]

The explication of Hebrew poetry requires above all else a discernible strategy marked by a systematic, complete, and logical progression. This strategy consists of six steps. The first is to identify the sub-genre. For example, is the poem a psalm, and if so, what type (e.g., a psalm of praise, a psalm of worship, or a psalm of lament)? We may ask the same question of prophecy in poetic form or of wisdom literature. Knowing the sub-genre of the poem helps explain the poem's organization, for each type carries its own structure.

---

[21] Ryken, *Words of Delight,* 162.
[22] Ibid., 207.
[23] Ibid.
[24] Ibid., 207–11.

Second, try to determine the situation of the poem. This allows its dynamics to become more understandable. The setting of the poem may become apparent as the poem unfolds. If the author is assumed to be in exile, or in a life-threatening situation, the dynamics of the poem make more sense.

Third, determine the topic and theme of the poem to be able to recognize the message of the poem. The topic is what the poem is all about, while the theme is the poet's assertion concerning the topic. The poet's topic in Ps 23 is God's providential care. The theme, however, is the satisfaction and contentment that come from trusting in that providence.

Fourth come structure and unity. The structure develops the theme and assumes a unified whole. Most poems have their particular units bracketed by ideas or images. Moving from one unit to another assures a systematic flow of thought in explication. Four types of material can account for structure. (a) If the poem describes a person, a scene, or an event, it has a descriptive structure. (b) The poem has an expository structure if it presents a series of emotions or ideas. (c) If the units present occurrences of events in succession, the poem has a narrative structure. (d) The poem is dramatic in structure if it is an address by a speaker. The reader should be cautioned, however, that although one of these structures may dominate, an overlapping or a combining of structural elements usually occurs. While these four are the main structural forms that guarantee unity, Ryken does offer others, two of which need mention here. A poem has a catalogue structure when it primarily lists aspects of a single topic. The other structural element is best described as psychological. A poem will have this structure when the poem evidences that it was composed during great emotional moments, with the speaker's or writer's consciousness jumping from one topic to another. The only point of unity is the writer's consciousness.

Fifth, isolate the details of a poem—the literary devices and figures of speech (e.g., metaphors, hyperboles, similes, and personification). These devices are bearers of the message. These details make up what is usually referred to as *poetic texture*. The exploration of their meanings is not an option, but a necessity, and may occupy most of the reader's time. When analyzing the poem, the reader must ask why a particular literary device occurs in a particular context. An examination of the figures within a poem should follow the structure of the poem itself.

Finally, the reader should not ignore the sheer artistic excellence and beauty of the poetic parallelism and imagery. Any explication that neglects the aesthetic dimension of the poem is incomplete.

Hebrew Prophecy

Since we have already discussed both narrative and poetry, we confine our remarks here to the arrangement of the prophetic texts and to some of the forms through which the prophetic messages are communicated. Generally, the prophetic texts of the Hebrew Bible are not chronological but are collections of materials. These materials were initially preserved together in larger or smaller collections and only at a later time became the groundwork for the prophetic texts. Collectors had a wide variety of material at their disposal. Primarily oracles, other sayings, larger prophetic compositions, and short narratives about episodes in the life of the prophet were collected. In many cases, the utterances were not preserved in their original form, but are in the form of free summaries or abstracts.

The principles that guided the collectors vary. The most dominating factor was similarity in subject matter. Antithetical ideas such as righteousness and unrighteousness or judgment and salvation also governed the association of passages. Passages consisting of the same structure often occur in a series, like woe-speeches and sermons beginning with "hear." Catch-words were also used in grouping different passages; and often, but not always, passages were grouped chronologically.

As a rule, the collectors did their work after the death of the prophet whose teachings and utterances they recorded. They frequently recorded in writing, but smaller collections may have circulated in oral form. The main intention was to preserve the prophecies for posterity and to adapt them for practical use.

Redactional (editorial) work occurred after the work of the collectors. Our present prophetic books are not identical with the original collections, for these have undergone changes and transformations of different kinds. There are numerous examples of additions, enlargements, and comments showing that the texts were subjected to alterations in accordance with the tastes and needs of later times. The texts remained fluid for many centuries.

The redactors of the prophetic books (collections) developed the prophets' original words in order to bring out their significance for a later age. This accounts for the presence of unfulfilled prophecies. For example, Micah's prediction in the eighth century B.C.E. of the fall of Jerusalem, which appears to conflict with the prophecies of Isaiah that the city would be protected by God, was regarded as unfulfilled as late as Jeremiah's time (Jer 26:17–19). Yet, Micah's prophecies were preserved.

Clements comments that "very significantly an important aspect of the redactional work on the prophetic books was to adapt and reinterpret prophecies in the light of later historical circumstances."[25] This indicates that the question of the truth of prophecy was seen to be a larger truth than could be contained within a simple prediction-fulfillment formula. Hosea, whose message was originally directed to the northern kingdom, is an example. Sometime later, however, slight editing—the insertion of the name "Judah" at several places—gave Hosea's message a new address to the southern kingdom. Von Rad offers the following explanation:

> It was never presumed that the prophet's oracles were addressed to one set of people and one only, and were thereafter to be wrapped up in their rolls and deposited among the records. There must have been people who never forgot that a prophet's teaching always remained relevant for a coming day and generation, and who themselves played their part in making it appear relevant—in many cases their work can be clearly seen in the various secondary additions which they made.[26]

Several rhetorical and literary forms are present in the prophetic texts, and like other texts, the message of the prophetic texts or singular oracles within them is inseparable from the form. Probably the most common form used to convey the prophetic message was the **messenger formula**. The Hebrew prophets usually prefaced this formula with another form designed to draw the recipient's attention to the message. This preface to the message was a designation of those for whom it was intended. Von Rad comments: "In the case of a divine threat, what was prefixed was a diatribe; in the case of a promise, an exhortation. These two, the messenger formula and prefixed clause, must both be present before we have the literary category of prophetic oracle."[27] As a rule, the prophets (until the time of Jeremiah) drew a clear distinction between the messenger formula and the diatribe or exhortation which introduced it. The messenger formula was the Word of God, while the prefaced form was an editorial addition by the prophet. This prefaced form had the purpose of leading up to and preparing the way for God's Word and gave it its reference.

But the messenger formula is only one among many forms in the prophetic texts. There was no hesitation in using multiple forms to clothe the messages. There are exhortations to repent, reproaches, woe

---

[25] R. E. Clements, *Prophecy and Tradition* (Atlanta: John Knox, 1975), 53.

[26] Gerhard von Rad, *Old Testament Theology* (2 vols.; New York: Harper & Row, 1965), 2:43.

[27] Ibid., 37.

and satire, lamentations, hymns, prayers, judicial debating, and ritual utterances. There are short messages and extended sermons, historical retrospects, parables and allegories, similes, and wisdom sayings.

By choosing a particular form, these prophets intended to attract attention. For example, when a prophet drafted into service a time-hallowed sacral form, his purpose was to shock the audience. In Isa 40–55, the author drew from the priestly oracle of weal and, by reshaping it into something more sweeping, made it the form of his preaching. Other messages were clothed in the form favored by wisdom teachers (Amos 3:3–6) or popular songs (Isa 5:1–7). A vivid example of the way a prophet would take a well-known form or a literary device and drastically change it to the point of almost non-recognition is the dirge. The later prophets actually turned it upside down and parodied it (Isa 14:4–23; 23:1–14; Ezek 19; 27:2–36; Amos 5:1).

The prophets thus attired their prophetic messages and oracles in non-prophetic, secular garb. However, the reverse is also true: The prophets also tailored their messages to the forms. Ezekiel derives a number of subjects from folk tales and songs (cf. Ezek 14:12–23; 16:1–43; 17:1–10; 19:1–14; 21:13–23; 23:1–27; 26:19–21; 28:1–10; 31:1–18; 32:17–32). Isaiah utilizes the type of the love song (5:1–7) and a wisdom instruction (28:23–29).

All of this means, of course, that interpretation must address the texts of the prophets with their multiple forms and sub-genres. While the prophetic texts differ from the narrative texts we discussed earlier (there is really no narrative or story world in the strict sense), they are replete with forms constitutive of meaning.

Summary

This chapter has described the genres of Hebrew narrative, poetry, and prophecy. Regardless of the genre in which the authors chose to write, communication was the primary goal. But communication proceeds differently through each genre. Each genre combines techniques, sub-genres, and literary devices in characteristic ways in order to convey an ethical, cultic, historical, or social message. Narrative communicates through plot, characterization, and setting; poetry through images and word pictures; and prophecy through arranging collected materials according to subject matter or around some literary device. A knowledge of the sub-genres within these three genres and an appreciation for the manner in which these sub-genres are strategically arranged and presented are prerequisites to successful interpretation. While all three of these genres share some common elements with narrative and poetry in general, they also have their distinctive characteristics. Not only was the world which produced the works of the Hebrew Bible different from ours, but the world within the texts differs from our real world. To impose modern expectations (whether theologically, doctrinally, or ethically generated) upon these texts while neglecting their generic worlds and literary qualities is to treat them irresponsibly.

REVIEW & STUDY

Key Terms and Concepts

allusion	narrative
characterization	narratology
chiastic patterns	narrator
complication	order
conflict	parallelism of thought
direct dialogue	plot
duration	point of view
frequency	protagonist
hebrew poetry	real author
histoire	real reader
historical narrative	real world
implied author	*récit*
implied reader	repetition
interior monologue	resolution
leitwort	setting
messenger formula	story world
mimetic narrative	themes
mood	truth value
motif	type scenes
narratee	voice

Study Questions

1. The book of Jonah has been described as a series of descents. Read this brief work and see if there might be merit in this description. Should these events be taken literally? If your answer is yes, does this vitiate the mimetic quality of the work? Why or why not?

2. In *The Art of Biblical Narrative,* Robert Alter refers to Hebrew narrative as "fictionalized history" or "historicized fiction." If he is correct, does this mean that the narratives are untrue? Explain.
3. Read the story of Judah and Tamar in Gen 38 and comment on the following:
   a. difference between *récit* and *histoire*
   b. narrative voice
   c. duration
   d. distance
   e. perspective
   f. voice
   g. setting
   h. characterization
   i. quotation
4. Is there a betrothal type scene in the book of Ruth? If so, how does it differ from the paradigm?
5. Read the book of Numbers. Identify the motif of "water" and offer a brief discussion of its function within the text.
6. Read Isa 53:8–12. List the parallelisms and identify the type of each. For each parallelism, name the type of focusing and comment on the poet's theological assumptions based upon the poet's identification of terms through the device of focusing.

Suggestions for Further Reading

Alter, Robert. *The Art of Biblical Narrative.* New York: Basic, 1981.
———. *The Art of Biblical Poetry.* New York: Basic, 1985.
Bellinger, W. H. *Psalms: Reading and Studying the Book of Praises.* Peabody, Mass.: Hendrickson, 1990.
Berlin, Adele. *Poetics and Interpretation of Biblical Narrative.* Sheffield: Almond, 1983.
Fisch, Harold. *Poetry with a Purpose: Biblical Poetics and Interpretation.* Bloomington: Indiana University Press, 1988.
Kort, Wesley A. *Story, Text, and Scripture: Literary Interests in Biblical Narrative.* University Park, Penn.: Pennsylvania State University Press, 1987.
Rosenberg, Joel. *King and Kin: Political Allegory in the Hebrew Bible.* Bloomington: Indiana University Press, 1986.
Sternberg, Meir. *The Poetics of Biblical Narrative.* Bloomington: Indiana University Press, 1985.

Chapter

6

HOW THE NEW TESTAMENT COMMUNICATES AS LITERATURE

When critics talk about the literary artfulness of the Bible, the reference is generally to the Hebrew Bible. From Origen to Dibelius to Sternberg, the New Testament is regarded as less artistic, less literary than the Hebrew Bible. The fact is, however, that while some literary conventions and theological bases differ from those of the Hebrew Bible, the majority of the literary characteristics of the New Testament are also recognizable as Hebraic. More simply put, the literary forms in the New Testament are, to a great degree, modifications of existing literary forms and strategies. The New Testament writers make extensive use of the Hebrew Bible, suggesting a firsthand familiarity with most of its genres and sub-genres. With their plots, characters, conflicts, complications, and resolutions, the Gospels and Acts remind us of the narratives of the Hebrew Bible; Revelation also shares the properties of Old Testament apocalypse.

Throughout the New Testament, we find language that transcends the simple expository and descriptive, a language embellished with literary devices and pregnant with imagery. Any hermeneutical approach that consciously or unconsciously neglects this literary nature of the New Testament is incomplete and unbalanced.

Our examination of the literary context of the New Testament involves two primary considerations: (1) the development of the defining structures of the three major genres—narrative, **epistle**, and apocalypse; and (2) a discussion of the sub-genres and literary forms within these three genres.

The Gospels and Acts

The New Testament's four Gospels and Acts can be classified as narrative. While they do compare significantly to both Hellenistic

biography and historiography, the Gospels are not biographies of Jesus in the strictest sense; neither are they history in the modern sense. They are above all else **story**. In order to counter any confusion over this statement, let's review the earlier discussion concerning story and then demonstrate the way in which the Gospels fall into this category.

Every effective story must necessarily have a beginning, middle, and end. A story must have established limits within which the elements such as plot, characterization, setting, conflict, complication, and resolution are employed. This requirement naturally assumes that the author recognizes the utter impossibility (indeed futility) of incorporating every minor detail. So what do authors do? First, authors know what truths they wish to communicate. They then select, arrange, and interpret events, characters, and settings through the literary forms and devices that most effectively and artistically convey those truths.

Understanding this process of selection and arrangement is vital. The author (storyteller) does not flatly state the case, but through the selective process, seeks to guide the reader into the construction of the message. The author invites the reader, therefore, to become involved in and engaged by the story. The author seeks to move the reader from one event or scene to another, leaving sufficient gaps of information so that the reader can make necessary inferences. Story does not allow the reader to remain static.

This suggests that the world in the story points to a reality beyond itself. That is, meaning does not reside just in the events within a story, but in the reality that the story asks the reader to help create. The story is itself really one half of a metaphor, the other half being the interpretation to which the story leads. The story is like a map to a truth outside the world of the story. Story is not story for story's sake, but an invitation to encounter some truth about the real world or perhaps about the world to come. For example, in the book of Job, there is a beginning, middle, and end, with characters involved in dialogues, thought, and events. But is this all the story tells us? Certainly not! It asks the perennial question, "Why do bad things happen to good people?" Whether it offers an answer is debatable. The point is that in interpreting a story, the reader must move beyond what is said *in* the story to what is said *through* the story. Movement from the referential level to the mimetic level must occur.

Again, the Gospels are stories. This statement does not imply that the Gospels are fictional. The historical validity of the events need not be rejected in order to read the Gospels as story; however, as we will demonstrate below, the telling of objective, chronological history was

furthermost in the writers' minds. If there is any doubt concerning this
assumption, one need only read the Gospels side by side and note the
different contexts within which a single event is found. For example,
the passage in which Jesus foretells the temple's destruction occurs
in Luke at 13:34–35 *before* Jesus' arrival in Jerusalem, while in Matt
23:37–39, it occurs *during* his final visit to the city.

Ultimately, where should we direct our attention in the interpretation of the Gospels? Should we direct it to Jesus' teaching or to the evangelists' narrative of Jesus' words and actions within a particular context? For instance, both Matthew and Mark record a time when Jesus
teaches in parables. Yet, while Mark places it near the beginning of
his gospel (ch. 4), Matthew records it in the middle of his (ch. 13), and
John does not even mention that Jesus spoke in parables! Perhaps more
illustrative is John's placement of the temple cleansing by Jesus at the
beginning of his gospel (ch. 2), whereas the authors of the Synoptics
place it during the passion week, at the end of their narratives. We may
conclude, therefore, that the Gospels paint verbal portraits of Jesus and
the events surrounding his ministry, giving individual interpretations
of his person and mission. The evangelists accomplish this through selection, emphasis, and arrangement. While each gospel presents the
"good news" of Jesus, each does so in a particular way. Consequently,
we must allow each gospel to stand on its own and approach it as a
single literary whole. As Gordon Fee rightly observes, "the Gospels in
their present form are the word of God to us; our own reconstructions
of Jesus' life are not. Many of the Gospel materials owe their present
context to the evangelists."[1] Leland Ryken similarly notes: "The individual Gospels have their own characteristic ideas, images, settings,
and emphases. Knowing that individual Gospel writers build their own
world in this way can go a long way toward unifying our experiences
of the Gospels."[2]

Nevertheless, some qualifying discussion is in order. While the Gospels are not strictly biographies of Jesus, but complete and unified literary narratives, they are not entirely unique narratives. The Gospels may
be unique in their christological emphasis, but they are not unique as to
their form of presentation. Indeed, it is inconceivable that the evangelists would not capitalize on the modes of literary production current in
their day. Charles Talbert has argued brilliantly that Luke-Acts is pat-

---

[1] Fee and Stuart, *How to Read the Bible,* 113.
[2] Ryken, *Words of Life,* 34.

terned after the Hellenistic biography,[3] and in a somewhat neglected work, Elizabeth Haight discusses the parallels between the Gospels/ Acts and the Hellenistic genre of **romance**.[4]

Since a detailed treatment of the Hellenistic biography and romance would take us too far afield, I offer the following summary of elements found within these two genres with brief comments, and encourage the interested reader to pursue the subject further. In the words of Helmut Koester, the Hellenistic biography:

> grew out of an increasing interest in the lives of famous poets and philosophers. Greek biography was born when one began to inquire into the relationship between the works and the life (*bios*) of such persons, and when one began to search for examples for the right conduct of the wise man. . . . Thus it was the purpose of these biographies to present the principles of philosophical doctrines, conduct of life, and formation of character in the form of a *bios*.[5]

Included in these biographies were biographical anecdotes, legends, panegyric (extravagant praise), aretology (miracle stories), thematic approach, amplification, and comparison. Exploring the Gospel of Matthew alone would reveal countless examples of each of the above, but two will illustrate that Matthew was versed in the genre of the Hellenistic biography. Matthew uses the thematic approach. The Sermon on the Mount (chs. 5–7) deals with righteousness. Matt 10 relates the sending of the Twelve and the cost of discipleship. And the parables in ch. 13 concentrate on the kingdom of God. The emphasis upon the progressive disclosure of Jesus' identity mentioned in Matt 14:1–16 is one example of amplification. A second, according to Shuler, is the treatment of events surrounding the death of Jesus.[6] Both examples emphasize supernatural phenomena and the additional testimony of eyewitnesses.

The various generic forms within Hellenism seem to have been concentrated in the genre of romance. The identifying elements of the Hellenistic romance are legion. The chart below lists some of the elements within the Hellenistic romance that have parallels in the Gospels and

---

[3] Charles Talbert, *Literary Patterns, Theological Themes and the Genre of Luke-Acts* (SBLMS 20; Missoula: Scholars Press, 1974).

[4] Elizabeth Haight, *Essays on the Greek Romances* (Port Washington, N.Y.: Kennikat, 1943).

[5] Koester, *Introduction to the New Testament*, 1:133.

[6] See Philip I. Shuler, *A Genre for the Gospels: The Biographical Character of Matthew* (Philadelphia: Fortress, 1982).

Parallels between Hellenistic Romance and the Gospels and Acts

Hellenistic Romance	Gospels and Acts
Travel Motif	Luke 9:51–19:44; Acts 19:21–21:16, 27:1–28:16
Aretology	Numerous in Gospels and Acts
Prevention of suicide	Acts 16:25–34
Dreams	Matt 1:20–25; 2:13; 27:19
Visions	Luke 1:22; 24:23; Acts 9:10, 12; 10:3, 10–19; 11:5; 16:9–10; 18:9
Courtroom scenes	Matt 26:57–67; 27:11–26; Luke 22–23; Acts 22–26
Letters	Acts 15:23–29; 23:26–30
Crowd motif	Seen surrounding Jesus in all the Gospels and the disciples in Acts (e.g., 2:14 and 19:35)
Speeches	Matt 5–7; Acts 2:14–36; 7:1–53; 17:22–31
Storms	Matt 14:22–33; Acts 27:13–26
Shipwreck	Acts 27:27–44
Narrow escapes	Matt 2:13–20; Acts 12:1–18; 14:19–20; 17:5–10; 21:27–32; 27:42–44
Ethnography	John 4:1–27; Acts 8:26–27; 14:11–13; 17:21: 28:1–6
Origin and birth of hero	Matt 1–2; Luke 1–3; John 1:1–18
Historical characters	Pilate, Festus, Herod the Great, Felix, Herod Agrippa, etc.
Divine direction	Throughout Gospels and Acts

Acts.[7] These are only a few of parallels that the New Testament shares with Hellenistic romances. When the parallels are placed side by side, there is an obvious similarity between the Gospels/Acts and the Hellenistic biography/romance. Thus, we might at least conclude that the evangelists employed several elements common in the biography and romance. Indeed the messages of the Gospels and Acts may be unique, but the form(s) may not be.[8]

---

[7] Albin Lesky, *History of Greek Literature* (New York: Thomas Y. Crowell, 1966), 858–67; and Koester, *Introduction to the New Testament,* 1:137.

[8] In his book *The New Testament in Its Literary Environment* (Philadelphia: Westminster, 1989), David Aune offers a detailed and coherent discussion of the Greco-Roman biography and historiography. In his excellent discussion, Aune demonstrates that the Gospels of Mark, Matthew, and John share most

If we accept each individual gospel as a story, as a literary whole, with a distinct purpose determining a particular framework, then the most plausible interpretation of any portion will be that one which seeks to relate the part to the whole. While the individual units (like the Sermon on the Mount in Matthew) may be rhetorically self-contained, in some fashion they must be understood *now* within the context of the gospel's world. Since some find it difficult to think of the smaller units in light of the whole story, a brief discussion of the Gospel of Matthew as a literary whole should help. This discussion is followed by a look at the different sub-genres that are the tools for constructing the Gospels.

The Gospel of Matthew: A Model

If Mark paints Jesus as the suffering messiah and defines disciple-ship as following in this path of suffering, Matthew portrays Jesus as the great teacher, fulfiller, and personification of the **Torah.**[9] Matthew's chronological arrangement is based upon Mark's; however, the additional material and arrangement of all the material is Matthew's.

Concerning Matthew's setting, recent scholarship has suggested that Matthew was consciously composed in dialogue with rabbinic Judaism. It was written during the last quarter of the first century when the church was struggling for its identity as an institution apart from Judaism, yet appropriating the actual symbols of Judaism as a means of definition. The foremost symbol of Judaism was the Torah. How does Matthew present Jesus as the fulfillment, interpretation, and personification of the Torah? And how does the resultant definition of discipleship fit within this context?

Matthew accomplishes his purpose with structural patterns. The first concerns Matthew's polemic against Pharisees and experts in the Law. The combining of the piety of the Pharisees with the legal expertise of the scribes defined rabbinic Judaism developing during the period immediately before and after the fall of Jerusalem in 70 C.E. This polemic against rabbinic Judaism surfaces in ch. 23, where Matthew has creatively placed it between the Jerusalem controversies (22:15–46)

---

of the constituent parts of the Greco-Roman biography and some of the *topoi* characteristic of the Hebrew biographical writings. He argues that Luke-Acts is closely akin to Greco-Roman historiography and shares some of the characteristics of Hebrew historiography.

[9] Johnson, *Writings of the New Testament,* 185.

and Jesus' private eschatological instruction to the disciples (24:1–25:46). The polemic contains seven woes (23:13, 15, 16, 23, 25, 27, 29). Polemical statements are directed against the Pharisees and scribes throughout Matthew, but the polemic here in ch. 23 assumes a formal, more caustic nature. Johnson suggests that ch. 23 brings the polemical elements together here in a kind of crescendo.[10]

Within this polemical emphasis, Matthew presents Jesus as the true and perfect teacher or interpreter of the Torah. Matthew accomplishes this is in two ways. First, throughout his narrative, Matthew presents Jesus in strategic settings that reveal him to be the authoritative interpreter of Torah. These settings include confrontations with the Pharisees and experts in the Law in which Jesus consistently challenges his opponents' understanding of the Torah by asking, "have you not read [in the law/Scripture]?" On one occasion he challenges his opponent to "go and learn what this means" (9:13).

Second, the section of discourse commonly referred to as the Sermon on the Mount functions paradigmatically as the true interpretation of the Torah. Appealing to the Torah five times (5:21, 27, 31, 33, 38) and to midrash once (5:43), Jesus illustrates how the Torah is to be truly interpreted. The Law is not a legalistic code to be observed outwardly, but its true interpretation is an internalization; true obedience to the Torah brings about an inner disposition.

But Jesus is more than the true interpreter of the Law; he is also its fulfillment. The third structural element supports this conclusion. Fifty-seven times Matthew refers directly to the Hebrew Scriptures and some thirty times indirectly. Matthew's approach is an interesting one. He identifies particular moments in the life of Jesus with Old Testament texts in such a fashion that the events or moments in Jesus' life interpret the Scriptures. Jesus is the real meaning of the Law. But the coin has two sides—the Torah also reveals Jesus, that is, Jesus and Torah are mutually interpretive.

Besides being the true interpreter and the fulfillment of the Torah, Matthew's Jesus is also the personification of the Torah. Matthew completes the three-dimensional portrait by inviting the reader to make connections between Jesus' words and the Torah in rabbinic Judaism. Some of these connections are illustrated in the chart on the next page. Indeed, the reader is led to conclude that Jesus is the very personification of the Torah. The reader is left to observe other implicit associations between Jesus and the background material in the chart.

---

[10] Ibid., 189–90.

Parallels Between Jewish Understanding of Torah and Matthew's Portrait of Jesus

Wisdom or Rabbinic Reference	Matthew's Parallel
1. Wisdom personified (cf. Wis 7:25–27) and Wisdom identified with Torah (cf. Bar 4:1).	When Jesus is ridiculed for associating with sinners, he responds: "Yet wisdom is vindicated by her deeds" (11:19).
2. Torah is eternal (Bar 4:1).	In the Sermon on the Mount, Jesus says, referring to the Torah, "until heaven and earth pass away, not one letter, not one stroke of a letter, will pass from the law until all is accomplished" (5:18). Later he says, "heaven and earth will pass away, but my words will not pass away" (24:35).
3. Torah is the yoke of the kingdom (Sir 6:19–31; *Pirqe 'Abot*). See also Acts 15:10.	Jesus describes his "yoke" as "easy" (11:28–30).
4. Torah provides God's rest for those who study it (Wis 8:16; Sir 6:28; 51:26–27).	As Torah brings one into God's Sabbath, so Jesus says, "I will give you rest" (11:28).
5. The Shekinah is found among so few as two or three gathered to study Torah (*Pirqe 'Abot* 3:2).	Jesus says, "For where two or three are gathered in my name, I am there among them" (18:20).

The final structural device in Matthew pertains to the entire work. Scholars have long noted Matthew's placement of Jesus' teachings into five major groupings, each ending with the formula "When Jesus had finished these sayings . . ." or something very similar. Preceding each block of discourse is narrative material. Many have suggested skeletal structures similar to the following:

Prologue: Birth narrative and the Spirit's activity (chs. 1–2)

Division I: Narrative material (3:1–4:25)
                Discourse on the Mount (5:1–7:27)
                Formula (7:28–29)

Division II: Narrative material (8:1–9:35)
                Discourse on mission and discipleship (9:36–10:42)
                Formula (11:1)

Division III: Narrative material (11:2–12:50)
Discourse on kingdom (13:1–52)
Formula (13:53)

Division IV: Narrative material (13:54–17:21)
Discourse on church administration (17:22–18:35)
Formula (19:1)

Division V: Narrative material (19:2–22:46)
Discourse on eschatology (23:1–25:46)
Formula (26:1)

Epilogue: Last Supper and resurrection (26:3–28:20)

Is it possible that Matthew intended this arrangement to suggest the five books of the Pentateuch along with its primeval prologue and epilogue (the farewell speech by Moses in Deuteronomy)? An affirmative response would see this structure as being consistent with Matthew's portrayal of Jesus as Torah discussed above. If further evidence is needed, I should point out the very subtle Mosaic overtones in Matthew. First, whereas Mark begins his gospel with "the beginning of the good news of Jesus Christ, Son of God," Matthew begins with "the book of the genesis of Jesus Christ" (Matt 1:1, literal translation; cf. Gen 5:1). Second, consistent with Old Testament usage, the genealogy in Matthew suggests the beginning of a new epoch in history. This is further supported by Matthew's record of the Spirit's activity in the birth of Jesus, perhaps recalling the activity of the Spirit of Yahweh at creation. Third, Herod's order to have all male children who were two years old or under killed (2:16) is reminiscent of Pharaoh's order to have all male children killed (Exod 1:22). Fourth, Moses received the law on Mount Sinai, and Jesus interprets the law on the mountain (5:1–7:27). Fifth, Jesus performs ten miracles in chs. 8–9, as Moses performs ten marvels in Exod 7–10. Finally, the account of the transfiguration in Matt 17:1–4, with its reference to the appearance of Jesus' face, immediately recalls the description of Moses' face when he came down from the mountain (Exod 34:29–34).

Before moving to the sub-genres, a brief glance at the disciples in Matthew will be illuminating. The experts in the Law and the Pharisees were the interpreters of Torah. But if Jesus is the personification of the Torah, who will be *his* interpreter? For Matthew, there must be an equivalent to the "experts in the Law" who will interpret *the* Torah. The most likely candidates, of course, are the disciples, who after the resurrection (i.e., only after the new Torah is complete) are instructed by Jesus to make disciples of all nations, teaching them to observe all the commandments they have received (28:16–20). The new Torah requires the authoritative interpretation of the disciples. Therefore, the disciples become the new interpreters of the new Torah.

The foregoing discussion of the Gospel of Matthew is in no sense to be taken as comprehensive or definitive. It illustrates, though, the literary nature and creative artistry of the work as a whole. However, wholes are constructed by weaving smaller units or parts together. The whole can be meaningful only through the parts, and the parts must be interpreted in light of the whole. This seems to be asking, "Which comes first, the chicken or the egg?" Welcome to the infamous hermeneutical circle. More will be said concerning this circle (which is actually a spiral) in the next unit. For the present, our purpose is to introduce the reader to the literary forms (the parts) used by the authors of the Gospels to produce coherent, narrative wholes.

Sub-Genres in the Gospels

Sayings and Sayings Stories

Most scholars are convinced that many sayings of Jesus were collected quite early in the life of the church and were later circulated. One of these hypothetical collections is referred to as Q (from German *Quelle,* meaning "source"). Most scholars feel that it was a source for the evangelists. In particular, Matthew and Luke are believed to have drawn on Q for their respective "sermons" of Jesus, each one providing his own context for the various sayings. We may classify these sayings into **apophthegms**, proverbs, **legal sayings**, and **prophetic sayings**.

The apophthegm or pronouncement story is a brief episode or event that precipitates a saying of Jesus. It originates in the anecdote about a well-known person. The anecdote climaxes in a significant statement or declaration. The episode or event exists for the saying and not vice-versa. One example is the saying, "I have come to call not the righteous but sinners" (Mark 2:16–17; Matt 9:10–13; Luke 5:29–32). The setting for the narrative is a meal where Jesus is eating with tax gatherers and sinners. No details, such as time and place, are given about the meal. Such matters were irrelevant since the saying was the focal point; the meal served only as a point of anchorage. Care should be taken not to so concentrate on some hidden meaning in the story as to neglect the saying given birth by it. The story may be nothing more than a pretext for the saying.

The proverbs, or wisdom sayings, in the Gospels are probably best described as aphorisms—terse, succinct statements easily remembered. The **proverb** is quite similar to the Old Testament **wisdom saying**. Examples are:

> For those who want to save their life will lose it. (Mark 8:35a)

> No one tears a patch from a new garment and sews it on an old garment. (Luke 5:36b)

> But many who are first will be last, and the last will be first (Matt 19:30).

A proverb is open-ended. It demands contemplation because it is filled with universal applicability or speaks of a universal principle of truth. Frequently a proverb uses figurative language such as **metaphor**, hyperbole, or simile to ensure a broad range of meaning.

The legal sayings are those which have a juridical ring to them. They usually have to do with an area of ministry or ecclesiastical order. Below are three examples:

> laborers deserve their food. (Matt 10:10b)

> If anyone will not welcome you or listen to your words, shake off the dust from your feet as you leave that house or town. (Matt 10:14)

> Truly I tell you, whatever you bind on earth will be bound in heaven, and whatever you loose on earth will be loosed in heaven. (Matt 18:18)

The prophetic sayings are usually salvific or judgmental.

> Two women will be grinding meal together; one will be taken and one will be left. (Matt 24:41)

> The days are coming when you will long to see one of the days of the Son of Man, and you will not see it. They will say to you, "Look there!" or "Look here!" Do not go, do not set off in pursuit. For as the lightning flashes and lights up the sky from one side to the other, so will the Son of Man be in his day. (Luke 17:22–24)

Parables

A **parable** is a short narrative comparing one thing to another. In this sense, a parable is an extended metaphor. A parable generally employs familiar situations, persons, or events to illustrate or illuminate an unfamiliar or unrecognized truth. The parable is a successful teaching tool because it is told in terms which people readily understand and remember.

Adolf Jülicher separates the parables into four types: the parable as similitude, as story, as example story, and as allegory.[11] When the parable is a similitude, it has a customary sense about it that draws attention to some commonly recurrent event. Some examples include the growth of the mustard seed, the leavening of bread, or the properties of salt. In this type of parable, the reader must ascertain the relationship between the event and the more abstract issue being illuminated.

The parable as story is a pericope with beginning, middle, and end. It will usually revolve around one or two characters engaged in some action and will be marked by brevity of detail. The action will move swiftly to a conclusion, inviting the reader to make a single comparison between the culminating action and the "point" of the story. Examples of such parables are the parable of the Two Sons, the parable of the Friend at Midnight, and the parable of the Lost Sheep.

Jülicher's third parable type is the example story. In this type, the central character exhibits exemplary behavior. The central point is "look at this person and act likewise." One of the most familiar example stories is the parable of the Good Samaritan. His moral behavior is exemplary and should thus be emulated.

The final of the four types is the parable as allegory. Actually this type is nothing more than a series of metaphors, which means that this parable (unlike the others) necessarily has a number of comparative points. For an example of this type see the discussion of allegory in ch. 4. Examples of this type include the parable of the Tares, the parable of the Net, and the parable of the Sower.

By the time the parables were recorded in the Gospels, their original settings had been lost. Therefore, the idea that a parable focuses on a single comparison must be qualified. Most of the parables told by Jesus concerned the kingdom (reign) of God, which itself is presented as a parable.[12] While parables do offer a comparison, the comparison is told in terms of imagery, necessitating a consideration of multiple images and themes.

When readers encounter a parable in the Gospels, they need to ask not only what Jesus' point is, but what literary function the parable has for the evangelist. For instance, in Mark's version of the parable of the Sower (Mark 4:1–9) and Matthew's parable of the Tares (Matt 13:24–30), each

---

[11] Adolf Jülicher, *Die Gleichnisreden Jesu,* vol. 1 (Tübingen: Mohr, 1910).

[12] Hans Conzelmann and Andreas Lindemann, *Interpreting the New Testament* (trans. Siegfried S. Schatzmann; Peabody, Mass.: Hendrickson, 1988), 78.

original parable is given an allegorical interpretation by the evangelist. The original settings of these parables cannot be discovered and indeed are irrelevant to their interpretation as they now stand in their present contexts. Furthermore, in Mark's gospel the parables function almost exclusively to separate the insiders from the outsiders. Mark accomplishes this by reversing the parable's purpose. Whereas the parable is supposed to make some point more easily understood, the parables in Mark become a means by which information is clothed in mystery as far as the disciples and those outside are concerned. This use is illustrated in Mark 4:10–13:

> When he was alone, those who were around him along with the twelve asked him about the parables. And he said to them, "To you has been given the secret of the kingdom of God, but for those outside, everything comes in parables; in order that 'they may indeed look, but not perceive, and may indeed listen, but not understand; so that they may not turn again and be forgiven.'" And he said to them, "Do you not understand this parable? Then how will you understand all the parables?"

The disciples, who should understand the parables, are the very ones who do not. The astute reader of Mark's gospel soon recognizes that the disciples consistently do not understand the parables and that those who think themselves to be insiders may actually be outsiders. This understanding of Mark's use of the parables at once causes modern readers to examine their own status within the circle of Christ.

Jülicher's paradigm, however, has been challenged by a number of New Testament scholars. Craig Blomberg argues for a quasi-allegorical approach to the parables based upon (1) the many allegorical elements in (which he assumes have their genesis in Jesus) the parables, (2) the similarities between the allegorical rabbinical parables and the parables of Jesus, and (3) the assumption that since first century audiences were accustomed to allegory, they would have sought allegorical elements in Jesus' parables.[13]

John Dominic Crossan describes the parables of Jesus as "poetic metaphor" in which Jesus teaches about the kingdom of God through stories concerning first century peasant life. In other words, the subject or referent of the parables is the experience of God's rule as Jesus conceptualized it.[14]

---

[13] See Craig L. Blomberg, *Interpreting the Parables* (Downers Grove: InterVarsity, 1990), 29–69.

[14] See John Dominic Crossan, *In Parables: The Challenge of the Historical Jesus* (New York: Harper & Row, 1973).

In 1967, Dan Otto Via Jr. introduced his view of the parables as "freely invented stories." Since they are fictional narratives, they operate the same as other narrative fictions and should be interpreted in the same manner as fictions in general are studied.[15] Via approached the parables as fictions having plots, characterization, settings in which form and function are inseparable—somewhat reminiscent of the New Criticism. All the parts work together to form a unified whole whose meaning is not to be sought in the world outside the parable, but in the aesthetic world created by the parable. Furthermore, the meaning of a parable is not what Jesus may have intended by it, but is to be determined by the structures of the parable itself. In other words, a parable speaks for itself in terms of its artistic structure. Via also assumes the mimetic quality of the parables when he claims that parables, like any good fiction, offer readers insight into the human condition; i.e., they teach us how to be human in the world, how we may live as humans. Consequently, their significance transcends the first-century listener and embraces readers of all ages.

More recently, Charles Hedrick has offered an interesting assessment of the parables and their interpretation. For Hedrick, the parables are "brief, freely invented first century narrative fictions, comprised of beginning, middle, and end, dramatizing a common human experience or some incident from nature."[16] His treatment of the parables turns upon four crucial assumptions (1) Readers cannot know how or within what contexts Jesus used his parables; (2) The comparative frames in the Gospels are not part of the original parables, but are "literary settings . . . [representing] later Christian interpretations rather than a historical memory of the original social context"[17] supplied by the evangelists; (3) interpretation of and response to the parables are identical; and (4) the parables are not necessarily figurative, i.e., since we cannot know how Jesus used them nor what he intended by them, we cannot conclusively know that they originally carried a figurative significance.

With this definition and assumptions in place, Hedrick then offers a six step interpretive process for the parable:[18]

---

[15] See Dan O. Via Jr., *The Parables: Their Literary and Existential Dimension* (Philadelphia: Fortress, 1976).

[16] Charles W. Hedrick, *Many Things in Parables: Jesus and His Modern Critics* (Louisville: Westminster John Knox, 2004), 9.

[17] Ibid., 11.

[18] Ibid., 89–95.

Step One: Separate the parable from its literary context. In this step, Hedrick puts on the hat of the genetic/historical critic. According to Hedrick, this step is absolutely essential in that it demands that readers divest themselves of two thousand years of Christian history. The assumption is that the parables in the Gospels are hidden beneath layers of church tradition and that the evangelists, who had no idea of the original contexts of the parables, contextualized them within their theological concerns imposing comparative frames that were not part of the originals. The necessity of separating the parable from its literary contexts within the Gospels is clear if the goal is to read, appreciate, and understand it as an open-ended first-century narrative fiction demanding reflection and contemplation from the reader.

Step Two: Establish the textual history of the parable. In this step, Hedrick encourages the reader to become acquainted with the textual history (i.e., the transmission history) of the parable. The primary task here is for the reader (in particular the reader who cannot deal with the critical apparatus in the Greek New Testament) to decide which version of the New Testament has most likely preserved the most authentic version in terms of variants. For the multiple-version parables (parables found in more than one gospel), readers must decide with the help of available aids which version to investigate.

Step Three: Consider the elements of the story line by line, word by word. At first glance, this step seems to suggest a formalist reading of the text. However, as the reader soon realizes, it involves further historical work by inviting the reader to jump from his or her world squarely into the world of first century Palestine in order to "hear the elements of the parable as a part of Jesus' world and not as a part of the modern reader's world."[19] Tools such as Bible dictionaries and commentaries may be consulted to "gather raw data about the ancient world"[20] and to help determine the manner in which each element of the parable fits into the first century world.

Step Four: Examine the literary features of the narrative. In this step, Hedrick asks his readers to step inside the story as a piece of literary artistry and examine it in the same way, asking the same questions that we might put to any piece of narrative fiction. But he also cautions that the literary reader should resist the temptation to pass moral judgments on characters or their actions.

---

[19] Ibid., 93.
[20] Ibid.

Step Five: Consider the hypothetical response(s) of a first-century Jewish audience. Hedrick recognizes that this step is probably the most difficult of the six and advises readers to become familiar with sources that will assist in understanding that audience. His use of "hypothetical" alone suggests the ineluctable fact that without the original contexts of Jesus' parables, re-constructions of responses will always be provisional.

Step Six: Ask how the reader responds to the parable. In a sense, Hedrick defines the meaning of the parable as the "voice" that resonates in its own way for each reader: "A reader's response occurs in the nexus between the parable and the life experience the reader brings to it."[21] So meaning becomes synonymous with understanding, and as there is the possibility of numerous understandings, meaning is virtually unlimited. Earlier in the book, Hedrick accounts for this protean quality of the parables by claiming that they are polyvalent which he defines as describing "an innate ambiguity found in all narrative, a feature facilitating multiple responses (or meanings) from readers."[22]

Poetry

Since we have already discussed poetic parallelism, suffice it here to say that the evangelists were quite adept at its use. An excellent example is the two-stanza poem in Luke's instruction concerning prayer:

Ask, and it will be given you;
search, and you will find;
knock, and the door will be opened for you.

For everyone who asks receives, and
everyone who searches finds, and
for everyone who knocks, the door will be opened (Luke 11:9–10).

Hymns

While most New Testament hymns are in the Epistles, there are a few in the Gospels—the Magnificat (Luke 1:46–55), the Benedictus (Luke 1:68–79), the Nunc Dimittis (Luke 2:29–32), and the Song of the Angels (Luke 2:14). All the hymns have a distinct and pervasive lyric quality. They consist of language which is highly structured, cadenced, compressed, intense, economical, and with unusual grammatical features. These qualities become significant for interpretation.

---

[21] Ibid., 95.
[22] Ibid., 13.

Midrashim

When scholars use the word **midrashim** in reference to the New Testament, they usually have in mind those instances where the author interprets an Old Testament passage in light of contemporary circumstances. Since the term "midrash" actually has a plethora of definitions, to tease out a common one is problematic. What one scholar means by midrash is not necessarily what another means. For this reason, our discussion of midrash is a bit more involved than our discussion of most of the other sub-genres. First, we review the possible definitions of midrash, finally focusing upon one of these in some detail. Second, we offer some illustrations of the use of midrash in the New Testament.

The term "midrash" is generally used in one of three ways. First, it may refer to an exegetical method of interpreting the Hebrew Bible. This method may include the rewriting of a text within a new situation or the explaining of a text or portion of it within a new situation. Examples of the former are the Chronicler's rewriting of the history in Samuel and Kings and the translation of the Hebrew Scriptures into Greek (Septuagint). In the Hebrew text of Exod 24:10, we read that Moses and Aaron "saw the God of Israel." In the Septuagint's rendering of the same verse, however, it is paraphrased to read that Moses and Aaron "saw the place where the God of Israel stood." Why the change? It was probably an attempt by the translators to convey in Greek Israel's unspoken assumption concerning the impossibility of seeing God and remaining alive.[23] An example of explaining a text or portion of it within a new situation is the exegesis of Old Testament texts at Qumran. Notice the prophetic application of the following interpretation of Num 21:18.

> But God remembered the Covenant with the forefathers, and He raised from Aaron men of discernment and from Israel men of wisdom, and He caused them to hear. And they dug the Well: the well which the princes dug, which the nobles of the people delved with the stave.

> The *Well* is the Law, and those who dug it were the converts of Israel who went out of the land of Judah to sojourn in the land of Damascus. God called them all *princes* because they sought Him, and their renown was disputed by no man. The *Stave* is the Interpreter of the Law of whom Isaiah said, *He makes a tool for his Work* (Isa liv, 16); and *the nobles of the people* are those who come to dig the *Well* with the staves with which the *Stave*

---

[23] Jacob Neusner, *What Is Midrash?* (Philadelphia: Fortress, 1987), 25.

ordained that they should walk in all the age of wickedness—and without them they shall find nothing—until he comes who shall teach righteousness at the end of days.[24]

Second, it may refer to the fruit of the method, i.e., to a compositional unit resulting from exegesis such as the above exegesis of Num 21:18. Two or more of these compositional units are called "midrashim." And third, the collection and arrangement of these midrashim into a compilation may also be called midrash. It is the first two of these definitions that we want to expand upon and illustrate.

Underlying the midrashic exegesis of Scripture are two crucial presuppositions: (1) The Scriptures were given by God and are consequently relevant for all subsequent generations; and (2) each part of the Scriptures (sentences, phrases, words, even single letters) has an autonomy independent of the whole. These two presuppositions then have an interesting corollary: Since the Scriptures were given by an infinite God, a particular passage in part or whole may have an infinite number of applications.

There are basically three approaches within midrashic exegesis. Neusner calls them paraphrase, prophecy, and parable.[25] Paraphrase is simply a re-reading of a particular passage. This type of midrash is designed to amplify or clarify a passage in which the meaning is unclear. Clarification may be made by supplying a synonym, telling an illustrative story, giving a word-for-word explanation, or introducing another verse. In the first five verses of the Gospel of John we find a re-reading of the first few verses of Genesis. This is an example of midrash by paraphrase.

Prophecy as midrash (according to Neusner) identifies a contemporary event or situation with a scriptural passage. The original meaning or historical frame of reference are not lost, but the reference does inform the present or the future. Thus we may find in Scripture (even historical sections) the meaning of what is happening now. As Neusner explains, "Midrash as prophecy treats the historical life of ancient Israel and the contemporary times of the exegete as essentially the same, reading the former as a prefiguring of the latter."[26]

In the New Testament, Matthew is known to engage in midrash as prophecy. For example, quoting from Isa 7:14 he says, "All this took

---

[24] G. Vermes, *Dead Sea Scrolls in English* (rev. ed.; Baltimore: Penguin, 1968), 102–3.
[25] Neusner, *What Is Midrash?* 7–11.
[26] Ibid., 7.

place to fulfill what had been spoken by the Lord through the prophet: 'Look, the virgin shall conceive and bear a son, and they shall name him Emmanuel'" (Matt 1:22–23). Another example involves the interpretation of a historical reference from Hosea as applying to an event in the life of Jesus: "Then Joseph got up, took the child and his mother by night, and went to Egypt, and remained there until the death of Herod. This was to fulfill what had been spoken by the Lord through the prophet, 'Out of Egypt I have called my son.'" (Matt 2:14–15). Of particular note is that Hos 11:1 is referring to the exodus of Israel as a nation (the son) from Egypt!

A special type of midrash as prophecy is called pesher. This type of midrash assumes that what was written in the Scriptures was intended specifically for the contemporary situation. A given statement in Scripture has its significance in a contemporary event. In a classic example of a pesher interpretation, Peter interprets a prophecy of Joel in Acts 2:16–21 to refer to the events of Pentecost ("This is that . . .").

Midrash as parable is similar to, if not identical with, allegorical interpretation. The more profound or authentic meaning of a statement or event is not the obvious historical or literal one. Scripture is interpreted in terms which the author never intended. This is possible because of the presuppositions mentioned above. The real meaning of Scripture is hidden beneath the literal one and must speak in such a way as to offer guidance to everyday living. This last type is probably the most characteristic of rabbinic midrash. While these three types of midrash differ somewhat in method and results, they share a common purpose: All midrash attempts to interpret the Scriptures in order to make them authoritatively applicable and therefore binding upon the smallest everyday details of the life of a people. "Thus the task of midrash is never merely reproductive; it is always productive of new understanding. It is a way of keeping the Bible open to the histories of those who answer its claims."[27]

While we will discuss the literary forms within the Epistles below, to avoid repetition, it should be said that midrashim are also present among the New Testament Epistles. Examples include Rom 10:5–13, 1 Cor 10:1–11, and 1 Pet 2:4–8, to name a few. The authors of the epistolary literature also compiled Scriptures together in a midrashic fashion (cf. 1 Pet 2:4–8). Perhaps the most obvious midrashim appear in

---

[27] Gerald L. Burns, "Midrash and Allegory: The Beginnings of Scriptural Interpretation," in *Guide to the Bible* (ed. Robert Alter and Frank Kermode; Cambridge, Mass.: Harvard University Press, 1987), 629.

the Epistle to the Hebrews. Passages from the Psalms, the Pentateuch, and the Prophets are so radically applied to Jesus and the new covenant that the original context has completely disappeared. Passages that originally referred to Yahweh, David, and others are now applied to Jesus (e.g., Heb 1:5–14; 5:4–6; 7:11–22). If modern exegetes recognize that the ancient authors were using an acceptable exegetical method, they will be in a better position to allow the authors to communicate their messages in their own exegetical medium.

Other literary forms, such as controversy stories, genealogies, Old Testament quotations, apocalyptic addresses, extended discourses, and Beatitudes, should become part of the reader's repertoire. Excellent discussions of these can be found in almost any good New Testament introduction.

Epistolary Literature

Since matters such as authorship, destination, and audience were dealt with in unit I, attention will be given here only to the literary character of the Epistles. Obviously, once we move from the Gospels and Acts into the Epistles, we are hard pressed to find what we have previously referred to as a narrative world or the world within the text. Terms such as characterization, plot, setting, story line, and narrative time become inappropriate if not meaningless. We are in a different genre. Nonetheless, just as the Gospels as narrative have uniquely definable structures, so does the genre of New Testament epistolary literature. That the Epistles are not mimetic history does not diminish their literary qualities. The qualities are simply of a different sort.

Letter writing in the Hellenistic tradition followed a stereotypical form:

1. Opening or Prescript. This consists of three parts: the author, the addressee, and a greeting. The greeting is often a wish for good health or a prayer-wish. Various other information may be offered concerning the writer or addressee.

2. Body. Here the purpose of the letter is elaborated. It may be exceptionally brief or rather long. The **body** proper is quite often prefaced with a prayer to the gods, an expression of thanksgiving, mention of the author's circumstances, or some mention of a favorable remembrance of the addressee. These preliminary statements serve as a transition from the opening to the body and lay the basis for the relationship

between the writer and the addressee. However, in many instances, these transitional matters are foregone and the writer moves directly to the body. Attached to the end of the body proper may also be a request for reciprocal communication, notification of a prospective visit, or a challenge to action.

3. Closing. The **closing** usually consists of a final greeting. It may also include a second wish for health for the addressee and/or other persons. A word of farewell (*errōsthe*) is usually placed at the end along with the date.

Before discussing the letters in the New Testament and their similarities to and differences from the Hellenistic letter, we need to examine some characteristics of the Hellenistic letter besides its form. The letter expressed a relationship of friendship between two parties. The letter was to have a certain "presence" about it, substituting for the actual presence of the writer. Thus a person would write to someone as if he or she were present.

The Hellenistic letter is extremely stereotyped. The **salutation**, final greeting, and prayer (or wish for health) appear in Hellenistic letters with almost predictable wording. David Aune, describing what he calls the private or documentary letter with its three-part structure, observes that the basic structure of the letter varied only slightly over the centuries.[28] Within the basic three-part structure, however, there was room for modifications. For example, within the *prescript* of the typical letter occur three elements—the superscription, adscription, and salutation. Each of these could be expanded; and epithets, titles, geographical references, a health wish, or a prayer might be added. Aune goes on to describe two other categories of Greco-Roman letters, which he calls official letters and literary letters. Official letters, very similar to the private letter, were from a government official to someone else, often in a government position. Literary letters were "preserved and transmitted through literary channels and were valued either as epistolary models, as examples of literary artistry, or as vignettes into earlier lives and manners."[29] These letters are further categorized into: (1) Letters of recommendation written by educated persons who had no intention of publishing them. These allowed an influential person to recommend a friend for a particular political or civil position. The framers of such letters made their recommendations on the basis of moral traits rather

---

[28] Aune, *The New Testament*, 162.
[29] Ibid., 165.

than on vocational ability. (2) Letter-essays are proper treatises rather than formal letters because they use the standard epistolary structure in a limited fashion. While they may display the customary opening and closing, these letters are actually philosophical or ethical treatises (e.g., Quintilian's *Institutes* and Plutarch's *On Tranquility*). Epicurus, Diogenes Laertius, and even Plato and Aristotle used the letter as a means of philosophical instruction. (3) Pseudepigraphical letters were fictional presentations of stories about great men of the past.[30] Other fictional letters, which Aune terms imaginative letters, were written in the names of the past, often in an explicit attempt to capture the worldview of people from the past.

While it seems that the personal letter was the norm in Hellenism, there were instances (Epicurus, Seneca) where ethical questions were addressed in the form of the letter. These were actually treatises and not letters in the strict sense, as they were probably written with the intention of producing a highly literary document. This observation has led some scholars to make a distinction between letter and epistle.[31] This distinction is based upon the private or public audience; a letter is seen as being non-literary and written for an individual or particular audience, whereas an epistle is regarded as literary and written for posterity or the public. Second Peter, 1 John, and James are cited as examples of the epistle. For instance, neither James nor 2 Peter has a final greeting or a specific addressee. Gabel and Wheeler suggest that genuine letters differ from epistles in that "an epistle is an artificial or make-believe letter, written for publication rather than for mailing."[32] These scholars feel that the most distinctive aspect of New Testament letters is their occasional nature. They were not written for posterity but were intended to address the particular and actual situations of the audience. Like their Greek and Roman counterparts, their basic purpose was to convey information between two people or audiences. They are not essays. As Ryken explains, "It would be wrong, therefore, to regard the epistles as systematic and expository. Like letters in general, the New Testament Epistles (with the exceptions of Romans and Hebrews) are not systematic arguments."[33] Most scholarship today, however, has reached what

---

[30] Ibid., 165–69.
[31] Gabel and Wheeler, *Bible as Literature;* and Fee and Stuart, *How to Read the Bible.*
[32] Gabel and Wheeler, *Bible as Literature,* 216.
[33] Ryken, *Words of Life,* 90–91.

William Doty regards as a balance.[34] The letters of the New Testament fall somewhere between documents as purely occasional responses to local situations and documents as purely theological treatises intended to express Christian theological ideologies that extend beyond historical situations.

The Structure of the New Testament Epistle

Paul's letters are the earliest in the New Testament and set the standard epistolary form. While both formal and conceptual variations are found in the New Testament Epistles, they generally follow the basic Pauline structure:

I. Salutation (sender, addressee, greeting).
II. Thanksgiving (possibly a blessing or accompanied by intercession).
III. Body (may include introductory formulae and statement of future plans).
IV. Paraenesis (ethical exhortation and instructions).
V. Closing (peace wish, greetings, benediction, writing process).

In order to understand how Paul adapted and expanded the form of the Hellenistic letter, we need to examine each of the parts of the genuine Pauline letter.

Opening. The standard Greek salutation often contained the word *chairein* (greeting) followed by a formulaic wish for well-being. Paul changed the word to *charis* (grace) and expanded the salutation to include references to his apostleship and fellow workers. He might also refer to the status of his addressees:

> Paul, called to be an apostle of Christ Jesus by the will of God, and our brother Sosthenes, To the church of God that is in Corinth, to those who are sanctified in Christ Jesus, called to be saints, together with all those who in every place call on the name of our Lord Jesus Christ, both their Lord and ours: Grace to you and peace from God our Father and the Lord Jesus Christ. (1 Cor 1:1–3)

Notice that Paul has not only substituted *charis* for *chairein* but also inserted "peace." *Shalom* (peace) was the traditional Jewish epistolary

---

[34] William G. Doty, *Letters in Primitive Christianity* (Philadelphia: Fortress, 1973), 26.

greeting. So Paul has expanded and modified the traditional formulaic Hellenistic salutation to include both his Jewish and Christian heritage. In the opening of Romans, Paul's expansion includes a summary of his gospel. Since Paul did not found the church at Rome and had not visited it, he probably felt the need to establish his authority to speak.

Thanksgiving. Most work done today on the Pauline **thanksgiving** is little more than commentary on the efforts of Paul Schubert.[35] Schubert contends that the thanksgiving serves three functions: it terminates the salutation, gives the basic purpose of the letter, and may offer an outline of the primary topics in the body of the letter. Hellenistic letters frequently have thanksgivings where the writer gives thanks to the gods or informs the addressee that mention is made of him or her before the gods. With the exception of Galatians, Paul follows this tradition. In that letter, Paul is anxious to move on to the problem and therefore contravenes the convention. But in 1 Thessalonians, Paul's thanksgiving section is so disproportional to the rest of the letter (it consumes well over half the letter) that the letter seems convoluted. While Paul follows epistolary custom with the inclusion of a thanksgiving, he does inject modifications based upon his religious perspective. For instance, the thanksgiving becomes the occasion to offer praise for the faithfulness of the addressees and to express a wish that this faithfulness will continue.[36]

As indicated above, the Pauline thanksgiving tends to announce at least some of the major topics of the body. Consider the thanksgiving in 1 Cor 1:4–9:

> I give thanks to my God always for you because of the grace of God that has been given you in Christ Jesus, for in every way you have been enriched in him, in speech and knowledge of every kind—just as the testimony of Christ has been strengthened among you—so that you are not lacking in any spiritual gift as you wait for the revealing of our Lord Jesus Christ. He will also strengthen you to the end, so that you may be blameless on the day of our Lord Jesus Christ. God is faithful; by him you were called into the fellowship of his Son, Jesus Christ our Lord.

Notice that Paul refers to the charismatic gifts of speech and knowledge and to the "day of our Lord." Both of these subjects are primary

---

[35] Paul Schubert, *Form and Function of the Pauline Thanksgivings* (Berlin: Alfred Töpelmann, 1939).

[36] See Jack T. Sanders, "The Transition from Opening Epistolary Thanksgiving to Body in the Pauline Corpus," *JBL* 81 (1962): 352–62.

concerns in the body of 1 Corinthians, where Paul puts the charismatic enthusiasm in perspective by emphasizing the eschatological nature of the day of the Lord.

Paul also seems to include in his thanksgivings liturgical elements, such as the note in the thanksgiving of 2 Corinthians: "Blessed be the God and Father of our Lord Jesus Christ" (2 Cor 1:3a). As James Robinson has successfully demonstrated, while Paul follows the general epistolary form, he also adapts elements from his liturgical tradition to it, resulting in some essentially new patterns.[37]

Body. The material within the bodies of the Pauline letters is diverse. The controlling factor is a need or problem of the recipients. The reader would not logically expect any rhyme or reason within the variegated Pauline landscape called the body of the letter. But this is only partially the case. Among the variety of topics in Paul's letters, there is a recurring pattern of formal features. Here are some of these formal features:

(a) The request or injunction formula. Look at the following example:

> Now I appeal to you, brothers and sisters, by the name of our Lord Jesus Christ, that all of you be in agreement and that there be no divisions among you, but that you be united in the same mind and the same purpose. (1 Cor 1:10)

A verb occurs, followed by a direct address and the actual request. This request or appeal formula, however, also occurs in other places within the body of the letter, especially where new material is introduced.

(b) The disclosure formula. Examples are: "I want you to know that" or "We do not want you to be unaware" (Rom 1:13; 2 Cor 1:18; 1 Thess 2:1; Phil 1:12; Gal 1:11). According to Doty, this formula (as well as the request formula) provides a heading "for the following paragraph(s) and states briefly its contents, analogous to a newspaper headline and subtitle."[38] As with the request formula, the disclosure formula introduces new material within the body of the letter (e.g., 1 Cor 11:3; 1 Thess 4:13; 1 Cor 10:1; 12:1; Rom 11:25).

(c) The joy formula. Expressions of joy ("I have indeed received much joy") were usually a result of some pleasing information which

---

[37] James M. Robinson, "The Historicality of Biblical Language," in *The Old Testament and Christian Faith* (ed. Bernhard W. Anderson; New York: Harper & Row, 1963), 132–49.

[38] Doty, *Letters,* 34.

the apostle had received. An example is Paul's joy over Philemon's Christian progress.[39]

(d) Autobiographical notes. Near the beginning of the body in most of his letters, Paul remarks on his activities. Paul recollects his former ministry among the Corinthians in 1 Cor 1:10–17, and in Phil 1:12–26, he talks about an imprisonment (cf. Gal 1:10–2:21 and 2 Cor 1:8–2:12). These autobiographical notes are not unrelated miscellany but have integral meanings within his arguments. They reinforce Paul's demands upon his addressees.

(e) The **travelogue**. Toward the end of the body of the letters (with the exception of Galatians), Paul alludes to a possible future visit by himself or an emissary (cf. Rom 15:14–33; 1 Cor 4:14–21; 2 Cor 12:14–13:13; Gal 4:12–20; Phil 2:19–24; 1 Thess 2:17–3:13; Phlm 21–22). Roetzel suggests that the function of the travelogue is to add punch to the message of the letter by promising an apostolic visit.[40]

Paraenesis. Paul was especially adept at tailoring general ethical materials to specific situations. That Paul utilizes traditional materials (from Jewish and Hellenistic sources) should not obscure the fact that he did not intend to develop a new Christian moral system. As Roetzel observes, "these act not as a rulebook for solving every problem, rather, they are examples or illustrations of how the gospel is to take effect. These ethical sections, or **paraenesis**, provide practical guidance, but they also convey information, make requests and issue reminders."[41]

The paraenetic sections consist of three types of ethical materials. First, Paul combines various moral statements which have very little inherent connection. For example, Rom 12:9–13 encompasses the topics of love, hate, evil, good, brotherly affection, the bestowing of honor, zeal, spiritual aliveness, service, hope, patience, constancy in prayer, liberality in giving, and hospitality. Paul presents each topic in the form of a moral injunction. Most probably Paul received this material from an existing tradition.

The second type of material is found in lists of vices and virtues, where there is borrowing from both Jewish and Hellenistic traditions. The lists vary in length and do not necessarily reflect the situation at any particular church (e.g., Rom 1:29–31; 1 Cor 5:10–11; 2 Cor 6:6–7, 14; Gal 5:19–23; Phil 4:8). A list of vices may stand alone, as in Rom 1:29–31, or

---

[39] Ibid., 35.

[40] Calvin J. Roetzel, *The Letters of Paul: Conversations in Context* (Atlanta: John Knox, 1982), 35.

[41] Ibid., 36.

it may be paired with a list of virtues, as in Gal 5:19–23. Doty suggests that rules for the household which offer specific domestic duties (*Haustafeln*) should be included in this type of paraenesis.[42]

Third, Paul employs what can be called homiletical exhortations centering around a particular topic. Most of 1 Cor 5–15 is taken up with a series of homiletical exhortations on a variety of topics. Another example of this type of paraenesis is Paul's discussion of the resurrection in 1 Thess 4:13–18. More will be said about the forms within the paraenetic sections when we discuss the literary forms in the New Testament letters.

Closing. The closing normally includes a peace wish, greetings, a benediction, and sometimes an apostolic pronouncement. Most often these are prefaced with a list of final instructions. The greetings occur between the peace wish and benediction. While these may be stock meanings within the conclusion of the Pauline letter, they are not simply meaningless formalities. In the peace wish, Paul returns to the major concern(s) of the letter. Note this return in 1 Thess 5:23: "May the God of peace himself sanctify you entirely; and may your spirit and soul and body be kept sound and blameless at the coming of our Lord Jesus Christ." The coming of the Lord and the readiness of the saints are major concerns of the letter. The peace wish in Gal 6:16 ("As for those who will follow this rule—peace be upon them, and mercy, and upon the Israel of God") returns to Paul's concern with the bondage of circumcision versus freedom in Christ and the true Israel.

The benediction ("the grace of the Lord Jesus be with you") varies little in Paul's letters, but it has taken on a distinctly Christian perspective. However, sometimes Paul prefaces the benediction with a warning or exhortation (see 1 Cor 16:22; 1 Thess 5:27; and Gal 6:17).

Conceptual Differences in the Epistles

In addition to the formal variations already mentioned, scholars recognize that there are also conceptual differences among New Testament Epistles. Such differences are due in part because of differences in originating circumstances, the use of amanuenses, and changing conditions in the life of the church. For example, the **Pastorals** (1, 2 Timothy and Titus) are recognized by most scholars today as the products of a church well on its way to becoming an institution. The

---

[42] Doty, *Letters,* 58.

outlook of the Pastorals is advanced in their concern for the survival of the institution. In the earlier Pauline letters, the author is constantly on the offensive, where both internal and external problems are confronted with an almost fever-pitched debate. In the earlier Pauline letters, faith is defined as a trust in God, a belief in Jesus as the Messiah. In the Pastorals, faith is a body of received truth to be defended. Furthermore, in the earlier Pauline letters, the Parousia, or coming of Jesus, is imminent, whereas in the Pastorals it becomes more distant.

Not only is the outlook in the Pastorals different from the earlier letters, but linguistic differences also exist. Approximately twenty percent of the vocabulary in the Pastorals is *hapax legomena* (lit., "once said," meaning terms that occur only once in the New Testament) and about thirty percent of the vocabulary in the Pastorals is not found in the earlier letters. When we add to this the absence in the Pastorals of very key words of the earlier letters, we get the sense that we are without a doubt in a world with highly different theological interests from the earlier letters.

Along with the differences in outlook and vocabulary, we may also make reference to a difference in form. The paraenetic, or ethical, section virtually dominates the Pastorals.

Some of the same observations pertaining to vocabulary and outlook given above for the Pastorals could be applied to Ephesians, Colossians, and 2 Thessalonians. In Ephesians (which contains about one-third of Colossians) we find a summary of Pauline theology while 2 Thessalonians modifies Paul's eschatological thought.

The **Catholic Letters** have the character of more conscious literary production. While 2 and 3 John appear in traditional letter form, 1 John has moved entirely away from the traditional letter toward the form of an essay on Christian love. James, Jude, and 2 Peter retain little of the letter form. For example, James retains the salutation, but this is followed by a list of moral admonitions and exhortation. It appears to be a moral tractate and not a letter.

While 1 and 2 Peter and Jude employ epistolary conventions, they also move in the direction of the theological tractate. Doty remarks,

> these writings are best understood as tracts expressing support for those undergoing persecution for their religion—persecution both from the state and from deviant Christians. Theological reflections now revolve around the sacred Christian traditions, not around the necessary shaping of the religion in specific contexts.[43]

---

[43] Ibid., 70.

Sub-Genres in the New Testament Epistolary Literature

When we examine the literary forms of the New Testament letters, it becomes obvious that the authors were well-versed in the broad spectrum of Hellenistic and Jewish literary practices. An acquaintance with these forms is indispensable for the hermeneut, especially since content (and therefore, message) must be tailored to form. The catalogue given below is intended to introduce the student to the literary forms in the Epistles. The discussion is by no means comprehensive, but perhaps enough interest will be sparked to encourage further specialized study.

The *Topos*

The *topos* was a particular rhetorical device used by Hellenistic Cynic and Stoic itinerant preachers. These itinerant preachers developed standardized responses to frequently asked questions on certain topics. Most often the topic concerned vice or virtue. These *topoi* (plural) could be strung together with no apparent controlling principle or arranged by the use of some *Leitwort*. David Bradley has identified two *topoi* in Paul's letters—Rom 13 and 1 Thess 4:9–5:11.[44]

Lists of Vices and Virtues

We have already referred to these lists above, so only a few comments are necessary here. Attempts to identify **lists of vices and virtues** with particular ecclesiastical communities will probably result in frustration or at best be nothing more than speculation. More likely the authors adapted these lists to describe general moral behavior and problems. An example of a list of vices is 1 Cor 5:10–11:

> not at all meaning the immoral of this world, or the greedy and robbers, or idolaters, since you would then need to go out of the world. But now I am writing to you not to associate with anyone who bears the name of brother or sister who is sexually immoral or greedy, or is an idolater, reviler, drunkard, or robber. Do not even eat with such a one.

An example of a list of virtues is Col 3:12–14:

---

[44]See David G. Bradley, "The *Topos* as a Form in the Pauline Paraenesis," *JBL* 72 (1953): 238–46.

As God's chosen ones, holy and beloved, clothe yourselves with compassion, kindness, humility, meekness, and patience. Bear with one another and, if anyone has a complaint against another, forgive each other; just as the Lord has forgiven you, so you also must forgive. Above all, clothe yourselves with love, which binds everything together in perfect harmony.

Other lists include: Rom 1:29–31; 1 Cor 6:9–10; 2 Cor 6:6–7; Gal 5:19–23; Eph 6:14–17; Phil 4:8; Titus 1:7–8; Jas 3:17; 1 Pet 4:3; 2 Pet 1:5–8; Rev 9:20–21.

List of Circumstances

These lists reflect details about careers of the apostles. For example in 2 Cor 12:10 we find this list: "Therefore I am content with weaknesses, insults, hardships, persecutions, and calamities for the sake of Christ; for whenever I am weak, then I am strong." Another such list is found in 2 Cor 11:23–28.

Lists of Rules for Behavior within the Christian Community

These lists show a concern with articulating how Christians should live in the world on a day-to-day basis. These lists of relationships are not unique to the New Testament writings, but as part of the general Hellenistic cultural milieu, they became part of the daily life of the church. Most of these lists occur in the later letters of the church (e.g., Eph 5:21–6:9; Col 3:18–4:1; 1 Tim 2:1–15, 5:1–21; Titus 2:1–10; 2 Pet 2:13–3:7).

Proverbs

Since proverbs, or wisdom sayings, have been discussed in the gospel section, I simply list some examples here:

A little yeast leavens the whole batch of dough. (Gal 5:9)

Bad company ruins good morals. (1 Cor 15:33b)

making the most of the time, because the days are evil. (Eph 5:16)

Confessional Statements

These formulaic statements are professions of belief. They are compact summaries of theological understanding and doctrine which were most likely used and recited within liturgical situations, like baptism.

Terms such as "confess" or "believe" suggest confessional statements. Also a rhythmic quality may indicate a **confessional statement** (but this is also a quality of a hymn or what Ryken calls patterned rhetorical prose). The following typify the confessional statement:

> because if you confess with your lips that Jesus is Lord and believe in your heart that God raised him from the dead, you will be saved. (Rom 10:9)

> He was revealed in flesh,
> vindicated in spirit,
> seen by angels,
> proclaimed among Gentiles,
> believed in throughout the world,
> taken up in glory. (1 Tim 3:16b)[45]

Hymns

The present discussion by scholars on hymnic material within the epistolary literature of the New Testament is considerable and far too extensive to discuss at any length here. Therefore, I give the general qualities of the New Testament hymn. The hymnic material is marked by a pronounced and recognizable rhythm. The reader should also look for types of parallelisms. For example, in the confessional statement above (1 Tim 3:16 might be considered a hymn) the aorist passive is used in every verb. Also in every expression except one, *en* (in) precedes a noun in the dative singular. The rhythmical quality and the parallelism are unmistakable. Again, there is a fine line (often an invisible one) between confessional statements, hymns, and patterned rhetorical prose (to be discussed below).

Metaphor

The Epistles are saturated with metaphors evidencing a poetic impulse. Some examples are:

> You are God's field, God's building. (1 Cor 3:9b)

> These are waterless springs and mists driven by a storm. (2 Pet 2:17a)

> the tongue is a fire. (Jas 3:6a)

> your body is a temple of the Holy Spirit. (1 Cor 6:19a)

---

[45] Because of the rhythmical quality of the latter example, it might also fall within Ryken's definition of patterned rhetorical prose.

Paul especially attests to a distinct trust in the power of metaphor to convey meaning. As P. C. Sands observes, the diction of Paul "is continually enlivened by metaphor, 'gluing yourselves to the good,' 'boiling with the spirit,' 'buying up the opportunity,' 'let the love of Christ make its home in you,' 'let the peace of Christ be umpire in your hearts.' "[46]

Diatribe

A **diatribe** is a type of argument in which a writer/orator creates a hypothetical inquirer or objectioner (a dialogue partner, often referred to as the interlocutor). The writer or orator then proceeds to answer the objections of this imaginary questioner. While the inquirer may be hypothetical, the issue at stake is not. An example is in Rom 6. Here the inquirer asks, "What then are we to say? Should we continue in sin in order that grace may abound?" Paul then goes on to answer this challenge in verses 2–14. Apparently this inquirer is persistent, because another question is asked in verse 15: "What then? Should we sin because we are not under law but under grace?" The answer is recorded in 6:14c–7:6. This type of argumentation continues with further questions in 7:7, 13 and 9:14, 19, 30. Another example is Jas 2:18–22, which begins with, "But someone will say, 'You have faith and I have works.'" The author then proceeds with an elaborate retort. The hypothetical opponent may even be an abstract personification, as in 1 Cor 12:15–21 (the speakers are body parts) and Rom 2:21–22 (the speaker is righteousness).

Captatio benevolentiae

In *captatio benevolentiae,* the author offers flattery by assuming that the reader will be familiar with a particular corpus of knowledge. Note the flattery and assumption in Rom 7:1: "Do you not know, brothers and sisters—for I am speaking to those who know the law—that the law is binding on a person only during that person's lifetime?" The same assumption underlies 1 Cor 9:24: "Do you not know that in a race the runners all compete, but only one receives the prize?" (cf. Acts 24:2–3).

---

[46]P. C. Sands, *Literary Genius of the New Testament* (New York: Oxford University Press, 1932), 153.

Word Chains

By linking concepts together (usually in some causal manner) in a **word chain** the author produces a climatic effect. In Rom 5:3–5 we read,

> And not only that, but we also boast in our sufferings, knowing that suffering produces endurance, and endurance produces character, and character produces hope, and hope does not disappoint us, because God's love has been poured into our hearts through the Holy Spirit that has been given to us.

A similar chain is found in 2 Pet 1:5–7:

> For this very reason, you must make every effort to support your faith with goodness, and goodness with knowledge, and knowledge with self-control, and self-control with endurance, and endurance with godliness, and godliness with mutual affection, and mutual affection with love.

Other literary devices such as rhetorical questions (e.g., Rom 8:31–32), personifications (Jas 1:15), and patterned rhetorical prose are common. The last of these is illustrated especially by the author of Ephesians:

> There is one body
> and one Spirit,
> just as you were called
> to the one hope
> of your calling
> one Lord,
> one faith,
> one baptism,
> one God and Father of all,
> who is above all
> and through all
> and in all. (Eph 4:4–6)

And again, by Paul:

> For I am convinced that neither death,
> nor life,
> nor angels,
> nor rulers,
> nor things present,
> nor things to come,
> nor powers,
> nor height

nor depth,
nor anything else in all creation,
will be able to separate us
from the love of God
in Christ Jesus our Lord. (Rom 8:38–39)

In the first example, the word "one" occurs a seven times. It has the effect of a drum beat—one body, one Spirit, one hope, one Lord, one faith, one baptism, one God. The word "all" has the same effect at the end of the passage—of all, above all, through all, in all. The immediate context of this passage is concerned with unity within the body of Christ. By repeating the word "one" followed by the repetition of "all," the author drives home the point of doctrinal unity within the church.

In light of the many literary forms in the Epistles, it is no wonder that recent scholarship has recognized the high literary nature and creative artistry of the New Testament epistolary literature. Ryken neatly encapsulates this view:

> The New Testament epistles represent a mingling of the traditional and the innovative. Like ordinary letters, they exist to convey information to an audience and are prompted by a specific occasion. Their religious focus makes them distinctive. They also differ from other ancient letters by being more consistently literary in their form and style, but this very quality makes them similar to other literature and actually enhances their accessibility for a modern reader.[47]

Apocalyptic Literature

The third literary genre in the New Testament is **apocalyptic literature**. While apocalyptic passages exist in the Gospels, the single sustained apocalypse is the final work in the New Testament canon—the book of Revelation. The Gospels may remind modern readers of a novella; the Epistles of contemporary letter correspondence; but when modern readers enter the world of apocalypse, they usually find themselves stumbling around amidst lamp stands and horses, wondering what this all means! Since apocalyptic writing presents the greatest interpretive difficulties to modern readers, we will briefly examine its basic characteristics and then discuss the artistry of the book of Revelation.

---

[47] Ryken, *Words of Life,* 97.

Apocalyptic literature occurs in both the Hebrew Bible and New Testament. Portions of Ezekiel, Isaiah, Zechariah, and the book of Daniel are apocalyptic. Since most readers are more familiar with the book of Revelation, however, I have chosen to discuss apocalypse here in the New Testament section and encourage the readers to examine apocalypse in the Hebrew Bible at their own leisure.

Characteristics of Apocalyptic Literature

Although apocalypse is not a modern literary genre, it was a common type of writing in Judaism during the middle Hellenistic period (second century B.C.E.–second century C.E.). *Second Esdras, Ethiopic Enoch,* and the *Syriac Apocalypse of Baruch* are the purest representatives of this genre outside of the Bible. Since apocalypse as a genre is generally unfamiliar to modern readers, a brief discussion of the major characteristics should be helpful.

First, the scope of apocalypse is cosmic, having characters moving with ease between heaven, earth, and hell. Conflict involves angels and immense human armies pitted against the powers of deity. This conflict and ultimate victory by the deity is most commonly a result of a small group's persecution and vindication. After this minority experiences a time of extreme, hyperbolized suffering, the deity will eventually rescue them, replacing this present age with a utopian one.

Second, apocalyptic cosmology is dualistic. Working within the universe are an evil and a good force, almost equally matched. In the end, however, the good force triumphs over the evil. The personification of this evil force is typical of apocalypse.

Third, apocalypse is generally, but not always (e.g., the *Shepherd of Hermas*) eschatological; that is, its focus is on the end of history and the final stages of human existence. However, a discrete distinction should be maintained between eschatology and apocalypse. Whereas eschatology is concerned exclusively with the doctrine of the end of the age, apocalypse refers to a revelation and a particular type of writing which discloses that revelation. In addition, apocalypse could be used to communicate a body of knowledge which has nothing to do with end time concerns. An apocalypse of this type is the *Shepherd of Hermas,* which is concerned with proper Christian living. In other words, the symbolism of apocalyptic literature might be used without its eschatological character.

Fourth, the mode of presentation is usually an ecstatic vision, dream, or supernatural journey experienced by the author, who is normally a great person from Israel's history. This vision is filled with images (usually very concrete in nature), which incarnate meaning through symbolism and allegory. For example, in Dan 8, the visionary observes a male goat with one horn, which breaks off and is replaced by four other horns. This is followed by the appearance of a small horn growing out of one of the previous four. This small horn then overthrows the other horns. When the vision is explained in 8:19–26, the goat represents the Greek kingdom and its horn is the first Greek king, Alexander the Great. The horns represent the four kingdoms into which Alexander's kingdom is divided, and the little horn is the most fierce king from among these four kingdoms.

Finally, and most significantly, apocalyptic literature is extremely symbolic. In fact, the basic sub-genre in apocalypse is symbolism. Accordingly, throughout apocalypse, the author uses metaphoric images and events to point to something else. Christ, for example, is represented as a lamb or a lion in Revelation. Apocalypse is imagery at its best.

No other genre of the Bible has been so fervently read with such depressing results as apocalypse, especially the books of Daniel and Revelation. This genre has suffered from a disastrous history of misinterpretation due to a fundamental misunderstanding of its literary forms, structure, and purpose. Because of its very claim to reveal what is shortly to happen, apocalypse has been viewed as a road map into and a blueprint of the future. The tragic flaw in this view is the assumption that the book's frame of reference is the reader's contemporary age rather than the author's. This misguided approach to apocalypse (particularly Revelation) treats the work as if it were a cryptogram by which contemporary events can be used to interpret the symbols of the text.[48]

With the above characteristics and observations in mind, some basic guidelines for reading apocalyptic literature in general and Revelation in particular can be offered.

Guidelines for Interpreting Apocalyptic Literature

First, the interpreter must recognize that apocalyptic literature communicates its messages through symbolism. To interpret a symbol literally when it is metaphoric is simply to misinterpret. The issue is not whether the events in apocalypse are historical. The events may be historical; they may have really happened, or might happen. But the author

---

[48] Johnson, *Writings of the New Testament,* 513.

presents events and communicates meaning through images and archetypes. In Rev 12, we find the following:

> A great portent appeared in heaven: a woman clothed with the sun, with the moon under her feet, and on her head a crown of twelve stars. She was pregnant and was crying out in birth pangs, in the agony of giving birth. Then another portent appeared in heaven: a great red dragon, with seven heads and ten horns, and seven diadems on his heads. His tail swept down a third of the stars of heaven and threw them to the earth. Then the dragon stood before the woman who was about to bear a child, so that he might devour her child as soon as it was born. And she gave birth to a son, a male child, who is to rule all the nations with a rod of iron. But her child was snatched away and taken to God and to his throne. (Rev 12:1–5)

A careful reader recognizes this passage as a description of the incarnation of Christ. The woman with the twelve-starred crown is Israel, the child who will rule the nations is Christ, and the dragon is Satan who was unsuccessful in his attempt to destroy Christ and his mission. To view the symbols and images in such passages as self-referential is to consign interpreters to a literalist prison. The writer does not describe the incarnation here literally, but figuratively, symbolically, calling to mind the historical or spiritual reality. The extra-referentiality of the symbols in general (e.g., the horses in 6:1–8, the soiled garments in 3:4, and the sword of Jesus' mouth in 2:16) can be taken as a rule of interpretation or decoding for the book of Revelation and for apocalypse as a genre.

Second, look for archetypes. Apocalyptic literature in general and Revelation in particular will also be pregnant with what in literature is called the archetype. As we have already seen, an archetype is an image, plot, motif, character type, or concept which appears with repeated regularity. It becomes a master image around which reality in the literary imagination is organized. Explanation of the significance of archetypes is usually unnecessary because the master images themselves immediately elicit a whole world of perception and understanding. Archetypes such as light, darkness, blood, lamb, water, sea, throne, war, gold, and bride organize meaning in apocalyptic literature.

Third, recognize that apocalypse always originates in periods of oppression or persecution imposed upon the Hebrews by foreign powers. The literature that emerges is intended to encourage faith and hope. Regardless of how hopeless things may now seem, according to apocalyptic works, God is going to bring about the redemption of his people by intervening on a cosmic level. Even though God's people are undergoing persecution, God will eventually manifest his justice and mercy by vindicating his chosen people. The hermeneut must keep this redemptive and vindicative purpose in mind when explicating apocalyptic literature.

Fourth, when interpreting the book of Revelation, look for Old Testament allusions. Since symbols in Revelation have roots in the Hebrew Bible, the reader will find a thorough knowledge of the Hebrew Bible to be indispensable. The book of Revelation is a creative reworking and reapplication of the Hebrew Scriptures. Revelation is heavily dependent upon the canonical prophetic texts and especially upon apocalyptic works like Zechariah, Daniel, and Ezekiel. The following chart provides some examples of this grounding in the Old Testament imagery.

Old Testament Imagery in Revelation

Item	OT Reference	Revelation
Archangel Michael	Dan 10:13, 21; 12:1	12:7
Vision of God	Dan 7:9, 13, 22; Ezek 1:26–28	4:2–9
Lamb imagery	Isa 53	5:6–14; 7:9; 13:8; etc.
Heavenly beings	Ezek 1:10; 10:14	4:6–8
Shadowy horses	Zech 1:8; 6:1–6	6:1–8; 19:14
Locusts	Joel 1:4–2:11	9:1–11
Resurrection of dead for judgment	Dan 12:2–3	20:4–6
The holy city	Ezek 40:1–48:35	21:2–22:5
Horns	Dan 7:7–8; Zech 1:18–21	9:13; 12:3; 13:1; 17:3,7, 12, 16

Most of the symbols and concrete images in Revelation actually had a long history of literary significance before they were adapted by the author of Revelation. We also may assume that the Apocalypse's original audience had a sufficient familiarity with the symbols and their history of conventional use. Even if we assume that Revelation is a report of historically grounded visionary experiences, these experiences have been artfully crafted into apocalyptic conventions.

One final observation concerning apocalypse is necessary. Apocalypse is one literary genre while classical Hebrew prophecy is another. To interpret apocalyptic literature as prophecy is simply to misinterpret. The following distinctions should be kept in mind. First, prophecy carries with it a contingency: the outcome in prophecy depends upon the actions of a certain group of people. This is not the case with apocalypse. In apocalypse, this evil age is so far beyond redemption that a predetermined and unchangeable course has been mapped out for human history. Second, the prophetic future is a continuation of the present and is itself part of the course of history. In apocalypse, the future is a decisive break with the present age brought about by the direct intervention of God. History will in fact terminate. And third, at least in written form, prophecy is poetic while apocalypse is narrative—albeit highly figurative—prose.

Summary

In this unit we have discussed the world within the text and have found that the storehouse from which the authors pull their material is large, diversified, and well-stocked. Without some knowledge of the materials, modern travelers of this textual world will soon become lost and unable to read, much less follow, the road signs, and will eventually find themselves groping for meaning and direction. A familiarity with genre, sub-genre, conventions, and strategies by which the author engages the reader must receive as much consideration as the world behind the text. This world of the text is constructed by and must be understood in relationship to its constituent parts. But the parts must be interpreted under the scrutiny of the whole. The individual literary units of a writing are meaningful only in the context of the literary whole. Thus if the individual literary unit has meaning, it is at once dependent upon and in the service of the whole. The biblical text must be interpreted as a structural unity, with each part seen as integral to the whole and as modifying the meaning of the whole. McKnight observes:

> Interpretation, then, involves bringing all parts of the text into a meaningful relationship to the entire text. Whenever possible, one unit in the text is seen as standing in metaphoric relation to other units and to the total work.[49]

A reader makes sense of words, sentences, and paragraphs of a text only to the degree that the codes or conventions of the natural language have been mastered. In a similar fashion, readers ascertain the literary meaning or significance of a text only through a mastery of the codes or conventions of the literary languages which co-exist with

---

[49] McKnight, *Postmodern Use of the Bible,* 132.

the codes of the natural language. Consequently, a reader must see a text as the interaction of the types of codes—those of the natural language plus those of literary languages in genre and sub-genre. This means that different readers, depending upon their competence in these languages, may construe meaning at different levels. The best-equipped readers feel at home in the genres and sub-genres, and, when confronted simultaneously by the multiple levels of the linguistic and literary structures, they are capable of applying the multiple codes. The reader thus is not an innocent bystander upon whom the text acts. Rather, the reader plays an integral role in actualizing the meaning of a text. The reader is neither disinterested nor inactive. The text means nothing until someone means something by it. It is to this complex role of the reader in the production of meaning that we now turn.

REVIEW & STUDY

Key Terms and Concepts

apocalyptic literature	midrashim
apophthegms	parable
biography	paraenesis
body	pastorals
captatio benevolentiae	prophetic sayings
Catholic Letters	proverb
closing	romance
confessional statement	salutation
diatribe	story
epistle	thanksgiving
hapax legomena	*topos*
legal sayings	torah
letter	travelogue
lists of vices and virtues	wisdom saying
metaphor	word chain

Study Questions

1. Read the resurrection narrative in all four gospels, noting the differences. What do these differences suggest about the authors' use of traditional material and about the mimetic quality of the Gospels?

2. Suggest some explanations for the differences discovered in the above question.

3. In *An Introduction to the New Testament* (Peabody, Mass.: Hendrickson, 1989), Charles Puskas sets up the following scenario: Suppose that you were working in the great Ptolemaic library in Alexandria in the first century C.E. Upon receiving copies of the four gospels, the head librarian instructed you to catalogue and shelve these works according to genre. Puskas suggests three categories—biography, history or tragic drama. We might add a fourth—romance. How would you catalogue the Gospels and what would guide you in your decision?

4. Read Gen 14:17–20. Now read Heb 6:16–7:17. What type of midrash is the author of Hebrews offering on Gen 14:17–20?

5. Basing your response upon the New Testament writers' practice of midrash upon the Hebrew Bible, what implications do you see for the modern interpretation of the New Testament?

6. Read 1 Thessalonians and 1 Timothy. Identify the paraenetic sections in each. In what ways do they differ? What conclusions might be offered based upon your observations?

7. Both the book of Revelation and the prophecy of Ezekiel contain a vision of a holy city. Read both accounts (Ezek 40–48 and Rev 21:2–22:5) and note the main characteristics of each. There is at least one glaring omission in the vision in Revelation. Try to identify it and offer an explanation for it. Based upon your comparison of the two visions, do you think that the vision might be a literary device capable of being modified by the author?

8. Many scholars have recognized that the author of Mark consistently portrays the disciples as "insiders," but he consistently depicts women and Gentiles as "outsiders." Read the Gospel of Mark and see if you can identify the treatment or characterization of each group. What might such characterization suggest about Mark's theological purpose?

Suggestions for Further Reading

Aune, David. *The New Testament in Its Literary Environment.* Philadelphia: Westminster, 1989.
Doty, William G. *Letters in Primitive Christianity.* Philadelphia: Fortress, 1973.

Johnson, Luke T. *The Writings of the New Testament: An Interpretation.* Philadelphia: Fortress, 1986.

Neusner, Jacob. *Invitation to Midrash: A Teaching Book.* San Francisco: Harper & Row, 1989.

———. *What Is Midrash?* Philadelphia: Fortress, 1987.

Petersen, Norman. *Literary Criticism for New Testament Critics.* Philadelphia: Fortress, 1978.

Shuler, Philip I. *A Genre for the Gospels: The Biographical Character of Matthew.* Philadelphia: Fortress, 1982.

Talbert, Charles. *Literary Patterns, Theological Themes, and the Genre of Luke-Acts.* SBLMS 20. Missoula: Scholars Press, 1974.

ILLUSTRATIVE METHODS THAT FOCUS ON THE WORLD WITHIN THE TEXT

The backbone of text-centered criticism is its spotlight on artistic strategies, literary forms, and textual coherence. Practitioners of those methods that may be called text-centered assume that the text must be viewed spatially, that is, as a whole. Because of this concept of wholeness, text-centered critics are dedicated to demonstrating how the parts of the text *cohere* in order to produce the whole.[1] But the understanding of the whole conditions our understanding of the individual parts. Many critics examine texts in terms of how one text makes use of prior texts, assuming that texts are produced in conversation with prior texts and that prior texts are renewed or reconfigured as they are appropriated by later texts. Other critics examine the manner in which texts can be grouped according to genres (literary conventions), and still other critics focus on the myths reflected in texts. In each case, the focus falls squarely on the text and its structures (literary, generic, or mythical).

Redaction Criticism

Redaction criticism represents a movement towards a more concentrated focus upon the text as a whole. A basic assumption underlying redaction criticism is that the authors were guided in their adaptation, modification, and arrangement of their sources by theological purposes. The theological purpose of an author can be discovered by examining how that writer uses sources. Writers arranged and altered their sources and traditions according to their own theological purposes or those of their community. This, of course, means that source and form criticism are presuppositions for redaction criticism. Sources and individual units of tradition must be available before an interpreter can determine to

---

[1] Donald Keesey, "Formal Criticism: Poem as Context," in *Contexts for Criticism* (4th ed.; ed. Donald Keesey; Boston: McGraw Hill, 2003), 77.

what extent and in what ways an author has adapted and reapplied them. It follows that redaction criticism inherently focuses on four concerns: (1) selection of traditional material and sources; (2) adaptation and modification of the material; (3) arrangement of the material; and (4) the extent of the author's own theological contribution to the text.

When a text's sources are available to the interpreter, conclusions about the author's theological purposes reflected in the obvious modifications, selections, and arrangement are relatively simple to make. For example, if Markan priority is assumed when studying Luke, we can easily observe the ways in which Luke modifies his source. Consider the followings passages from Mark and Luke:

Mark 8:27–33

Jesus went on with his disciples to the villages of Caesarea Philippi; and on the way he asked his disciples, "Who do people say that I am?" And they answered him, "John the Baptist; and others, Elijah; and still others, one of the prophets." He asked them, "But who do you say that I am?" Peter answered him, "You are the Messiah." And he sternly ordered them not to tell anyone about him. Then he began to teach them that the Son of Man must undergo great suffering, and be rejected by the elders, the chief priests, and the scribes, and be killed, and after three days rise again. He said all this quite openly. And Peter took him aside and began to rebuke him. But turning and looking at his disciples, he rebuked Peter and said, "Get behind me, Satan! For you are setting your mind not on divine things but on human things."

Luke 9:18–22

Once when Jesus was praying alone, with only the disciples near him, he asked them, "Who do the crowds say that I am?" They answered, "John the Baptist; but others, Elijah; and still others, that one of the ancient prophets has arisen." He said to them, "But who do you say that I am?" Peter answered, "The Messiah of God." He sternly ordered and commanded them not to tell anyone, saying, "The Son of Man must undergo great suffering, and be rejected by the elders, chief priests, and scribes, and be killed, and on the third day be raised."

Some differences are striking—the setting is different; "people say I am" vs. "crowds say I am." Both rebukes are missing in Luke's account. The redaction critic must ask why the source was modified. Why does Luke soften Mark's treatment of the disciples? Why the different settings for the same event? Why crowds instead of people? Why "one of the ancient prophets has arisen" instead of simply "one of the prophets?" and why the answer, "the Messiah of God" rather than "the Messiah?" The answer most redaction critics quickly offer is that the differences are due to Luke's theological interests. Luke has something to say *through* his narrative that is theologically different from that of Mark.

But what happens if the interpreter has no available sources which underlie that text, or when there is evidence that the author has simply incorporated a unit of tradition without any modification? Mark is a case in point; what are Mark's sources? The answer lies in the more modern approach of redaction critics to view a text as an entity within itself. This approach supposes that a final redactor has produced a final version of a text and the text itself supplies the primary evidence for discovering the author's theological purpose. The interpreter must examine in detail the way in which each individual part of a text relates to the other parts and consequently, the way in which the text as a whole presents its message. This observation obviously vitiates any attempt to harmonize texts which make use of the same or similar traditions. The Gospels should not become only sources for constructing a homogenized gospel story.[2] Each gospel is a biased (Ger. *Tendenz*) narrative which has its own message to communicate. In the Hebrew Bible, both the Chronicler and the author of Samuel–Kings have their own messages, and attempts to harmonize these two accounts of the same period stand in opposition to redaction criticism.

Resources

Bornkamm, Günther, Gerhard Barth, and Heinz Joachim Held. *Tradition and Interpretation in Matthew.* Translated by Percy Scott. Philadelphia: Westminster, 1963.

Hayes, John, and Carl R. Holladay. *Biblical Exegesis: A Beginner's Handbook.* Atlanta: John Knox, 1987.

Marxsen, Willie. *Mark the Evangelist.* Translated by James Boyce et al. Nashville: Abindgon, 1969.

---

[2] Ibid., 105.

Literary Criticism

By literary criticism here, I refer to an approach that interprets the biblical texts as literature. It is an approach grounded in the assumption that the biblical authors were imaginative, creative crafters of art employing structural elements and literary devices usually associated with the poetics of literature (i.e., the creation of literature) and genre.

Broad structural elements include the three basic components of literary texts: first, plot with its five components of exposition, complication/rising action, climax, crisis, and resolution/*dénouement;* second, setting, which includes the time, the place, and all the objects included in the time and place; and third, characterization, the manner in which the various characters populating a text are portrayed either as rounded, static, dynamic, flat, full-fledged, or stereotypical. Other more narrow structural elements of literary works are style, tone, atmosphere, point of view, syntax, and diction.

Authors employ a number of literary devices to enhance the reading experience. Most of these devices create informational gaps that the reader must fill. For example, a metaphor asks the reader to make a comparison between two items (sometimes between two concrete items and sometimes between a concrete item and an abstract one). The author also creates a gap by alluding to another text, cultural object, historical event or person. These allusions ask the reader to place prior information into a new context and to think about the significance of the allusions. Other literary devices that authors regularly employ are simile, myth, hyperbole, symbol, understatement, synecdoche, parallelism, and personification. Rhetorical techniques usually fall under three general categories—ethos, pathos, and logos (see the section on rhetorical criticism in the appendix).

Perhaps the most important issue within literary criticism is genre. While texts may share common literary devices (listed in the previous paragraph), different types of texts operate according to different literary conventions. For example, readers generally do not expect to find complex plot development within poetry. Literary critics also claim that readers approach different types of texts in different ways with different expectations. For example, readers of the Bible do not approach a proverb with the same expectations as for the book of Genesis. The literary critic approaches the Pentateuch as theological history and the Proverbs as a collection of aphorisms. In the Hebrew Bible, the genres include theological history (e.g., the Pentateuch, Deuteronomic History,

Chronistic History), short story (e.g., Ruth, Jonah, Esther), prophecy (e.g., Isaiah, Jeremiah, Amos), and poetry (e.g., Psalms, Proverbs, Song of Songs). The latter genre, however, is complicated by the fact that there is poetry within most of the books of the Hebrew Bible, especially the prophetic books. Consequently, with the prophetic books, for example, the reader is faced with the responsibility of interfacing the genre conventions of both prophecy and poetry. The New Testament genres include gospel, apocalypse, and epistolary literature.

In addition to assumptions about structure, devices, and genre, literary critics generally assume that a text is a unified whole in which the parts must be understood in terms of the whole and the whole in terms of the parts. This assumption is based upon the prior assumption that authors select and arrange their materials according to a predetermined plan or idea. Such a plan or idea contributes to the possibility of the text being a unified whole and therefore being read as an autonomous literary object.

Although this latter idea may suggest univalence, literary critics claim that the best pieces of literature are multivalent, that they have the capacity to generate and legitimate a number of plausible understandings. Take the book of Jonah as an example. A reader might read Jonah and see that God has done a supernatural thing in causing the great fish to swallow the prophet. From a modern scientific perspective, such a thing is impossible or at least improbable. Yet the reader might assume that this story teaches that natural laws and human possibilities do not bind God and that God will at times intervene in lives miraculously. This is a legitimate reading of Jonah. Reading the same book, another reader might notice that when Jonah decides to flee from God, he heads to Tarshish, which in ancient reckoning was a metaphor for paradise. This reader might also notice that Jonah's trek to what he thinks is paradise is actually a descent into death, denoted by a series of downward movements: Jonah goes down to Joppa, down into the belly of the ship, down into the belly of the fish, and down to Sheol. While Jonah thinks his flight is to paradise, his flight from God is actually a flight into death. Again, this reading is both suggested and legitimated by the text itself. Finally, a third reader may focus upon Jonah's actions at the end of the account. Jonah's problem seems to be a theological one. Nineveh had perpetrated unspeakable atrocities upon Jonah's people and deserved judgment. But Jonah knows that a single act of repentance can erase a lifetime of sins. Jonah's problem is that he does not want to live in a world where God's grace is always poised to win out over justice. God is just, but God's grace is always superabundant. Did the author intend for readers to arrive at all these possibilities? It is impossible to know for certain. The point is that a text such as Jonah and the others that we have looked at depend upon readers to make sense of them and this sense-making may be pluralistic.

Resources

Hayes, John, and Carl R. Holladay. *Biblical Exegesis: A Beginner's Handbook.* Atlanta: John Knox, 1987.
Soulen, Richard N., and R. Kendall Soulen. *Handbook of Biblical Criticism.* 3d ed. Louisville: Westminster John Knox, 2001.

Genre Criticism

Genre criticism focuses on a text's literary type as the source of its meaning. The biblical texts are commonly categorized by genre as historical narratives, prophecy, biblical poetry, psalms, wisdom literature, apocalypse, epistle, and gospel. Genre critics assume that the context for understanding a piece of literature is not reality, history, or authorial intention but literature itself. Literature is best comprehended by reading it in the context of literary conventions, and unless readers know these conventions, they cannot fully appreciate literature.

The defining assumption of genre criticism in classifying texts is that there exist formal or technical characteristics among texts of the same kind irrespective of time, place, author, or subject. An equally important assumption is that readers cannot fully appreciate and understand a text unless they approach it with some understanding of its genre. Since all literature (all art for that matter) is conventional, it can only be rightly understood by individuals who are familiar with the conventions. For example, if the Gospel of Luke is read as a romantic comedy, it will simply be misread (although it does manifest some of the generic characteristics of Hellenistic romance, biography, epic, and historiography). Although a particular text may not conform absolutely to its conventional framework and thus may be unique, if it does not conform to some degree—if it is completely unique—it would simply be unintelligible.

Genre critics generally assume that if readers know the genre of a text, they will read it in a particular way because the knowledge of the genre creates a set of expectations with which the reader approaches the text. Critics such as E. D. Hirsch argue that the accuracy of a reader's understanding depends upon the accuracy of his or her identification of the genre.[3] Plausible understanding occurs only to the extent that the reader operates under the same genre expectations as the author. If readers approach the book of Revelation with the same expectations that they have for the Song of Songs, misunderstanding of Revelation will result.

Because of the interconnectedness between form and content in literature, literary criticism must concern itself with both aspects at the same time. This concern entails understanding the conventions of genre. Even the casual reader knows that a poem must be read and interpreted differently from a recipe. When readers approach texts, they identify those texts, whether unconsciously or consciously, in terms of their literary type.

Rules of grammatical construction and syntax govern the way we group words or symbols, thus ensuring communication. Similarly, rules govern or identify literary genres. Consequently, we read different genres with different expectations and interpret them differently. Knowing the genre of a text allows the reader to know what type of questions can sensibly be asked of the material.

Resources

Alter, Robert. *The Art of Biblical Narrative*. New York: Basic Books, 1981.

Bakhtin, Mikhail. *The Dialogic Imagination: Four Essays*. Edited by Michael Holquist. Translated by Caryl Emerson and Michael Holquist. Austin and London: University of Texas Press, 1981.

Fowler, Alistair. *Kinds of Literature: An Introduction to the Theory of Genres and Modes*. Cambridge, Mass.: Harvard University Press, 1982.

Gilbert, Sandra, and Susan Gubar. *The Mad Woman in the Attic: The Woman Writer and the Nineteenth-Century Literary Imagination*. New Haven: Yale University Press, 1979.

Hayes, John, and Carl R. Holladay. *Biblical Exegesis: A Beginner's Handbook*. Atlanta: John Knox, 1987.

Hirsch, E. D., Jr. *Validity in Interpretation*. New Haven: Yale University Press, 1967.

---

[3] E. D. Hirsch Jr., "Objective Interpretation," *PMLA* 75 (1960): 471.

Unit III

THE WORLD IN FRONT OF THE TEXT

Chapter

7

WHAT HAPPENS WHEN WE READ?

This unit is devoted to examining aspects of the world in front of the text (the world of the reader). In this chapter, we look at the complex process of reading. In ch. 8, we observe the role of the reader's pre-understanding and presuppositions. This discussion is continued in ch. 9, with an examination of the vital role that methodological presuppositions play in the hermeneutical enterprise. Chapter 10 will use a test case from the Gospel of Mark to show how the three worlds of author, text, reader intersect to produce meaning.

Without an author, there is no text; without a reader, a text does not communicate. In a real sense, an unread text carries no meaning, because it can mean nothing until there is a mutual engagement between reader and text. Meaning involves a process of signification in the act of reading. The creative role of the author has already been established in unit I. In the same unit, I argued for the essential adjunctive role of historical research. The reader, however, is the person who must make key decisions about what the text says. Perhaps Robert Morgan and John Barton overstate their case, but their metaphor speaks to the problem:

> A text has no life of its own. It "lives" only as an electric wire is alive. Its power originates elsewhere: in a human author. There is another point of comparison: however powerful the author's act of creation, the text lies impotent until it also comes into contact with a human reader. Only then can the human power, imagination, and intellect carried by the marks on a page strike a light, communicate warmth, or give a nasty shock. The medium itself is important, and determines how much of the source's power is communicated. Old wires can give unreliable service and cause accidents. But it is the source that gives the wire its potential for illumination or destruction. Without this, there is no live wire. Once this is present, however, those at the receiving end are in control. It is they who decide what to do with the powerful resource they possess—whether and how to use it. They have all power in their hands.[1]

---

[1] Robert Morgan with John Barton, *Biblical Interpretation* (New York: Oxford University Press, 1988), 269.

If written discourse is communication between author, text, and reader, then what role does the reader play in determining meaning at the receiving end of the process? Communication has not occurred until the message (text) has reached its final destination.[2] For this reason, the reception of a text by the reader should be a primary consideration in any hermeneutic.

Just as the author (sender) brings his or her worldview and understanding of reality to a text, allowing the text to mirror at least some elements of that worldview and reality, so the reader (receiver) brings to the text his or her worldview and conception of reality. Texts must be read and made sense of within the reader's complex and multifaceted world. We understand another person's discourse only by relating it to what we already know and by putting questions to the text from within our own world. As we read a text we infer meaning, and that meaning is in some measure determined by our understanding of our own world. The interpreter's world intrudes into the process of actualizing meaning. We may recognize just how significant this circumstance is when we realize the gulf of time, language, and culture, and when we acknowledge the presuppositions that exist between the biblical texts and ourselves. This means that all sorts of values, preunderstandings, and presuppositions impinge upon the reader and the interpretive process. Consequently, the reader's world is as constitutive of textual meaning as the world of the author. These observations are summarized in the following chart:

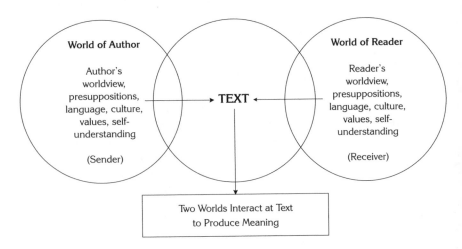

[2] Bernard C. Lategan and Willem S. Vorster, *Text and Reality: Aspects of Reference in Biblical Texts* (Philadelphia: Fortress, 1985), 68.

These observations lead to a number of perplexing but legitimate questions: Does meaning exist within the text apart from the subjective reception of the reader? How does one interpretation of a text influence subsequent interpretations of the same and other related texts? If every reader approaches the text with varying viewpoints, presuppositions, aims, preunderstandings, and methodologies, does a text have only one meaning? If, on the one hand, the answer to this last question is *yes*, then we are faced with what Japp calls a **hermeneutic of reduction**, i.e., a text has only one objective meaning. If the answer, on the other hand, is *no*, then we must be willing to accept what Japp calls a hermeneutic of unfolding, which allows the text in dialogue with the reader to have a multiplicity of possible meanings.[3]

Without question the biblical texts were born within specific historical contexts. There is also no question that authors of the biblical texts directly refer to and allude to specific historical events within their real world. But do the texts refer only to historical facts? Do they not also refer to realities which transcend historical events and facts? If they do, then the texts refer to realities which must be "construed by the readers in their situation (ancient readers as well as modern ones)."[4] This means that a biblical text has at least two levels—an original meaning and a contemporary significance.[5] We might go so far as to suggest that authors even expect readers to construe meaning based upon the readers' own circumstances and needs. When this happens, meaning becomes, in part, the significance construed by the reader. The early church not only told and wrote the stories of Jesus, they also retold and rewrote them. The existence of four gospels is evidence that Jesus and his message could be applied in a variety of ways, each with a particular emphasis. Simply put, the story and message were dynamic. The events in Israel's history were also told and retold, applied and reapplied by subsequent generations in such a way that the events spoke to these generations. The "meaning" of the texts for these readers was the significance which spoke to their lives. The texts were more than mere repositories of historical information; they were living organisms capable of interpretations that reached beyond their own historical and cultural milieu. Depending upon the needs of the readers, the texts contained an overflow, a surplus of meaning significance.

---

[3] U. Japp, *Hermeneutik: Der theoretische Diskurs, die Literatur, und die Konstruktion ihres Zusammenhanges in den philologischen Wissenschaften* (Munich: Fink, 1977), 47.

[4] McKnight, *Postmodern Use of the Bible*, 107.

[5] Ibid.

While readers may enhance the reading experience through excursions into the author's world, we should never naively suppose that we as readers can divorce ourselves from the influences of our own worlds. Just as authors assimilate, internalize, and then synthesize their cultural experiences, adding to these experiences individual evaluations and expressions, so readers do the same.

Reading is not a pure activity. Readers are not simply innocent bystanders, sponges who soak up a text. The text at the **artistic pole** (composition) of the communicatory continuum may be complete, but the work at the **aesthetic pole** (reading) must be created with the help of the reader. A passive reading never allows room for the active participation of the reader in the creation of meaning.

Reading is not a monological process (i.e., a process by which the text speaks to the reader), but a dialogical one (i.e., reading is a process through which the text and reader engage in an ongoing dialogue). What readers do to a text is just as constitutive of meaning as what the text does to the readers. The text and reader question and answer each other, just as in most forms of dialogue. The reading process is diachronic, that is, it takes place through time. When we consider that this diachronic process is affected both by textual and by reader-responsive considerations, we suddenly come face to face with the realization that the reading process is anything but static. Reading is dynamic, open-ended, always subject to modification, change, evaluation, and rereading.

The Dialectics of Discourse

Before examining the particulars of the reading process and the implications for hermeneutics, an understanding of the **dialectics of discourse** will help clarify some of the issues involved. In oral discourse, a speaker addresses a message to a hearer. The oral message has at least two levels of meaning—the speaker's and the speech's. The two meanings may or may not be identical, for the speech's meaning may not objectively represent the speaker's **conceptualization**. A gap is then created between the speaker's conceptualization and the speech's meaning. This gap is the first dialectic in oral discourse. The conceptualization is private, while the speech becomes public.

If we concentrate only on the utterance's meaning, there arises a second dialectic—the dialectic between meaning and **reference**. The meaning of a sign (whether the sign is a single word or an entire discourse) is the object, event, or concept which the sign names in the real world; while the reference of a sign is concerned with the thing to which the sign refers. For example, if I utter the word "snake," the meaning of the sign "snake" is a crawling reptile, while the reference may be to a particular person with a particular personality trait. Paul Ricoeur states that "meaning is *what* a statement says, reference is *that about which* it says it."[6] A major problem in hermeneutics is that the term "meaning" is also used in the same sense as reference, especially in the case of written discourse; what a text means is synonymous with what a text is about. This double use of meaning is perhaps unavoidable (as has been the case in this text). Therefore, I will continue to use the term "meaning" to refer to the actualization by a reader of what a text is about. The distinction of the two terms should be kept in mind, however, because the distinction has serious implications for interpretation. For example, if a text's (sign's) reference has to be construed by a reader, then there exists the possibility of multiple interpretations.[7] Further, if a sign has multiple referents, then there will be multiple interpretations, depending upon which referent the reader assigns the sign. The Gospel of Matthew includes individuals, events, and places which existed or happened in first-century Palestine. The meaning (on the first level discussed above) of the text occurs in first-century Palestine. But to whom do the Pharisees, disciples, publicans refer? To what do the events and places refer? What is the reference of the text? Or I suppose we might ask about the "real" meaning of the text.

A third dialectic concerns the reader in written discourse. We have already suggested that there is not necessarily a one-to-one correspondence between an author's conceptualization (the original intentional object) and the **inscripturation** (the literary **concretization**) of that conceptualization. The former is private, while the latter is public. A similar dialectic exists on the reader's part between understanding (the reader's conceptualization of the text) and subsequent explanation. The former is private, while the latter is public. There simply is no guarantee that a reader's explanation adequately represents the reader's understanding. This dialectic is further complicated since different readers understand texts differently due to a wide range of elements within readers' worlds. With the above remarks in mind, we are now ready to examine two other dialectic pairs within the reading process which more directly impinge upon interpretation.

---

[6] Paul Ricoeur, "Biblical Hermeneutics," *Semeia* 4 (1975): 81.
[7] See Lategan and Vorster, *Text and Reality,* 27–65.

First, there is the dialectic between the original languages and the translations. Biblical hermeneutics involves a special problem: the languages of the texts are not the same as those of modern readers. If readers use a translation, they are already working with an interpretation, because all translations are themselves interpretations. It is impossible for a translation to have a one-to-one correspondence to the original. Therefore, any interpretation of a biblical text based upon a translation is actually an interpretation of an interpretation; i.e., the interpretation based upon a translation is an interpretation of the translator's understanding of the original. There always exists a linguistic gap between any translation and the original text. Why is this the case? In any society there exists a system of phonological, morphological, and syntactical rules. Most of these rules are not objects which are consciously analyzed by the members of the society, but are simply learned, internalized, and then used intuitively. The system that makes any act of speech possible and comprehensible is called *langue* (in this case Hebrew or Greek; see the discussion of structuralism in ch. 9). The system that makes particular speech acts (*parole*) possible can never be completely mastered or internalized by an individual within a culture, much less by someone outside that culture.

> Hence the *full* meaning of a language is never translatable into another. We may speak several languages, but one of them always remains the one in which we live. In order completely to assimilate a language, it would be necessary to make the world which it expresses one's own, and one never does belong to two worlds at once.[8]

Obviously, if the individual speech act has its meaning only against this *langue,* and if this *langue* can never be completely assimilated by an individual outside the culture, then no translation can completely capture that nonverbal dimension of another language. Of course the nonverbal dimension of language is crucial in the formation and meaning of individual speech acts. No natural language can ever be equivalent to another, thus no individual speech act within one system can ever be the exact equivalent of a speech act within a translation.

As we explained earlier in ch. 4, every literary text actually employs a multiplicity of languages—the natural language, which is governed by syntactical and linguistic conventions, and literary languages,

---

[8] Maurice Merleau-Ponty, *Consciousness and the Acquisition of Language* (trans. Hugh J. Silverman; Evanston: Northwestern University Press, 1973), xv–xvi.

which likewise involve literary conventions. As readers we acquire levels of competency in the codes and conventions of a text's natural language. A familiarity with grammatical, lexical, and syntactical conventions enables readers to determine what a sentence, unit, or entire text says. It is at this level that readers also give attention to historical events, persons, and places within the real world of the text. In literary texts, however, literary languages are superimposed upon the natural language. This entails, consequently, that readers of literary text must coordinate the conventions of the natural language and the conventions of the literary languages. This balancing act by the readers is described well by Edgar McKnight:

> Readers are confronted simultaneously by the multiple levels of the linguistic and literary structures of the writing being read, and they must apply multiple codes. In the case of letters, for example, readers must keep in mind the first-century letter form and the form of the smaller units (the "hymn," for example) used within the letter. In addition, the systematic ordering on the basis of content must be considered. Since appeal is being made to the reader's will as well as to his or her intellect, rhetorical structures (not necessarily ordered by, but not unrelated to, ancient rules of rhetoric) coexist with structures related to subject matter and the different levels of literary genre.[9]

As we saw in unit II, genres and sub-genres carry their own poetics, their own literary languages. A reader lacking any appreciable understanding of the dynamics of these literary languages tends to read primarily on the level of the natural language. This type of reader will generally unconsciously make no distinction between what the text says and what it is about, i.e., the meaning and the reference are not perceived as differing. The failure to recognize the literary languages within the texts of the Bible has generated questions such as, Why did Eve not think it strange when the serpent talked to her? When was "in the beginning"? What kind of fish could have swallowed Jonah? These types of questions derive from a failure to understand that the biblical texts are literary documents, which by their nature overcode the natural languages with literary ones. More literarily competent readers (those readers familiar with the literary languages) approach the biblical texts open to the texts as potential literary documents.

This brings us to the final and most significant dialectic for the reading process and to its impact upon meaning. This is the dialectic

---

[9] McKnight, *Postmodern Use of the Bible,* 137.

between text and work. No other theorist has been more successful in explaining the dynamics of the reading process than Wolfgang Iser. According to Iser, the meaning which readers infer from texts results from the tension between "the role offered by the text and the real reader's own disposition."[10] The following discussion of this process of production is based upon the model offered by Iser:

When approaching a literary text, the reader must take into account two factors: the text and the response to the text. The **literary work** is not synonymous to the text, but is created in the act of reading. The work exists somewhere between the artistic pole (the text created by the author) and the aesthetic pole (the realization accomplished by the reader). The text exists on paper; the work is born out of the interaction between the text and the reader. Since dispositions of readers vary and since a single reader's disposition may change between readings, the literary work can never be precisely pinpointed.

Iser asserts that **gaps of indeterminacy** and the completion of these gaps by the reader is *the* central factor in literary communication. Language is such that it allows itself to be broken up and then reconstructed. The place where the language is broken up and reconstructed "is marked by gaps in the text—it consists in the blanks which the reader is to fill in. . . . Whenever the reader bridges the gap, communication begins. The gaps function as a kind of pivot on which the whole text-reader relationship revolves."[11]

As we observed in unit II, authors engage in the process of selection when producing texts. This process of selection leaves some things unsaid. An author cannot possibly incorporate every detail from the real world into the text, for the text would become unmanageable. There are, therefore, gaps of silence within the text. In fact, if a narrative does not leave enough blank spaces through which to engage the reader's imagination, the reader's interest is lost. Because of these gaps, readers of texts are required to "fill them in" by drawing from their own repertoires.

Iser speaks of gaps existing in different textual elements and on different levels: syntax, semantics, pragmatics, narrative flow, character action, even the role assigned to the reader. Iser describes the reading process as establishing connections—filling the gaps—among these different levels and phases of the text. Before discussing in more detail

---

[10] Wolfgang Iser, *The Act of Reading: A Theory of Aesthetic Response* (Baltimore: Johns Hopkins University Press, 1978), 37.
[11] Ibid., 169.

Iser's theory of "gap filling," some examples of the basic types of gaps readers are required to fill should be helpful.

Grammatical and Syntactical Gaps

Many of the gaps occurring in texts are due to the inherent **ambiguity** of language. In Gal 1:16, Paul states that God "was pleased to reveal his Son to me." In what sense are we to understand the sense of Paul's statement: "to me," "through me," "in my heart," or "to me in particular"? The dative case of the preposition *en* (trans. NRSV as "to") may indicate any of these relationships.[12] When statements such as "the love of God" occur, are we to treat them as objective (God being the object of love) or subjective (God's love) genitives? Thus, does this phrase refer to the love a person has for God, or the love that God has for a person? The text does not always supply the answer, and this means that the reader must make a decision to fill in the grammatical gap; the reader must solve the ambiguity of (disambiguate) the text.

Other instances of gaps due to grammatical ambiguity occur when a particular word may be translated in two or more ways. For example, a word may in form be either indicative or imperative. In 1 Cor 12:31a, should we translate the word *zēloute* as an indicative ("you are striving for") or an imperative ("strive for")? The manner in which the reader fills this grammatical gap affects the interpretation of the rest of the passage.

Another example of gap filling due to syntactical ambiguity arises from the pronoun and its antecedent. In Luke 11:8, the reader is confronted with a barrage of pronouns: "I tell you, even though he will not get up and give him anything because he is his friend, at least because of his persistence he will get up and give him whatever he needs." If we concentrate on the first few words of the last clause—"yet because of *his* persistence *he* will get up"—who are the antecedents for these two pronouns? Notice the question: "Who are?" This question itself assumes that the two pronouns have different antecedents. This assumption is based upon the word "persistence." The man outside the house asking for bread must be the one who is persistent. Further, the man outside the house is thought to be persistent because the reader will read back into the parable the persistence usually associated with the poem which follows. If, however, the word translated "persistence"

---

[12] For an excellent discussion of such examples, see McKnight, *Postmodern Use of the Bible,* 223–35.

(a *hapax legomenon*) were to be translated "sense of integrity," then both pronouns would refer to the man inside the house! As McKnight suggests:

> Normally, the ambiguity involved in the subordinate grammatical and syntactical structures can be handled by the reader because one actualization fits the total linguistic and literary context better than the others. When different actualizations fit the same context equally well, the reader may process the text in different ways allowed by the ambiguity.[13]

The antecedent of a pronoun is not always easily determined. In John 3:2, Nicodemus says to Jesus, "Rabbi, we know that you are a teacher who has come from God." What is the antecedent for "we"? Is Nicodemus referring to the Sanhedrin, to his colleagues, or to some other group? The antecedent is unclear.

Poetic or Literary Gaps

Generally, filling gaps created by literary structures is not as easy as filling those created by the ambiguities of syntax and grammar. James 1:13b reads: "for God cannot be tempted by evil, and he himself tempts no one." The reader may want to add to the end of this sentence the words "with evil." The context seems to suggest that the reader should supply what is only hinted at by the text. This is an example of poetic omission. Intentional omission of words or even phrases is part of the stock and trade of literary artists. The result is the involvement of the reader in the completion of the sense of the text. When the writer in Eph 5:21–22 says, "Be subject to one another out of reverence for Christ, wives . . . to your husbands as you are to the Lord," the reader must supply the missing verb in the second part of the sentence, since it is not present in the original language.

In Hebrew poetic parallelism, verbs are often omitted and must be supplied by the reader: "They shall beat their swords into plowshares, and their spears into pruning hooks" (Isa 2:4b). The reader must understand that the same verb "beat" is understood in the second clause. There are also times when the reader must supply information not discernible from the immediate context. Such information includes religious, cultural, and geographical matters.

There are also paratactic constructions with which the reader must deal. Paratactic constructions include grammatical clauses joined with no indication of their syntactic relationship. In the New Testament,

---

[13] Ibid., 226.

phrases and clauses are often joined by the conjunctive *kai* ("and"), and the reader must determine whether the relationship between the clauses is causal, circumstantial, conditional, etc. Consider Ps 23:1: "The LORD is my shepherd, I shall not want." The second clause is the result of the first. The reason that the Psalmist lacks nothing is because the Lord is his shepherd.

Literary devices such as simile, hyperbole, and metaphor (discussed in ch. 4) may also be ambiguous. Hyperbole, if taken literally, certainly results in misreading. Indeed, if the reader does not hold a body of information in common with the author, the hyperbole may not have its desired effect. The same is true for simile and metaphor. Both forms are comparative figures of speech; i.e., simile and metaphor require that a reader compare two objects that are in real life incongruous. In Matt 5:13–14, Christians are called light and salt, the latter metaphor being partially unintelligible to the modern reader. Peter Cotterell and Max Turner observe:

> The use of metaphor is a creative act, and there can be no certainty that the interpretation of the metaphor will follow the intention of its creator. The receiver must search through his own experience, and must employ his own imagination, and if necessary engage his own research, and only so can the meaning of a metaphor be realized. But that experience and that imagination are his, and not those of the creator of the metaphor, so that the use of metaphor inevitably opens up the way to misunderstanding.[14]

In order for metaphor or simile to operate, there must exist a commonality of perception between the metaphor's creator and the hearer. Without this commonality, the reader or hearer may misunderstand the force of the metaphor or simile. Cotterell and Turner offer a striking example illustrated by the metaphor of "burning coals" in Rom 12:20: "You will heap burning coals on their heads." This metaphor demands a comparison where both the *vehicle* and the *tenor* of the metaphor are not immediately apparent to the modern reader.[15] If the reader bases the interpretation of this metaphor upon other references to burning coals in the Bible, judgment is perceived to be the primary idea (e.g., Gen 19:24; Lev 10:2; Ps 11:6). But does the idea of judgment fit the context of the metaphor? The force of Rom 12:14–21 concerns forgiveness, not judgment. According to William Klassen, in the *Stories of the High Priests of Memphis,* a repentant person is depicted as going to

---

[14] Cotterell and Turner, *Linguistics and Biblical Interpretation,* 300–301.
[15] Ibid., 302–5.

the person he had wronged, bearing a clay dish containing burning coals on his head.[16] This better explains the source of the metaphor in Prov 25:21–23:

> If your enemies are hungry, give them bread to eat;
> and if they are thirsty, give them water to drink;
> for you will heap coals of fire on their heads,
> and the LORD will reward you.
> The north wind produces rain;
> and a backbiting tongue, angry looks.

Since the last verse describes the rain pattern in Egypt, the origin of the metaphor of "burning coals" probably has its source in Egypt also. With this in mind, the meaning of the metaphor in Proverbs is that if a person acts in a forgiving way towards an enemy, the enemy will come to repent. This is almost certainly the meaning of the metaphor in Paul's usage. Without this contextual background, the modern reader may very well assign to the metaphor a meaning of retribution instead of forgiveness.

According to Iser, the various **textual segments** (sentences, lexical units, etc.) present different perspectives within the text. But the segments point to something beyond what is said. This something is what is left unsaid. This is the "unwritten text" and is actually the unstated connections between the textual segments or components. The reader must infer these unstated connections. As a reader joins these segments, a referential field results in which the reader holds the segments in tension. This tension gives rise to the need for a common framework that allows the reader to grasp the similarities and differences according to a pattern. To some extent, the text provides no such framework; the reader must supply it; however, things are not quite this simple.

Meaning is the result of a dialogue between a reader and a text. This dialogue depends on a pair of structures—**structures of effect** and **structures of response**. While readers clearly bring their unique individual symbolic worlds to the text, responses are not entirely arbitrary because the structures of response as well as the structures of effect are textually determined. Since these structures are interactive, we will not attempt to discuss them separately but in their dialogic relationships.

First, we must consider the relationship between reality and thought systems. Every age has its own dominant thought system that reduces

---

[16] William Klassen, "Coals of Fire: Sign of Repentance or Revenge?" *NTS* 9 (1962–1963): 337–50.

the contingencies and complexities of reality to a meaningful and manageable structure. What any one epoch considers to be reality is not reality in its totality, but rather an order imposed upon reality. Every system imposes an order upon contingent reality, thereby providing a framework for living as well as for a set of social norms that lays claim to a universal validity. But when a system becomes dominant, it does so through a reduction of the complexity of reality. While it foregrounds some possibilities, it necessarily backgrounds or excludes others. The negated or neutralized possibilities are not eliminated, but only deactivated, waiting to be resurrected or reactivated. Literature is the means of resurrection. Literature attempts to bring to light the possibilities neutralized or excluded by the dominant system. Literature interferes with the existing ordering of reality, drawing attention to its deficiencies. The result of such interference is the bringing to light of the system's inability to deal with the multifarious nature of reality. Once literature attacks the system at its seams, a rearrangement of the meaningful structures of the system is called for. The excluded possibilities are the focus of literary works.[17] But how does a literary text accomplish the work of a gadfly?

What Iser calls the repertoire of a text consists of **schemata** and **strategies**. The schemata consist of social norms and **literary allusions** while the strategies consist of narrative techniques (especially perspectives) and gaps of indeterminacy.

Social Norms

The negated or neutralized possibilities of the dominant thought system constitute the focal point of a literary text. At the same time, however, in order to establish this focal point, the text must incorporate implicitly the framework of the contemporary system. The text accomplishes this by "explicitly shading in the areas all around that system."[18] On the one hand, when a text incorporates elements of the current thought system, these elements are recoded in such a way that the familiar elements lose their validity. On the other hand, the text does not formulate an alternative validity, but presents the elements in such a way that readers must discover or construct the intention of recoding. Consequently, the readers are called upon to be partners in constructing meaning. Now if the readers are contemporary with the text, they are provided with the possibility of a fresh look at the system

---

[17] Iser, *The Act of Reading,* 71–78.
[18] Ibid., 73.

that they have to this point accepted without question. If the readers, however, are no longer involved in the thought system of the text, they are able to reconstruct the framework from the text, to experience the system's deficiencies, and to discover the alternative answers implicit in the text. So the historical distance between a text and later generations of readers does not vitiate a text's power. The contemporary reader is confronted with defamiliarized norms, necessitating a reassessment of the norms and possibilities negated by such norms. The result is the construction of meaning. Later readers experience a reality that is not theirs and are able to transcend their own world or *Sitz im Leben,* resulting in a reassessment or broadening of their reality.[19]

Literary Allusions

The schemata of the text also consists of past literary elements and entire traditions that are intertwined with the social and cultural norms.

> If the function of the incorporated norms is to bring out the deficiencies of a prevailing system, the function of literary allusions is to assist in producing an answer to the problems set by these deficiencies.[20]

These literary allusions offer the reader past answers to the problems presented by the social norms, but answers that are no longer valid. So what is the value of the allusions? Since the allusions are now stripped of their original context, the reader should assume that their function is more than simple reproduction but that they serve as guides or points of orientation for discovering a new meaning. Since the literary elements are depragmatized by a new context, the original or old context recedes into the background, but does not disappear. The old context serves as a backdrop that throws the now implied significance into relief. It is only against the background of the old context that the reader is able to construct new possibilities and their significance.

The **repertoire of the text** (schemata and strategies) constitutes the context for the dialogue between the text and the reader. The repertoire provides the reader with the wherewithal to produce an answer to the questions raised in the text. But before we move to textual strategies, it is necessary to make a more thorough examination of the relationship between the schemata and the role of the reader.

The social norms incorporated within a text originate in a historical thought system, while the literary allusions have their origin in past

---

[19] Ibid., 78–79.
[20] Ibid., 79.

reactions to problems. Since the norms and allusions are not equivalent, a problem for the reader arises when the norms and allusions are joined together. The fact that they are joined together suggests that they are related in some fashion. So the reader is called upon to look for a system of equivalences between the two even if their marriage is designed to highlight differences. However, since a text always refers to something beyond itself, the reader is also called upon to create a system of equivalences between the work and the real world. The role of the schemata is to organize the reader's reaction to the problem implied within the text. But the schemata's structure must be realized through reading. The degree to which the structures of meaning are optimized will depend upon the reader's awareness of these structures and the degree to which the reader is willing to open up to an unfamiliar and sometimes threatening experience. But according to Iser, "the meaning must inevitably be pragmatic, in that it can never cover all the semantic potentials of the text, but can only open up one particular form of access to these potentials."[21] This is tantamount to saying that the schemata present a range of organizational possibilities, and these can be realized in a number of ways. It is here that the reader's unique individual disposition and background come into play. Meaning originates, then, from the interplay between the reader's own decisions and the attitude that the text provokes in the reader toward the problems that the text implies. Nevertheless, the organizational structure of the schemata guards against indiscriminate meaning assembly by the reader by providing the context in which to assemble the meaning.

For Iser the most determinate guide relating to the schemata is **negativity**, which is actually a basic form of what he calls gaps of indeterminacy (a concept that we will discuss in detail in relation to textual strategies). For Iser, negativity is "the basic regulator of the human condition."[22] Human beings are incapable of knowing how they experience one another. Because of this basic knowledge gap, we create our own conceptions of how others experience us and then substitute these conceptions for reality. Indeed, we even base our actions and reactions to others upon our projections. We create an imaginary picture and base all our communication upon this fiction. But projections are exactly that—projection—and not reality. Consequently, we spend our lives bridging a fundamental double gap by formulating imaginary projections based upon imaginary perceptions.

---

[21] Ibid., 85.

[22] Wolfgang Iser, *Prospecting: From Reader Response to Literary Anthropology* (Baltimore: Johns Hopkins University Press, 1989), 142.

Negativity is responsible for stimulating the processes of imagination that can bridge the knowledge gap. When applied to the text and reader, negativity must be understood in terms of negation. When a text incorporates familiar social norms and literary allusions, it does so in order to negate them, to cancel them out. These negated norms and allusions, however, remain in the background and serve to stimulate the reader to assume a posture or attitude toward the text. In other words, when the norms are negated, the reader is expected to look for the positive "elsewhere than in what is negated and this demand is nearly always accompanied by a number of signposts to point the way."[23] The alternatives to the negated norms and literary conventions are only implicit in the text and the reader must discover what they are. This is where the concept of negativity is important, for there is, Iser assumes, a hidden motive behind the many negations and deformations within the text. This motive is negativity, and it can be discovered only by the constitutive activity of the reader in recognizing that something is being withheld that must be discovered. There is no doubt that the negative slant given to the knowledge offered induces the reader to ideate the as yet hidden cause governing the negation—and in so doing he formulates what had been left unformulated.[24]

The meaning of the text is never that which is manifest, but exactly that which is latent. But what is stated serves as the primary context for what is unstated. So the reader is engaged in a constant switch between what is manifest or present and what is unstated or absent. It might be said that the reader must always distinguish between what a text says and what it might actually be about. And that "aboutness" is never explicit, but will always come into being through the protracted attempts of the reader to initiate and engage in the play of the text. Such an engagement should not strike readers as an unfamiliar process, for it is exactly this process that ensures everyday instances of communication. What is spoken or manifest is always accompanied by the unspoken. In other words, **absence** is always co-present with presence. The spoken is always impregnated with associations that cannot be dispensed with, and every object to which the spoken refers is one that has already been described in countless ways, so that whatever is said about it can only be a selection from the possibilities, thus defining itself by what it excludes.[25]

---

[23] Ibid., 140.
[24] Iser, *The Act of Reading,* 214.
[25] Iser, *Prospecting,* 102.

So when we as readers are sucked into the text through negativity, we are engaged in a drama that mirrors the drama of life itself. More complex texts tend to make the signposts that point the reader to discovering the hidden motive more ambiguous, thus dismantling any specific frame of reference from which the reader is to view the negations. When this occurs, the play of the text manifests itself in a multiplicity of possibilities.

Strategies

While the repertoire of the text consists of the social norms and literary allusions that produce negativity, it also includes textual strategies. On the one hand, the schemata create the context within which the reader must actualize a system of equivalences between the norms and allusions and between the text and the real world. On the other hand, the textual strategies function to organize the readers' actualization, without making them feel as if they are being led by the nose. As Iser puts it:

> [The strategies] provide a meeting-point between the repertoire and the producer of those equivalences, namely the reader himself. In other words, the strategies organize both the material of the text and the conditions under which that material is to be communicated.[26]

The strategies not only govern the structures of the text but also the acts of comprehension triggered in the reader. Put another way, it is the function of the strategies to carry the schemata (the primary code of the text) to the reader and to guide the reader's creation of the aesthetic object (the second code) by providing the meeting place for the schemata and the individual reader's own social and cultural code.

The textual strategies include those devices normally associated with the conventions of genre. For Iser, however, the emphasis falls upon the unmanifested dimension of the text, which we refer to as seams, but which he refers to as gaps. Literary texts offer readers only enough information to keep them "oriented and interested." Inferences that are to be drawn from the information are left up to the imagination of the reader. The resulting empty spaces or gaps within the text must be filled by the reader.

> The gap functions as a kind of pivot on which the whole text-reader relationship revolves. Hence, the structured blanks of the text stimulate

---

[26] Ibid.

the process of ideation to be preformed by the reader on terms set by the text.[27]

How are such gaps strategically created and subsequently filled by readers? To answer this question, we must look at Iser's treatment of textual perspectives.

There are generally four perspectives in a literary work (especially the novel)—the perspectives of the narrator, the characters, the plot, and the implied reader. The point of their convergence is the meaning of the text. This point of convergence is not provided by the text, but must be supplied by the reader. In other words, the convergence of the perspectives must emerge from a vantage point beyond the four perspectives, but pre-structured by the text. The real reader, then, is a mediator between the various perspectives, including that of the implied reader. This mediating activity is created by gaps between the perspectives, gaps that Iser refers to as blanks. Between perspectives there is a "suspension of connectability," an empty space that must be filled by the reader.

> In other words, between the "schematized views" there is a no-man's land of indeterminacy, which results precisely from the determinacy of each individual view in its sequence. Gaps are bound to open up, and they offer a free play in the interpretation of the specific ways in which the various views can be connected with one another. These gaps give the reader a chance to build his own bridges, relating the different aspects of the object which have thus far been revealed to him.[28]

These blanks function to impede textual consistency or coherence. While they are actually empty spaces, they do stimulate the reader's involvement; indeed, they are responsible for the very dialogue between reader and text. The blanks between the perspectives also serve as the referential field for the reader's attention in any one moment of the reading process. When two or more perspectives must be related by the reader, it is the blank that makes such a relation possible.

The perspectives have the function of stimulating the production of the aesthetic object. Consequently, the aesthetic object is never congruent with a single perspective. The aesthetic object is produced through the consistency-building activities of the reader. Since all the perspectives are interactive and this interaction is continuous throughout the

---

[27] Iser, *The Act of Reading,* 86.
[28] Iser, *Prospecting,* 9.

work, the reader is called upon to mediate between the shifting perspectives in order to produce a consistent viewpoint.

> Authorial comment, dialogue between characters, developments of plot, and the positions marked out for the reader—all these are interwoven in the text and offer a constantly shifting constellation of views.[29]

As the readers are confronted with the shifting and interacting perspectives, they are faced with the task of making them consistent. When we consider that this task is one carried out during the time flow or on the temporal axis of reading, the real reader's role is actually that of a **wandering viewpoint**. As the reader's attention shifts in the time flow of reading from one **perspective** to another, it is incapable of embracing all the perspectives at once. The perspective with which the reader is involved at any one moment is the **theme**. But this theme is set in relief by the previous perspectives with which the reader has been concerned. The previous segments constitute what Iser calls the "horizon." "It [the horizon] is made up of all those segments which had supplied the themes of previous phases of reading."[30]

These complementary concepts of theme and horizon point up a strategic element in literary texts pertaining to the wandering viewpoint—the relationship between expectation and memory, or **protension** and **retention**. Every segment or perspective (theme) is viewed within the context of a horizon; but in the time flow of reading, a theme is immediately transformed into the background, thus becoming part of the horizon from which the next theme will be viewed. Therefore, while the horizon influences the theme, the theme will also modify the horizon. The horizon always arouses expectations of things to come (e.g., how a problem will be resolved), while the theme will either satisfy the expectations or frustrate them. In addition, each new theme not only answers or frustrates expectations, but gives rise to new ones. In most literary texts, the theme serves to modify the expectations of the horizon or even to frustrate them. As a result, the theme has a retroactive influence upon the horizon, because the reader must go back and reconsider the previous segments and their relationship. So reading becomes an interplay between protension and retention. It is through this process of protension and retention that the wandering viewpoint continually seeks to relate the perspectives. Iser describes the process as follows:

---

[29] Iser, *The Act of Reading,* 96.
[30] Ibid., 97.

Every articulate reading moment entails a switch of perspective, and this constitutes an inseparable combination of differentiated perspectives, foreshortened memories, present modifications, and future expectations. Thus, in the time-flow of the reading process, past and future continually converge in the present moment, and the synthesizing operations of the wandering viewpoint enable the text to pass through the reader's mind as an ever-expanding network of connections. This also adds the dimension of space to that of time, for the accumulation of views and combinations gives us the illusion of depth and breadth, so that we have the impression that we are actually present in a real world.[31]

Since the shifting perspectives challenge the reader to produce a consistent viewpoint (i.e., create meaning), consistency building is a configurative, productive activity. The wandering viewpoint travels through the text of interconnecting perspectives making connections that will (at least for the reader) result in a mediated, consistent meaning. In other words, the wandering viewpoint seeks patterns of consistency. Now since readers differ in terms of memory, mental capacity, training, and interest, patterns of connections may be realized to varying degrees. Hence, the intersubjective structure of the text is capable of generating a multiplicity of subjective actualizations. As Iser puts it:

> This network of connections potentially encompasses the whole text, but the potential can never be fully realized; instead it forms the basis for the many selections which have to be made during the reading process and which, though intersubjectively not identical—as is shown by the many different interpretations of a single text—nevertheless remain intersubjectively comprehensible in so far as they are all attempts to optimize the same structure.[32]

Iser, however, is careful to guarantee a modest degree of determinacy created by the gaps of indeterminacy. He does this by redescribing the concept of horizon by calling it a **vacancy**, thus transforming the horizon into a type of controlling or governing gap (a determining indeterminant). While the blanks are the empty spaces, the missing links between perspectives, the vacancies develop when a segment fades from relevance, thus forming the background for the next theme. Against this background of the vacancy, each new thematic segment must be approached.

---

[31] Ibid., 116.
[32] Ibid., 118.

As the vacancy is structured by the sequence of positions in the time-flow of reading, the reader's viewpoint cannot proceed arbitrarily; the thematically vacant position always acts as the angle from which a selective interpretation is to be made.[33]

What Iser actually wants to ensure is a dialogic balance between the text and the reader, a free-play that produces an aesthetic object that is a product of both the governing structures of the text and the creative imagination of the reader. Perhaps this is no better stated than in his famous essay, "The Reading Process":

Thus, the reader, in establishing these interrelations between past, present and future, actually causes the text to reveal its potential multiplicity of connections. These connections are the product of the reader's mind working on the raw material of the text, though they are not the text itself—for this consists just of sentences, statements, information, etc. . . . The literary text activates our own faculties, enabling us to recreate the world it presents. The product of this creative activity is what we might call the virtual dimension of the text, which endows it with its reality. This virtual dimension is not the text itself, nor is it the imagination of the reader: it is the coming together of text and imagination.[34]

The aesthetic object is not a well-defined kernel of meaning placed in some manner by the author into a text. Neither is the aesthetic object the result of the free-play of the reader's imagination. In terms that recall Gadamer's definition of meaning, the aesthetic object is given birth when the horizons of reader and text converge (and perhaps sometimes clash). Until that convergence takes place, the meaning of the text (if indeed we should even be referring to the meaning of the text!) is only virtually present. It is not that the reader activates the meaning structures of the text to formulate meaning. Nor is it that the text simply activates the creative activities of the reader. The aesthetic object comes into being through the mutual interaction of the text's structures and the reader's imaginative activities. Without either there simply is no aesthetic object produced. When either pole of this dialogue is absent, communication between a piece of literature and a human mind is impossible. Where there is, on the one hand, no strategic provision on the part of the text for the free-play of the creative human imagination, or, on the other hand, no willingness on the part of the

---

[33] Ibid., 202.

[34] Wolfgang Iser, *The Implied Reader: Patterns of Communication in Prose Fiction from Bunyon to Beckett* (Baltimore: Johns Hopkins University Press, 1974), 278–79.

reader to allow the imagination to play (and to be played by) the text, the game of literary communication never gets off the ground.

Iser's central idea of gaps of indeterminacy has been progressively adopted and applied by biblical scholars. For example, McKnight observes:

> A reader makes sense of one segment and then confronts another segment. What is the relationship between the first segment and the succeeding segments? The text itself does not fill in the connections. The reader must progressively fill in the gaps or blanks and thereby form the segments of the text. The reader is provided potential by the text, but the reader must determine or actualize meaning.[35]

McKnight then offers John 7:1–9 as an example which necessitates the filling of gaps. Jesus is portrayed as going about in Galilee instead of Judea because of danger in Jerusalem. When his brothers encourage him to "leave here and go to Judea so that your disciples may also see the works you are doing" (v. 3), Jesus responds, "Go to the festival yourselves. I am not going to this festival" (v. 8). In the very next segment, however, the text indicates: "But after his brothers had gone to the festival, then he also went, not publicly but as it were in secret" (7:10). A reader will make sense of the first segment by assuming that Jesus simply did not want to go. The next segment forces a complete re-evaluation of what the reader considered the only possible reading of the initial segment. What the reader encounters in the second segment demands that the first segment and its meaning be reconsidered.

Perhaps the most notable proponent of gap filling in the area of biblical studies is Meir Sternberg.[36] He suggests that reading is a copy of life. Just as we move through life groping and stumbling, trying to make sense of events, constructing some pattern by which all the events fit together into a meaningful whole, learning through trial and error, so we do the same thing in reading. The omniscient narrator knows everything, but refuses to tell the reader everything. The narrator creates gaps between segments which the reader must fill by perpetual **introspection** and **retrospection**, constantly engaging in a process of evaluation and reevaluation of the partial information supplied by the narrator. Reading thus becomes a drama, a drama similar to that of living, in which the reader is the principal character. For example, if one reads the sordid story of David and Bathsheba in 2 Sam 11, the man-

---

[35] McKnight, *Postmodern Use of the Bible*, 237.
[36] Sternberg, *Poetics of Biblical Narrative*, 186–229.

ner in which the gaps are filled is central. Why does Uriah not go down to his house after David brought him home from the war? Does Uriah know about his wife's affair with David? Does Uriah think David knows that he knows? Does David suspect that Uriah knows about the affair? The text does not allow an unequivocal answer. The gaps may be filled legitimately by both affirmative and negative answers. Each hypothesis is supported by a number of arguments, but other arguments indicate a flaw and support the opposite answer. This situation, according to Sternberg, is deliberate. The text demands that both hypotheses be utilized to shed their different light on details in the text. The text requires the reader to maintain both hypotheses simultaneously. The text and the reader profit from such an interaction. Sternberg concludes that the meaning of a text is inexhaustible because no context can provide all the keys to all of its possibilities.[37]

Wallace Martin's summary of the effect that readers experience during the process of reading is well stated:

> When a perspective on life proves inadequate, the reader tends to question the entire repertoire of conventional assumptions on which it is based. If open to the experience the text provides, we are likely to find negations of some of our own views; as a result, the self that begins reading a book may not be quite the same as the one that finishes it.[38]

Reading in this sense is a transforming experience, a confrontational dialogue with the possibilities offered by the text. Reading is an engaging, life-changing, rebirthing phenomenon.

Obviously, within this view of the actualization of meaning (where the work is a function of the text), the reader actively participates in the process of communication and in the construction of meaning. If different readers bring different dispositions, skills, preunderstandings, competencies, and traditions to the reading of the text, different readers will experience the text and actualize the work differently. This observation, along with the above description of the reading process, obviously has the potential to introduce a certain amount of subjectivity into the hermeneutical enterprise. This leads us to the flip side of the coin. Just as a reader has a repertoire from which to draw (to be discussed in chs. 8 and 9), texts as written discourse also have what might be called a **literary repertoire**. As Lategan points out,

---

[37] Ibid., 228.
[38] Wallace Martin, *Recent Theories of Narrative* (Ithaca, N.Y.: Cornell University Press, 1986), 162.

inscripturation implies the molding of the message in a specific form. Syntactic and semantic relationships become fixed and cannot be altered at will. Genre, point of view, minor and major stylistic features—all imply a definite choice to the exclusion of other possibilities.[39]

The process of communication operates under the direction of rules which are part of the literary repertoire. A communicatory act simply cannot mean what the rules will not allow. Since written discourse is also communication, with the reader being the author's counterpart in the communication process, there are limitations that the text itself imposes upon the reader. While we may claim that readers can never disco assumptions about the readinver the author's intention, we may, however, assert that any author makesg audience. The assumptions include knowledge about the author's symbolic world and how that symbolic world is reflected in the language. Authors assume that readers bring with them a level of competency. Umberto Eco refers to this body of competency demanded by the text as the text's "encyclopedia," each element of which places restrictions on the reader. We close this chapter with a discussion of Eco's concept of the text's encyclopedia as a means of offering a balance to the tendency towards subjectivity inherent in Iser's process of reading.

Eco is quite aware that literary texts (as well as other artistic productions) are open, lending themselves to a multiplicity of interpretations:

> We see it (the work of art) as the end product of an author's effort to arrange a sequence of communicative effects in such a way that each individual addressee can refashion the original composition devised by the author. . . . As he reacts to the play of stimuli and his own response to their patterning, the individual addressee is bound to supply his own existential credentials, the sense conditioning which is peculiarly his own, a defined culture, a set of tastes, personal inclinations, and prejudices.[40]

The openness of a text does not mean that the text will allow any interpretation whatsoever. The text dictates (at least for the competent readers) the limits of interpretative creativity. What are these textual encyclopedic restraints on the reader? Eco offers seven of them.[41]

---

[39] Lategan and Vorster, *Text and Reality,* 75.

[40] Umberto Eco, *Role of the Reader* (Bloomington: Indiana University Press, 1979), 49.

[41] Ibid., 18–23.

Constraints upon the Reader

Basic dictionary. In our discussion of "gap filling," we learned that the text requests that readers supply information in order to fill out the text. This process begins at the most elementary level of words or the reader's **basic dictionary**. In Luke 7:12 we read, "As he approached the gate of the town, a man who had died was being carried out. He was his mother's only son, and she was a widow." When confronted with the word "widow," the reader immediately knows that the widow is a woman. But a word like "widow" is more complex. For instance, not only is a widow a woman in the physical sense, she is also a woman whose husband is deceased. "At this point the reader does not know as yet which of these *virtual* properties must be *actualized.*"[42] The reader will make a decision only based on further information offered by the text. The terms within a sentence imply properties commonly associated with the terms, and these associations imply still others. When a text involves a highly technical vocabulary, the reader will make associations within strictly defined parameters. Authors are aware of this imposition upon readers and consciously choose their vocabulary in order to place readers within a particular frame of reference.

Rules of co-reference. Since words within any language can have multiple meanings (think of the various meanings of the word "lot"), the meaning of a word at any point within the text must be determined by what Eco calls **rules of co-reference**. Initially, the reader makes sense of terms based upon co-textual relations, i.e., upon the relationships which a word has with the other words within a sentence. As reading progresses, terms that remain ambiguous will be disambiguated through other textual clues.

Contextual and circumstantial selections. As we saw in ch. 1, co-text is concerned with the relationship between words, sentences, and units of a text in the text's linear development. Eco defines contextual selections as "coded abstract possibilities of meeting a given term in connection with other terms belonging to the same semiotic system."[43] Thus, a term may have one connotative meaning in one language system while having a different meaning within another.

Circumstantial selections relate a term with external circumstances. The reader is asked to connect the term or phrase with circumstances in

---

[42] Ibid., 18.
[43] Ibid., 19.

the "extraverbal environment." "Thus 'aye' means 'I vote yes' in the framework of certain types of formal meetings and 'I will obey' in the framework of the Navy."[44] The reader is to infer information implicit within the text but not explicit. The reader fills in the gap, but the **contextual and circumstantial selections** limit the possible inferences which the reader can make.

Rhetorical and stylistic overcoding. When a reader approaches the literary devices of a text, some literary competence is expected. Figures of speech and rhetorical devices require that readers avoid naively applying literal interpretations to these devices and figurative constructions. While figures of speech may lend themselves to polysemy, they also limit denotative interpretations.

Along with the rules governing rhetorical constructions, we may include here the rules of genre. Since we have discussed these rules in some detail in unit II, they should not detain us here. We should be reminded, however, that there is an inseparable link between the way something is said (genre) and what is said (content). The reader should recall the distinction between the natural language and the literary languages of genre and sub-genre that are superimposed or overcoded upon the natural one. By employing a particular genre, or literary device—**rhetorical and stylistic overcoding**—an author sets parameters within which interpretation must take place.

Inferences from common frames. A frame refers to a situation in life which is generally understood throughout a particular culture. Authors may assume that some information or knowledge pervades a culture. Possible frames of common, cultural references include rules of etiquette, agricultural practices, religious traditions and practices, legal concerns, and literature. If an author either consciously or unconsciously refers to one of these frames of reference, it enables the informed reader to recollect an entire body of knowledge. The reader may then perform a correlation between the frame of reference and the elements within the text. A single term may find its significance within a particular frame of reference. When the New Testament authors use the term "circumcision," the entire historical and religious matrix of the practice of circumcision is immediately called to mind. **Common frames of reference**, thus, may supply the context, which limits the reader's interpretation.

---

[44] Ibid.

Inferences by intertextual frames. As Eco claims, "no text is read independently of the reader's experience of other texts."[45] While common frames of reference are usually limited to an individual's culture, **intertextual frames of reference** are the result of an amalgamation of the various literary traditions with which the reader is familiar. When an author alludes to another text or literary tradition, the reader is asked to make inferences based upon a tradition outside the author's own tradition. Through allusions to another tradition or text, the author asks the reader to "overcode" a secondary frame of reference upon the primary one. When the author of 2 Peter makes reference to Isa 53, the reader is expected to overcode the present frame of reference with inferences originating in the context of the suffering servant theme in Isaiah. The reader is in a sense guided in the process of filling in the gaps by the author's intertextual frame of reference.

Ideological overcoding. Every reader confronts a text under the influence of some ideological perspective. The reader may be unaware of this influence, but it is there nonetheless. The counterpart to the structures of the reader's ideological perspective are the structures of the text's ideological perspective. The convergence of these two can be termed **ideological overcoding**. The ideological orientation of the reader is always present and can no more be absent from the interpretive process than stripes from a zebra. They may be suppressed, but not dismissed. An informed reader, however, is aware of the influence that the ideological orientation of the author has upon interpretation. The ideological perspectives of a text are reflected in both textual structure and language. The vocabulary of a text may be such that it seeks to persuade or dissuade a reader in specific areas. In this way, a text shapes and to a great extent seeks to determine a reader's response.

Summary

In developing his theory of the reader's role in relation to the text's encyclopedia, Eco focuses on what he calls the "model reader." The fact is, however, none of us are model readers. Moreover, no two readers are identical; neither are we ever individually the same reader twice. While some readers may share common areas of agreement, each reader has an individual imagination and as such fills out a text in individualistic

---

[45] Ibid., 21.

ways. To compound this sense of subjectivity, literary texts are self-referential. Given this self-referential quality of literary (what we have already referred to as mimetic) texts, the reader is invited, indeed, required to become intimately involved in creating the literary *work*. This is a requirement because the literary *work* (the aesthetic object) comes into being only through the imaginative interaction between the text (the artistic object) and the reader. Some readers, however, are more informed and therefore more competent than others; i.e., some readers are more cognizant of the restraints placed upon the process of reading by the linguistic, figurative, and ideological structures of the text. Authors of truly mimetic texts know their trade well. They know that competent readers read in particular ways, and therefore structure their presentation in ways that either validate the poetics of reading or frustrate them. They can impose one intertextual frame of reference upon another one, demanding that the reader make the connection; they can withhold information at strategic places in the plot; they can provide information in order to foreshadow some other event further along in the story; they can deliberately decontextualize a literary device.

Perhaps we have reached something close to a balance here. It may be a disturbing balance, however, to those who tend to demand something of literary texts and language that is simply unachievable— complete objectivity. Literary texts as specific instances of *parole* have an inherent **polyvalence** because the systems (*langue*) from which they originate are polyvalent. The best which we may claim for such texts is that they establish parameters which may constitute one interpretation more or less legitimate than another. Not all interpretations are equally plausible, just as not all readers are equally skilled. While we assert that readers confront texts with a given repertoire, we may also claim that these same readers should be cognizant of the text's repertoire. If a reader ignores the text's repertoire, an aesthetic object will be actualized, but it will be an inferior one.

REVIEW & STUDY

Key Terms and Concepts

absence	literary work
aesthetic pole	negativity
ambiguity	parole
artistic pole	perspective

basic dictionary
common frames of reference
conceptualization
concretization
contextual and circumstantial
  selections
dialectics of discourse
gaps of indeterminacy
hermeneutic of reduction
ideological overcoding
inscripturation
intertextual frames of reference
introspection
langue
literary allusions
literary repertoire

polyvalence
protension
reference
repertoire of the text
retention
retrospection
rhetorical and stylistic overcoding
rules of co-reference
schemata
strategies
structures of effect
structures of response
textual segments
theme
vacancy
wandering viewpoint

Study Questions

1. Read Gen 2:4–8 in the NRSV. Notice the words in verse 8, "And the LORD God planted a garden in Eden." What creative order do you notice in verses 8 and 9? Now read the same reference in the NIV, noting the words in verse 8, "Now the LORD God had planted a garden in the east, in Eden." What creative order do you notice here? Why do you think the translators of the NIV changed the tense? What does this suggest about translations?

2. Read Judg 5:24–31 in the NRSV. Based upon our discussion of gaps, what are some of the types of gaps you as a reader must fill in for this passage? Now read Judg 4:17–22. Notice that this is a prose account of the events described in 5:24–31. Now reread 5:24–31. In what ways does your second reading differ from the first one?

3. What reasons can you give for judging an interpretation (reading) of a text better than another interpretation?

4. What are some reasons you might give for the importance of genre considerations in the process of reading?

5. In terms of common frames, how might a familiarity (or lack of it) with an author's world influence interpretation?

6. In terms of intertextual frames, what value for interpretation is there in a person being versed in a variety of literary traditions?

7. In concluding this chapter, I have suggested that interpretations of a text might be multiple. I have also suggested that the parameters imposed by the text upon reading make one interpretation more plausible than another. We might refer here to a limited subjectivity. In terms of an individual reader and a text, construct a diagram that illustrates this limited subjectivity.

Suggestions for Further Reading

Croatto, Severino. *Biblical Hermeneutics: Toward a Theory of Reading as the Production of Meaning.* Maryknoll: Orbis, 1987.

Eco, Umberto. *The Role of the Reader: Explorations in the Semiotics of Texts.* Bloomington: Indiana University Press, 1984.

Iser, Wolfgang. *The Act of Reading: A Theory of Aesthetic Response.* Baltimore: Johns Hopkins University Press, 1978.

———. "The Reading Process: A Phenomenological Approach." In *Reader-Response Criticism: From Formalism to Post-Structuralism.* Edited by Jane Tompkins. Baltimore: Johns Hopkins University Press, 1980.

Lategan, Bernard C., and Willem S. Vorster. *Text and Reality: Aspects of Reference in Biblical Texts.* Philadelphia: Fortress, 1985.

McKnight, Edgar V. *The Bible and the Reader.* Philadelphia: Fortress, 1985.

WHAT THE READER BRINGS TO THE TEXT: THE ROLE OF READER PRESUPPOSITIONS

According to Heidegger, interpretation is always grounded in three things—something we have in advance, or "a fore-having," something we see in advance, or "a fore-sight," and something we grasp in advance, or "a fore-conception."

> Whenever something is interpreted as something, the interpretation will be founded essentially upon fore-having, fore-sight, and fore-conception. An interpretation is never a presuppositionless apprehending of something presented to us. If, when one is engaged in a particular concrete kind of interpretation, in the sense of exact textual interpretation, one likes to appeal to what "stands there," then one finds that what "stands there" in the first instance is nothing other than the obvious undiscussed assumption of the person who does the interpreting.[1]

Any interpreter brings to the act of interpretation a **fore-structure**. This fore-structure includes the interpreter's **preunderstanding**, a vast array of **presuppositions**, and the purpose and aim for interpretation. Just as authors write within their social locations, readers interpret within theirs. A **social location** is a matrix of contexts (ideological, cultural, literary, religious, etc.) within which individuals understand, make judgments, value, and think. Contemporary literary and cultural theorists assume that both authors and readers perform their respective tasks within their social locations, never quite able to step outside them to perform objective actions. To put the matter another way, all texts are granted significance by readers making sense of language. Since language is naturally equivocal, capable of generating a number of understandings and responses, misinterpretation is always possible. Standing behind these interpretations and misinterpretations are the

---

[1] Martin Heidegger, *Being and Time* (trans. John Macquarrie and Edward Robinson; New York: Harper & Row, 1962), 191–92.

social locations of readers who, in the case of the biblical texts, are separated from the authors and original readers by time, culture, and ideology, in other words, by social locations. It becomes important, therefore, for interpreters to examine their social locations as much as possible to make an honest assessment of their **interpretive agenda**.

The Role of Preunderstanding

Every reader approaches a text under the guidance of a perspective. Any text is read, perceived, and interpreted within a preexistent structure of reality. All understanding and interpretation proceed from a prior understanding or a system of making sense of reality. There is no such thing as a pure reading, an objective interpretation. Since reality is infinite, no person can reach outside the realm of time and space to give an objective account of reality. As part of the structure of reality, I can never completely escape the present. I am always being affected by my present horizon of understanding, a horizon within which and from which all things are intelligible to me. Without this horizon of understanding, this world of preunderstanding, discovering meaning would be simply impossible. Without a preunderstanding, understanding is impossible.

A reader may approach a text without presupposing the results of reading, but the same reader will never engage a text without some preunderstanding, some specific questions about the text, or some idea about what the text itself is about.[2] Readers always wear tinted glasses and make sense of a text according to the particular shade of the lenses. New Testament exegete Günther Bornkamm recognizes this:

> Only the bearing of life on relevant matters that makes itself felt in pre-understanding can establish communication between the text and the interpreter and make possible a proper examination of the text, allowing the interpreter to ask himself about the text and to revise it on the basis of his own self-understanding.[3]

This is especially true for canonical texts, because they impose upon readers a receptivity that other texts do not.

---

[2] Rudolf Bultmann, *Existence and Faith* (ed. and trans. Schubert Ogden; London: Hodder & Stoughton, 1961), 289–96.

[3] Günther Bornkamm, "The Theology of Rudolf Bultmann," in *The Theology of Rudolf Bultmann* (ed. Charles W. Kegley; London: SCM, 1966), 7.

When the believer and believing community read the Scriptures, they do so as "believers." This means they already accept the faith presented and presumed by the text and thus hear the sacred text in light of the prior faith. The text is thus approached with a "preunderstanding." The text is heard within the context of the faith. A secondary consequence of this pre-understanding and contextual hearing is the tendency to ignore or indulge differences, inconsistencies, and problems within the text. The reader fills out and smooths over differences and difficulties within the text in light of the overall cohesion of the canon and in terms of the community's faith perspective.[4]

The community of faith provides the colored lenses through which the reader views the text.

Reader Presuppositions

Perhaps Terry Eagleton is correct in his idea of textual rewriting.[5] Every time a text is read, it is in essence unconsciously rewritten by the reader under the pressures of presuppositions attending the reader's horizon of understanding. The presuppositions through which any act of perceiving and interpreting reality is filtered are many. Since it is not within the purview of this text to enumerate the almost infinite number of possible presuppositions, I simply offer several categories of presuppositions and then discuss two of these categories: theological and methodological.

Presuppositions might be more appropriately called assumptions. Presuppositions, however, are not synonymous with beliefs or convictions. Presuppositions are axiomatic, a priori, unconscious assumptions. They are not generally subjected to examination or exegesis, but they impact exegesis and interpretation profoundly. Once a reader realizes that he or she holds a certain presupposition, then it may become a belief which is open to examination and modification. Nevertheless, the presupposition which becomes a belief still exerts a powerful control on interpretation. When these presuppositions and beliefs are taken as a whole at any one point in the hermeneut's career, we have the framework within which all texts are perceived and interpreted. This **interpretive framework** consists of presuppositions, beliefs, and attitudes that are ethical, doctrinal, denominational, philosophical, theological,

---

[4] Hayes and Holladay, *Biblical Exegesis,* 123.
[5] Eagleton, *Literary Theory,* 12.

and methodological. Obviously, these classifications constitute the elements of a person's worldview; they are not consciously categorized but exist in an ever-changing process of interrelatedness.

Theological Presuppositions

The biblical texts speak to different people in different ways in each historical period because people hold different worldviews. Also, biblical truth is discovered and expressed within a particular universe of meaning. Interpretations, therefore, must be consistent with the established interpretive framework of the interpretive community. The worldview of the interpretive community sets the parameters within which interpretations are accepted or rejected.

Theological presuppositions are varied and numerous. Traditionally, however, they have focused on the Bible itself. This focus, therefore, crucially influences interpretation. Some of the areas of central focus have been the concepts of faith, **revelation**, **word of God**, and inspiration, including issues of authority and history.

Faith

Duncan Ferguson makes the following claim:

> Faith is the necessary preunderstanding for the interpretation of the Christian faith. . . . Faith is firmly rooted in historical probability, though it is born not of historical knowledge but of God. Historical evidence may suggest that God is present and acting in the events of history, but it cannot supply the personal experience of trust in and commitment to the risen Lord.[6]

What allows Ferguson to make such a claim? Central to his view is the idea that faith originates in an experience. This experience is confrontational. A person experiences deity on a personal, mystical level, thereby receiving a knowledge of God; not a cognitive knowledge, but an experiential knowledge, a participatory knowledge. An individual does not receive this faith knowledge through a study of God or the Bible. The assumption, however, is more complex than this. The faith knowledge originating in God centers in the Christ event. The assumption is that knowledge of God comes from God's self-disclosure in

---

[6] Ferguson, *Biblical Hermeneutics*, 63–64.

Jesus Christ. But the Christ event *is* historically grounded. Further, the primary source for understanding this historically grounded Christ event is the Bible. Faith knowledge obviously influences how we will read and interpret the biblical account of the Christ event. Therefore, from this perspective, a person must necessarily claim that faith knowledge and historical study are standard assumptions for doing hermeneutics. These two assumptions obviously create a circularity. A pre-posture of faith means that we read with a predetermined attitude; and what we read impacts our faith knowledge by enlarging, modifying, or changing it in a variety of ways.

Not all interpreters accept the idea that faith is a necessary presupposition to interpretation. It is suggested that a person does not require (or desire) an experience of God in order to rationally interpret a written document. Even if the author claimed such an experience, the written document generated by the experience communicates with literary, religious, and philosophical categories of the author's culture. To interpret requires only a knowledge of those categories, not an experience similar to the author's.

Revelation

In the context of biblical hermeneutics, revelation is understood as the process of God's self-disclosure to humans. This initiative by God presupposes in humans the capacity to respond. The concept of divine revelation has been categorized in numerous ways—historical, temporal revelation, natural revelation (God has revealed himself in the world of nature), and personal revelation, which constitutes the faith knowledge discussed above. The concept of revelation, however, is closely associated with the Bible. This is especially the case if the Bible is in one way or another equated with the word of God.

Word of God

A common position is that God's revelation is his word. But how does this concept relate to the Bible? First, I might assume that the word of God (the content of revelation) is the same as the Bible. In this view, the Bible is the standard for the Christian's faith and practice.

A second position concerning the relationship between the word of God and the Bible depends upon the identification of God's word and God's saving activities throughout history, culminating in the Christ event. These activities are recorded in the Bible, and God speaks through

these activities. Actually, the Bible is a record of God's redemptive activities, and human responses to them. According to this view, the
Bible is not God's word, but gives access to it. God speaks to humanity
through the Bible, but the Bible is not God's word.

Third, there is the position that Jesus is God's ultimate revelation,
the living Word of God. The Bible is the essential historical witness to
this supreme revelation of God in Jesus, but it is not itself God's revelation. The Bible constitutes *the* access to God's supreme revelation or
word in Jesus.

A fourth position claims that the Bible *becomes* the word of God in
proclamation. As the Bible is proclaimed, so it is assumed, the Spirit
of God uses it to produce a faith response. A faith-hearing results in a
movement towards conformity to a distinctive Christian lifestyle (which
is, of course, defined by the particular community of faith in its interpretation of the Bible).

Each of these positions affects how an individual community interprets the Bible. If I assume that the Bible is synonymous with the
word of God, my interpretive approach may be characterized by a
sense of literalism along with the deification of the Bible. If the Bible
is a record of God's word to humans in history, I will probably fall
squarely within the historical-critical camp. If the Bible is the primary
access to God's supreme revelation in Jesus Christ, my interpretive
method will concentrate on the New Testament and those passages in
the Hebrew Bible which I perceive to pertain to Jesus as the Messiah.
If the Bible becomes the word of God in proclamation, then the interpretive community must define a proper pedagogy for proclamation.
An interpretive community cannot countenance just any proclamation. There must be a proclamational canon. But where does one secure
such a canon? From the Bible, of course. Further, if proclamation creates a response, how do we judge the difference between an acceptable
and unacceptable response? By recourse to the Bible, naturally.

Inspiration

The assumption that the Bible is "inspired" centers in the claim
that in some manner, God superintended the writing of the Scriptures.
Just what this idea of superintendence entails is a debated issue. Terms
such as "infallible," "inerrant," "plenary inspiration," **verbal inspiration**," and "clarity" are used to describe this superintendence or the result of it. To claim verbal inspiration for the Bible presupposes that this
superintendence goes beyond the concepts or ideas in Scripture to in-

clude the very words themselves. Such a view does not preclude the possibility that the words reflect the style and personality of the writer. So, for example, Luke's style and diction may reflect a more sophisticated level of literary and academic training or talent than does the Gospel of Mark.

Verbal inspiration differs from the **dictation theory** in that the latter holds that God dictated each and every word of Scripture to each individual author and that they wrote Scripture in a robotic fashion, faithfully and inerrantly recording exactly what was received. Each author simply functioned as a stenographer. Part of this view assumes that the Scriptures are clear in their presentation and that the goal of all interpretation is to articulate this plain sense.

A third view of inspiration might be called **conceptual inspiration**. According to this view, God communicated a message to an individual through a dream, vision, mental impression, or some other means, and left the author free to choose the form in which this message would be conveyed. Between the divine act of inspiration and the human act of inscripturation, there exists a gap. This gap allows for the creativity of the author in choice of genre, literary devices, and strategies. This also allows for the different levels of authorial competence and takes into account that human agents differed in personality and historical setting. Each author composed by choosing from a personal vocabulary, literary repertoire, and experience those words, forms, and genres that best conveyed the message.

One interesting assumption relating to divine inspiration is that since God is the author of language, the language of God's revelation (the Bible) is transparent and unambiguous. Those who claim such transparency and non-ambiguity for divinely inspired texts usually do not make the same claim for other, secular texts. These assumptions force the interpreter to further assume that sacred texts must be interpreted differently than secular ones. Other scholars, however, ask on what basis we should presume to interpret sacred texts differently from secular ones if the authors of the former did not consciously write with such a view in mind. Indeed, if we assume that God is the "ultimate" author, why should we also assume that God reveals or speaks through language any differently than any human author? Why should the poetics of a sacred text be different from that of similar secular texts of the same historical matrix? Even God himself cannot transcend the conventions of communication if he wishes to be understood. Why claim linguistic transparency for sacred texts and ambiguity for secular ones? If God is *the* author of language (as some claim) and if language is ambiguous (as most claim), then why would we ever assume that God would transcend his own authorial ambiguity? For a more detailed discussion of social location, see Ideological Criticism in the Appendix.

Summary

Theological preunderstanding and presuppositions as components of a person's worldview are constitutive of meaning. Any single understanding and explanation of a text proceeds from a prior understanding and set of presuppositions. In a sense, then, all interpreters peer "through a glass darkly."

The range of theological presuppositions is as varied and extensive as the range of religious communities. Concepts such as scriptural authority, the Bible's relation to history, progressive revelation, and canonicity are part of a long and growing list. A discussion of theological presuppositions, not to mention the other presuppositional categories, would fill volumes. Nevertheless, since methodological presuppositions exert such a powerful influence upon interpretation, a detailed treatment of these follows in ch. 9.

REVIEW & STUDY

Key Terms and Concepts

conceptual inspiration
dictation theory
fore-structure
interpretive agenda
interpretive framework
presuppositions

preunderstanding
revelation
social location
verbal inspiration
word of God

Study Questions

1. In the Apocrypha, read Judith 13:1–26. Now read Judg 4:17–22 and 5:24–27. Did you read these texts differently? If so, was it due to presuppositions concerning the nature of the two books? Explain.

2. Suppose a person were to ask you the following: "Do you believe the Word of God is inspired?" How would you answer? If you were to answer *yes,* can you be certain that you both mean the same thing? Why or why not?

3. Speculate on the following statement: There is something inherently unique about the writings of the Bible that requires that they be interpreted differently than other writings.

Suggestions for Further Reading

Barr, James. *The Bible in the Modern World.* New York: Harper & Row, 1973.

Childs, Brevard S. *Biblical Theology in Crisis.* Philadelphia: Westminster, 1970.

Ferguson, Duncan. *Biblical Hermeneutics: An Introduction.* Atlanta: John Knox, 1986.

Merleau-Ponty, Maurice. *Consciousness and the Acquisition of Language.* Translated by Hugh J. Silverman. Evanston: Northwestern University Press, 1964.

Morgan, Robert, with John Barton. *Biblical Interpretation.* New York: Oxford University Press, 1988.

III

ILLUSTRATIVE METHODS THAT FOCUS ON THE WORLD IN FRONT OF THE TEXT

Formalist critics—those critics who claim that the text itself provides the objective standard of meaning—tend to view the text as static, an autonomous literary object which somehow contains within itself meaning awaiting to be grasped. In the view of text-centered critics, textual meaning is independent of both author and reader. Once the text leaves the hands of the author, the author's intention and entire matrix of originating circumstances lose any claim of being constitutive of meaning. Reader-centered critics, however, have called into question the formalists' presupposition of textual autonomy. The pendulum of interpretive emphasis swings in the direction of the reader's role in the construction of meaning. Affective critics (as some reader-response critics are called) have begun to ask significant questions: Why do we value some texts above others? Why do we continue to read and value texts even if the originating circumstances are irretrievable? Is it really legitimate to talk about meaning apart from a consideration of what happens when we read? What *does* happen when we read? Why do we respond to certain texts in certain ways? Reader-centered theories of interpretation in various ways and degrees attempt to answer these and similar questions as they pertain to the dynamic interaction between text and reader, an interaction with a resultant reader response.

The so-called affective critics constitute a multifarious group. Along a continuum between text and reader, affective critics may be placed according to the relative role which each critic ascribes to the text in the determination of meaning.[1]

---

[1] See Donald Keesey, "Reader-Response Criticism: Audience as Context," in *Contexts for Criticism* (4th ed.; ed. Donald Keesey; Boston: McGraw Hill, 2003), 129–37.

Reader-Response Criticism

Since we discussed in detail the reading process in ch. 7, in order to avoid duplication, I only summarize the reader-response approach to criticism here.

When a tree falls in the forest, is a sound produced if there is no one present to hear it fall? The falling tree produces sound waves which must pass over someone's eardrum creating a vibration before sound is produced. This might be expressed in the equation, waves + eardrum = sound. The sound is the result of the interaction of two objects—waves and eardrum. In a similar fashion, reader-response critics view literary meaning as bipolar. Meaning is produced through the interaction between a text and a reader. Until a reader picks up a text and begins reading it, a literary work does not exist. Most reader-response critics define a literary "work" as the product of the interaction between a literary "text" and a reader. This literary work exists only as a potentiality, a virtual entity somewhere between the text (artistic pole) and the reader (aesthetic pole).

Within a narrative, time does not correspond exactly to real time. Neither does narrative sequence necessarily correspond to the actual sequence of events of the real or narrative world. Literary devices—flashback, summary, expansion, or even digression—may confront the reader. The reader is then called upon to sort through this narrative, sequencing it to form a "story." The narrative is the text; the story is the literary work. The equation is similar to the one above: artistic pole + aesthetic pole = artistic work.

Not only does a narrative text require a sequential reformulation by the reader, but authors frame their texts with the intention of involving readers. In a sense, authors expect readers to enter into a literary covenant with them in order to jointly create an artistic work. Most reader-response critics agree that authors allow for reader involvement by creating gaps within the text which readers must fill.

The two ideas of sequencing a text and filling in gaps (discussed in ch. 7) may seem innocent until we realize that this process varies with each individual reader. For reader-response critics, not only does a text exist in a state of indeterminacy, but so does a reader. As the literary work is always coming into being, the reader is also coming into being. Both literary work and reader are only possibilities.

Not only do reader-response critics reject the idea that a text is an autonomous object, they also reject the idea that readers are autonomous and free to read as they please. Readers are always submerged within social contexts exerting profound influences. An individual's entire social context and degree of involvement within that social context profoundly affect the way that person will actualize the text, what questions will be put to the text, and how that individual will perceive and fill in the gaps presented by the text. The end product of this dual indeterminacy (of text and reader) is a plurality of interpretations. If both the artistic and aesthetic poles are ultimately indeterminate, there exists the possibility of an infinite number of "artistic works."

Iser, whom we have already discussed, moves further away from the text toward the reader with his theory of the "implied reader." According to Iser, there exists within a text a potential reader who

> embodies all those predispositions necessary for a literary work to exercise its effect. These predispositions are laid down, not by an empirical outside reality, but by the text itself. Consequently, the implied reader as a concept has its roots firmly planted in the structure of the text; he is a construct and in no way to be identified with any real reader.[2]

The implied reader would possess the necessary competence in the conventions assumed by the text in order to "decode" the text. Within every text there are those "gaps of indeterminacy" which the reader must fill. In the process of such gap filling, the resultant interaction between reader and text produces the "work." But the work is always in a virtual state, because real readers can only approximate the competence of the "implied reader." Meaning, consequently, can never be reduced to a single, objective meaning latent within the text. Rather, it exists in the interaction between the text and the reader. According to Iser, however, the text presents several perspectives between which the reader shuttles. Together with the gaps, these perspectives, or textual clues, guide the reader in formulating the "work." Obviously, while Iser moves toward more reader involvement in the construction of meaning, the text remains crucial in its role of establishing parameters for reading. His theory also allows for one reading to be more plausible than another, depending upon how closely the real reader approximates the competence of the ideal reader.

Autobiographical Criticism

Also known in the area of biblical criticism, autobiographical criticism encourages critics to include their personal experiences in their

---

[2] Iser, *The Act of Reading,* 34.

readings of literary texts. Its method of persuasion is to call upon other readers to "believe this, because it happened to me."[3]

In the early 1990s, Jane Tompkins and Nancy K. Miller pioneered this form of criticism in Tompkins's "Me and My Shadow" in *The Intimate Critique: Autobiographical Literary Criticism*[4] and Miller's *Getting Personal: Feminist Occasions and Other Autobiographical Acts.*[5] While autobiographical critics differ in many aspects, they agree on the key concepts of autobiographical criticism.

First is the focus on the critic's life as a major contributing factor to understanding the diversity of interpretations. Each critic perceives a text through a different social location with a number of identity markers including race, ethnicity, geography, class, religion, gender, age, education, physical characteristics, marital status, and employment status. One critic/reader will emphasize a certain aspect of the text while another will downplay that aspect. Thus, for autobiographical criticism to be taken seriously, it must entail an "outspoken involvement on the part of the critic with the subject matter."[6] It requires personal self-exploration, self-reflection, and self-analysis.

Second is the implication of choosing one interpretation over other possible and legitimate ones. By recognizing the positive role of the interpreter's personal voice, one can see that interpreters choose among equally legitimate and plausible interpretations.[7] The key responsibility of the interpreter is to recognize how he or she came to value or configure aspects of the text rather than how another interpreter has understood the same aspects. This internal dialogue should occur not only between two interpreters but between two interpretations by the same critic as well. The openness to the personal voice in autobiographical criticism can cause an interpreter's critique to change with each rereading because of the new experiences brought to the table. In other words, each time a critic/reader reads the text, his or her personal

---

[3] Ibid.

[4] Jane Tompkins, "Me and My Shadow," in *The Intimate Critique: Autobiographical Literary Criticism* (ed. Diana Freedman et al.; Durham: Duke University Press, 1993), 23–40.

[5] Nancy K. Miller, *Getting Personal: Feminist Occasions and Other Autobiographical Acts* (London: Routledge, 1991).

[6] Mary Ann Caws, *Women of Bloomsbury: Virginia, Vanessa, and Carrington* (London: Routledge, 1990), 2.

[7] Daniel Patte, "The Guarded Personal Voice of a Male European-American Biblical Scholar," in *Personal Voice in Biblical Interpretation* (ed. Ingrid Rosa Kitzberger; New York: Routledge, 1999), 22.

voice picks a different aspect to focus on. Consequently, the choice of one interpretation over another, whether between two critics or two interpretations, is completely subjective and must be determined by the individual.

The third key deals with the personal voice of the critic/reader. The personal voice is characterized by a certain pattern of relationships with others and is explained by clarifying for whom the interpretation is performed. It involves acknowledging that the interpretations are as constructed, partial, and selective as the personal voice is tentative, changing, and fleeting. Expressing one's personal voice is not easy, however, because of the intimacy involved. "To write about how our personal lives, economic situations, and prejudices affect our interpretation . . . is to reveal the tenuousness and interested nature of our exegetical moves."[8]

Fourth, in autobiographical criticism, not only is the critic's identity important, but so is "the question of identity in the interaction between author and reader," which is usually referred to as the autobiographical pact. The pact claims to be referential even though Kitzberger believes an awareness exists that, to a degree, everything that represents oneself is at the same time "fictional and constructed."[9] This realization that the critic is sharing his or her identity allows the reader to trust that what is written actually refers to the critic's real self. The critic sharing his experiences results in the reader acknowledging and responding to the critic's interpretation, which develops the mutual agreement of the critic and reader.

Fifth is the mode of interpretive expression, the form in which an interpretation is conveyed. According to Olivia Frey, traditional academic interpretations assume a predictable form, which she refers to as adversarial. Frey characterizes this method as reflecting the critic's sarcasm and condescending attitude. The goal of this method is "to establish cognitive authority not only by demonstrating the value of one's own idea but also by demonstrating the weakness or error in the ideas of others. At the heart of the literary critical enterprise seems to be competition, not cooperation."[10] Further, according to Frey, most of the signals that

---

[8] Janice Anderson and Jeffery Staley, "Taking It Personally: Introduction," *Semeia* 72 (1995): 12.

[9] Ingrid Rosa Kitzberger, "Pre-liminaries," in *Autobiographical Biblical Criticism* (Leiden: Deo, 2002), 7.

[10] Olivia Frey, "Beyond Literary Darwinism: Women's Voices and Critical Discourse," in *The Intimate Critique: Audibiographical Literary Criticism* (ed. Diana Freedman et al.; Durham: Duke University Press, 1993), 48.

young scholars receive from their profession "indicate that this is our business—to refute, repudiate, or attack."[11] Consequently, any criticism of texts that are driven by the adversarial method always "treats literature as problems to be solved, and critics will frequently go to great lengths to solve them, sometimes at the expense of knowledge and understanding."[12] In addition, "we direct all of our creative efforts toward protecting ourselves and defending our theories."[13] Within this framework, creative thinking suffers. To counter this adversarial method, Frey calls for a "relational ethic" in which essays about literature should be "personal, revelatory, non adversarial. They are non hierarchal and mixed-genre, often validating a variety of voices—the critic's, her students', other critics' voices."[14] Frey further argues that literary critical activity is and should be intensely personal, motivated by the desire to "connect with someone else in a meaningful way."[15] Literary criticism, i.e., reading and writing about literature, should be forms of creation and should be expressed in a variety of forms other than the philosophical, persuasive essay (e.g., by hymn, poetry, letter, journal, diary). This language of expression should be "accessible, concrete, and real" and absolutely one's personal voice.

A final key has to do with structure. Fernando Segovia argues that

> structure should not be seen as residing in the text itself . . . but rather in the interchange between the text and reader, or that structure should not be approached as fixed and stable but rather as variable and dependent on readers.[16]

The focus on a universal reader gave way to a concern for the real reader, which resulted in the understanding that real readers can only be approached in terms of "the manifold and highly complex dimensions of human identity."[17] Segovia claims that this realization allowed critics to recognize that an objective and impartial reader does not exist, so interpretation is always contextual and ideological.[18] When

---

[11] Ibid.

[12] Ibid., 60.

[13] Ibid.

[14] Ibid., 58.

[15] Ibid.

[16] Fernando F. Segovia, "My Personal Voice: The Making of a Postcolonial Critic," in *Personal Voice in Biblical Interpretation* (ed. Ingrid Rosa Kitzberger; New York: Routledge, 1999), 28.

[17] Ibid., 30.

[18] Ibid., 31.

readers interpret, these contextual and ideological factors are brought to the text, resulting in diverse reactions.

In the last two decades, autobiographical criticism has found a home in biblical studies. According to Staley, "autobiographical interests have found their way into biblical studies as scholars have begun to think and write about the social and ideological constraints that have formed them as real readers of the Bible."[19] According to Kitzberger, "autobiographical biblical criticism implies the choice of one interpretation over other possible and legitimate ones. Taking over responsibility for one's interpretations, one's knowledge about the meaning of a text, and entering into dialogue with others who have chosen other interpretations is thus a truly ethical practice."[20] A goal of autobibliocriticism (the name that Staley gives to autobiographical criticism applied to biblical studies) is "to raise personal voices in biblical studies precisely so that we all might be more aware of how we can bring crucial understanding to bear upon the ordinariness of all our readings."[21] Furthermore, the acknowledgment of the personal voice in interpretations should not undermine in any way the authority the Scriptures possess.[22] Instead, it should complement the study of the Bible and further people's understanding. Mark Brett sets forth five reasons for inserting the personal voice into biblical interpretation:

1. showing how one's life can be configured by a biblical narrative;
2. using one's life story to form a hypothesis about literary structure;
3. exploring the ways in which personal experience might lead us to formulate questions and methods of research;
4. describing how a change in political commitments provoked the rereading of a particular text; and
5. evaluating the norms expressed through biblical texts.[23]

---

[19] Jeffery L. Staley, "Autobiography," in *Handbook of Postmodern Biblical Interpretation* (ed. A. K. M. Adam; St. Louis: Chalice, 2000), 14.

[20] Kitzberger, "Pre-liminaries," 5.

[21] James Staley, "What Is Critical about Autobiographical Biblical Criticism?" in *Autobiographical Biblical Criticism* (ed. Ingrid Rosa Kitzberger; Leiden: Deo, 2002), 19.

[22] Patte, "The Guarded Personal Voice," 17.

[23] Mark G. Brett, "Self Criticism, Cretan Liars, and the Sly Redactors of Genesis," in *Autobiographical Biblical Criticism* (ed. Ingrid Rosa Kitzberger; Leiden: Deo, 2002), 117–18.

When these reasons are considered, the personal voice becomes a tool that allows critics to feel free to contemplate the relationship between the biblical text and personal experience. It also points the way to a self-reflective and contextualized biblical criticism.[24]

Since most biblical interpretation is about the primary text, readers inevitably reconstruct the text out of the materials of their own identities and interpretative traditions.[25] For example, Mikeal Parsons offers autobiographical reflections on the Parable of the Prodigal Son in Luke 15 as well as his own homecoming story. He tells of the time in his life when he was figuratively eating with the pigs and how he came out of this to reunite with his father after many years of bitterness. Below is an excerpt:

> I thought of my own life, how this wound of my father was . . . a part of his legacy to me. And, I realized how my own sense of inadequacy as a man had helped sign the death warrant on several significant relationships. I got a piece of myself back that day that made me a little more whole. The Prodigal Father and the Wandering Son wept and embraced each other. And rejoicing in that which was lost and was now found, they made their way, hand in hand, back home.[26]

Resources

Anderson, Janice, and Jeffery Staley. "Taking It Personally: Introduction." *Semeia* 72 (1995): 7–16.

Brett, Mark G. "Self Criticism, Cretan Liars, and the Sly Redactors of Genesis." Pages 114–32 in *Autobiographical Biblical Criticism*. Edited by Ingrid Rosa Kitzberger. Leiden: Deo, 2002.

Carlton, Peter. "Rereading Middlemarch, Rereading Myself." Pages 237–44 in *The Intimate Critique: Autobiographical Literary Criticism*. Edited by Diane P. Freedman, Olivia Frey, and Frances Murphy Zauhar. Durham: Duke University Press, 1993.

Caws, Mary Ann. *Women of Bloomsbury: Virginia, Vanessa, and Carrington*. London: Routledge, 1990.

Freedman, Diane P., Olivia Frey, and Frances Murphy Zauhar, eds. *The Intimate Critique: Autobiographical Literary Criticism*. Durham: Duke University Press, 1993.

---

[24] Anderson and Staley, "Taking It Personally," 11–16.

[25] Brett, "Self Criticism," 114.

[26] Mikeal C. Parsons, "Hand in Hand: Autobiographical Reflections on Luke 15," *Semeia* 72 (1995): 137.

Frey, Olivia. "Beyond Literary Darwinism: Women's Voices and Critical Discourse." Pages 41–65 in *The Intimate Critique: Autobiographical Literary Criticism*. Edited by Diane P. Freedman, Olivia Frey, and Frances Murphy Zauhar. Durham: Duke University Press, 1993.

Jouve, Nicole. *White Woman Speaks with Forked Tongue: Criticism as Autobiography*. London: Routledge, 1991.

Kaufman, Linda S. "The Long Goodbye: Against Personal Testimony, or an Infant Grifter Grows Up." Pages 258–77 in *American Feminist Thought at Century's End*. Edited by Linda S. Kaufman. Cambridge, Mass.: Blackwell, 1993.

Kitzberger, Ingrid Rosa. "Pre-liminaries." Pages 1–11 in *Autobiographical Biblical Criticism*. Leiden: Deo, 2002.

Murfin, Foss, and Supryia Ray. "Personal Criticism." Page 339 in *The Bedford Glossary of Critical and Literary Terms*. Boston: Bedford/St. Martin's, 2006.

Parsons, Mikeal C. "Hand in Hand: Autobiographical Reflections on Luke 15." *Semeia* 72 (1995): 125–52.

Patte, Daniel. "The Guarded Personal Voice of a Male European-American Biblical Scholar." Pages 12–24 in *Personal Voice in Biblical Interpretation*. Edited by Ingrid Rosa Kitzberger. New York: Routledge, 1999.

Segovia, Fernando F. "My Personal Voice: The Making of a Postcolonial Critic." Pages 23–37 in *Personal Voice in Biblical Interpretation*. Edited by Ingrid Rosa Kitzberger. New York: Routledge, 1999.

Staley, Jeffery L. "Autobiography." Pages 14–19 in *Handbook of Postmodern Biblical Interpretation*. Edited by A. K. M. Adam. St. Louis: Chalice, 2000.

———. "What Is Critical about Autobiographical Biblical Criticism?" Pages 12–33 in *Autobiographical Biblical Criticism*. Edited by Ingrid Rosa Kitzberger. Leiden: Deo, 2002.

Tompkins, Jane. "Me and My Shadow." Pages 23–40 in *The Intimate Critique: Autobiographical Literary Criticism*. Edited by Diane P. Freedman, Olivia Frey, and Frances Murphy Zauhar. Durham: Duke University Press, 1993.

Voelz, James W. "A Self-Conscious Reader-Response Interpretation of Romans 13:1–7." Pages 156–69 in *Personal Voice in Biblical Interpretation*. Edited by Ingrid Rosa Kitzberger. New York: Routledge, 1999.

Zauhar, Frances Murphy. "Creative Voices: Women Reading and Women's Writing." Pages 103–16 in *The Intimate Critique: Autobio-*

graphical Literary Criticism. Edited by Diane P. Freedman, Olivia Frey, and Frances Murphy Zauhar. Durham: Duke University Press, 1993.

Feminist Criticism

A wide variety of interpretive methodology occurs within feminist criticism. In what follows, I attempt to capture the essence of feminist criticism by referring to several of its most notable proponents. Yet while a variety of methodological emphases exist, all feminist critics proceed from a common assumption and several underlying principles. The common assumption is that all the biblical texts were written in the contexts of patriarchal cultures and have been subsequently translated and interpreted within patriarchal cultures. These patriarchal contexts have dehumanized and marginalized women, treating them as second-class, inferior beings. Within these contexts, women traditionally function on a secondary level and are significant as human beings to the degree that their actions and lives support and further the superior function of men. Women are treated as a means to patriarchal ends, rather than as ends within themselves. All feminist interpretation in one way or another seeks to depatriarchalize not only the biblical texts but also theological traditions and systems that are based upon patriarchal interpretations of the patriarchal texts. The interpretive principles of feminist hermeneutics are threefold:

1. Virtually all feminist critics place extreme importance upon the feminist consciousness.[27] Briefly put, this feminist consciousness concerns recognizing women's own unique experience as a way of understanding Scripture. Two primary convictions function within feminist consciousness: equality and mutuality. The conviction of equality demands that women's interests and aims (including interpretive ones) are as valid as those of men. Any inequality in gender must be rejected out of hand. The conviction of mutuality demands that women (indeed all persons) be viewed as both autonomous and rational beings. Each person stands as an individual, but because all are primarily rational, there exists a universal bond between persons—a bond which transcends roles. Any interpretation

---

[27] See Margaret A. Farley, "Feminist Consciousness and Scripture," in *Feminist Interpretation of the Bible* (ed. Letty M. Russell; Philadelphia: Westminster, 1985), 41–51.

which vitiates this feminist consciousness is to be rejected as having no binding authority.

2. All women are fully human and are to be valued as such. Any biblical passage or interpretation which devalues the humanity of women cannot be accepted as binding revelation. Elisabeth Schüssler Fiorenza states it clearly: "only the nonsexist and nonandrocentric traditions of the Bible and the nonoppressive traditions of biblical interpretations have the theological authority of revelation."[28]

3. Because women have found that traditional interpretations of their identity regularly contradict their own identity consciousness and self-experience, the basic criterion for judging truth is women's experience. "New understandings must be tested for truth (for accuracy and adequacy) against the reality of women's lives as revealed in women's experience."[29] Rosemary Ruether defines women's experience as the premier interpretive key:

> that experience which arises when women become critically aware of these falsifying and alienating experiences imposed upon them as women by a male-dominated culture. . . . Women's experience, then, implies a conversion experience through which women get in touch with, name, judge their experiences of sexism in patriarchal society.[30]

Within that group of feminist critics who see the Bible as a vital part of their faith experience, there exists a plurality of approaches and interpretations.

Katharine Doob Sakenfeld and Rosemary Radford Ruether. Katharine Doob Sakenfeld lists three optional approaches to the biblical texts: (1) Feminist critics may use texts about women in order to offset the famous (or infamous) texts which have been traditionally used "against" women; (2) feminists may refer to the Bible in general (as opposed to specific texts) in order to discover a theological perspective which in turn may be employed against patriarchalism; and (3) feminists may look to bib-

---

[28] Elisabeth Schüssler Fiorenza, "A Feminist Biblical Hermeneutics: Biblical Interpretation and Liberation Theology," in *The Challenge of Liberation Theology: A First-World Response* (ed. Brian Mahan and L. Dale Richesin; Maryknoll: Orbis, 1981), 108.

[29] Farley, "Feminist Consciousness and Scripture," 50.

[30] Rosemary Radford Ruether, "Feminist Interpretation: A Method of Correlation," in *Feminist Interpretation of the Bible* (ed. Letty M. Russell; Philadelphia: Westminster, 1985), 114–15.

lical texts about women in order to "learn from the intersection of history and stories of ancient and modern women living in patriarchal cultures."[31] These are not exclusive options, but rather, broad categories within which critics may move back and forth.

Approaches within the first option may reinterpret texts that marginalize women or they may bring to bear on these texts other texts which seem to portray women in a more positive light. For example, Gen 2–3 may be reinterpreted in such a way that women and men are seen as equal, and mutual subjection can be claimed as the import of Eph 5. Gal 3:28 may be brought to bear on texts such as 1 Tim 2:13–14 and 1 Cor 14:34–35.

The second option contains approaches that attempt to extrapolate from the Bible in general a perspective which is in its essence Christian. Exactly what this central witness or perspective is varies from critic to critic. One of the best-known approaches is that of Rosemary Ruether. Ruether examines the entire biblical text and discovers a prophetic principle (what we might call a prophetic consciousness or prophetic impulse) which is present at different places and times within the biblical canon. According to Ruether, this prophetic principle rejects every "elevation of one social group against others as image and agent of God, every use of God to justify social domination and subjugation."[32] She describes this principle as follows:

> By the prophetic-messianic tradition I mean to name not simply a particular body of texts, which then would be understood as standing as a canon within the canon. Rather, what I mean by the prophetic-messianic tradition is a critical perspective and process through which the biblical tradition constantly reevaluates, in new contexts, what is truly the liberating Word of God, over against both the sinful deformations of contemporary society and also the limitations of past biblical traditions, which saw in part and understood in part, and whose partiality may have even become a source of sinful injustice and idolatry.[33]

Ruether asserts that religion (along with sacred texts and interpretations of such texts) throughout history has sanctioned existing social orders

---

[31] Katharine Doob Sakenfeld, "Feminist Uses of Biblical Materials," in *Feminist Interpretation of the Bible* (ed. Letty M. Russell; Philadelphia: Westminster, 1985), 56–64. See also idem, *Faithfulness in Action: Loyalty in Biblical Perspective* (Philadelphia: Fortress, 1985).

[32] Rosemary Radford Ruether, *Sexism and God Talk: Toward a Feminist Theology* (Boston: Beacon, 1983), 23.

[33] Ruether, "Feminist Interpretation," 117.

which divide human beings into classes in which the superior rules over the inferior. But this religious sanction of the existing social order is counteracted by an alternative principle—the prophetic principle. God periodically speaks through the prophetic person in order to criticize and condemn the society that, in the name of religion, perpetuates injustices upon some social groups. Therefore, the prophetic principle criticizes both society's injustices and its religious justification of them.[34] True religious and divine experiences do not support such social injustice, but rather expose structures that lead to injustices. The emphasis of feminist criticism in a very real sense parallels this prophetic principle because of the former's concentration on the structures which perpetuate the marginalization of women.

However, the prophets in the biblical texts were limited in their perspective as to precisely who those oppressed persons were. They were, according to Ruether, unaware of the oppression of women and slaves. Or put another way, due to the limited view dictated by the prophets' social context, women and slaves were not included within the prophets' range of perception. The result is a limitation of the prophetic consciousness. Furthermore, after the initial prophetic renewal, because of its limited perspective, the renewed perspective may itself become the catalyst for subsequent social stratification.[35] This recognition that the prophetic consciousness is tied to its social context means that the prophetic consciousness requires perpetual reinterpretation. This is the pattern, in fact, that we see in the biblical texts themselves and in church history (e.g., the initial messianic freedom of the Christian experience was deformed to marginalize Judaism; the freedom-giving servanthood of Jesus is deformed when the language of servanthood is identified with human roles of power).[36] Feminist critics like Ruether correlate the feminist consciousness with this prophetic consciousness and call for the reinterpretation of texts and traditions within new contexts. At the same time, they take steps to guarantee that the fruits of feminist interpretation should always be a viable part of Christian communities.

Within Sakenfeld's third option, all texts (positive or negative) are viewed as speaking realistically to the condition of women as oppressed persons yearning for freedom.

> The Bible is viewed as an instrument by which God shows women their true condition as people who are oppressed and yet who are given a

---

[34] Ibid., 118.
[35] Ibid., 119.
[36] Ibid., 120–21.

vision of a different heaven and earth and a variety of models for how to live toward that vision.[37]

Elisabeth Schüssler Fiorenza. By observing how women of the past have been treated within androcentric cultures, women today may identify with these women in their oppression and struggle for freedom. Schüssler Fiorenza argues that the Bible has been employed as a weapon against women's struggle for freedom. Accordingly, a feminist hermeneutic challenges the authority of the patriarchal texts and their use as a weapon against women's struggle. It will also examine ways in which the Bible may be employed as a positive resource in women's struggle for freedom. In order to explain how this hermeneutic works, Schüssler Fiorenza has set forth five key elements within it:[38]

First, feminist critics must assume a posture of suspicion rather than acceptance of biblical authority. This task is twofold: (1) The critic must recognize any oppressive, sexist, or racist elements within the Bible and refuse to explain these elements away; and (2) honest attempts should be made to uncover any antipatriarchal undertones in the biblical texts, undertones which may be hidden within the androcentric language of the texts.

Second, critics must evaluate rather than correlate. This means that some texts and interpretations must be rejected if they perpetuate and legitimate patriarchal structures.

Third, interpretation is inseparable from proclamation. Texts or traditions that perpetuate patriarchal oppressive structures should not be proclaimed as "word of God" for people today. Before texts are translated with inclusive language, a careful selection process should be engaged. Texts that support patriarchal structures should not be allowed proclamational status. Only texts that affirm persons as equals should be allowed into the lectionary.

Fourth, texts that do perpetuate and legitimate patriarchal structures of oppression should not be abandoned. Furthermore, these texts should become resources for remembering how women were oppressed and marginalized. Schüssler Fiorenza refers to this reclamation of suffering as a hermeneutic of remembrance. While feminists may recognize these texts as reflecting reality, they do not equate this with acceptance

---

[37] Sakenfeld, "Feminist Uses of Biblical Materials," 62.

[38] See Elisabeth Schüssler Fiorenza, "The Will to Choose or to Reject: Continuing Our Critical Work," in *Feminist Interpretation of the Bible* (ed. Letty M. Rusell; Philadelphia: Westminster, 1985); and idem, *Bread Not Stone: Introduction to a Feminist Interpretation of Scripture* (Boston: Beacon, 1985).

of the validity of that reality. This hermeneutic of remembrance should allow critics to reconstruct the origin and history of early Christianity from a feminist perspective. The biblical canon retains only scattered remnants of the early nonpatriarchal Christian community, but these remnants give evidence that patriarchal structures were not originally part of the Christian community.

Fifth, interpretation must include celebration and ritual. This actualizes the text into the present. Bible stories are retold from the perspective of the feminist imagination, especially the reconstruction of those nonpatriarchal remnants. Included within this imaginative reconstruction are creative tools such as music, dance, drama, and literary creativity. As the church through history has ritualized parts of the biblical text and traditions in order to celebrate "forefathers," so the present church should engage in the creative formulations of rituals that will celebrate our "foremothers."

Resources

Farley, Margaret A. "Feminist Consciousness and Scripture." Pages 41–51 in *Feminist Interpretation of the Bible*. Edited by Letty M. Russell. Philadelphia: Westminster, 1985.

Fiero, Gloria. *The Humanistic Tradition.* 6 vols. Boston: McGraw-Hill, 2002.

Fiorenza, Elisabeth Schüssler. "A Feminist Biblical Hermeneutics: Biblical Interpretation and Liberation Theology." Pages 91–112 in *The Challenge of Liberation Theology: A First World Response.* Edited by Brian Mahan and L. Dale Richesin. Maryknoll: Orbis, 1981.

Gelfand, Elissa. "Feminist Criticism, French." Pages 44–50 in *Encyclopedia of Contemporary Literary Theory: Approaches, Scholars, Terms.* Edited by Irena R. Makaryk. Buffalo: University of Toronto Press, 1993.

Ruether, Rosemary Radford. "Feminist Interpretation: A Method of Correlation." Pages 111–24 in *Feminist Interpretation of the Bible.* Edited by Letty M. Russell. Philadelphia: Westminster, 1985.

———. *Sexism and God Talk: Toward a Feminist Theology.* Boston: Beacon, 1983.

Sakenfeld, Katharine Doob. *Faithfulness in Action: Loyalty in Biblical Perspective.* Philadelphia: Fortress, 1985.

———. "Feminist Uses of Biblical Materials." Pages 55–64 in *Feminist Interpretation of the Bible.* Edited by Letty M. Russell. Philadelphia: Westminster, 1985.

Weedon, Chris. "Feminist Materialists." Pages in 41–42 in *Encyclopedia of Contemporary Literary Theory: Approaches, Scholars, Terms.* Edited by Irena R. Makaryk. Buffalo: University of Toronto Press, 1993.

INTEGRATING THE THREE WORLDS

MARK'S GOSPEL AND THE MERGING OF THREE WORLDS

I once read an anecdote about a woman who suffered from insomnia. Desperate for sleep, she sought the advice of her pastor, who naturally offered her what he felt to be a foolproof solution. He told her to go home, close her eyes, open her Bible at random, and point to a spot on one of the open pages. The verse to which she pointed would be her answer from God. Complying with her pastor's advice, the woman randomly pointed to a passage. Upon opening her eyes she read, "Behold, I show you a mystery; We shall not all sleep, but we shall all be changed" (1 Cor 15:51). The woman was so pleased with the outcome that she actually laughed herself to sleep!

On the one hand, we laugh at the naïveté of such an approach to reading the Bible. While the woman's problem was solved, we can safely assume that this passage of Scripture has absolutely nothing to do with insomnia. Both the approach and result are ludicrous. On the other hand, it is no laughing matter when we assume that when one person speaks to another, the speaker intends to communicate something to the listener(s). That something may be trivial or profound, but it is something nonetheless. It is an equally safe assumption that authors intend to communicate something to readers. On the one hand, authors may choose to be as clear and precise as possible, diminishing the possibility of misunderstanding; put another way, an author may consciously attempt to erase the gap between intention and understanding. On the other hand, authors may try to be opaque and ambiguous, using language in such a way as to elicit the cooperation of their readers in producing meaning. The latter especially characterizes what I have referred to as mimetic texts. While all texts communicate according to genre conventions and presuppose certain kinds of readers, mimetic texts create a role for the reader which is more complex and imaginative than texts that we might refer to as propositional.

As we have argued throughout this book, literary meaning is the result of a conversation between a text and a reader. This conversation is informed by knowledge of the author's world. In this chapter, we will use the Gospel of Mark as a text case to show how the three worlds of author, text, and reader merge to produce meaning. We intend not to offer a detailed commentary on Mark but only to demonstrate how the three worlds merge. Consequently, we will focus on how the narrative structures of plot (the world of the text) set the stage for a reader to make interpretive decisions (the world of the reader) based upon some knowledge of the worldview of ancient Judaism (the world of the author).

We will argue that Mark's plot (the emplotment of episodes) invites the reader to make a decision about the goal of Jesus' ministry. Nowhere does Mark make the goal explicit. He does, however, through the literary strategies of plot, ask the reader to infer that Jesus is redefining the concept of the people of God. In other words, Mark invites the reader to **assemble meaning**. While Mark's plot creatively implies in a number of ways that Jesus is redefining the people of God, we will demonstrate this assumption by looking at only three narrative strategies: (1) Mark's use of **literary allusion**, (2) his use of **intercalation**, and (3) Jesus' relationship to his contemporary worldview as it is assumed by Mark. While all three are strategic elements of the narrative world within the text, the first two create sufficient gaps to engage the reader in making decisions, and the third requires some knowledge on the part of the reader of the author's world. I should emphasize that these plot strategies do not exhaust Mark's literary repertoire. We could have chosen to discuss other plot items such as multiple points of view, protension and retention, and a variety of motifs and structures of openness. Some matters, however, must be left to my readers to pursue.

Mark's Use of Literary Allusion

Any text must be read intertextually. **Intertextuality** refers to the notion that all communication takes place within contexts. All communication occurs in conversation with other texts. These "texts" are not all written ones. Included in what counts for texts here are such elements as prior written texts, oral traditions, social norms, language norms, religious norms, and literary norms. Intertextuality includes both ends of the communication process, both author and reader. Not only do authors communicate within these "texts" but so do readers. Therefore, any writing of a text is intertextual and any reading is intertextual. In other words, everything that goes into defining a culture is part of the text that a writer or reader uses and depends upon in the process of communication. Here we are concerned with the intertextuality of the text in terms of the author's use of prior literary texts.

Mark's Abrupt Beginning

Mark's extensive use of literary allusion invites the reader to make inferences about the purpose of Jesus' ministry. From the beginning of his story to the end, Mark alludes to events in the Hebrew Bible that are calculated to suggest to the reader some significance for defining the purpose of Jesus' ministry. Mark opens his story with a reversal of the Exodus story. The original story moves from the wilderness, to the Jordan, to Judea, and finally to Jerusalem (under David). In Mark the action is reversed: "And people from the whole Judean countryside and all the people of Jerusalem were going out to him, and were baptized by him in the river Jordan, confessing their sins" (1:5). The reversed movement is Judea, Jerusalem, and the Jordan. In the original story, Israel was tested in the wilderness for forty years, while in the reversed version, Jesus is tested in the wilderness for forty days. Only Jesus seems to take the reversal back as far as the wilderness.[1] Through this allusion, Mark may be giving the reader advanced warning that not only is Jesus reformulating the people of God, but that his reformulation will reverse some of the ways in which the people of God are currently defined. Mark hands the readers this allusion and asks them to make sense of it.

Allusions to Moses

The two feeding episodes (Mark 6:30–44 and 8:1–13) contain four different allusions to the Hebrew Bible. In both episodes, the feeding takes place in a deserted place and Jesus instructs his disciples to give the crowds something to eat. In both, the disciples respond with a question about the feasibility of obtaining enough food to feed such a large number. In the first feeding episode, the disciples seat the crowd in "groups of hundreds and of fifties" (6:40). Below are the passages in the Hebrew Bible to which Mark alludes.

---

[1] John Drury, "Mark," in *Literary Guide to the Bible* (ed. Robert Alter and Frank Kermode; Cambridge, Mass.: Harvard University Press), 408–9.

Num 11:13a   Where am I to get meat to give to all this people?

Num 11:22   Are there enough flocks and herds to slaughter for them? Are there enough fish in the sea to catch for them?

Exod 18:24–25 So Moses listened to his father-in-law and did all that he had said. Moses chose able men from all Israel and appointed them heads over the people, as officers over thousands, hundreds, fifties, and tens.

Equally fascinating is the similarity between Jesus' decision to speak in riddles to outsiders but clearly to the disciples (Mark 4:11) and Yahweh's pronouncement about Moses:

When there are prophets among you,
I the LORD make myself known to them in visions;
I speak to them in dreams.
Not so with my servant Moses;
he is entrusted with all my house.
With him I speak face to face—clearly, not in riddles;
and he beholds the form of the LORD. (Num 12:6b–8a)

An Allusion to Elisha

Second Kings 4:42–43 is an account of a miraculous feeding involving the prophet Elisha. The parallels with the two feeding episodes in Mark should be obvious:

A man came from Baal-shalishah, bringing food from the first fruits to the man of God: twenty loaves of barley and fresh ears of grain in his sack. Elisha said, "Give it to the people and let them eat." But his servant said, "How can I set this before a hundred people?" So he repeated, "Give it to the people and let them eat, for thus says the LORD, 'They shall eat and have some left.'"

An Allusion to Israel as Sheep

In the first feeding episode, the narrator refers to the crowd as being "like sheep without a shepherd" (6:34b). First Kings 22:17, 2 Chr 18:16, Isa 13:14, Jer 50:6, Ezek 34:12, Zech 10:2 all refer to Israel as being like sheep without a shepherd.

Allusion to Passover and Covenant

The reader is not surprised by Jesus' meal with the disciples on the first day of Unleavened Bread (Mark 14:12). But Jesus' actions during the meal (14:22–25) give the reader pause, for it suddenly becomes obvious that against the background of the feast that celebrates the very founding and deliverance of the people of God, Jesus is forming a new people. By allowing the bread and wine to symbolize his broken body and shed blood, Jesus identifies himself as the sacrificial lamb. When he says of his blood that it "is poured out for many" (Mark 14:24), the reader (and disciples) should think in terms of the sacrificial lamb at the original Passover (Exod 12:1–13) and of the blood of the original covenant (e.g., Exod 24:8 and Zech 9:11). Both speak of deliverance through death. Jesus becomes both founder and ratifying sacrifice of a new covenant.

The strength of allusion is its power of suggestion. It appears that Mark is inviting the reader to make a connection between what Jesus is doing in the two feeding episodes and what God has done in the past for Israel. Given the parallels between the feeding episodes and the above passages, we might conclude that Mark invites the reader to assume that Jesus is reformulating the people of God.

Mark's pervasive use of allusion creates a wide field of possibilities. As we have seen above, some allusions seem calculated to produce connections that enable readers to assemble meaning. Some, however, seem designed to create interpretive openness. Below are two examples.

An Allusion to Esther

One of the most puzzling allusions in Mark occurs in 6:21–23, the account of Salome's dancing before Herod. The account is an unmistakable allusion to the book of Esther. When compared to the conversation between Ahasuerus and Esther, the counterpart between Herod and Salome reveals some striking similarities:

Mark 6:22b: *aitēson me ho ean thelēs, kai <u>dōsō soi.</u>*
αἴτησόν με ὃ ἐὰν θέλῃς, καὶ δώσω σοι.

Mark 6:23b *ho ti ean me aitēsēs <u>dōsō soi heōs hēmisous tēs basileias</u>*
<u>*mou.*</u>
ὅ τι ἐάν με αἰτήσῃς δώσω σοι ἕως ἡμίσους τῆς
βασιλείας μου.

Esth 5:3b   *kai ti sou estin to axiōma; <u>heōs tou hēmisous tēs</u>*
              <u>*basileias mou.*</u>
              καὶ τί σού ἐστιν τὸ ἀξίωμα; ἕως τοῦ ἡμίσους τῆς
              βασιλείας μου.

Esth 7:2b   *kai <u>estō soi heōs tou hēmisous tēs basileias mou.</u>*
              καὶ ἔστω σοι ἕως τοῦ ἡμίσους τῆς βασιλείας μου.

Why such an allusion here? Is there really any similarity between
Esther and Salome that would warrant such an allusion? These and
similar questions may lead nowhere, since the context simply does not
provide the justification for the allusion. Perhaps it was this sense of
displacement that led Kermode to look outside the immediate context
for the purpose of the allusion. Kermode finds the allusion connected
to Jesus' use of "little girl" and Jairus (meaning "the awakener") in
Mark 5:21–43. "Little girl" is used of both Salome and Jairus' daughter, while the theme of sleeplessness occurs in Esther.[2] After observing
that Esther is a story of a beautiful young girl surviving death at the
hands of a sleepless king by enticing him to touch her with his golden
scepter, Kermode asks concerning the account in Mark 5, "is the story
of the little girl a transformation of that story?"[3] While an interesting
observation, it does not make a connection between Esther, Salome,
Herod, and John the Baptist. This is another example of the power of
allusion to invite interpretation.

An Allusion to Joseph

As puzzling as Mark's allusion to Esther is his allusion (14:52) to
Joseph's encounter with Potiphar's wife (Gen 39). At Jesus' arrest,
readers are introduced to a mysterious "young man" who was following Jesus "wearing nothing but a linen cloth" (14:51a). When the ar-
resting authorities attempt to subdue the young man, he evades them
by slipping out of his linen cloth and fleeing naked. A comparison of
this event to the account of Joseph's escape from the overtures of Potiphar's wife yields the following parallels:

---

[2] Frank Kermode, *The Genesis of Secrecy* (Cambridge, Mass.: Harvard
University Press, 1979), 133.
[3] Ibid.

Gen 39:12b   *kai <u>katalipōn ta himatia</u> autou en tais chersin autēs*
                 <u>*ephygen.*</u>
                 καὶ καταλιπὼν τὰ ἱμάτια αὐτοῦ ἐν ταῖς χερσὶν
                 αὐτῆς ἔφυγεν.

Mark 14:52   *ho de <u>katalipōn tēn sindona gymnos ephygen.</u>*
                 ὁ δὲ καταλιπὼν τὴν σινδόνα γυμνὸς ἔφυγεν.

At this point, interpretation is frustrated. Readers have sought and will continue to seek for significance in this allusion. What possible connection can there be between the circumstances of Joseph and those of this young man? What is the purpose behind such an allusion? Rereading the text, the reader might find a connection between the naked man among the tombs in Mark 6 and this young man, and even between the young man at the tomb (Mark 16), but a connection between the young man in Mark 14:52 and Joseph in Gen 36 makes no sense.

Mark's Use of Intercalation

Based upon the above examples, we have seen that Mark employs literary allusion to create interpretive openness that requires the reader to make decisions about the narrative in order to assemble meaning in making sense of the narrative. We have also seen that while some allusions suggest that Jesus is redefining the people of God, others generate an openness that is difficult to fill. Mark also uses a literary structural device called intercalation. Intercalation is the practice of sandwiching one story within another, or bracketing several textual segments with similar episodes. Mark does not inform the reader of any relationships between the two stories or the bracketing or bracketed episodes. The reader is invited to find the significance of the intercalation. Like his use of allusion, Mark uses intercalation to suggest that Jesus is redefining the people of God and to create a level of interpretive openness that goes beyond such a redefinition.

The Intercalated Stories of Jairus and the Hemorrhaging Woman

Mark 5:21–43 contains the intercalated stories of Jairus and the hemorrhaging woman. Both the woman and Jairus seek a miracle from Jesus, both seem to have faith in Jesus' healing ability, both fall down before Jesus, and in both instances Jesus is ridiculed. But there is one major difference between Jairus and the woman: the woman is ritually unclean, and thus a religious outsider, while Jairus is the ruler of the synagogue and thus a traditional **insider**. Is Mark's point here that the status of insider is defined not in traditional terms of clean and unclean (i.e., in terms of ceremonial purity) but in terms of faith in Jesus? Such an understanding is certainly plausible.

But some items in the intercalation beg a comparison between the woman and Jairus' daughter. Mark makes it a point to tell the reader that the woman has suffered for twelve years and that the girl is twelve years of age. In the story of the woman, the healing is public, but only the girl's parents, Peter, James, and John witness the second miracle. Jesus refers to the woman as "daughter" and to the girl as "child" and "little girl." What is the reader to make of this? Given that characters in the narrative consistently understand Jesus' activities as instances of teaching, the reader is probably expected to look beyond the surface of the narrative for clues of a deeper significance. The reader may safely assume also that these intercalated stories constitute a parable of the kingdom. While the woman may represent those who have been ceremonially marginalized by the old system, the young girl of twelve may represent the new seed of the kingdom. Out of the old (Jairus, whose faith is never questioned) comes a new seed, a "daughter" in danger of dying. Mark may be suggesting that Jairus, the woman, and the young girl constitute the remnant of the faithful from among the old system. This is especially suggested by Mark's use of the number twelve in the intercalation.

The Intercalated Stories of the Fig Tree and the Cleansing of the Temple

By means of intercalation, Mark does what any good storyteller does; he asks his readers to become involved in the story. The technique of intercalation is so pervasive that the text displays overlapping intercalations and intercalations within intercalations. Below is an outline of three overlapping and embedded intercalations:

11:12–14	Fig tree
11:15–19	Cleansing of the temple
11:20–25	Fig tree

11:15–19   Jesus enters temple

11:20–25   Fig tree

11:27–33   Jesus enters temple

11:1–11   Jesus enters Jerusalem and temple

11:12–25   First intercalation above

11:27–34   Jesus enters Jerusalem and temple

Such complex intercalation shows plainly that the narrative invites the readers to look for a relationship between what happens to the fig tree and what happens to the temple. The narrative also gives the readers pause when the narrator says that Jesus cursed the fig tree because of its lack of fruit even though "it was not the season for figs" (11:13b). Just as Jesus rejects the fig tree for its lack of fruit, is he rejecting the temple, the central religious symbol of the people of God? If Jesus is rejecting the temple as God's house, what is to take its place within the redefined people of God? Mark 11:22–25 may suggest that the people of God now have access to God directly instead of having to go through the priesthood and temple. Simple faith in God becomes the central religious symbol of the redefined people of God.

The Intercalated Stories of the Death of John the Baptist and the Disciples' Missions Trip

Just as Mark's literary allusions create interpretive openness that goes beyond the issue of Jesus' purpose, so does his use of intercalation. The placement of the account of John the Baptist's death between the commissioning of the disciples and their subsequent return (6:7–30) is one of the most problematic intercalations in Mark. The text does suggest a variety of associations between the account of John's death and episodes outside the intercalation. But readers have found it difficult even to formulate sensible questions about the intercalation. In what possible way do the two events interpret each other? Is the reader to make some connection between the disciples of Jesus and those of John? Or is the connection between Jesus and John? Does John's death at the hands of Herod foreshadow Jesus' death? Is the lack of fear of John's disciples to be contrasted with the fear of Jesus' disciples? The intercalation invites inferences without foregrounding any.

Jesus' Relationship to His Contemporary Worldview according to Mark

In Mark 4, Jesus tells the parable of the sower (4:3–9). When his disciples do not understand the parable (4:10), Jesus offers an interpretation (4:11–20); this is followed by a cluster of sayings (4:21–25), the parable of the growing seed (4:26–29), and the parable of the mustard seed (4:30–32). As Burton Mack has noted, the image of sowing seed constituted in Hellenistic society a popular analogy for the inculcation of culture (Greek, *paideia*).[4] A Hellenistic reader would recognize that Jesus was offering instruction designed to impart an understanding of culture. Similar analogies occur in other ancient writers, such as Hippocrates, Antiphon, Seneca, and Quintilian.[5] The correspondences within the analogy were sower to teacher, sowing to teaching, seed to words, and soils to students. Within the parable of the sower, the emphasis falls upon the acts of sowing and harvest, consequences beyond the control of the sower or reaper, rather than upon cultivation. When we move to the sayings involving the lamp and bushel basket (Mark 4:21–25), there seems to be a correspondence between the seed/word and enlightenment. As Mack points out, "the opposition is between 'hidden' and 'manifest.' "[6] The two parables suggest that while the new culture begins in a rather inauspicious manner, it eventually will become the greatest of all cultures (the image of the scrub from the mustard seed). The seed analogies recall the Greek *paideia,* while the mustard seed's becoming the great shrub whose branches offer habitation for all the birds of the air alludes to the imagery of the great tree of Daniel (Dan 4:10–12) that represents Israel. Mack is probably right when he observes that the point of the seed parable is that the kingdom will eventually succeed in displacing both Greek and Jewish cultures.[7] In other words, the secret of the kingdom that the disciples do not understand (Mark 4:10) is that Jesus is establishing a new culture, an alternative society in conflict with both Greek and Jewish ones. The movement within 4:13–25 in conjunction with 4:11–12 suggests (1) that the disciples should recognize that Jesus is instituting a new culture, (2) that

---

[4] Burton Mack, *A Myth of Innocence: Mark and Christian Origins* (Philadelphia: Fortress, 1988), 159.

[5] Ibid., 159–60.

[6] Ibid., 164.

[7] Ibid., 165.

they should move from hearing about such a culture to understanding its nature, and (3) that such insight is the condition for being a member of the new culture (an insider). The disciples are to understand that everything that Jesus teaches and does pertains in some way to the inculcating of the new culture.

Jesus Redefines the People of God by Challenging Social Boundaries

Social scientists have shown that cultures structure social identities by formulating **boundaries** around particular areas (e.g., cosmological, social, bodily). Ancient Mediterranean cultures often formulated these boundaries in terms of the categories of clean and unclean. As long as an action or event remained within the boundaries of its area, it was clean. When an action or event crossed its prescribed boundaries, it was unclean. Jerome Neyrey has shown that the boundaries of cleanness within Judaism focused on places, people, things, and times.[8] For example, for Judaism, the land of Israel was holier than any other land; the Holy of Holies was more holy than the other parts of the temple; the high priest (who alone has access to the Holy of Holies) was more pure than the other priests, who were more pure than Levites, who were more pure than Israelites. Animals and people with blemishes or deformities were unclean.[9] Body fluids such as spit, blood, and semen were unclean because they belonged inside the body. A woman was unclean throughout her menstrual period. Lepers were unclean because their bodies broke out in fluid that belonged inside. Most of these boundaries—cosmological (God on earth is located in the Holy of Holies), social (Jew vs. Gentile, male vs. female, orthodox vs. sinner), and bodily (abstinence from certain foods, avoiding contact with certain people, and ritual worship)—are referred to indirectly in Mark. Mark's plot presents Jesus as not only challenging these boundaries, but as erasing them. Jesus thus foregrounds possibilities that were backgrounded or even negated by the system founded upon the socio-religious categories of clean and unclean.

In Mark, Jesus as Son of God empowered by the Holy Spirit is not confined to a specific location, but comes in contact with uncleanness,

---

[8] See Jerome Neyrey, "The Idea of Purity in Mark's Gospel," *Semeia* 35 (1986): 91–128.

[9] See David Rhoads, "Social Criticism: Crossing Boundaries," in *Mark and Method* (ed. Janice Chapel Anderson and Stephen D. Moore; Minneapolis: Fortress, 1992), 151–53.

replacing it with wholeness (exorcisms of unclean spirits [6:7–13]). In addition, the plot presents the reader with John's claim that his successor is "mightier" (1:7), with Jesus' temptation by Satan (1:12–13), and with Jesus' parabolic claim that he is binding Satan and plundering his house (3:22–30). Taking as a cue Mark's reference to God's ripping open the heavens and empowering Jesus with the Holy Spirit (1:10–11), the reader can assume that the boundary between heaven and earth is abolished and that God's holiness is evidenced not in ritual protection, but in the bringing of new life to individuals, freeing them from the power of unclean spirits.

Thus far (Mark 1:1–8:33) the plot shows Jesus redefining socio-religious boundaries up to 8:27–33 by means of (1) miracles and (2) his controversies with the Jewish leaders or by his actions that lead to controversies. Jesus' healing miracles involve either those **marginalized** by society (i.e., those who are in some way unclean) or those not in compliance with ritual regulations:

1:29–31	Jesus heals Simon's mother-in-law on the Sabbath.
1:40–43	Jesus heals a leper.
3:1–6	Jesus heals on the Sabbath.
5:25–34	Jesus heals a hemorrhaging woman.
5:35–43	Jesus raises a dead girl.
7:24–30	Jesus heals the daughter of a Syrophoenician woman, a Gentile.
7:31–37	Jesus heals a deaf man with spittle.
8:22–26	Jesus heals a blind man.

Instances in which Jesus' actions deviate from the socio-religious norms in controversy with the Jewish teachers are summarized below:

2:14	Jesus calls a tax collector as his disciple.
2:15–17	Jesus eats with sinners and tax collectors.
2:18–22	Jesus rejects the whole socio-religious system in his defense of not fasting.
2:23–28	The role of the Sabbath is reversed in Jesus' defense of his disciples plucking grain on the Sabbath. There

are life situations which take priority over ceremonial norms.

3:31–35   Jesus redefines the family.

7:1–23   Jesus disagrees with the Pharisees over the tradition of the elders. He redefines cleanness in terms of morals rather than in terms of diet.

Until Mark 8:26, the plot presents Jesus as an itinerant teacher whose actions and conflicts with religious leaders are supplanting the culture of the day. Rather than avoiding those ritually unclean, Jesus and his disciples replace their uncleanness with wholeness. Jesus teaches a system that breaks down the boundaries. This is represented in the first half of Mark by Jesus' encounters in the synagogue and by his conflicts with the leaders of Judaism. The boundaries are either erased or extended to include those people, actions, and things traditionally excluded (e.g., women, Gentiles, lepers, sinners, tax collectors, physically afflicted, certain foods, Sabbath regulations). The plot invites the reader to consider this reformulated people of God.

The Redefined People of God Is Inclusive

Following the second feeding miracle in Mark 8, Jesus responds to the disciples' question about bread by firing a volley of questions at the disciples—questions that have to do with the numbers of the two crowds, the loaves of bread, and the baskets of fragments. Jesus caps this interrogation with the question, "Do you not yet understand?" (8:21). The disciples' silence suggests that they do not recognize the significance of the numbers. But the reader should know that the numbers twelve and seven have a history of symbolic significance. Twelve is the number of tribes that constituted the Jewish nation; and in Jewish reckoning, seven represents the number of nations from which Gentiles originated. Furthermore, Mark might expect the reader to correlate this symbolism with other items implicit in the text. Is there an instance in the text where the number twelve occurs? In 3:13–19 Jesus chooses from among his followers twelve whom he commissions as apostles and who will participate in and perpetuate Jesus' teaching and healing. The plot suggests that this group of twelve represents the core of a new people of God. Jesus is formulating a new Israel, a new culture that will replace the old (itself symbolized historically by the twelve tribes). Furthermore, given the significance of the numbers 12 and 7, it is interesting that the first feeding takes place in Jewish territory while the second (where seven baskets of fragments were collected) takes place in Gentile territory. It is possible that Mark is suggesting through the **narrative emplotment** that Jesus is reconstituting the people of God to include both Jews and Gentiles.

The People of God Redefined through Jesus' Controversies with Religious Leaders

Immediately after the first passion prediction (Mark 8:31), Jesus assumes the role of teacher in 8:34–9:1. Much of his teaching, however, takes place within controversies with the religious authorities. In each controversy, Jesus introduces a characteristic of the new culture with the old thought system as a backdrop. Jesus foregrounds what has been obscured or negated by the old system. Below is a summary of these controversies.

10:2–12   Using Gen 2:24 to refute the more relaxed view of the Pharisees, Jesus redefines the parameters governing divorce.

11:15–18   The narrator tells how the chief priests and scribes respond to the spellbinding effects of Jesus' teaching upon the crowds (the reader might assume that the teaching of the leaders did not have such an effect).

11:27–33   The three groups mentioned in Jesus' first passion prediction (8:31) question the source of Jesus' authority to act as he has in reference to the temple. Here Jesus creates the opportunity for the religious leaders to acknowledge his source of authority as divine. If the leaders answer that John's ministry is divinely ordained, they must admit that Jesus' authority is likewise divine. The reader already knows the source of Jesus' authority (1:2–11). As John Paul Heil points out, the reader should recognize that the episode serves to disclose "their [the leaders'] inadequacy to question his authority. . . . Jesus has thus masterfully exercised and demonstrated his own superior, divine authority over the Jewish leaders who stubbornly refuse to acknowledge and believe in the divine origin of John's baptism and hence of Jesus' authority."[10]

12:1–12   Jesus tells the parable of the Wicked Tenants to the leaders. Realizing that they are implicated by the parable, the leaders seek to arrest Jesus. While the readers should understand the referents in the parable and the fact that God himself is rejecting the old culture and replacing it with a new one, the extent of the leaders' insight is left in doubt. This episode is immediately followed by a series of dialogues between Jesus, the religious leaders, and the crowds in which Jesus demonstrates the inadequacy of the old system.

12:13–17   Jesus addresses the issue of taxes.

12:18–27   Jesus accuses the Sadducees of knowing neither God nor the Scriptures.

12:28–34   Jesus' definition of the law's essence challenges the traditional structures of clean and unclean. The new element here is the appearance of a scribe as an insider in his positive evaluation of Jesus' teaching. Again the status of insider is contingent upon insight into the nature of the kingdom rather than position within or conformity to the structures of the old system.

12:38–40   Jesus warns against the hypocrisy of the scribes who use the system in order to enhance their own reputation and material possessions while marginalizing those (represented by the widow) for whom the law instructs special care. The words "Beware of the scribes" remind the reader of Jesus' earlier warning to the disciples: "beware of the yeast of the Pharisees and the yeast of Herod" (8:15). All three parties are guilty of aborting the essential nature of the law. In fact, in 10:46–12:40, the entire range of Jewish leadership (chief priests, scribes, elders, Pharisees, Herodians, and Sadducees) engages Jesus in dialogue concerning basic religio-ethical matters and is found wanting.

---

[10] John Paul Heil, *The Gospel of Mark as a Model for Action: A Reader-Response Commentary* (New York: Paulist, 1992), 233.

Redefining the New People of God in Terms of Insiders and Outsiders

As we suggested above, Jesus consistently reaches out to the disenfranchised and marginalized of society. By presenting Jesus in such situations, Mark depicts Jesus as challenging, even erasing, the old boundaries that defined the insiders and outsiders among the people of God. This redefinition of insider/outsider status is suggested rather strongly when we compare Mark's treatment of the disciples with the treatment of other key individuals in the narrative.

Peter and the Disciples. Throughout the narrative, Mark portrays the disciples as comprehending neither the nature of Jesus' messiahship nor the nature of discipleship within the redefined people of God.[11] By the end of the narrative, Peter has accepted the possibility of Jesus' death and even announces his own willingness to die with Jesus (14:31). But when the moment of truth arrives, he and the other followers flee just as Jesus had predicted. When the council interrogates Jesus, Peter proclaims publicly what the reader has suspected all along: "I do not know this man you are talking about" (14:71b). Peter fails to recognize that the religious leaders' treatment of Jesus fulfills Jesus' predictions in 13:9–13 and 8:34–38. Because Peter and the disciples are as incapable of understanding this parable as they have been of all the other parables, they show themselves to be outsiders. But three characters in Mark's narrative appear to have some insight into the nature of the new people of God. Two of these are paradigm outsiders who become insiders, while the third is a paradigm insider who also becomes an insider within the new people of God.

The Syrophoenician Woman. In 7:1–23 Jesus tells a parable concerning the definition of defilement to the crowd. The disciples fail to comprehend the significance of the parable as a redefinition of a category of clean and unclean. Their incomprehension elicits a rebuke from Jesus: "Then do you also fail to understand?" (7:18a).

Immediately following this failure of the disciples, the reader encounters an episode underscoring the disciples' lack of understanding. A Syrophoenician woman (an ethnic outsider) readily solves Jesus'

---

[11] Since a full treatment of this major motif would take us too far afield, interested readers may consult the following references: Mark 4:10–13; 4:38–41; 5:30–31; 6:52; 7:17; 8:4; 8:14–21; 9:5–6; 9:10; 9:33–50; 10:13–16; 10:23–31; 10:35–41; 14:3–9.

riddle concerning children, food, and dogs (7:24–30). The point of the episode seems to have nothing to do with faith but with insight (i.e., the ability to solve the riddling language of Jesus), for Jesus responds to the woman's solution, "For saying that, you may go—the demon has left your daughter" (7:29). The woman has more insight into the scope of Jesus' new culture than do the disciples.

The Roman Centurion. Here is another individual with insight into the defining quality of sonship and kingdom. The narrative highlights his reaction to Jesus' suffering and death by juxtaposing it with the reactions of the religious leaders and crowds. While the latter group misunderstands the significance of the events and Jesus' words (e.g., 15:16–20, 25–32, 33–36), the Roman centurion concludes, "Truly this man was God's Son!" (15:39b). It is not the statement itself, however, that should shock the reader, but the reason that the narrator gives for the centurion's assessment: "Now when the centurion, who stood facing him, saw that in this way he breathed his last . . ." (15:39a). To what does "in this way" refer? It could not refer to the splitting of the temple curtain, since this bit of insight is given to the reader alone. As the Roman centurion "stood facing him," he heard the cry of abandonment, *"Eloi, Eloi, lema sabachthani,"* and the "loud cry" (Mark 15:34–37). It is upon these two cries of abandonment and death that the centurion bases his claim. He has seen in the suffering of Jesus, in the absence of God, the essence of sonship. The centurion does not make his assessment in response to healings, exorcisms, or any teaching, but solely upon these cries of abandonment. Is this what the voice from heaven means when it silences Peter with "this is my Son, the Beloved; listen to him!" (9:7b)? No voice from God silences the centurion. There is only the sound of ripping flesh and temple curtain. The outsider has understood that Jesus' sonship is essentially defined in terms of suffering and death and that such insight is the mark of an insider. The reader has only to think on the disciples' inability to gain such an insight to recognize that they are in danger of becoming outsiders. Mark does not make such a conclusion explicit, but invites the reader to make the inference.

Joseph of Arimathea. The other person of insight is Joseph of Arimathea, a member of the Jewish council and a paradigm insider, a member of the very body that accuses Jesus of blasphemy and sedition. Joseph requests the body of Jesus with the intention of giving Jesus a proper burial. The narrator informs the reader that Joseph was "also himself waiting expectantly for the kingdom of God" (15:43). Two things catch the reader's attention. First, the word "also" presupposes that someone else was "waiting expectantly" for the kingdom. The most likely referent is the group of women "looking on from a distance" (15:40–41). The narrator does not record their response to Jesus' death. Unlike the centurion, the women cannot see Jesus' face nor hear his shouts of abandonment. To respond with insight, the observer must see Jesus' face and hear his scream. If the above assessment is plausible, then the reader may assume that the women are closer to the kingdom than the disciples but have not arrived at the essential insight. Second, the plot pressures the reader to assume that Joseph's search for the kingdom leads him to Golgotha; i.e., he has found the kingdom in Jesus' death. Like the centurion (and perhaps the reader), Joseph has understood that the essence of the redefined people of God is found in suffering and death.

Conclusion: The Ending of Mark and the Predicament of the Reader

While this is the end of the story for Joseph, it is not for the readers, who must recall Jesus' three predictions of resurrection as well as the parable of the Buried Seed. The readers have been prepared for Jesus' resurrection by both the parable of the seed and Jesus' predictions. This brings us to Mark's controversial ending.

Jesus' address to his disciples in Mark 13 is calculated to prepare them for a time in which they would be responsible for perpetuating the new culture. Consequently, the reader must wonder about Jesus' promise to meet the disciples in Galilee (14:28) and the young man's reminder of such a meeting in 16:7. Is it possible for Jesus to simultaneously be absent and present with the disciples? Faced with this paradox, the reader suddenly realizes that the ending of Mark is not about the disciples in the story at all, but rather about the *readers-disciples*. Its focus is upon the readers who have struggled to **configure** the text's elements in a meaningful way. Whether or not the disciples ever solve the riddle of Jesus and his new culture is not the issue. The text holds out the possibility of these outsiders becoming insiders (16:7) just as the young man at the tomb finds insider status after his failure in 14:51–52. But the reader cannot return to Galilee except by way of the text. The disciples were not able to understand the essence of the new people of God. The ending invites the readers not only to understand but to return to the Galilee of the text and to walk again through the text. Are the readers willing to become the living and dying embodiment of the kingdom's essence?

Mark's open ending is the quintessential gap to be filled by each reader. The invitation of the gap is to consider the possibility of a social reordering of reality based upon the unpredictable. This new way must be traveled in the absence of Jesus. The reader's faith must be that of the centurion and Joseph of Arimathea. The disciples and other characters in the story had Jesus as guide; the reader has the text.

REVIEW & STUDY

Key Terms and Concepts

assemble meaning	marginalized
paideia	intertextuality
literary allusion	narrative emplotment
boundaries	insider
intercalation	configure

Study Questions

1. Read the episodes of the feedings in Mark 6:30–44 and 8:1–10. Then read 2 Kgs 4:42–44. Keeping in mind the suggestion that Jesus is reconstituting the people of God, what do you see as the significance of this allusion?

2. Read Mark through, giving special attention to the treatment of women. What role do you think the women play in the plot's point of view?

3. In Mark 4:11, Jesus tells the disciples that they have been given the secret of the kingdom of God. Have the disciples been given some information that the narrator has withheld from the reader? Reread chs. 1–3 to see if there is an occasion when the disciples receive such information. Now reread 4:1–12. What do you think the secret is?

4. In Mark 11:12–25 are the two intercalated episodes of the fig tree and the temple. Giving special attention to the narrator's comment

in 11:13 ("for it was not the season for figs"), draw from the inter-calation some inferences that you think are plausible.

5. Mark 14:53–15:47 contains numerous allusions to the Hebrew Bible. In a good reference Bible, look up these allusions. What do you think is the portrait of Jesus that the plot is asking the reader to recognize? Explain.

6. Find a recent book or journal article which deals with the social world of first-century Judaism. Read the appropriate portions and explain how such knowledge might influence your understanding of Mark's narrative.

7. We have mentioned briefly Mark's two motifs of incomprehension and insider/outsider. Read the gospel through giving attention to any reference to clothing. What purpose do you think this possible motif serves in the narrative?

Suggestions for Further Reading

Anderson, Janice Capel, and Stephen D. Moore, eds. *Mark and Method: New Approaches in Biblical Studies.* Minneapolis: Fortress, 1992.

Collins, Adela Yarbro. *The Beginning of the Gospel: Probings of Mark in Context.* Minneapolis: Fortress, 1992.

Eco, Umberto. *The Role of the Reader: Explorations in the Semiotics of Texts.* Bloomington: Indiana University Press, 1984.

Fowler, Robert. *Let the Reader Understand: Reader-Response and the Gospel of Mark.* Minneapolis: Fortress, 1991.

———. "The Rhetoric of Direction and Indirection in the Gospel of Mark." *Semeia* 48 (1989): 115–34.

Iersel, Bas M. F. Van. "The Reader of Mark as Operator of a System of Connotations." *Semeia* 48 (1989): 83–114.

Iser, Wolfgang. *The Act of Reading: A Theory of Aesthetic Response.* Baltimore: Johns Hopkins University Press, 1978.

Kermode, Frank. *The Genesis of Secrecy.* Cambridge, Mass.: Harvard University Press, 1979.

Kingsbury, Jack Dean. *The Christology of Mark's Gospel.* Minneapolis: Fortress, 1983.

Power, Mark Allan. *What Is Narrative Criticism?* Minneapolis: Fortress, 1990.

Resseguie, James L. "Reader-Response Criticism and the Synoptic Gospels." *JAAR* 52 (1984): 307–24.

Robbins, Vernon K. *Jesus the Teacher: A Socio-Rhetorical Interpretation of Mark.* Minneapolis: Fortress, 1992.

Waetjen, Herman C. *A Reordering of Power: A Socio-Political Reading of Mark's Gospel.* Minneapolis: Fortress, 1989.

Weeden, Theodore. "The Heresy that Necessitated Mark's Gospel." *Zeitschrift für die neutestamentliche Wissenschaft und de Kunde der älteren Kirche* 59:3–4 (1968): 145–58.

William, James G. *Gospel Against Parable: Mark's Language of Mystery.* Sheffield: Almond, 1985.

THE NEVER-ENDING STORY

The hermeneutical task basically involves mediating between the text and a present situation. Traditional hermeneutics has placed heavy emphasis on the distinction between the original, objective meaning of the text in its historical situation and the interpretive application of that meaning to present situations. Approaches that emphasize the historical dimensions of the author's world as the locus of meaning tend to view meaning as something that the author has consciously placed within the text. Meaning for their author-centered approaches is just lying there, waiting to be scientifically excavated. The text is regarded as a purely analytical object reflecting the mind of the author. From this perspective, hermeneutics is a reproductive exercise. It is a recognition of the author's cognition, and the text becomes nothing more than a channel to the author's or early community's mind. At least implicit in this approach is the idea that revelation has occurred once and for all and is unrepeatable. Written revelation becomes objectified, static, final.

With the advent of New Criticism, the locus of meaning shifted to the autonomous text, freed from its historical moorings. Meaning resides within the structure of the text, independent of author, and the text alone legitimates an interpretation. But try as they may, the New Critics discovered that they could not completely dislodge the text from its originating circumstances. Understanding the rhetorical art of the original languages became crucial, as did recognizing the peculiarities of the biblical genres and their embedded literary forms. A familiarity with the conventional system of the text is indispensable, and this familiarity is possible only through historical research, especially through the comparative study of other similar texts.

We have also seen that reader-centered methods of interpretation have produced a paradigm change. The reader is no longer an innocent bystander passively succumbing to the irresistible influence of the text. Reading becomes an integral, if not primary, activity in the creation of meaning. The idea of the reader's artistic activity in the creation of meaning suggests that meaning is the product of the interaction between a present creating intellect and the literary representation of another. The world of the reader (at least at the level of ideology) becomes as important as (if not more important than) the world of the author. Readers are called upon to create a world from the building materials supplied by the text. In the process, however, readers import their understanding of the real world.

If the interpreter takes any of these interpretive thrusts in isolation (i.e., author-centered, text-centered, or reader-centered), consciously or unconsciously excluding the other two, hermeneutics becomes an unbalanced discipline. Hermeneutics is not a monologue; i.e., the author does not simply address readers through the medium of the text, the text does not alone speak to the reader, and the reader does not address only a silent text. Hermeneutics is a dialogue between the text and reader where the text and reader enter into a conversational covenant informed by the world of the author. It should be obvious to the reader that throughout this book I have implicitly prescribed a hermeneutical model that calls for integrating three worlds: the worlds of the author, text, and reader. This approach rests upon a modified communication model in which the text and reader dialogue, and in which the world of the author offers preparatory, foundational information for the dialogue. If hermeneutics is willing to bring to bear upon interpretation the scholarship of the differing critical approaches, the dialogue will inevitably be more informed, constructive, and pertinent.

While background studies into the world behind the text (the discovery of historical, ideological, traditional, and social information) do not constitute interpretive ends within themselves, such studies do fulfill an important heuristic function within hermeneutics. The biblical texts did not generate themselves. While the author may not be present for questioning, the text certainly reflects the culture which gave it birth. This culture influenced the way in which the text itself speaks linguistically, conventionally, and ideologically. If methodologies such as source, form, and redaction criticism help to focus these influential forces, then they can certainly serve a preparatory function. Methods that attempt to get to the world behind the text are misused only when they fail to perpetuate the dialogue between the text and reader. They should inform the text/reader dialogue.

While the text may be the linguistic representation of an authorial object of consciousness, as an entity to itself, it begins to set its own agenda. It is a whole composed of parts. But the text is greater than the sum of its parts. We have suggested (ch. 4) that the language of literary texts is a special case of language. It is characterized by its rhetorical, metaphorical nature. If this observation is valid, then the connotative sense of the language is inexhaustible. In other words, language is unable to present completely what it represents. The words of the text individually and collectively continually reach beyond our interpretations. Consequently, any hermeneutic which searches for the final, absolute word expects something that language cannot yield. Should hermeneutics, then, concern itself with offering the definitive interpretation of texts? If hermeneutics supposes texts to be metaphorical and ultimately not sources of absolute knowledge, then texts will continue to escape our complete and final grasp. Yet as we saw in ch. 7, the text does impose restrictions upon interpretation. Perhaps we should refer to this paradoxically as a restricted infinity. While a metaphor can never be exhausted, it cannot mean just anything. It can mean an infinite number of things within parameters. The inexhaustibility of the text is similar to the number of points on a line segment between two end points. The interpretive methodologies focusing on the world within the text are more than instrumental in defining these parameters; they are rather absolutely essential. Without the insights of rhetorical criticism, New Criticism, and formalism, there simply is no context for a constructive dialogue between the text and reader. The text and reader might be speaking to each other, but it would be a language which the other cannot understand.

The metaphorical nature of the text has its counterpart in the person of the reader. Reader-response criticism, along with deconstructive criticism, has made modern readers aware of the metaphorical, rhetorical, non-objective nature, not only of the language of literary texts, but also of language in general. All readers live within a world represented by their words. Not only do we think in language, but we also evaluate, explain, and offer criticism of texts in language. When we move from the experience of reading to the task of conceptualizing that experience in language, we should not expect a precise correlation between the experience and the evaluation and description of it. Because readers bring to the text their own agendas, complete with communally approved methodology, structures of faith, ideological presuppositions, and interpretive purposes, individual text/reader conversations vary. Meaning takes place somewhere within this conversation and can never exist apart from the interpretive context of the reader. Individual interpretations are not propositions, issues to be decided for or against. They are individual conversations with the text and are always situated within some context. Interpretation is relational and involves understanding the text in light of who we are, and understanding ourselves in light of the text.

The words on the page never change, and in one sense neither do the worlds of texts. But readers must always approach the textual world and make sense of it in relation to their own world, a world constantly in flux. If hermeneutics is to be perpetually pertinent, we must allow for this flux and recognize that texts are interpreted in time. Time then becomes the "constant variable" within hermeneutics, the proverbial monkey wrench in the machinery of hermeneutics. The task of hermeneutics, therefore, can never be complete. If the ever-changing, never-ending character of hermeneutics tends to frustrate us at times, this frustration is counterbalanced by the possibilities that hermeneutics offers for personal growth.

Hermeneutics, then, is not an exercise whereby in some precise, scientific manner, we simply *reproduce* what lies in the text. It is rather a *productive* enterprise. It is undeniable that interpreters bring assumptions to the text. During the process of interpretation, however, the text itself may legitimate, deny, clarify, or modify those assumptions. This textual influence upon the reader is possible because while the text as signifier is inexhaustible, it does place parameters around interpretation, making one interpretation more or less plausible than another. The ideal, therefore, is a balance between interpretive dogmatism and individual solipsism. The discipline of hermeneutics should always seek to operate between these two limits. As Paul Ricoeur states,

> the logic of validation allows us to move between the two limits of dogmatism and skepticism. It is always possible to argue for or against an interpretation, to confront interpretations, to arbitrate between them and to seek agreement, even if this agreement remains beyond our immediate reach.[1]

The world within the text in this view is dynamic, a living organism, presenting itself differently on each reading. This also means that as readers we undergo continual change. When we read sacred texts we may have the sensation of experiencing God. But we are experiencing the Infinite through words. We experience the Word through words. But just as the Infinite can never be totally objectified in words, always transcending our finite definitions of God, perhaps the words themselves, at least in their totality, also always lie beyond our reach, escaping any

---

[1] Paul Ricoeur, *Interpretation Theory: Discourse and the Surplus of Meaning* (Fort Worth: Texas Christian University Press, 1976), 79.

final objective meaning. As the text discloses itself to us in ever-changing ways, perhaps we gain a vision of God who is not the "unmoved mover," the God of dogma, but the God who is dynamic, always relating to the changing world of humanity. If this is indeed the case, the experience of doing hermeneutics is not just a scientific discipline unrelated to the task of living; it is rather a continually life-changing and life-shaping experience. It can be an experience of God, and as such, it is redemptive.

SYNOPSES OF ADDITIONAL INTERPRETIVE METHODS EMPLOYED BY SCHOLARS

HOW METHODS AFFECT INTERPRETATION

Interpretive methods play a constitutive role in the determination of a text's meaning.[1] Interpretive methods control the questions that an interpreter puts to a text, and these questions determine the interpreter's focus. Methodological control means that some elements of the text, culture, social location of the interpreter, etc. are emphasized while other elements will be overlooked or at least deemphasized. Consequently, while interpretive methods guide the interpreter in one direction as opposed to another, they are certainly anything but innocent objects. They constitute interpretive frameworks within which interpreters operate upon the text.

By the late 1960s and early 1970s, biblical criticism had moved away from theological interests and shifted to an ever increasing number of literary methodologies. These methodologies tended to concentrate more on the world of the text and the world of the reader than on the world that produced the text. Standing between the critical methods concerned with the worlds of the author or the reader are narrative criticism, rhetorical criticism, structuralism, and linguistics. However, by the 1980s and 1990s, biblical criticism became the gathering ground for approaches that began to raise questions about an array of modern assumptions about meaning and understanding—reference, representation, objectivity, history, universals.[2] Perhaps the bridge between the historically oriented methods and the newer methods was reader-response criticism, which trained the interpretive gaze away from the text to the response generated in the reader and the reader's role in the process of meaning construction. With the advent of what we may classify as postmodern methods, the modern assumption (which in postmodern

---

[1] For a more complete presentation of interpretive terms and methods, see W. Randolph Tate, *Interpreting the Bible: A Handbook of Terms and Methods* (Peabody, Mass.: Hendrickson, 2006).

[2] George Aichele et al., *The Postmodern Bible* (New Haven: Yale University Press, 1995), 13.

reckoning was a myth) of disinterested, objective, apolitical meaning was called into question. From the perspectives of these methods, texts mean what interpreters intend them to mean. In other words, interpretation is always interested, subjective, political, and ideological. Not only have these methods called for a rereading of texts, but a rereading of readings under the assumption that not only were the biblical texts written within structures of patriarchy and in male metanarratives but they have been interpreted within systems of power that authorize and foreground some strategies and groups while marginalizing and disenfranchising others. These more recent methods, then, call for an openness to include issues of race, gender, ideology, and sexual preference as important parts of the praxis of biblical criticism.[3]

The aim of the interpreter is the deciding factor in interpretation. A text has no rights except those allowed by the interpreter. The text exercises controls over interpretation, but only to the degree that the interpreter chooses to permit such control. There is obviously the case where the interpreter is not even aware of the text's literary repertoire.

Interpreters use texts to fulfill their interests or aims. This means that interpretive purpose often differs from authorial intent. Consequently, given the possibility of this difference, hermeneutics must give appropriate attention to interpretive aims, for differences in interpretation may be due as much to differing aims as to textual ambiguity, interpretive competence, and matters of genre. As Robert Morgan points out, "Leviticus is read as religious law by Jews, as a source of religious history by historians and anthropologists, and by Christians maybe as typology or outdated theology coupled with some moral exhortation."[4] Depending upon what the aims might be, a text may mean different things to different readers at different times.

How does the issue of aims pertain to methodology? Literary aims or interests require literary methods; historical aims require historical methods; and theological aims may require a variety of methods. Interpretive aims dictate interpretive methods. These methods in turn influence the way in which interpreters perceive and use the data of the text.[5] We make sense of texts against the backdrop of our own world by employing methods determined and validated by that world. Every method is in turn anchored to a set of underlying presuppositions that determine the questions to be put to the text; and the answers are those expected in advance.

---

[3] Ibid., 14–15.
[4] Morgan and Barton, *Biblical Interpretation*, 12.
[5] McKnight, *Postmodern Use of the Bible*, 58.

Interpretive integrity should certainly require the hermeneut to articulate aims and examine methodology. The method should be consistent with aims. Aims may pertain to moral instruction, historical knowledge, justification of a liturgical practice, doctrinal support, or simply aesthetic enjoyment. There should be a viable relationship between the genre of the text, aims, and methodology. If the method of interpretation does not suit aim and genre, interpretation will be based upon presuppositions that are consistent with neither the aims nor the character of the text.

To interpret a text means to interpret in one way and not another. The hermeneut has no choice in this matter for interpretation proceeds from some method. The only choice that the hermeneut has is either to remain ignorant of the interpretive method and the attendant assumptions or to select consciously a particular methodology after examining the feasibility of the other alternatives. Since to interpret at all is to do so from one perspective rather than others, interpreters should be aware of the particular method they have selected and why.

Finding the most suitable method for interpretation is not an easy task. Sorting through the number and diversity of critical methods can be frustrating, especially to beginning hermeneuts. We find historical critics, feminists, Freudians, existentialists, structuralists, deconstructionists, narrative critics, reader-response critics, Marxists, redaction critics, canonical critics, New Critics, and formalists. How do we find our way through such a maze of competing and sometimes disparate methods?

Interpreters do not interpret without provocation and purpose. Provocation and purpose (what might be called interpretive aims) are objectified by interpretive methods. The interpreter will consciously (sometimes unconsciously) advocate the method that most nearly correlates with his or her interpretive aims. Interpretive aims dictate methods, which in turn, determine what kinds of questions the interpreter will ask of the text.

A hermeneut must use some method or a composite of several methods. There is no alternative in this matter; interpretation is based upon method. In many cases, however, the interpreter may be unable to articulate the method. Most often such inability produces haphazard, inconsistent results. The defense against such results, of course, is to examine the labyrinth of available methods and then to choose one or a mixture of methods that take into account the three worlds of hermeneutics—author-centered, text-centered, and reader-centered. Author-centered methods insist that since a text is the creation of an individual mind, any interpretation will be enhanced that takes into account anything that can be discovered about that mind or the world within which that mind thought. Text-centered methods tend to treat the text as a literary artifact that assumes a reality and life all its own once it leaves the hands of the author. The meaning of a text is exactly that— the meaning of the text, and the standard by which any interpretation of the text is measured is the text. The text is a coherent and complex whole, and any interpretation of the text must treat it as a coherent and complex whole. Reader-centered methods recognize that the text has no power to communicate meaning without the presence of a reader. In a number of creative ways, adherents of reader-centered methods locate meaning somewhere within the interaction between the reader and the text. The reader and text engage in a dialogue out of which meaning is created. These reader-centered methods are particularly interested in what actually takes place when an individual or community reads a text. The best hermeneutic will be the one that pulls from "something old and something new," the one that gives audience to a variety of interpretive approaches.

I

METHODS THAT FOCUS ON THE WORLD BEHIND THE TEXT

The world behind the text focuses on the fact that the biblical text was birthed within a particular culture, and is, therefore, an attempt to say something objective, definable, and communicable through conventions that reflect its culture.

Form Criticism

Form criticism proceeds upon the premise that parts (e.g., miracle stories, pronouncement stories, and sayings) of the early Christian and Israelite traditions circulated as individual oral units, were finally collected, and eventually became sources for the composition of the biblical texts.

Substantial efforts have been made to identify the individual forms of the biblical texts. This is true of both the Hebrew Bible and the New Testament. For example, the book of Psalms has been sub-divided into psalms of lament, thanksgiving, coronation, and hymns, among others. The prophetic books have also come under the scrutiny of form-critical studies—the prophetic address may be, among other things, judgment, exhortation, admonition, or promise. In the New Testament, much of form-critical activity has centered around the Synoptic Gospels. Some of the forms identified by Martin Dibelius, Rudolf Bultmann, and Vincent Taylor[1] include: paradigm (a brief account of an event which is designed to supply the context for a "pronouncement" of Jesus); miracle

---

[1] Martin Dibelius, *From Tradition to Gospel* (New York: Scribner, 1965); Rudolf Bultmann, *The History of the Synoptic Tradition* (rev. ed.; trans. John Marsh; Oxford: Basil Blackwell, 1963; repr., Peabody, Mass.: Hendrickson, 1993); Vincent Taylor, *The Formation of the Gospel Tradition* (London: Macmillan, 1960).

stories (which Bultmann claimed were designed for propaganda and apologetic purposes); legends (which Dibelius defined as "religious narratives of a saintly man in whose work and fate interest is taken");[2] and "sayings" of Jesus (which Bultmann divided into proverbial sayings, prophetic sayings, legal sayings, and parabolic sayings). Most of these general forms are further subdivided.

Form critics are concerned with the ways in which individual forms were utilized in the ancient culture of Israel and the life of the early church before the forms became fixed in writing. Underlying this concern is the assumption that small units of folk memory are the means by which a people's tradition is preserved and passed on. Form criticism seeks to isolate these small units of tradition and then discover how these units were used within the community. For example, the Psalms were produced in Israel within specific social contexts and in turn reflect social aspects of Israel's culture. The Epistles and Gospels in the New Testament contain units that reflect the faith and worship of the early church. As the individual stories were told and retold, they tended to be told within common settings, such as preaching, teaching, or worship. As a result, the pericopae assumed discernible forms which fit the settings. The forms, for example within the Gospels, received their shape within the Christian communities. Usage dictated form. This means that by the time the evangelists produced their gospels, the individual pericopae were already molded into definite shapes. Perhaps recognizing that a single story could assume different shapes in different settings might account for some of the variations of the same story as told by the evangelists.

Form criticism, however, goes further than correlating form with setting. Form criticism is the English translation of the German word *formsgeschichte*. Since *geschichte* means "history," form criticism is also concerned with the history of the individual forms, the way in which the forms were transmitted and adapted.[3] This concern is sometimes called "tradition criticism." This means that form criticism attempts to inquire as far back into the form as possible, even to the form's origin. Therefore, form criticism concerns itself with a process of development from origin to present context.

The concern with the origin and development of forms and traditions has led many scholars to assume that many of the gospel stories (or at least details of the stories) did not originate in the life of Jesus,

---

[2] Dibelius, *From Tradition to Gospel*, 104.
[3] Tuckett, *Reading the New Testament*, 101.

but were "invented" by the church. Debate continues concerning the extent to which early Christians modified existing traditions about Jesus or created new ones.

Form criticism has successfully called attention to the range of forms utilized by the biblical authors. With form criticism's insistence that the forms in the biblical texts were simply metaphors reflecting problems or events in the life of the early Christian communities, attention was diverted away from the text itself. For Bultmann and his followers, what actually happened in the life of Jesus was not important; in fact, historical certitude was impossible to obtain. What became foremost, therefore, was the discovery of the faith of the early believing community and the traditions through which that faith was expressed. This position would say, therefore, that the controversy between Jesus and the Jewish authorities over the Sabbath really describes the controversies between the early Christians and Jews. Positively, however, form criticism concentrates upon the stories and sayings as types of expressions rather than as historical events in the life of Jesus, a prophet, or a patriarch. Consequently, form criticism focuses upon the ways in which ancient religious communities used and shaped forms. Thus, "form criticism allows the interpreter to understand and appreciate the role and significance of the faith and practices of the believing community in the formation of the traditions that the community would hold sacred and declare canonical."[4]

Resources

Bultmann, Rudolph. *The History of the Synoptic Tradition.* Oxford: Basil Blackwell, 1963. Repr., Peabody, Mass.: Hendrickson, 1993.

Dibelius, Martin. *From Tradition to Gospel.* Translated by Betram Lee Woolf. New York: Scribner, 1965.

Hayes, John, and Carl R. Holladay. *Biblical Exegesis: A Beginner's Handbook.* Atlanta: John Knox, 1987.

Taylor, Vincent. *The Formation of the Gospel Tradition.* London: Macmillan, 1960.

Tuckett, Christopher. *Reading the New Testament: Methods of Interpretation.* Philadelphia: Fortress, 1987.

---

[4]Hayes and Holladay, *Biblical Exegesis,* 89.

Genetic Criticism

Genetic criticism may refer to any type of criticism that focuses on the author as the source of meaning or that grounds the meaning of a text in the mind of the author at the time of writing. Since the mind of the author is the source of meaning, the genetic critic must examine any object that may have influenced that mind. When other documents by the same author are available, the task of the critic becomes easier. But even when these documents or other sources which might cast light on the author's life and mind are not available, genetic critics claim that they can still gain much information from studying the world and time of the author. Consequently, the political, social, intellectual, economic, religious, and scientific milieus of the author's world become areas of examination in order to understand the life and times of an author.

In the nineteenth century, two interests converged to direct the study of literary texts toward a focus on the biographical and historical: the author as an individual creative mind and the individual character of the age. This is the reason even today that English and humanities departments in universities still offer courses on eighteenth-century English literature or Renaissance studies or the modern British novel. The circumstances of the text's composition and the assumption that a text could be understood in terms of the life and times of the author became central to literary study in the nineteenth century. Since the author is the product of an age, an understanding of that age should assist in understanding the mind that produces a text. The most valid interpretation of a text, then, is the one that invokes the most probable context relative to the author.[5]

Publishers continue to publish works on the "world" of the Bible, background studies of both the Hebrew Bible and the New Testament, the world of the early church, the "mind" of Paul and others, and the literary, cultural, and religious environments of the Bible. The assumption behind these works is that a knowledge of the various contexts within which the biblical texts were written produces more plausible interpretations. The Gospels are better understood if studied in their first-century Greco-Roman and Judaic contexts. The works of the Hebrew Bible should be studied in the light of their Mesopotamian con-

---

[5] See Donald Keesey, "Historical Criticism I: Author as Context," in *Contexts for Criticism* (4th ed.; ed. Donald Keesey; Boston: McGraw Hill, 2003), 11–12.

texts. While the reliability and extent of our historical knowledge are being challenged by many postmodern theories, the sense that genetic criticism has a "scientific" nature continues to have a profound attraction in biblical studies.

Resource

Keesey, Donald, ed. *Contexts for Criticism.* 4th edition. Boston: McGraw-Hill, 2003.

Tradition Criticism

Tradition criticism, also referred to as tradition history, history of traditions, and traditio-historical criticism, is the study of the history of both Hebrew and Christian oral traditions and their transmission.[6] It is a method of analyzing biblical literature in terms of tradition and its growth and development. It presupposes that many biblical texts have a "prehistory," i.e., that they are based upon and/or incorporate historical traditions and that these traditions are accessible. These traditions include story, creed, poetry, aphorism, hymn, and confession, and were circulated among and within communities in what critics call the "oral period," a period in which the stories and other forms were preserved and circulated, eventually developing into traditions which were then passed on from generation to generation.[7] Tradition criticism focuses upon the nature of the traditions and the manner in which the communities over time used and adapted them. The discipline operates upon the assumption, introduced by Hermann Gunkel (1862–1932), that ancient communities produced texts through a lengthy transmission process rather than a single author creating them. These traditions were handed down over a long period of oral transmission before later authors set them down in writing or incorporated them into other written documents. Tradition critics may also assume that since the traditions grow out of and reflect the symbolic world of the communities that produce the traditions, by studying the genesis, transmission, and recontextualization of the traditions, scholars can discover much about the way in which these communities defined themselves in terms of faith and self-understanding.

---

[6] Soulen and Soulen, *Handbook of Biblical Criticism,* 198.
[7] Hayes and Holladay, *Biblical Exegesis,* 93.

Gunkel was persuaded that scholars could systematically reconstruct the manner in which different communities defined their faith and religious practices. He believes five things about these reconstructions: First, it is possible to discover the original context of the stories. Second, the scholar should be able to reconstruct the various stages through which the stories developed. Since the different stages of a tradition may have developed at different locations and in different ways within texts, the scholar may conclude that these stages reflect different periods and theological viewpoints.[8] Third, from this reconstruction, it should be possible to get at the earliest form of each story. Fourth, on the basis of the first three steps, it should then be possible to trace the process through which the stories were combined into longer narratives. And fifth, since it is rarely possible to tease out reliable historical information from these stories or the process of transmission and development, the final goal is to say something meaningful about the faith and religious practices that defined these ancient communities. Some scholars go a step further and use the knowledge gained through tradition criticism to understand the biblical texts as we now have them. The assumption here is that by examining the manner in which an author has recontextualized a tradition or a portion of it, the exegete is in a better position to understand the text under examination. In other words, an author's recontextualization of traditional material is constitutive of meaning. For example, Pss 105 and 106 both incorporate the traditional story of Israel's sojourn in the wilderness. But whereas Ps 105 "translates" the story in such a way that emphasizes the faithfulness of Yahweh to the people, Ps 106 employs the story to stress the unfaithfulness of the people toward Yahweh. Furthermore, the author of Isa 40–55 uses the tradition to describe the return from exile as a new exodus, and Hosea uses the tradition to describe the condition of Israel as a return to Egypt.[9]

As these examples illustrate, Israel recycled and dialogued with its traditions and in the process continually (re)developed its self-understanding. Individuals and communities receive the traditions but subsequently reinterpret them in light of new situations and conditions and, in turn, transmit the reinterpreted traditions to successors.[10] So the tradition is always in a state of further development. Through a study of such recontextualizations, the biblical exegete can reach a more

---

[8] Ibid., 92.
[9] Ibid., 96.
[10] Ibid., 98.

plausible understanding not only of the text but of the development and use of the traditions as well. Although tradition criticism offers assistance in the former, its primary focus is the latter; i.e., it is concerned primarily with the manner in which the Hebrew and Christian communities participated in the process of transmission. Consequently, tradition criticism remains a historically focused discipline.

Resources

Gunkel, Hermann. *The Legends of Genesis: the Biblical Saga and History.* Translated by W. H. Carruth. New York: Schocken, 1964.

Hayes, John H., and Carl R. Holladay. *Biblical Exegesis: A Beginner's Handbook.* Atlanta: Westminster John Knox, 2007.

Soulen, Richard N., and R. Kendall Soulen. *Handbook of Biblical Criticism.* 3d ed. Louisville: Westminster John Knox, 2001.

Tate, W. Randolph. *Interpreting the Bible: A Handbook of Terms and Methods.* Peabody, Mass.: Hendrickson, 2006.

Appendix

II

METHODS THAT FOCUS ON THE WORLD WITHIN THE TEXT

The world of the text highlights the fact that the biblical text has been interpreted over time, but time is never static. Both the interpreter and the interpreter's world are in continual flux. Consequently, hermeneutical models must make allowances for a certain subjectivity, incompleteness, and open-endedness.

Formal Criticism

In formal criticism (sometimes referred to as New Criticism), lexical, historical, and social meanings become irrelevant because the literary context dictates meaning. The literary context can both create new meanings and eliminate old ones. The meanings of literary forms or strategies such as motif and archetype are conveyed *only* within the context of the text. The only meaning possible for a part of the text thus depends upon its function in the text as a whole. The text may or may not depict reality in the sense of describing accurately the political, social, or religious milieu of its author's time.

Two major assumptions of formalists deal with complexity and congruence. Literary texts (i.e., literarily coherent texts) are complex constructs employing a number of literary devices such as irony, metaphor, ambiguity, and tension. On the one hand, formal critics do not intend to divorce literary texts from human experience. Since texts generate experiences that we recognize as inherently human, formalists claim that this textual complexity presents us with a story world full of emotional and moral significance somewhat congruent to our own complex experiences of the real world. On the other hand, if the text somehow creates a congruence between the textual world and the real one, then the focus for interpretation is not the text alone, but those typical or definable human experiences of the real world as well. Because of selectivity and arrangement, the text can never be more than an imitation or redefinition of reality. Reading a literary work may be similar to the drama of living, but it is never a true copy of life because selection is made *for* us rather than *by* us.

One last crucial assumption warrants attention. When formal critics refer to form, the referent may be any part of the text—words, literary devices, and so on—in a particular order. What they do not mean by form is literary *type*. Generally they are not interested in genre—whether a satire, a comedy, or an epic. The reason for this indifference towards generic categories is that such considerations might distract attention away from the *particular* text to *intertextual* concerns. When we begin to compare an Aristophanean comedy with one by Molière, or Mark's Gospel with Matthew's, we are appealing to an interpretive context outside the text itself. A text constitutes its own interpretive domain, and it neither requires nor desires historical or generic contextualization. The meaning of a literary text is contingent only upon the unique form of the text itself. Meaning is textual meaning and it is inseparable from the unique form.

Resources

Brooks, Cleanth. "Literary Criticism: Poet, Poem, and Reader." Pages 392–405 in *Literary Criticism*. Edited by Lionel Trilling. New York: Holt, Rhinehart & Winston, 1970.

———. *The Well Wrought Urn*. New York: Reynal & Hitchcock, 1947.

Eliot, T. S. *The Sacred Wood: Essays on Poetry and Criticism*. New York: Harper & Row, 1972.

———. *The Use of Poetry and the Use of Criticism*. Cambridge, Mass.: Harvard University Press, 1933. Repr., London: Faber & Faber, 1970.

Ogden, C. K., and I. A. Richard. *The Meaning of Meaning: A Study of the Influence of Language on Thought, with Supplementary Essays by B. Milinowski and F. C. Crookshank*. New York: Harcourt Brace, 1923.

Richards, I. A. *Practical Criticism*. New York: Harcourt Brace, 1952.

———. *Principles of Literary Criticism*. New York: Harcourt Brace, 1925.

Wimsatt, William K., Jr. *Hateful Contraries*. Lexington: University of Kentucky Press, 1965.

———. *The Verbal Icon: Studies in the Meaning of Poetry.* Lexington: University of Kentucky Press, 1954.

Rhetorical Criticism

Rhetorical criticism focuses on the communication between an author and a reader by analyzing the strategies an author employs to influence a reader's view or shape a reader's response. Although rhetorical criticism is a collection of critical approaches, rhetorical critics share two assumptions: that, although imperfect, language is adequate to communicate human intentions and that a communicative act includes an intentional use of language, a response, and a rhetorical situation. Given that the ancient emphasis of rhetoric was on persuasion, it is not surprising that rhetorical criticism focuses on the interactions between the author, the text, and the audience. Consequently, rhetorical criticism is interested in the product, the process, and the effect of literary communication. It looks upon the text as an artistic object (also the concern of new criticism) but also as a structured object of communication. So rhetorical criticism is interested not only in what the text is but in what it does as well.

David Goodwin identifies three types of modern rhetorical criticism—traditional (neo-Aristotelian), transitional, and contemporary.[1] The focus of neo-Aristotelian criticism is on intentionally persuasive discourse, both written and oral. Neo-Aristotelian critics focus on the effect that the communicator and the communicator's time have on shaping the discourse, which generally depend upon classical models (especially those of Aristotle) for their interpretive principles. They analyze traditional genres such as public addresses, and examine the communicator's strategies, selection and arrangement of materials, as well as the structure of the argument. They also assume that Aristotle's rhetorical categories of *logos, ethos*, and *pathos* and his two types of proofs (artistic and inartistic) along with his five divisions of rhetoric (invention, arrangement, style, memory, and delivery) provide the most reliable theoretical basis for examining persuasive discourse.

Neo-Aristotelian rhetorical criticism examines a discourse in terms of its rhetorical unit, rhetorical situation, and arrangement of materials. The determination of the rhetorical unit involves establishing the boundaries of the discourse—the distinct beginning and end. With regard to the rhetorical situation, these critics assume that a particular

---

[1] David Goodwin, "Rhetorical Criticism," in *Encyclopedia of Contemporary Literary Theory: Approaches, Scholars, Terms* (ed. Irena R. Makaryk; Buffalo: University of Toronto Press, 1993), 174–78.

discourse exists because of some specific condition or situation and that it is the task of the critic to determine these conditions and situations. Furthermore, the critic must decide how the author arranged the materials to form a unified whole and to produce persuasion. The rhetorical strategies are present in the discourse because the author chooses between available options. Since persuasion, therefore, is by design, the traditionalist focuses upon this design.

The transitional type of rhetorical criticism criticizes the traditional approach's almost exclusive interest in the speaker/author and the original audience's response. Thus, transitionalists offer a transactional model in which the function of criticism is to examine the transactions between the rhetorical situation, the rhetorical strategies, and the rhetorical effects. Although they are more interested in how a discourse functions, they do assume that criticism should focus on discourse that is self-consciously persuasive.

Contemporary rhetorical critics are not a unified group. Some, such as Wayne Booth and Mark Klyn, assume that a single, systematic rhetorical method is possible and define rhetorical criticism as the examination of the product (discourse), the process (speaker/author intention), and the effect (audience response) of communicative activity. A particular text is not necessarily rhetorical by intention but becomes such because the critic approaches the text as a communicative event.

Other contemporary rhetorical critics advocate a pluralistic approach and share a handful of key assumptions about reality and the nature of language. First they assume that reality is a social and linguistic construct that is always fluid. Second, they assume that all discourse itself is a nonobjective entity conditioned by sociopolitical forces. The third assumption is that the critic, not the theory, is central to criticism. Consequently, critical theories should always remain fluid, reflecting activities of the critic rather than dictating method to the critic. And fourth, since reality itself is fluid and perennially escapes definition, there should be no definitive method that dictates the interpretive domain of the critic.

On the one hand, there is no single method that can be called rhetorical criticism. On the other hand, however, all rhetorical critics assume that reality in some fashion is a social phenomenon and that there is a mutually informing relationship between language and human activity. Consequently, most assume a rhetorical stance that borrows from a variety of theories and methodologies that can assist in analyzing the relationships between intentions and motivations of speakers/authors, discursive structures, and audience responses. Perhaps underlying this stance is the assumption that a responsible examination of words in their linguistic patterns and formulations will reveal something about the speaker's/author's thought and intention.

Resources

Booth, Wayne. *Rhetoric of Fiction.* Chicago: University of Chicago Press, 1961.
————. *The Rhetoric of Irony.* Chicago: University of Chicago Press, 1974.
Gerber, John. "Literature—Our Untamable Discipline." *College English* 28 (1967): 354.
Goodwin, David. "Rhetorical Criticism." Pages 174–78 in *Encyclopedia of Contemporary Literary Theory: Approaches, Scholars, Terms.* Edited by Irena R. Makaryk. Buffalo: University of Toronto Press, 1993.
Kennedy, George A. *New Testament Interpretation through Rhetorical Criticism.* Chapel Hill: University of North Carolina Press, 1984.
Trible, Phyllis. *Rhetorical Criticism: Context, Method, and the Book of Jonah.* Minneapolis: Fortress, 1994.

Speech Act Theory

Speech act theory is a natural language philosophy concerned with showing how speakers can succeed in what they do regardless of the various ways in which linguistic meaning underdetermines use. Speech act theory was developed between 1939 and 1959 and first introduced by John L. Austin, an Oxford philosopher. John R. Searle worked out corresponding rules for everyday speech events such as promising, requesting, stating, and ordering, while Austin articulated appropriate conditions for such ritualized performatives as marrying and christening.[2] There are many different kinds of speech acts, including utterances, performatives, propositional utterances, illocutionary utterances, and perlocutionary utterances.

Utterance

To utter is simply to speak a word or string of words—basically to say a word for the sake of saying a word. According to Searle, utter-

----

[2] Lynne Magnusson, "Speech Act Theory," in *Encyclopedia of Contemporary Literary Theory: Approaches, Scholars, Terms* (ed. Irena R. Makaryk; Buffalo: University of Toronto Press, 1993), 194.

ances have no intention of communication or meaning. A good example is of a reflex. When someone puts a hand on a hot pan or gets pinched, he or she may say "Oh!" or "Ouch!" This speech act is an utterance. There is no meaning or intended meaning. Even though Searle implies that an utterance has no meaning except to utter, John L. Austin says,

> Every utterance is in fact a speech act . . . Consider the utterance "Fire." This may function as the speech act of warning, and if it does, it is expandable into the explicit form "I warn you that there is a fire." By this argument, every apparently constative utterance is expandable into the speech-act "statement," since utterance can be prefaced by "I state that."[3]

Austin is saying that all linguistic behavior can be considered a speech action and that every utterance has a particular "force." All that one needs to do is classify these forces.[4]

Performative

Austin desribes performative or locutionary speech acts as "declarative sentences which do not describe, and in the case of which it makes no sense to ask whether they are true or false, namely those used in the making of speech acts."[5] Furthermore, "Speakers do not state facts; instead, given appropriate circumstances, speakers actually perform conventional actions with their words."[6] A performative or locutionary speech act accomplishes something through the words being spoken. For example, the confession of one's own faith is a performative act. Through the promise within the words, the action is found. Anthony Thiselton describes this kind of speech act as "self-involvement," and Briggs suggests that "the speaker 'standing behind' the words [gives] a pledge and personal backing that he or she is prepared to undertake commitments and responsibilities that are entailed in extra-linguistic terms by the proposition which is asserted."[7] When Isaac blessed his son Jacob, his utterance is a performative or locutionary act:

---

[3] Quoted by Kristin Malmkjaer, "Speech Acts," in *A Dictionary of Cultural and Critical Theory* (ed. Michael Payne; Cambridge, Mass.: Blackwell, 1996), 508.
[4] Ibid.
[5] Ibid.
[6] Magnusson, "Speech Act Theory," 193.
[7] Briggs, *Speech Act Theory*, 133.

May God give you of heaven's dew and of earth's richness—an abundance of grain and new wine. May nations serve you and peoples bow down to you. Be lord over your brothers, and may the sons of your mother bow down to you. May those who curse you be cursed and those who bless you be blessed." (Gen 27:28–29 NIV)

Isaac is not only uttering words; the act of blessing is implicit in the words.

Propositional Utterances

A propositional utterance makes reference to or describes a real or imaginary object. Austin uses the term "constatives" for descriptive sentences. Consequently, only constatives are true or false.[8] This type of speech act defines things that are real or imaginary, things that can be described through words. These words themselves hold no meaning; rather, the object they describe holds the meaning. In Exod 26:1, instructions are given: "Moreover you shall make the tabernacle with ten curtains of fine twisted linen, and blue, purple, and crimson yarns; you shall make them with cherubim skillfully worked into them." The rest of this chapter goes on to describe in detail the construction of the tabernacle and its furnishings. The word "tabernacle" itself holds no meaning but, rather, the description of the tabernacle. Further examples may include the ark that Noah built, heaven and hell, pagan idols, the fruit of the Spirit, and the ark of the covenant.

Illocutionary Utterances

Whereas a propositional utterance describes an object, an illocutionary utterance is spoken with the intention of making contact with a listener. Illocutionary utterances are sentences that usually contain a propositional utterance, but it is their intention that is of most importance. Georg Meggle describes the illocutionary utterance as having "two possible functions—or as speech act theoreticians would like to put it, two possible illocutionary forces—'to order' and 'to inform.' "[9] Illocutions, then, are spoken with the intention to create some kind of contact with the person to whom the requests or comments are directed.

---

[8] Malmakjaer, "Speech Acts," 507–9.

[9] Georg Meggle, "To Hell with Speech Act Theory," in *Dialogue: An Interdisciplinary Approach* (ed. Mercelo Dascal; Philadelphia: Benjamins, 1985), 211.

"Strong illocutions create social reality which is thus sustained above and beyond the power of the individual to make arbitrary declarations about the world around him or her."[10] So it is an illocutionary utterance that portrays to the listener the object, place, or person being described.

Briggs suggests that the "kingdom of God" is an illocutionary act.[11] Even though a parable of the kingdom of God is a propositional utterance in that it describes a real or imaginary object, it is spoken with the intention of making contact with the listener. Matt 13:24–26 says, "The kingdom of heaven may be compared to someone who sowed good seed in his field; but while everybody was asleep, an enemy came and sowed weeds among the wheat, and then went away. So when the plants came up and bore grain, then the weeds appeared as well." The story of the kingdom of heaven is a propositional utterance because it describes a "real or imaginary object"; however, it is also an illocutionary utterance because of its intention to persuade the listener.

Perlocutionary Utterance

The perlocutionary speech act attempts to affect change in the actions of the listener. This type of speech act is also an utterance because it includes a proposition but with the intention to interact with the receiver. Austin lists the perlocutionary utterance as a "deed performed in word."[12] A perlocution is not the action itself but the words used to initiate that action. Austin also refers to this type of speech act as a " 'behavitive' to our social behavior."[13] The perlocutionary utterance goes beyond simply making contact with the receiver to changing the actions of the receiver. For example, if someone asks a friend to get him or her a glass of water, the intention is not to make small talk, but to have the friend take the action communicated by the utterance. To further illustrate, Matt 9:6–7 says, " 'But so that you may know that the Son of Man has authority on earth to forgive sins'—he then said to the paralytic—'Stand up, take your bed and go to your home.' And he stood up and went to his home." Jesus is not simply describing an object, but, rather, he intends to affect a change in the action of the man listening to him. Another example of perlocution is in Mark 16:15: "Go into all the world and proclaim the good news to the whole creation." Jesus' words communicate the actions he expects in the lives of the disciples.

---

[10] Briggs, *Speech Act Theory*, 133.
[11] Ibid., 2.
[12] Magnusson, "Speech Act Theory," 194.
[13] Ibid.

Utterances, performatives, propositional utterances, illocutionary utterances, and perlocutionary utterances are all speech acts. Through such acts, people speak, perform actions, describe objects, make contact with other persons, and create a change in the actions of others. It is possible to apply all of these types of speech acts to biblical interpretation. Briggs warns, however, that "speech act theory is not a comprehensive solution to hermeneutical problems, is not a comprehensive philosophy of language, and is not a variety of antifoundationalism."[14] Briggs suggests that even though speech act theory can be used for biblical interpretation, it may not be the best source to fully understand the message and meaning.

Resources

Briggs, Richard S. *Speech Act Theory and Biblical Interpretation: Toward a Theory of Self-Involvement.* New York: T&T Clark, 2001.

Magnusson, Lynne. "Speech Act Theory." Pages 193–99 in *Encyclopedia of Contemporary Literary Theory: Approaches, Scholars, Terms.* Edited by Irena R. Makaryk. Buffalo: University of Toronto Press, 1993.

Malmkjaer, Kristin. "Speech Acts." Pages 507–9 in *A Dictionary of Cultural and Critical Theory.* Edited by Michael Payne. Cambridge, Mass.: Blackwell, 1996.

Meggle, Georg. "To Hell with Speech Act Theory." Pages 205–11 in *Dialogue: An Interdisciplinary Approach.* Edited by Mercelo Dascal. Philadelphia: Benjamins, 1985.

Mith, Barry. "Towards a History of Speech Act Theory." Pages 29–61 in *Speech Acts, Meanings, and Intentions: Critical Approaches to the Philosophy of John R. Searle.* Berlin: de Gruyter, 1990.

Reboul, Anne. "Conversational Implications: Nonce or Generalized." Pages 322–34 in *Foundations of Speech Act Theory: Philosophical and Linguistic Perspectives.* Edited by Savas L. Tsohatzidis. London: Routledge, 1996.

Structuralism

Source and form criticisms in one way or another seek to go behind the text to the stages of textual development—the traditions or sources underlying the text, the early believing communities that shaped the

---

[14]Briggs, *Speech Act Theory*, 132.

text, or the theological intention of the author. Even canonical criti-cism seeks to articulate meaning in terms of the process of canonical development. The discovery and articulation of meaning (authorial or textual) are central. With structuralism, this changes. Issues such as the author's identity and purpose, original audience, and originating circ-umstances are bracketed out as areas of concern. Structuralism is not concerned with *what* a text means, but with *how* a text means. There-fore, only the final form of the text is of interest to structuralists.

Structuralism in general is based upon the assumption that all hu-man social activity is nothing more than manifestations of underlying systems of abstract rules or conventions which govern the way humans order their existence into meaningful structures. These systems of rules exist on a subconscious level. For example, when I formulate a sentence, I do not consciously recite beforehand the syntactical and grammatical rules which underlie my sentence, just as I do not consult a commen-tary on dress codes before I attend a funeral. At a fundamental level, the principles in these systems are universal. In all areas, then, of social ac-tivity, "deep structures" can be found common to all human societies, regardless of other culturally identifying specifics.

Another assumption of structuralism is that all human activity is essentially a form of communication. Furthermore, communication is possible precisely because people adhere to basic rules. Language is a form of communication and is, therefore, governed by a subconscious set of rules or conventions.

Structuralism as applied to literary discourse is based upon three concepts, two from Ferdinand de Saussure[15] and one from Claude Lévi-Strauss:[16] (1) the distinction between *langue* and *parole*, (2) the definition of *sign*, and (3) the concept of binary opposition as it relates to the con-cept of myth.

Langue and Parole

According to Saussure, meaning depends on an underlying system of conventions and relationships, which Saussure refers to as *langue,* and on the individual instances of actual speech, which he terms *pa-role. Parole* refers to the individual, meaningful act of speech that is

---

[15] Ferdinand de Saussure, *A Course in General Linguistics* (trans. Wade Baskin, ed. Charles Bally et al.; New York: Philosophical Library, 1959; repr., New York: McGraw-Hill, 1966).

[16] Claude Lévi-Strauss, *Myth and Meaning* (New York: Routledge, 2001).

based upon the subconscious system of literary conventions and relationships. Now if all human activities are governed by basic systems of subconscious rules, and if all these activities are actually forms of communication, we might assume that literature is a form of communication and thus governed by a set of basic conventions or rules. This can be expressed in the following proportion:

$$\frac{langue}{literature/narrative} = \frac{parole}{text}$$

Since deep structures (basic underlying conventions) are common to all languages, we can assume that as a form of communication, there are likewise common deep structures within literature in general and the genre of narrative specifically. Since *parole* is an instance of individual speech, based on the underlying enabling system of *langue*, a narrative text is a specific manifestation based on the enabling system of narrative. This means that the limited set of conventions of narrative transcends cultures, literary traditions, time, and space. All narrative traditions share the same basic conventions. It is the explicit task and goal of structuralism to uncover these deep structures within individual narratives which produce what is referred to as a meaning effect upon readers. Since all narratives communicate through a shared system of conventions, interest in individual textual meaning is replaced by an interest in the effect an individual text has on the readers. These deep structures operate at levels of writing and reading alike. Not only have authors of narrative texts internalized these deep structures, but competent readers have also internalized them. This is the only means possible for understanding a narrative text.

According to structuralists, a text actually has three meaning effect levels which correlate to types of structures. The first level is the structures of enunciation. These structures are determined by features such as authorial intent, authorial *Sitz im Leben*, and audience (the concerns of the historical-critical method). Second are structures of culture. Culture's structures consist of the specific codes of a specific people at a specific time. The third level of meaning effect is determined by the text's deep structures that are universal in all human activity. On the level of any genre of literature like narrative, certain narrative and mythological structures are present. For more conservative structuralists, these three meaning effect levels with their accompanying structures combine to produce a composite meaning effect. Consequently, texts have the potential for a plurality of meaning.

Sign and Its Dual Character

The second of Saussure's concepts that structuralists build upon is that of sign and its dual character. Concerning linguistics, Saussure claimed that a language was comprised of a series of "signs" involving relationships between signs and what the signs refer to. Every sign consists of a signifier and a signified. The signifier is the "immediate object of perception" while the signified is "that which the perception evokes." For example, the word "rose" is a sign signifying a particular flower in the real word. The signifier is the word-sound "rose" and the signified is the flower. We might say that the real-world flower is denoted by the signifier "rose." This brings us to a crucial point for structuralism. The signified may have not only a denotative meaning but also a connotative one. For example, the signifier "rose" may refer both to the real-world flower and to a person who is as lovely as a rose.

Now if a text (e.g., a narrative one) is itself a sign, it may also have both denotative and connotative meanings. It is on the denotative level that we would expect to find manifestations of authorial intention. On the connotative level, however, there exists a subconscious system of conventions and convictions which precede authorial intention. Actually, it is more accurate to speak of a plurality of levels of connotative meaning. Deep within the text are three levels which structuralists attempt to excavate: narrative structures common to all narratives but manifested culturally at the surface level; universal mythical structures; and an author's semantic universe, a system of convictions which underlies the author's work. The bottom level can be reached only by analyzing the narrative and mythical structures.

Every narrative has a series of three sequences. The initial sequence is the crisis describing some disruption of the social order. Following the initial sequence is the plot proper which consists of one or more topical sequences involving attempts to restore the social order. In the final sequence, resolution (*dénouement*), the hero is successful in restoring the social order. The articulation of these sequences varies on the surface level from narrative to narrative, depending upon culture specifics; but on the deep level of the text, these three sequences will always be found.

Each of the sequences may involve up to six roles which structuralists call *actants*. These actants are related along three different axes. A sender sends an object to a receiver, the object is carried to the receiver by the subject, and finally the subject may receive assistance from helpers and be frustrated by opponents. The relationships among the actants within a sequence can be represented by the following diagram:

Every narrative can be examined as a series of sequences by using diagrams like the one above.

Mythical Structures and Binary Opposition

Along with examining these endemic narrative structures, structuralists go even deeper in an effort to identify the presence of mythical structures. Narratives may contain mythical elements even though they are not mythical in general; thus, a narrative may contain mythical elements even though the narrative (unlike a pure myth) is a conscious logical argument. Therefore, according to biblical scholars who apply structuralism to the interpretation of the Bible, the Bible can be analyzed according to mythical structures.

The structuralists employ Lévi-Strauss's idea that myths are attempts to deal with "binary oppositions" inherent in human existence. These fundamental oppositions cannot be logically mediated. Some of these oppositions are love/hate, life/death, youth/old age, sin/righteousness. Myths attempt to mediate the oppositions by offering parallel oppositions that are proportional to the binary ones and capable of reconciliation. Structuralists seek to uncover these mythic structures and, by arranging them in paradigmatic order, discover the author's semantic universe (the fundamental system of convictions upon which the author operated).

Resources

Blancy, Alain. "Structuralism and Hermeneutics." Pages 75–104 in *Structural and Biblical Hermeneutics*. Translated and edited by Alfred M. Johnson. Pittsburgh: Pickwick, 1979.

Clarke, Simon. *The Foundations of Structuralism: A Critique of Lévi-Strauss and the Structuralist Movement*. Totowa, N.J.: Barnes & Noble, 1981.

Culler, Jonathan. "Structuralism and Literature." Pages 288–97 in *Contexts for Criticism*. Edited by Donald Keesey. 4th ed. Mountain View, Calif.: Mayfield, 1998.

Greenwood, David C. *Structuralism and the Biblical Text*. Berlin: Moun-
    ton, 1985.
Lévi-Strauss, Claude. *Myth and Meaning*. New York: Routledge, 2001.
Patte, Daniel. *What is Structural Exegesis?* Philadelphia: Fortress, 1976.
Saussure, Ferdinand de. *A Course in General Linguistics*. Translated by
    Wade Baskin. Edited by Charles Bally, et al. New York: Philosophi-
    cal Library, 1959. Repr., New York: McGraw-Hill, 1966.

METHODS THAT FOCUS ON THE WORLD IN FRONT OF THE TEXT

The world in front of the text centers on the reader and the dynamics of the reading process. The reader's presuppositions form an essential part of the reader's world and are just as constitutive of meaning as the presuppositions of the author.

African-American Criticism

At the heart of African-American criticism are the assumptions that race is an essential element of literary analysis and that the American literary canon has been irreversibly informed and shaped by Africans and African-Americans. African-American criticism has "taken a variety of forms, often grounding itself in other approaches but always revising them according to its own concerns and agendas."[1] Specifically, as African-Americans have gained strength and visibility in society, their ideals and values have altered, thus initiating change in the ways in which they perceive their "blackness" as an important attribute of their culture, particularly in regard to literature and aesthetics.

First, African-American literary critics must begin with the premise that their writing must reveal the traditionally dismal and repressive plight of the black person, and through his or her plight, they hope to foster change in both the attitude and behavior of the oppressive majority. Thus, the African-American's establishment of literature as an art is "a deep realization of the fundamental purpose of art and of its function as a tap root of vigorous, flourishing living."[2] This attempt to

---

[1] Donald C. Goellnicht, "Black Criticism," in *Encyclopedia of Contemporary Literary Theory: Approaches, Scholars, Terms* (ed. Irena R. Makaryk; Buffalo: University of Toronto, 1993), 8.

[2] Alain Locke, "Art or Propaganda?" in *African American Literary Criticism, 1773–2000* (ed. Hazel Arnett Ervin; New York: Twayne, 1999), 50.

portray passionate living of the African-American as a way in which to foster change, however, is done under the guise of slave narratives, sermons, folklore, oral tradition, and language. Thus African-American authors use their fictional writings as a way to portray accurately deeply rooted social problems.

Second, African-American critics focus on the works in which the black person and his or her role in society are primary. According to African writer Asante, "literature by African or African-American writers must reflect and treat African peoples as subject, not objects; and African ideals, values, culture, history, traditions and worldviews must inform any such creation, analysis, or presentation."[3] Thus, there remains no subject more important in African-American writing than the individual—a notion referred to as Afrocentric aesthetics. The essential assumption here is that "meaning, ethos, motifs, technique, and form all emanate from the worldview of African peoples and reflect their own sense of beauty, goodness, and . . . truth."[4] Based on this notion, then, African-American critics focus on the ways in which writers of color incorporate spirituals, work songs, blues, jazz, tales, and Ebonics—all aesthetic elements unique to the African tradition—into many of their works. All of these criteria, according to Langston Hughes, "intend to express our individual dark-skinned selves without fear or shame."[5]

Houston Baker argues that "no analyst can understand the black literary text who is not conscious of the semantic levels of black culture."[6] Basically then, language is such an integral part of the African-American literary tradition that it cannot be separated from origin and cultural identity. "The linguistic exercise among African-Americans . . . and other 'colonized' people can be seen as one modest attempt among many to repossess their histories."[7] Consequently, if African-American

---

[3] Abu Shardow Abarry, "Afrocentric Aesthetic in Selected Harlem Renaissance Poetry," in *Language and Literature in the African American Imagination* (ed. Carol Aisha Blackshire-Belay; Westport, Conn.: Greenwood, 1992), 133.

[4] Ibid., 134.

[5] Langston Hughes, "The Negro Artist and the Racial Mountain," in *African American Literary Criticism, 1773–2000* (ed. Hazel Arnett Ervin; New York: Twayne, 1999), 85.

[6] Houston A. Baker, "Toward a Critical Prospect for the Future," in *The Journey Back: Issues in Black Literature and Criticism* (Chicago: University of Chicago Press, 1980), 115–64; excerpt repr. in *Agrapha 9 African American Literary Criticism, 1773–2000* (ed. Hazel Arnett Ervin; New York: Twayne, 1999), 197.

[7] Alamin Mazrui, "African Languages in the African American experience," in *Language and Literature in the African American Imagination* (ed. Carol Aisha Blackshire-Belay; Westport, Conn.: Greenwood Press, 1992), 79.

writers do not use language that reflects the culture, they will cease to be part of the culture's traditions. Seemingly, then, African-American critics look at the oral tradition of folklore, musical influence, and black linguistic patterns to determine in what ways African-American writers have preserved African origin and culture.

Some African-American critics, however, focus on texts in which the authors attempt to "shed their race" and thus adopt the ideologies of the white majority. Specifically, when African-American criticism began to fully establish itself in the 1960s, there were many critics who desired to establish their own literary canon separate from the white majority; this notion, however, proved futile as many writers strove for integration of black and white cultures. Similarly, contemporary critics appeal to the poststructuralist notion that "whatever African-American texts have in common, there is no such thing as an essential, innate 'Blackness' in their authors."[8] Essentially, many contemporary critics note that African-Americans are not different from other American writers; rather they develop their work under different cultural and historical origins.

And third, African-American critics recognize and tolerate different schools of thought within their ranks. While African-American literary critics differ in some of their basic principles, it is not the critics themselves but the time periods in which these critics live that dictate the primary ideological differences between the various influential critics of African-American literature. This idea is what influential contemporary critic Houston A. Baker refers to as "generational shifts."[9] Subsequently, Baker's primary assertion is that African-American writings must be understood within African-American culture of specific time periods.

Currently, one of the most influential theorists in African-American literary criticism is Henry Louis Gates Jr. In his critical works, Gates explores the relationship between African culture and Western culture and the role such cultures play in assessing literature. In contrast to Houston Baker, Gates asserts that both black and white literature are socially constructed. Moreover, Gates makes note of the patterns of repetition and revision among texts by black authors: "Many black authors read and revise one another, address similar themes, and repeat the cultural and linguistic codes of a common symbolic geographic.

---

[8] Hans Bertens, *Literary Theory: The Basics* (London: Routledge, 2001), 109.

[9] Goellnicht, "Black Criticism," 6.

For these reasons, we can think of them as forming literary traditions."[10] In his most influential work, *The Signifying Monkey,* Gates refers to the trickster figure common to African-American folktales in order to demonstrate how the vernacular informs and becomes the foundation for formal black literature. Signifying, he maintains, is the process of "intertextual relations . . . the troped revision, of repetitions and difference."[11] According to Gates, all black literature is intertextual because most African-Americans have encountered similar experiences that shape the ways in which they write.

Most African-American theorists assert that the study of race in regard to literature strengthens society and, therefore, is necessary to the preservation of not only African culture but American culture as well. The issue of race has been a dominate one in the African-American literary tradition. Not only does the issue dominate the secular interpretation of texts, but it has and still does provide African-American critics with an interesting and extremely relevant way by which to interpret biblical texts. Basing one's interpretation on the idea that African-Americans are an oppressed people group under constant domination from the white majority, one can easily conclude that the Bible, through the words and actions of Jesus Christ, glorifies people groups of similar circumstance, such as the poor, widows, prostitutes, tax collectors, lepers, Samaritans—all those groups marginalized in one form or another. African-Americans easily identify with these people who, like themselves, have had to fight for recognition from their oppressors; thus, the interpretation of biblical texts from an African-American perspective is natural, expected, and necessary. James Cone, the father of black theology, defines the demand for this type of biblical interpretation as "a desperate need . . . a theology whose sole purpose is to apply the freeing power of the gospel to black people under white oppression."[12] the African-American literary critic, therefore, has a duty to both race and faith to understand biblical texts from the perspective of the oppressed.

Interpreting texts under the label of "black theology," theologians such as Howard Thurman, Emilie Townes, and James Cone have insisted that African-Americans must interpret texts through the lens of

---

[10]Bertens, *Literary Theory,* 109.

[11]Henry Louis Gates Jr., *The Signifying Monkey: A Theory of Afro-American Literary Criticism* (New York: Oxford University Press, 1988), 2.

[12]James H. Cone, *Black Theology and Black Power* (New York: Seabury, 1969), 31.

the suffering and redemption of Christ. Cone asserts that the black theology movement in the United States symbolizes Jesus as the black messiah, the strong believer and liberator who "took upon himself the suffering of all oppressed people and transformed oppression to triumph through his resurrection."[13] Additionally, black theology affirms that God reveals himself in his blackness by liberating black humanity from the powers of white racism and oppression in America; it is, therefore, essential that African-Americans see Jesus as black. Only then, states Cone, can the African-American truly relate to a normally oppressive, predominantly white version of Christianity.[14]

Many African-American critics, however, have questioned whether there is indeed legitimate truth to be found in the Christian Bible, as it was under the guise of Christianity that Africans were forced into slavery. Cone maintains that there is such a truth and glorifies the black experience while condemning the oppression by the white majority. Specifically, Cone's ideals are immersed in the black experience of liberation, as "Jesus' work of liberation;"[15] protest, also known as the "political hermeneutics of the gospel" by which Christianity becomes a religion of "protest against the suffering and affliction of man;"[16] and slavery, as the black church was "born in slavery" and symbolizes a people "who were completely stripped of their African heritage as they were enslaved by the 'Christian' white man."[17]

Contrasting somewhat with Cone's ideas of black power and scripture are the ideas of theologian DeOtis Roberts, who seeks liberation through reconciliation that "takes place between equals"[18] rather than through the doctrine of black power. He maintains that "[liberation] cannot exist with a situation of White over Blacks."[19] To foster social change through biblical interpretation, the African-American literary critic applies methods like those used by African-Americans in interpreting texts of a secular nature to advance their race ideologically, socially, and politically.

---

[13] Anthony Simmons, "African Theology and Black Theology." Online: http://www.BlackandChristian.com/articles/academy/simmons-02-04.shtml (accessed 3 March 2008).

[14] Ron Rhodes, "Black Theology, Black Power, and the Black Experience." Online: http://home.earthlink.net/~ronrhodes/BlackTheology.html (accessed 12 March 2008).

[15] Cone, *Black Theology*, 35.

[16] Ibid., 37.

[17] Ibid., 91.

[18] Rhodes, "Black Theology," 13.

[19] Ibid.

Resources

Abarry, Abu Shardow. "Afrocentric Aesthetic in Selected Harlem Renaissance Poetry." Pages 133–46 in *Language and Literature in the African American Imagination*. Edited by Carol Aisha Blackshire-Belay. Westport, Conn.: Greenwood, 1992.

Baker, Houston A. "Toward a Critical Prospect for the Future." Pages 115–64 in *The Journey Back: Issues in Black Literature and Criticism*. Chicago: University of Chicago Press, 1980. [Excerpt repr. on pages 192–97 in *African American Literary Criticism, 1773–2000*. Edited by Hazel Arnett Ervin. New York: Twayne, 1999.]

Bertens, Hans. *Literary Theory: The Basics*. London: Routledge, 2001.

Blackshire-Belay, Carol Aisha. "Afrocentricity and Literary Theory: The Maturing Imagination." Pages 3–7 in *Language and Literature in the African American Imagination*. Edited by Carol Aisha Blackshire-Belay. Westport, Conn.: Greenwood, 1992.

Cone, James H. *Black Theology and Black Power*. New York: Seabury, 1969.

DuBois, W. E. B. "Criteria of Negro Art." Pages 39–43 in *African American Literary Criticism, 1773–2000*. Edited by Hazel Arnett Ervin. New York: Twayne, 1999.

Gates, Henry Louis Jr. *The Signifying Monkey: A Theory of Afro-American Literary Criticism*. New York: Oxford University Press, 1988.

Goellnicht, Donald C. "Black Criticism." Pages 5–10 in *Encyclopedia of Contemporary Literary Theory: Approaches, Scholars, Terms*. Edited by Irena R. Makaryk. Buffalo: University of Toronto Press, 1993.

Guerin, Wilfred et al., eds. *A Handbook of Critical Approaches to Literature*. 4th ed. New York: Oxford University Press, 1999. [See especially pp. 256–60.]

Holmes, Carolyn L. "Reassessing African American Literature through an Afrocentric Paradigm." Pages 37–51 in *Language and Literature in the African American Imagination*. Edited by Carol Aisha Blackshire-Belay. Westport, Conn.: Greenwood, 1992.

Hughes, Langston. "The Negro Artist and the Racial Mountain." Pages 44–48 in *African American Literary Criticism, 1773–2000*. Edited by Hazel Arnett Ervin. New York: Twayne, 1999.

Locke, Alain. "Art or Propaganda?" Pages 49–50 in *African American Literary Criticism, 1773–2000*. Edited by Hazel Arnett Ervin. New York: Twayne, 1999.

Mazrui, Alamin. "African Languages in the African American Experience." Pages 75–90 in *Language and Literature in the African American Imagination*. Edited by Carol Aisha Blackshire-Belay. Westport, Conn.: Greenwood, 1992.

Neal, Larry. "The Black Arts Movement." Pages 122–28 in *African American Literary Criticism, 1773–2000*. Edited by Hazel Arnett Ervin. New York: Twayne, 1999.

Norrell, Robert J. "Race Does Matter." *Virginia Quarterly Review* 77, no. 2 (2001): 289.

Prahlad, Anand. "Guess Who's Coming to Dinner: Folklore, Folkloristics, and African American Literary Criticism." *African American Review* 33, no. 4 (1999): 565.

Rhodes, Ron. "Black Theology, Black Power, and the Black Experience." Online: http://home.earthlink.net/~ronrhodes/BlackTheology.html (accessed 12 March 2008).

Simmons, Anthony. "African Theology and Black Theology." Online: http://www.BlackandChristian.com/articles/academy/simmons-02-04.shtml (accessed 3 March 2008).

Washington, Robert E. *The Ideologies of African American Literature: From the Harlem Renaissance to the Black Nationalist Revolt*. Lanham, Md.: Rowman & Littlefield, 2001.

Williams, Sherley A. "The Blues Root of Contemporary Afro-American Poetry." Pages 179–91 in *African American Literary Criticism, 1773–2000*. Edited by Hazel Arnett Ervin; New York: Twayne, 1999.

Cultural Criticism

An increasing number of methods in one way or another hinge on the assumption that both texts and interpretations reflect their cultures and are often grouped under the heading of cultural studies. Texts and their interpreters are at the same time both products and producers of culture in terms of a mix of cultural systems such as art, economics, race, gender, sexual orientation, and politics. In other words, since texts, interpretations, and interpreters are cultural phenomena, the writing and interpreting of texts will never be independent of cultural forces and systems within which human communities operate. According to cultural critics, therefore, methods that claim objectivity by bracketing out or simply ignoring these cultural systems are faulty from the beginning because they fail to make room for the fundamental fact that all human activity and understanding take place under the pressure of culture.

Since so many methods have developed out of the focus on the role that culture plays in the writing and interpretive process, only a few representative methods are presented below. The resources listed contain a more exhaustive treatment of these methods that focus on the world in front of the text as it relates to the influence of culture on the enterprise of interpretation.

Adam, A. K. M., ed. *Handbook of Postmodern Biblical Interpretation*. St. Louis: Chalice, 2000.
Hayes, John, ed. *The Dictionary of Biblical Interpretation*. Nashville: Abingdon, 1999.
Tate, W. Randolph. *Interpreting the Bible: A Handbook of Terms and Methods* Peabody, Mass.: Hendrickson, 2006.

In these texts the reader will find essays on Postcolonial feminist criticism, gender criticism, race criticism, mujerista criticism, Asian/ Asian American criticism, queer theory, gay/lesbian criticism, materialist criticism, and socio-economic criticism, to name a few.

Deconstruction

Hermeneutics is, for him [Derrida], the process whereby we encounter the ambiguity in texts and in all cultural products and find in the very ambiguity new possibilities for thought and action.[20]

Jacques Derrida, the French philosopher most associated with deconstruction, consciously rejects any reference to his work as a system. Moreover, in order to militate against the tendency of scholars to define his work as a system, Derrida has adopted a strategy of employing terms in such an ambiguous and inconsistent manner that his critical thought is not easily classified by terminology. In order to speak at least coherently about deconstruction, however, I concentrate on select terms (used by Derrida and other deconstruction critics) that will assist in characterizing deconstruction.

Almost central to Derrida's thought on meaning is his concept of "writing" (*écriture*). "Writing" for Derrida is not the inscription of thought, but the fundamental human activity which precedes such inscription. In most Western hermeneutical thinking, individuals are able to write a text because they have previously "read the world." Or put another way, the world of reality that we variously encode within our texts already exists as a metaphysical reality. Derrida rejects this assumption by claiming that the world we are capable of knowing comes into being through the act of "writing." There is no world waiting to be

---

[20] Walhout, "Texts and Actions," 35.

read. Language is not rooted in a perceivable reality that precedes it; on the contrary, language itself sets the parameters of thought and, therefore, our world. If this is the case, we cannot be aware of the "presence" of that which is beyond our thoughts, but only of its "absence."[21]

In Derrida's estimation, since all human activity takes place in time, such activity is historically bound. Now this does not mean that human activity is solely historically or culturally determined. Human activity also determines and perpetually reshapes and redefines culture. Culture does not exist prior to individual acts of "writing." Prior assumptions about reality may exist, but these are themselves products of cultural "writings." This is the reason Derrida can assert that "writing" precedes speech. It is simply impossible to know something which exists prior to what is known.

Two other terms which help to explain the concept of "writing" are *trace* and *mark*. Each and every human action leaves a mark on culture, and each and every mark gives witness to its originating human action, an action which itself escapes complete specification. Therefore, writing's mark leaves a trace of the indeterminate origin of the writing.

If every human action has both a culturally specific mark and a trace of the moment of origination, then every human action has not only a determinate meaning, but also an indeterminate meaning. More simply put, if every human action is shaped by culture, while at the same time shaping the culture, the culture is constantly and infinitely undergoing modification and change while in a reciprocal fashion influencing the actions that change it. This complex of mutual influence gives rise to both continuity and discontinuity between the action and the culture. Therefore, interpretations of human actions (including literary ones) must focus on both the way in which an action is shaped by culture (i.e., the action's continuity with the culture) and the way in which an action is discontinuous with the culture.

This brings us to another of Derrida's focal terms—*différance*. This word is a deliberate misspelling of the word différence, combining two other words—*differing* and *deferring*. Using Saussure's definition of *sign*, Derrida says that a text derives meaning in its *differences* from other texts. But every text also evidences the *trace* of an indeterminate origination. Since this indeterminate quality creates change within the culture, meaning is always *deferred*. Interpretation itself becomes an activity laden with ambiguity. Interpretation is a human action with a determinate and in-

---

[21] Ibid., 36.

determinate meaning. Every hermeneut approaches a text within a culture, both influenced by and exerting influence upon the culture. Since this is an infinite process of shaping and reshaping, interpretation is an endless, ever-changing process. Interpretation is an infinite process of creation. All meaning is bound by cultural context, but that context becomes boundless.

Deconstruction critics assume that language, rather than being transparent, is inherently ambiguous, metaphorical, and rhetorical. Consequently, a text as a linguistic object is not a unified and coherent whole, but radically rhetorical and metaphorical. Actually, deconstruction is more a way of analyzing interpretive methods and philosophical systems than a method of interpretation itself. It is a backward analysis of the historical development of a tradition so as to arrive at its hidden presuppositions and bases. Derrida is interested in deconstructing Western philosophy and its metaphysical foundations.

If deconstruction critics are correct in their claims that all language is inherently metaphorical and that there exists no metaphysical reality outside our "writing," then all hermeneutics which seek a grounding either in linguistic objectivity or in a world of reality beyond language, of which language is simply the linguistic representation, are like the proverbial house built upon the sand. But do we really have a choice? Can we communicate (i.e., think and speak) in any other way except through language? Can we interpret outside the confines of some system? The answer to these questions must be negative. Nevertheless, while we may interpret within some system, we should take the reminders of the deconstruction critics in a constructive sense. At best, interpretive systems rest on theoretical bases. We should be willing to subject our methodological bases to scrutiny, for if the base is faulty, so are our subsequent interpretations.

Resources

Adamson, Joseph. "Deconstruction." Pages 25–31 in *Encyclopedia of Contemporary Literary Theory: Approaches, Scholars, Terms.* Edited by Irena R. Makaryk. Buffalo: University of Toronto Press, 1993.

Bloom, Harold, Paul de Man, Jacques Derrida, Geoffrey H. Hartman, and J. Hillis Miller. *Deconstruction and Criticism.* New York: Seabury, 1979.

Bressler, Charles E. *Literary Criticism: An Introduction to Theory and Practice.* 2d ed. Englewood Cliffs, N.J.: Prentice Hall, 1994.

Cahoone, Lawrence. *From Modernism to Postmodernism: An Anthology.* Cambridge, Mass.: Blackwell, 1996.

Culler, Jonathan. *On Deconstruction: Theory and Criticism after Structuralism.* Ithaca, N.Y.: Cornell University Press, 1982.

Derrida, Jacques. *Margins of Philosophy.* Translated by Alan Bass. Chicago: University of Chicago Press, 1982.

————. *Of Grammatology.* Translated by Gayatri Chakravorty Spivak. Baltimore: Johns Hopkins University Press, 1977.

————. *Writing and Difference.* Translated by Alan Bass. Chicago: University of Chicago Press, 1978.

Lynn, Steven. *Texts and Contexts: Writing about Literature with Critical Theory.* New York: Harper Collins, 1994.

Miller, J. Hillis. *Fiction and Repetition: Seven English Novels.* Cambridge, Mass.: Harvard University Press, 1982.

Moore, Stephen D. "Deconstructive Criticism: The Gospel of Mark," Pages 110–45 in *Mark and Method: New Approaches in Biblical Studies.* Edited by Janice Capel Anderson and Stephen D. Moore. Minneapolis: Fortress, 1992.

Odell-Scott, David W. "Deconstruction." Pages 55–61 in *Handbook of Postmodern Biblical Interpretation.* Edited by A. K. M. Adam. St. Louis: Chalice, 2000.

Saussure, Ferdinand de. *A Course in General Linguistics.* Edited by Charles Bally and Albert Sechehaye. Translated by Wade Baskin. New York: McGraw-Hill, 1959.

Stevens, Bonnie Klomp, and Larry L. Stewart. *A Guide to Literary Criticism and Research.* 3d ed. Fort Worth: Harcourt, 1996.

Walhout, Clarence. "Texts and Actions." Pages 31–77 in Roger Lundin, Anthony C. Thiselton, and Clarence Walhout, *The Responsibility of Hermeneutics.* Grand Rapids: Eerdmans, 1985.

New Historicism

New historicism developed in the United States in the 1980s. It was most succinctly defined by Stephen Greenblatt in 1982[22] and has spread to several fields of study, including biblical studies. Catherine Gallagher suggests that both adherents and opponents of the theory would probably agree that new historicism views literary and nonliterary texts as "constituents of historical discourses that are both inside and outside of texts and that its practitioners generally posit no fixed

---

[22] Stephen J. Greenblatt, *Renaissance Self-Fashioning: From More to Shakespeare* (Chicago: University of Chicago Press), 1980.

hierarchy of cause and effect as they trace the connections among texts, discourses, power, and the constitution of subjectivity."[23]

Historical criticisms that have recently rejected the ahistorical critical approaches that developed with New Criticism have been heavily influenced by Marxist criticism, deconstruction, and postmodern criticism. These historical approaches distinguish between history (the past) and historiography (the writing about the past) and reject the older historicists' claim that they can objectively reconstruct the past by reading its artifacts. While new historicism cannot be classified as a single, unified critical approach (some critics refer to their work as sociological poetics, others as cultural studies, still others as cultural criticism), the critics who practice it do share some common concerns, including the subjectivity of history, the historian's and the critic's ideologically tainted situation in writing and reading, the relationship between historiography and fiction, the relationship between discourse and ideology, and the textuality of the past.

First, according to new historicists, all history is subjective. Those who are dominant in culture tend to write it, suppressing the minority voices and leaving a biased record of the events. Consequently, new historicism presupposes the "historicity" of texts and the "textuality of history." By the former is meant that all texts are both written and read within historically and ideologically determined contexts. The latter claim means that the only access that readers or historians have to the past is through texts, which are themselves subject to the pressure of ideological context. Consequently, there is no direct access to the past, only that one mediated by texts.

Second, the new historicists see a direct connection between a text and its socio-historical context. A text of any kind is a product of social causes as well as a cause of social effects. Histories are not objective reconstructions of the past but are textual constructs of critics and historians within specific historical and literary institutions. As such, literary texts do not transcend their socio-historical contexts to tap into some transcendent realm of mimetic truth and knowledge. These critics are keenly aware that we cannot examine the past except through the lenses of the present. Neither historians nor literary critics occupy some objective, transcendent position from which to examine the past. They cannot find any natural, non-historical sources for their foundational

---

[23] Catharine Gallagher, "Marxism and New Historicism," in *New Historicism and Cultural Materialism* (ed. Ryan Kiernan; London: Arnold, 1996), 45.

assumptions. They can discover no natural givens, only their own historically constructed ideas that have no essence, only a history. Historians, literary artists, critics, and readers are all implicated in the act of writing and/or reading. Since texts are written and interpreted within specific historical, sociopolitical, and literary institutions, the histories and interpretations of texts are as much constructs by historically constructed subjects as are the past objects to be examined. This dilemma is complicated by the fact that since the original contexts of past events and texts cannot be fully reconstructed, historians and critics must construct interpretive contexts.

Third, new historicists tend to blur the line between historiography and fiction, viewing the former as the narrative arrangement of past events. Since historians must supply the contexts for most past events and objects as well as include select events while excluding others, an account of the past is always a misrepresentation. A text's context is itself a construct of the historian or critic. In other words, the historian/critic constructs a context and then assumes that it is a representation of the circumstances of the text's composition. From this perspective, then, the contextual communities (e.g., Matthean community, Essene community, Johannine community, or Priestly community) which scholars employ to say something meaningful about biblical texts are fictional creations of the scholars themselves. Historians, critics, and readers of all sorts fail to make a distinction between the actual past and their representations of the past. In other words, there is a fundamental misconception that their constructions are reconstructions. The new historicists, recognizing this basic epistemological blind spot, argue that the literary products of historians and scholars are just as fictive as texts that profess to be such.

The fourth concern of new historicism is the relationship between discourse and ideology. Historical and critical discourses are soundly rooted in ideologies. Rather than being objective, reflecting the way things were, accounts of the past reflect a particular present ideological perspective. In other words, they are attempts to legitimate the present or at least some aspect of it. A discourse is what an institution defines as truth, and this definition is an agreed-upon set of operational practices that themselves are beyond question or scrutiny and circumscribe the knowledge presented by the historian or critic. Since historians and critics are located within ideologies (socioeconomic, political, theological), historical and critical analyses of the past or of texts are not value-free. Such an assumption militates against the possibility of objective historical narratives and introduces into the practice of historiography and criticism the issue of ethical practice. Both historical and literary texts display and enforce existing rules of conduct, etiquette, and laws. Literary texts and their interpreters do not transcend the historical moment but are inevitably part of a complex ideological grounding. What past historians and critics have assumed to be universals (e.g., gender, race, and sexuality) are in reality social and historical constructs. In other words, both historical and literary texts are implicated in ideological agendas. It is clear, then, that new historicism is deconstructive in that it has been quite effective in challenging foundationalist and essentialist claims, deconstructing ideologies, and demonstrating that almost everything that humans consider to be universal, natural, or timeless is actually historically contingent and socially constructed.

Historical criticism has been a part of the study of biblical texts for years. Two aspects that unify new historicists in biblical interpretation are a rejection of traditional approaches and "a fundamental questioning of the kind of historiography represented both by the writings in the Bible and by those contemporary biblical historians whose books may be regarded as the continuation of the biblical narratives by other means."[24] New historicists believe that a new approach is needed that focuses on the subjectivity of history and on the marginalized voices that have been left out by the utopian religious viewpoints of the biblical writers. For instance, historicists studying the Pauline Letters have constructed ideas of what the communities were like that received them (Corinthians, Ephesians, etc.). New historicists claim that it is impossible to know what those cultures were like because they can only be accessed through secondhand historicity and textuality. They also claim that the accounts of ancient Israel's history have silenced other cultures which may have actually been more dominant, such as Palestine. Ultimately, many new historicists want repressed texts that are discovered (e.g., Nag Hamaddi) to be included in the canon, a goal that would be seriously opposed by many Christians.

Resources

Adam, A. K. M., ed. *Handbook of Postmodern Biblical Interpretation*. St. Louis: Chalice, 2000.

Carroll, Robert P. "Poststructuralist Approaches: New Historicism and Post-modernism." Pages 50–66 in *The Cambridge Companion to*

---

[24] Ibid., 55.

Biblical Interpretation. Edited by John Barton. London: Cambridge University Press, 1998.

Gallagher, Catharine. "Marxism and New Historicism." Pages 45–54 in *New Historicism and Cultural Materialism*. Edited by Ryan Kiernan. London: Arnold, 1996.

Greenblatt, Stephen J. *Renaissance Self-Fashioning: From More to Shakespeare*. Chicago: University of Chicago Press, 1980.

————. "Resonance and Wonder." Pages 55–60 in *New Historicism and Cultural Materialism*. Edited by Ryan Kiernan. London: Arnold, 1996.

Keesey, Donald, ed. *Contexts for Criticism*. 4th ed. Boston: McGraw-Hill, 2003.

Shea, Victor. "New Historicism." Pages 124–30 in *Encyclopedia of Contemporary Literary Theory: Approaches, Scholars, Terms*. Edited by Irena R. Makaryk. Buffalo: Toronto University Press, 1993.

Soulen, Richard N., and R. Kendall Soulen. *Handbook of Biblical Criticism*. 3d ed. Louisville: Westminster John Knox, 2001.

Young, R. V. *At War with the Word*. Wilmington, Del.: ISI, 1999.

Postcolonial Criticism & Liberation Theology

As the literary child of postcolonialism, postcolonial criticism focuses on the relationship between literature, literary canon, and imperialism. It emphasizes diversity as each critic brings his or her own emphasis to the discourses that center on several basic assumptions before branching out into the rich multiplicity inherent in this theory. A basic assumption of postcolonial critics is that the dominating culture wrote the literature and decided what literature was canonized. This literature, even the very language that was used, affected society by propagating the differentiation and subsequent oppression of the colonized.[25]

This basic assumption dictates to postcolonialists their main tasks, the first of which Alfred J. López calls "a reckoning with the colonial past."[26] This task involves the critique of the Western assumptions of what literature has been canonized as well as the reinterpretation of

---

[25] Donald E. Hall, *Literary and Cultural Theory: From Basic Principles to Advanced Applications* (Boston: Houghton Mifflin, 2001), 268–69.

[26] Alfred J. López, *Posts and Pasts: A Theory of Postcolonialism* (Albany: State University of New York Press, 2001), 7.

the texts with an awareness of their imperialist assumptions. The second task consists of a call for due attention to be given to the literature of marginalized people. And the third task is to discuss postcolonial diasporas, pan-nationalism, and nationalism.[27] This task includes discourses on the production of culture and the complexity of identity—the inherent hybridity of both the colonist and the subjugated people. Postcolonialists employ many theoretical approaches, most often psychoanalysis and deconstruction, and are commonly influenced by Marxist and feminist criticism.

Edward Said, one of the founders of postcolonialist thought, is concerned with the duty of the critic in the face of the Eurocentrism and cultural elitism of literary scholarship. He argues that the task of the critic is "oppositional criticism" against domination, for the goal of "noncoercive knowledge in the interests of human freedom."[28] Said's most significant contribution to the field is his book *Orientalism*, in which he examines Western images of the Orient—both in the academic disciplines, such as anthropology, and in popular representation in movies, literature, etc.[29] Said states that these representations of the oriental "other" are projections of the West, having little to do with the actual nature of the people represented. These constructions foster biases and justify Western domination of third-world cultures.[30]

This theme of imperialist representations of other cultures is common among postcolonial theorists. Gerald Vizenor directs similar attention to the portrayal of Native Americans in the academic world and popular culture. This portrayal "proved" the Native Americans' natural inferiority and helped to justify the ideology of "manifest destiny"—an ideology of spreading over the continent and subjugating the Native Americans.[31]

A residual phenomenon arising in the wake of colonialism, cultural imperialism encompasses the effects of colonization in language,

---

[27] Aparajita Sagar, "Post-colonial Studies," in *A Dictionary of Cultural and Critical Theory* (ed. Michael Payne; Cambridge, Mass.: Blackwell, 1996), 424.

[28] M. A. R. Habib, "Said, Edward William," in *A Dictionary of Cultural and Critical Theory* (ed. Michael Payne; Cambridge, Mass.: Blackwell, 1996), 480.

[29] George Aichele, "Edward W. Said," in *The Norton Anthology of Theory and Criticism* (ed. Vincent B. Leitch; New York: Norton, 2001), 1988.

[30] Habib, "Said, Edward William," 481.

[31] Jeanne Garane, "Gerald Vizenor," in *The Norton Anthology of Theory and Criticism* (ed. Vincent B. Leitch; New York: Norton, 2001), 1075.

culture, religion, and economic and political structures. Within this context, Frantz Fanon explores the use of language to dominate a people group after colonialism, specifically with regard to his home country, Martinique. Fanon notes the superior status attributed to French over Creole, which is seen as a degenerative local language.[32] He says that this acculturation dehumanizes the locals, forcing them to forget their own culture and history. Fanon called this the "whitening" of his race.

In her controversial essay "Can the Subaltern Speak," Gayarti Spivak levels criticism at postcolonialist efforts at emancipating cultures. Spivak claims that postcolonialists can easily be condescending to the people to whom they are claiming to give a voice. They do this in the very notion that third-world cultures must lead the fight against cultural imperialism, assigning them value only as far as they follow Western scripts.[33] Theorists can also do this by romanticizing the oppressed, essentializing them, and replicating the colonists they criticize.

Spivak's pragmatic application of her theories to real-life political (in her case, feminist) goals is characteristic of many postcolonial theorists. It seems to be common among these critics to see art as propagating social values. They often go beyond recommending academic measures (such as Achebe's call for writing from the perspective of the oppressed and Ngugi's call for the abolition of the English department) to advocate practical political steps. Homi Bhabha asserts that theory should be accompanied by political activism, not separated from it,[34] and Edward Said relates his criticism to real-world politics and is strategically involved with the Palestinian situation.[35] Literary and social commentary is often accompanied by social action in the field of Postcolonialism.

Postcolonial criticism has deep significance in how we view literature and society, and its value has been extended to other disciplines, including the field of biblical studies. Interpretive theory in the field of biblical studies has traditionally been dominated by Western interpre-

---

[32] Jeanne Garane, "Fanon, Frantz," in *A Dictionary of Cultural and Critical Theory* (ed. Michael Payne; Cambridge, Mass.: Blackwell, 1996), 190.

[33] Gayarti Chakravorty Spivak, "Can the Subaltern Speak," in *The Norton Anthology of Theory and Criticism* (ed. Vincent B. Leitch; New York: Norton, 2001), 2201–3.

[34] Homi K. Bhabha, "The Commitment to Theory," in *The Norton Anthology of Theory and Criticism* (ed. Vincent B. Leitch; New York: Norton, 2001), 2379–97.

[35] Habib, "Said, Edward William," 481.

tations of Scripture to the exclusion of other voices. Fernando Segovia asserts that postcolonialism has "particular importance and relevance for biblical criticism" as it calls for more diverse theories from the margins.[36] It has been argued that Western Christian missions have historically been an arm of Western imperialism. Since the early colonialism of the fifteenth century, the West has viewed itself as not only the political center but also the religious center. Segovia states that the West's view has been that those "culturally subordinated to the center must be brought into religious submission as well."[37]

Postcolonialists focus on what Sugirtharajah calls "discourse[s] of resistance"—critical theories from indigenous peoples.[38] These theorists of the developing world use "their own cultural resources to illuminate biblical narratives," offering valuable insights into the discourses on biblical interpretation.[39] Postcolonialists also focus on the reality of ancient imperialism (Assyrian, Roman, etc.) throughout the biblical narratives and discuss how this reality colored the writing of texts.

Postcolonial thought, however, extends beyond the texts to modern readings and interpretations of the texts. The West's imperialist heritage colors our worldview, causing us to see reality in terms of binary opposites. This seeing of people in terms of "us/them" or "center/ margins" extends to our religion. For example, categorizing people as "believers/pagans" can be interpreted as being the product of this imperialist mentality, which sees humanity in terms of "the West/everyone else."[40] Postcolonial theory also analyzes the readers of the texts in how they position themselves in regard to this binary opposition, comparing it with how marginalized people position themselves.

Liberation readings are a popular ideological interpretive stance in biblical studies. There are many examples of these readings from people outside the center, such as Native American and African-American readings, as well as a host of readings from people groups all over the world (e.g., the contemporary Jewish reading of Exodus).

Liberation theology has often focused on the biblical narrative of the Israelites' exodus from Egypt. Usually the marginalized or oppressed

---

[36] Fernando Segovia, *Decolonizing Biblical Studies: A View from the Margins* (Maryknoll: Orbis, 2000), 125.

[37] Ibid., 128.

[38] Rasiah S. Sugirtharajah, *The Bible and the Third World: Precolonial, Colonial and Postcolonial Encounters* (New York: Cambridge University Press, 2001), 5.

[39] Ibid., 7.

[40] Segovia, *Decolonizing Biblical Studies*, 126.

group relates itself to the Israelites in their achievement of freedom from bondage in Egypt and their resulting autonomy. Contemporary Jewish theologians often relate the formation of the modern state of Israel to this account, comparing the Diaspora to Egypt, and the Palestinians to the ancient Canaanites who have to be driven out of the promised land.[41] This is the prominent reading of the text, but dissident voices of Jewish and Christian Palestinian theologians argue that the modern state of Israel, with its economic and political oppression of a people and expropriation and occupation of a land, is more directly related to Egypt in the biblical narrative. The Palestinians, then, would ironically be related to the ancient Israelites in this marginalized reading. This has profound ramifications on the theology regarding Israel and is an example of the rich possibilities of decentralizing our biblical interpretations.

Resources

Adam, A. K. M., ed. *Handbook of Postmodern Biblical Interpretation*. St. Louis: Chalice, 2000.

Aichele, George et al. *The Postmodern Bible*. New Haven: Yale University Press, 1995.

———. "Chinua Achebe." Pages 1781–83 in *The Norton Anthology of Theory and Criticism*. Edited by Vincent B. Leitch. New York: Norton, 2001.

———. "Edward W. Said." Pages 1986–90 in *The Norton Anthology of Theory and Criticism*. Edited by Vincent B. Leitch. New York: Norton, 2001.

Bhabha, Homi K. "The Commitment to Theory." Pages 2379–97 in *The Norton Anthology of Theory and Criticism*. Edited by Vincent B. Leitch. New York: Norton, 2001.

Garane, Jeanne. "Fanon, Frantz." Page 190 in *A Dictionary of Cultural and Critical Theory*. Edited by Michael Payne. Cambridge, Mass.: Blackwell, 1996.

———. "Gerald Vizenor." Pages 1075–77 in *The Norton Anthology of Theory and Criticism*. Edited by Vincent B. Leitch. New York: Norton, 2001.

Habib, M. A. R. "Said, Edward William." Pages 479–81 in *A Dictionary of Cultural and Critical Theory*. Edited by Michael Payne. Cambridge, Mass.: Blackwell, 1996.

---

[41] Aichele, *The Postmodern Bible*, 292.

Hall, Donald E. *Literary and Cultural Theory: From Basic Principles to Advanced Applications.* Boston: Houghton Mifflin, 2001.

López, Alfred J. *Posts and Pasts: A Theory of Postcolonialism.* New York: State University of New York Press, 2001.

Sagar, Aparajita. "Postcolonial Studies." Pages 423–28 in *A Dictionary of Cultural and Critical Theory.* Edited by Michael Payne. Cambridge, Mass.: Blackwell, 1996.

Said, Edward W. *Orientalism.* New York: Pantheon, 1978. Repr., New York: Vintage, 2003.

Segovia, Fernando. *Decolonizing Biblical Studies: A View from the Margins.* Maryknoll: Orbis, 2000.

Spivak, Gayarti Chakravorty. "Can the Subaltern Speak." Pages 2197–208 in *The Norton Anthology of Theory and Criticism.* Edited by Vincent B. Leitch. New York: Norton, 2001.

Sugirtharajah, Rasiah S. *The Bible and the Third World: Precolonial, Colonial, and Postcolonial Encounters.* New York: Cambridge University Press, 2001.

Thiong'o, Ngugi, Wa Tababn Lo Liyong, and Henry Owuor-Anyumba. "On the Abolition of the English Department." Pages 2092–96 in *The Norton Anthology of Theory and Criticism.* Edited by Vincent B. Leitch; New York: Norton, 2001.

Reception Theory

Hans Robert Jauss, the principle architect of reception theory, claims that in order to get a new reading of a text, the reader must step outside his or her own historical praxis and view the work without any preconceived notions.[42] However, Jauss believes such a step is virtually impossible because a reader comes to the text with a certain horizon of expectation. The traditional focus on historical objectivism must be replaced by an approach to literature that prioritizes issues of reception rather than the impact on the reader.

For Jauss, the author, work, and reader form a fundamental triangle in the literary process, and current criticism gives import to the reader and the manner in which the reader is influenced by history. For Jauss, the reader (the public) is more than "a chain of mere reactions";

---

[42] Hans Robert Jauss, *The Aesthetic Experience and Literary Hermeneutics* (trans. Michael Shaw; vol. 3 of *Theory and History of Literature*; Minneapolis: University of Minnesota Press, 1982).

the reader is a formative part of history, and the literary work has no historical life without the active participation of its audiences.[43] The reader judges the aesthetic value of the work by comparing it to previously read texts. The latter historical implication lies in the observation that the understandings of the first readers will be inscribed in the receptions of future generations.

According to Jauss, history is mere opinion. For example, if history (or, better, historiography) is objective, all of the gospels should be exactly the same. The fact that the gospels are not the same but rather have irreconcilable differences does not mean that one or more of the texts is wrong. Jauss views history as a perspective of a certain group or individual. Consequently, history is in no way objective but is jaded by the perspective of the writer.

Jauss offers seven theses in his description of the aesthetics of reception.[44] The first deals with the problem of objectivity in reading a literary work: As a reader engages a text, preconceived ideas (originating from a number of sources—past text, status, economics, etc.)[45] are present in either the reader's conscience or subconscience. In other words, certain receptions of past reading experiences are triggered with each new reading, and these past experiences in turn influence any literary work a public reads. A literary work does not exist objectively by itself, offering to every reader in every period the same view. A work is more like an orchestration that strikes each reader differently. The historical contexts of both work and reader create a horizon of expectation, a horizon which the reader believes will happen based upon his or her historical background. Consequently, the possibility of comprehending and representing a literary work in its unique historicity is dependent upon the objectification of the horizon of expectation.

Jauss's second thesis concerns the manner in which one's horizon of expectation is continually evolving. What a reader expects a text to do will change as the reader reads other texts and accumulates more life experience. This change also applies to the rereading of a text. When certain understandings are established in the first reading, a subsequent reading allows for new questions to be raised and old lingering questions to be answered. For example, a person studying the Gospel

---

[43] Hans Robert Jauss, "Literary History as a Challenge to Literary Theory," in *Critical Theory since 1965* (ed. Hazard Adams and Leroy Searle; Tallahassee: University of Florida Press, 1986), 164.

[44] Ibid., 165.

[45] Ibid., 166.

of Mark with little critical reading background may sense an uneasiness with the manner in which the author portrays the disciples. If this same reader then reads a book or books that point out the literary role that the imperceptiveness of the disciples plays, not only will old questions be answered, but new ones will be generated, only to be answered upon further critical reading.

The third thesis argues that since readers and the conditions within which readers engage a text change, the text will have different effects at any historical moment. A work that is intended for a specific society at a specific time will not mean the same thing to that society twenty years later. Jauss calls this phenomenon the horizontal change. But the opposite can also happen. An author may write a work not intended for a particular audience but have a significant influence on a later society. For example, numerous texts in the Hebrew Bible had a formative impact upon the writers of the New Testament.

The fourth thesis concerns the reconstruction of the horizon of expectation and the production of a literary work. Reconstructing the horizon of expectation of the author and contemporary audience enables the contemporary reader to discover how he or she should view and understand the work.[46] It points up the hermeneutic difference between the past and the current understanding of the text. Jauss argues that a reader who is not part of the author's original audience must learn what the horizon of expectation might have been for the original audience by considering the reading and writing style of the period and the social, environmental, geographical, religious, and political contexts.

The fifth thesis points out the evolution of the horizon of expectation of the text. After a reader's theories and expectations have been upset, many questions may possibly arise that the text has not answered. As a reader engages other texts, however, these original questions may be answered and new meaning found in the first text. Thus, a text can be read hundreds of times with meaning always evolving.

In his sixth thesis, Jauss argues that not only does a text change over time for a particular reader; it also takes on new meaning with each generation. One generation passes down its understanding of the text, with the next generation beginning where the preceding one ended. Consequently, a text's meaning is always evolving diachronically across time.

In his seventh thesis, Jauss further develops his idea that social influences modify interpretations. Every social influence (from government

---

[46] Ibid., 171.

programs to job pressures) has an impact on interpretation. While general assumptions may be made dependent upon the major factors in a reader's life, the plethora of influencing factors precludes any predictability of the way a reader will interpret a text at any given moment.

It is obvious that Jauss based his theory on the triangle of interpretation, the points of which represent the three major constituents of interpretation—author, text, and reader. The author has his or her own interpretation of the text, the text holds the possibility of any number of interpretations, and the audience may create further interpretations. For Jauss, since each point of the triangle plays a significant part in the interpretive process, no point should be neglected or prioritized in any act of interpretation.

Resources

Jauss, Hans Robert. *The Aesthetic Experience and Literary Hermeneutics.* Vol. 3 of *Theory and History of Literature.* Translated by Michael Shaw. Minneapolis: University of Minnesota Press, 1982.

————. "Literary History as a Challenge to Literary Theory." Pages 164–83 in *Critical Theory since 1965.* Edited by Hazard Adams and Leroy Searle. Tallahassee: University of Florida Press, 1986.

————. *Question and Answer: Forms of Dialogic Understanding.* Minneapolis: University of Minnesota Press, 1989.

————. *Toward an Aesthetic of Reception.* Vol. 2 of *Theory and History of Literature.* Translated by Timothy Bahti. Minneapolis: University of Minnesota Press, 1982.

Womanist Criticism/Theology

Alice Walker, seeking an alternative word for organizing people's thinking about black women's "self-definitions, relationships, activities, and history, and their meaning for the black experience,"[47] coined the term "womanist" in 1982. In her book *Sisters in the Wilderness,* Delores William defines womanist theology in the following way:

Womanist theology is a prophetic voice concerned about the well-being of the entire African American community, male and female, adults and

---

[47] Cheryl Townsend Gilkes, *If It Wasn't for the Women: Black Women's Experience and Womanist Culture in Church and Community* (Maryknoll: Orbis, 2001), 10.

children. Womanist theology attempts to help black women see, affirm, and have confidence in the importance of their experience and faith for determining the character of the Christian religion in the African American community. Womanist theology challenges all oppressive forces impeding black women's struggle for survival and for the development of a positive, productive quality of life conducive to women's and the family's freedom and well-being. Womanist theology opposes all oppression based on race, sex, class, sexual preference, physical ability, and caste.[48]

Delores Williams also articulates four hermeneutical principles of womanist methodology. (1) It is intentionally multidialogical, practicing itself in community with others beyond the African-American women's community. (2) It is informed by liturgical intent, both accountable and challenging to the black church. (3) It is informed by a didactic intent, offering new ethical, spiritual, and moral insights to church and society. (4) It is committed to reason and black women's experience as related in their imagery and metaphoric statements.[49]

Womanists assume that God's revelation is directed to them and that God's revelation in the Bible must be read and heard in the context of their experience.[50] God is spirit and historically has been seen as a "deliverer" who lifts one "out of the miry bog."[51] However, womanists relate mostly to God in Jesus, because he identifies with "the least," and they feel that black women in U.S. society most appropriately represent "the least."[52]

Black women have viewed the Bible as a significant source of spiritual, ethical, and political empowerment and have used social-service clubs, educational systems, and advocacy organizations as bases for social activism. This focus is especially evident in the works of some distinguished African-American women activists of the twentieth century, such as Mary McLeod Bethune, Nannie Helen Burroughs, and Marian Wright Edelman.[53] The central hermeneutical principle for womanist theology is that "the Bible must be read and interpreted in the

---

[48] Delores Williams, *Sisters in the Wilderness: The Challenge of Womanist God-Talk* (Maryknoll: Orbis, 1995), 67.

[49] As summarized in Linda A. Moody, *Women Encounter God: Theology Across Boundaries of Difference* (Maryknoll: Orbis, 1996), 85.

[50] Ibid., 89.

[51] Karen Baker-Fletcher, *Sisters of Dust, Sisters of Spirit: Womanist Wordings on God and Creation* (Minneapolis: Fortress, 1998), 110, 112.

[52] Moody, *Women Encounter God*, 103.

[53] Cheryl J. Sanders, ed., *Living the Intersection: Womanism and Afrocentrism in Theology* (Minneapolis: Fortress), 126–27.

light of black women's own experience of oppression and God's revelation within that context."[54] Accordingly, there are four black women
in the Bible that womanists give special attention: Hagar (Gen 16:1–
15; 21:8–20), Zipporah (Exod 2:21–22; 4:24–26; Num 12:1), the queen
of Sheba (1 Kgs 10:1–13; 2 Chr 9:1–9), and Candace, queen of the
Ethiopians (Acts 8:27).[55] Of these four women, the most written about
is Hagar, the slave of Sarah and Abraham and mother of Ishmael.
Hagar is considered passive—barely a participant in her own story.
Womanists feel that the story is not about Hagar or even Sarah but
rather about Abraham.[56] In this biblical story, Hagar stands in as a
surrogate mother for Sarah, "who in her impatience and unfaithfulness, lost sight of who she was in relation to the sovereign Word of God,
and so doing, lost sight of reality itself."[57] The liberation in Hagar's
story is not by God; rather, it is found in human initiative. Consequently, the womanist draws a connection between the trials of black
women of the past and Hagar. "As Hagar learned how to survive and
acquire an appropriate quality of life for herself and her son, so also
did the African slaves, accommodating the Bible to the urgent necessities of their lives."[58] Womanists view both Hagar and Sarah as victims
of a societal system that privileged men and valued women only in
terms of their relationship to those men—as daughter, wife, mother,
and sister, unable to stand alone and with no identity to claim for
themselves.[59]

Black women also look to other females in the Bible, such as Phoebe,
Priscilla, and Mary—coworkers with Paul—and interpret the experiences of these women in ways that reflect womanists' interests, noting
especially that the ultimate allegiance of these women was to God, not
to men.[60] Womanists also look to the mothers of the Bible (e.g., the
mothers of Isaac, Moses, and Samson) as role models for motherhood
because they are "more than bodily receptacles through which great
men were born."[61]

---

[55] Moody, *Women Encounter God*, 90.

[56] Sanders, *Living the Intersection*, 131.

[57] Diana Hayes, *Hagar's Daughters: Womanist Ways of Being in the World*
(New York: Paulist, 1995), 6.

[58] Ibid., 7.

[59] Ibid., 57.

[59] Ibid., 7.

[60] Emilie M. Townes, *In a Blaze of Glory: Womanist Spirituality as Social
Witness* (Nashville: Abingdon, 1995), 33.

[61] Ibid.

Delores Williams devised a hermeneutic intended to help theologians understand the ways that "contemporary Hagars," the most marginalized of black women, are excluded from the liberation motif of black (male) liberation theology.[62] The bottom line seems to be that womanist theology "aims at reassuring the humanity of black women by disclosing forms of false and illusionary consciousness among black women and in the black community."[63]

While womanist theology is an expression of black women and their past, not all black women are womanists. But at the same time, "the potential is embedded in all Black women's experience."[64] The womanist feels that it is necessary "to ground Black women's analysis in multiple voices"—in order to have the diversity, richness, and power of black women's ideas as part of a "long standing African-American women's intellectual community."[65]

Resources

Anderson, Victor. *Beyond Ontological Blackness: An Essay on African American Religious and Cultural Criticism.* New York: Continuum, 1995.

Baker-Fletcher, Karen. *Sisters of Dust, Sisters of Spirit: Womanist Wordings on God and Creation.* Minneapolis: Fortress, 1998.

Douglas, Kelly Brown. *Sexuality and the Black Church.* Maryknoll: Orbis, 1999.

Gilkes, Cheryl Townsend. *If It Wasn't for the Women: Black Women's Experience and Womanist Culture in Church and Community.* Maryknoll: Orbis, 2001.

Hayes, Diana. *Hagar's Daughters: Womanist Ways of Being in the World.* New York: Paulist, 1995.

Johnson, Patricia-Anne. "Womanist Theology as a Counter-Narrative." Pages 197–214 in *Gender, Ethnicity, and Religion: Views from the Other Side.* Edited by Rosemary Radford Ruether. Minneapolis: Fortress, 2002.

Moody, Linda A. *Women Encounter God: Theology across the Boundaries of Difference.* Maryknoll: Orbis, 1996.

---

[62] Moody, *Women Encounter God*, 30.

[63] Victor Anderson, *Beyond Ontological Blackness: An Essay on African American Religious and Cultural Criticism* (New York: Continuum, 1995), 111.

[64] Gilkes, *If It Wasn't for the Women*, 186.

[65] Hayes, *Hagar's Daughters*, 4.

Sanders, Cheryl J., ed. *Living the Intersection: Womanism and Afrocentrism in Theology*. Minneapolis: Fortress, 1995.

Townes, Emilie M. *In a Blaze of Glory: Womanist Spirituality as Social Witness*. Nashville: Abingdon, 1995.

Walker, Alice. *In Search of Our Mother's Gardens: Womanist Prose*. San Diego: Harcourt Brace Jovanovich, 1983.

Williams, Delores. *Sisters in the Wilderness: The Challenge of Womanist God-Talk*. Maryknoll: Orbis, 1995.

METHODS INVOLVING MORE THAN ONE WORLD

Meaning results from an active conversation between the world of the text and the world of the reader, a conversation informed by the world of the author. The locus of meaning is not to be found exclusively in either world or in a marriage of any two of the worlds, but in the interplay between all three worlds.

Ideological Criticism

Ideological criticism attempts to uncover the ideology of a text and the ideological influences during the history of its interpretation. Ideology refers to the "social structures marked by patterns of dominance and subordination, i.e., race, ethnicity, gender, religion, etc."[1] The central focus of ideological criticism is to offer an approach to examining texts that asks readers to be aware of and account for not only the ideological frameworks of the author and the text, but their own ideological frameworks. Consequently, there are at least three areas to which ideological critics may direct their attention: (1) the ideological context in which an author produces a text, (2) the ideology reproduced within the text itself, and (3) the ideology of a text's readers.

An author's ideology, consisting of beliefs and assumptions on such issues as social class, economics, gender, and race, affect the way in which he or she writes, not to mention the content of the writing. Thus the reader can better understand the text by attempting to grasp the content of an author's ideology. Additionally, many hold to the notion that the text itself implies a certain ideology. Again, the astute reader will look for such things as the oppression of groups or the patriarchal

---

[1] Soulen and Soulen, *Handbook of Biblical Criticism*, 84.

dominance of women. Finally, readers must be aware of their own ideological biases that they bring to the reading of a text.

Although ideological criticism is varied in expression, the common thread running through all its expressions is the assumption that texts are not value-neutral but, rather, reflect to different degrees the relations and structures of race, gender, and class, which empower some persons and disenfranchise others. Ideological criticism, therefore, demands that interpreters of texts not only read from a posture of suspicion, but also that they critically examine their own interpretive traditions. In other words, in ideological criticism, readers cannot divorce themselves from ethical issues that become inherent in the act of interpretation.

Resources

Adam, A. K. M. *What Is Postmodern Biblical Criticism?* Minneapolis: Augsburg Fortress, 1995.

Aichele, George et al. *The Postmodern Bible.* New Haven: Yale University Press, 1995.

Elliot, Gregory. "Ideology." Pages 252–57 in *Dictionary of Cultural and Critical Theory.* Edited by Michael Payne. Cambridge, Mass.: Blackwell, 1996.

Fewell, Danna Nolan, and Steven L. McKenzie. *To Each Its Own Meaning.* Louisville: Westminster John Knox, 1999.

Soulen, Richard N., and R. Kendall Soulen, *Handbook of Biblical Criticism.* 3d ed.; Louisville: Westminster John Knox, 2001.

Walhout, Clarence, and Leland Ryken, eds. *Contemporary Literary Theory: A Christian Appraisal.* Grand Rapids: Eerdmans, 1991.

Intertextual Criticism

Intertextual criticism is based upon Julia Kristeva's term "intertextuality," which she introduced in 1969 in a critique of the modern assumptions that texts contain meaning and that critics can objectively excavate that meaning. Kristeva also used the term "text" to include anything that might be read, such as a text, person, ritual, or anything in culture that must be interpreted. According to Kristeva, a text is a centerless convergence of various signifying systems, an intersection of other texts. Every text is a conjunction of other texts of which it is a rereading.[2] So a text is a kind of patchwork quilt constructed from pieces of other texts, which are themselves constructed through the interweaving of other texts and discourses.

It becomes a truism, then, that interpretations can never exhaust what may be said about texts. A single interpretation can never be the last word, but simply one possible way among an infinite number of ways to configure the indeterminacy of the text's intertextuality. This means that any interpretation (or method of interpretation, for that matter) exists only at the expense of excluding other possibilities. To use the terminology of Umberto Eco, any interpretation results from a process of "blowing up" parts of the text while "narcoticizing" other parts.[3] In other words, interpretation is a matter of tracing intertextual relations guided by ideological and methodological agenda, personal interests, and affiliatory expectations (academic, theological, philosophical, etc.). The object of any textual analysis, then, is not necessarily meaning in terms of the relationship between the language of the text and an extratextual referent but signification in the sense of unlimited semiosis, that is, the relationship of signs and texts to other signs and texts as indeterminate objects.

Some critics, however, have extended the definition of intertextual criticism to mean something much broader. For example, Donald Keesey[4] sees intertextual criticism as having a twofold focus. First, he includes what other critics call genre criticism under the umbrella of intertextual criticism. Accordingly, literary texts do not imitate life but other texts of the same genre. Authors do not transform reality but transform the conventions of the genre within which they are working. For example, in writing the *Aeneid*, Virgil expected his readers to recognize that he was writing an epic that would look a lot like Homer's *Odyssey*. While his epic is structurally very similar to Homer's, it is an interpretive appropriation of the *Odyssey*. If Virgil's readers did not recognize this appropriation, they would be unable to grasp his purpose. While any single work may not conform exactly to its genre, it would be unintelligible if it were absolutely unique. So, when a reader analyzes a

---

[2] Julia Kristeva, "The Bounded Text," in *Desire in Language: A Semiotic Approach to Literature and Art* (trans. Thomas Gora et al.; New York: Columbia University Press, 1980), 36.

[3] Umberto Eco, *The Role of the Reader: Explorations in the Semiotics of Texts* (Bloomington: Indiana University Press, 1979), 228.

[4] See Donald Keesey, "Intertextual Criticism: Literature as Context," in *Contexts for Criticism* (4th ed.; ed. Donald Keesey; Boston: McGraw Hill, 2003), 265–77.

text by relating it to other texts of the same genre, the reader is practicing a type of intertextual criticism. A parable, for example, is best read in light of all other parables ever written. Similarly, the best reading of the wisdom literature in the Hebrew Bible occurs in the context of all other wisdom literature.

The last observation points to the second focus of intertextual criticism—the reciprocal nature of intertextuality. First, since texts are constructed from prior texts, the most plausible reading of any text is the one which recognizes an author's intertexts and the manner in which the author appropriates these texts. For example, a reading that takes into account Mark's appropriation of texts from the Hebrew Bible is an intertextual reading. Since Mark recontextualizes these texts, a reading that does not or cannot recognize such appropriation is impoverished. This idea of one author appropriating or alluding to other texts has become an important part of biblical intertextual criticism. The interest in the idea of intertexts is reflected in recent studies that claim that the authors of the Synoptic Gospels used Greco-Roman epics such as Homer's *Iliad* and *Odyssey* and Virgil's *Aeneid* (see McDonald; Bonz) as intertexts. If the appropriated texts are themselves networks of appropriated texts, then the act of interpretation potentially extends indefinitely. There simply is no backward boundary for the interpretive process. Interpretation may end, but it is never finished.

Intertextual reciprocity also extends into the indefinite future. Not only do former texts inform the reading of later texts; the reversal is true as well. That is, reading later texts informs the reading of former texts. For example, one's reading of Alexander Pope's *Rape of the Lock* and John Milton's *Paradise Lost* makes for a more plausible reading of Virgil's *Aeneid*, which in turn informs one's reading of Homer's *Odyssey*. If some modern critics are correct in their claim that the author of Luke-Acts constructed his work in conversation with Greco-Roman epic (especially Virgil's *Aeneid*), then one's reading of Luke-Acts would be greatly enhanced by reading epics such as *The Rape of the Lock* and *Paradise Lost*, which were written centuries after Luke-Acts. Consequently, when a text becomes an intertext for other texts, its literary signification extends beyond itself. The intertextual critic, therefore, is also interested in examining how other texts have appropriated a given text and then using this information in a reexamination of the appropriated text. Clearly then, a text is really never completed but is always in the process of being written; it is always in an intertextual process of production, which includes both past and future texts.

So intertextual criticism may focus on the issue of genre and linguistic and literary conventions, but it will always be concerned with the reciprocity of intertextuality and indeterminacy, which it naturally inscribes. Michael Riffaterre sums up intertextuality by defining it as the relationship between readers and their recognition of a text's relationship to texts that precede or follow it.[5]

Resources

Bonz, Marianne P. *The Past as Legacy: Luke-Acts and Ancient Epic.* Minneapolis: Fortress, 2000.

Culler, Jonathan. "Presupposition and Intertextuality." *Modern Language Notes* 91, no. 6 (1976): 1380–97.

Fewell, Danna Nolan, ed. *Reading between Texts: Intertextuality and the Hebrew Bible.* Louisville: Westminster John Knox, 1992.

Hand, Sean. "Missing You: Intertextuality, Transference, and the Language of Love." Pages 79–91 in *Intertextuality: Theories and Practices.* Edited by Michael Worton and Judith Still. Manchester, Eng.: Manchester University Press, 1990.

Keesey, Donald, ed. *Contexts for Criticism.* 4th ed. Boston: McGraw-Hill, 2003.

Kristeva, Julia. "The Bounded Text." Pages 36–63 in *Desire in Language: A Semiotic Approach to Literature and Art.* Translated by Thomas Gora, Alice Jardine, and Leon S. Roudiez. New York: Columbia University Press, 1980.

McDonald, Dennis R. *The Homeric Epics and the Gospel of Mark.* New Haven: Yale University Press, 2000.

Riffaterre, Michael. "Compulsory Reader-Response: The Intertextual Drive." Pages 56–78 in *Intertextuality: Theories and Practices.* Edited by Michael Worton and Judith Still. Manchester, Eng.: Manchester University Press, 1990.

———. *Text Production.* Translated by Terese Lyons. New York: Columbia University Press, 1983.

Tull, Patricia K. "Rhetorical Criticism and Intertextuality." Pages 156–80 in *To Each Its Own Meaning: An Introduction to Biblical Criticisms and Their Application.* Edited by Steven L. McKenzie and Stephen R. Hayes. Louisville: Westminster John Knox, 1999.

---

[5] Michael Riffaterre, "Compulsory Reader-Response: The Intertextual Drive," in *Intertextuality: Theories and Practices* (ed. Michael Worton and Judith Still; Manchester: Manchester University Press, 1990), 56–78.

Marxist Criticism

The Marxist critic holds that art serves as an ideological mechanism, legitimating and perpetuating the system of social values, beliefs, and relationships by which one class dominates the others. Central to Marxism is the assumption that individual human consciousness, cultural experience, and even society itself are products of discrete, material processes and can be understood in scientific terms. For Marx and Engels, the founding fathers of Marxism, the underlying dynamic of social change was the struggle for dominance between economic classes. Every change in the economic structure of a society was invariably accompanied by a corresponding change to its social order. This relationship led them to believe that the economic form in which one class has power over the others determines the ways in which the social hierarchy develops.

In recent Western history, for example, this class struggle has taken the form of capitalism. In a capitalistic economy, the modes of production are controlled by a ruling class but operated by a working class. Because the modes of production—the way in which production is carried out and the structures that control it—are owned by the ruling class, workers are dependent upon them for survival. In other words, self-sufficiency is not so much a result of an individual's ability to procure material necessities as it is an individual's ability to enter into a relationship with those who control the distribution of material necessities.

However, in order for this system to work, the number of workers must exceed the number of jobs. There must be a measure of unemployment. Because there are more workers than jobs, laborers are forced to compete with each other for employment. Competition for jobs, in turn, drives down job wages because those who have no work become willing to work for less in order to obtain employment. In this way, workers are not paid for the full value of their labor. In some of the less regulated forms of capitalism, this wage atrophy advances to the point where a harmony is struck between the minimum cost of survival and a worker's income, reducing the working force into what has been called "wage slaves." In the end, an artificial disparity is created between the market value of a product and the actual cost of production. This artificial disparity is called the surplus value of labor and is absorbed by the bourgeoisie as profit by mere virtue of the fact that they own the means of production and are able to leverage this economic ordering to their benefit. The individual worker, in order to survive, has no choice but to participate in this exploitive social structuring and is essentially powerless to remedy his or her situation.

Marx and Engels also asserted that the social, cultural, and physical environment one is born into determines, to a large degree, the development of the individual consciousness. In other words, society creates the individual rather than the other way around.

If the social structure of a society is in some way determined by its economic structure, then consciousness derives ultimately from that economic structure as well. This synthesis between the views of the economic basis of social structure and the development of consciousness results in a bipartite formulation of society according to which society is composed of two divisions: the base, which is the economic structure, and the superstructure, the collective social consciousness that develops in the context of the economic base. It is much like an all-inclusive ideology or worldview and includes such things as religion, morality, aesthetics, philosophy, politics, and law.

However, because the superstructure derives from an exploitive economic base, it creates a false consciousness that functions to legitimate the existing social structures. In other words, it is "the complex structure of social perception which ensures that the situation in which one class has power over the others is seen as 'natural' or not seen at all."[6]

The base and superstructure are so interrelated that changes within one will have recursive effects upon both itself and in the other. Consciousness is not only an object within a particular environment; it is also an integral element in the total composition of that environment. However inextricably bound the two components are, it is ultimately the base that determines the nature of the superstructure, since it is the base that grants one class power over the other classes. The superstructure merely exists to obscure the fact that the exploited classes are the victims of exploitation.

Marxist criticism is an application of the theory of superstructure to art, in which art itself exhibits in its very composition the ideology of the dominant class. According to Terry Eagleton, a leading if not the foremost neo-Marxist critic, ideology, as it is used here,

> is not in the first place a set of doctrines; it signifies the way men live out their roles in class-society, the values, ideas and images which tie them to their social functions and so prevent them from a true knowledge of society as a whole. In this sense . . . it shows a man making sense of his

---

[6] Terry Eagleton, *Marxism and Literary Criticism* (Berkeley: University of California Press, 1976), 5.

experience in ways that prohibit a true understanding of his society, ways that are consequently false.[7]

Marxist criticism is concerned with the complex relations uniting a work of literature to the ideology in which it originated. A non-simplistic understanding of a work must not overlook the several elements of the base-and-superstructure model—an author's class position, ideological forms and their relation to literary forms, spirituality and philosophy, techniques of literary production, aesthetic theory, and the economic base—which typify a period and how these elements converge to produce a literary specimen. A literary work, after all, is an elaborate concoction of values, images, and ideas specific to a time.

The Marxist wishes to expose the falsities and unnatural arrangements that endorse one class' power over the others. For the Marxist, all literature can be scrutinized for ideological ingredients, but good literature will typify the ideology of its period in such a way that ideology becomes consciously visible rather than just unconsciously present. Good literature will communicate a sense of realism and faithfulness to the social experience while exposing and implicitly challenging the limitedness, inadequacy, and artificiality of the very real structures that have been imposed upon it. In this way, it is able to generate a universal appeal and relevancy to all readers across time while being firmly rooted in its own context. In the end, a Marxist critique examines all aspects of a piece of literature—from form and style to characterization and plot, and even to the mode of production in which it was published—for social authenticity in order to expose the falseness of prevailing ideologies.

Approaching it from a non-theistic point of view, the Marxist sees the Bible as any other text subject to the same criticisms as all other texts. From a Marxist point of view, it would be difficult to construe the traditional ideas of inerrancy and infallibility as anything but pillars in the ideological mechanism sanctioning the structures that empower sacred authority. More devastating to an individual's hope of eschewing these social structures is the concept of original sin, whereby the lot of humanity is consigned to eternal punishment. The only escape, of course, is obsequious submission to the Almighty's authority, which he has, in his ever merciful wisdom, seen fit to vest in the institution of the church.

Eagleton has applied these techniques to an interpretation of the biblical book of Jonah in his essay "J. L. Austin and the Book of

---

[7]Ibid., 17.

Jonah."[8] According to Eagleton's essay, God sends Jonah to prophesy to Nineveh because God is really too maudlin to destroy the city himself and needs an excuse to spare the city in order to save face. Jonah sees right through God's self-deception and realizes that his own part in the narrative is only superficial. Consequently, Jonah is disturbed by what he judges to be God's manipulative motives, especially when Nineveh miraculously repents. Eagleton further concludes that the source of Jonah's despair is his recognition that as long as God is providentially guiding and directing everything, individual human action is meaningless. But then Jonah thinks that God may have put him up to this task just to make him question the meaningfulness of action. He realizes that he cannot even know if he knows whether action is meaningless or not. This realization plunges Jonah from existential despair into aimless subjectivism. The story ends with God reproaching Jonah's despair suggesting, according to Eagleton, that despite the prophet's earlier assessment, the divine propensity to mercy is, in fact, fickle and absurd.

Eagleton is painting Jonah's plight against the ideological backdrop of history. Jonah's relation to God, in this interpretation, is an allegory of the individual's relation to the Marxist conception of history. To what degree does human action matter if action is inseparable from history and that which is acted upon? And to what degree can we even know if human action matters? By raising these questions, Eagleton entices the reader to glimpse the individual's inescapable connection to history and the subjectivity that results.

Such as it is, this interpretation is not a traditional Marxist reading of the book of Jonah, but then again Eagleton is not a traditional Marxist. What is important is the insight provided by the illumination of ideological elements—the conjunction of Jonah's well-founded reluctance, the meaninglessness of his action, his subsequent despair, and God's ever present and unpredictable "otherness" present a realistic image of social experience characteristic of false consciousness. Eagleton summarizes this dilemma: "The Book of Jonah leaves its protagonist caught in a transitional stage between false consciousness and some new, currently unnamable style of identity; and to this extent we have made little advance upon it."[9]

---

[8] Terry Eagleton, "J. L. Austin and the Book of Jonah," in *The Postmodern Bible Reader* (ed. David Jobling, Tina Pippin, and Ronald Schleifer; Malden, Mass.: Blackwell, 2001), 177–82.

[9] Ibid., 181.

Resources

Eagleton, Terry. "Introduction Part I." Pages 1–15 in *Marxist Literary Theory: A Reader*. Edited by Terry Eagleton and Drew Milne. Cambridge, Mass.: Blackwell, 1996.

————. "J. L. Austin and the Book of Jonah." Pages 177–82 in *The Postmodern Bible Reader*. Edited by David Jobling, Tina Pippin, and Ronald Schleifer. Malden, Mass.: Blackwell, 2001.

————. *Marxism and Literary Criticism*. Berkeley: University of California Press, 1976.

Kellner, Douglas. "Marxist Criticism." Pages 95–99 in *Encyclopedia of Contemporary Literary Theory: Approaches, Scholars, Terms*. Edited by Irena R. Makaryk. Buffalo: University of Toronto Press, 1993.

Macey, David. *The Penguin Dictionary of Critical Theory*. London: Penguin, 2000.

Mimetic Criticism

Mimetic criticism finds the meaning of a text in the relationship between the text and reality. Almost any verbal representation seems to force some type of comparison with our experience. The mimetic critic, then, judges the worth of a literary text by its ability to represent or reflect some aspect of the world outside the text. Good literature, claims the mimetic critic, reveals some truth about the way humans experience nature. In one way or another, all mimetic critics appeal to a shared human common sense or experience of the world and the text's imitation of that common sense or experience as the locus of meaning.

From the time of the ancient Greeks to the eighteenth century, the idea that literature was essentially mimetic was an unchallenged premise. Literature revealed truth about life.[10] In his *Poetics*, Aristotle argued not only that the heart of tragedy was its catharsis of pity and fear but that tragedy produced in the viewer or reader an insight experience. Such an experience was what the reader or viewer of the tragedy recognized as the truth that the text revealed about some aspect of the human condition, i.e., an insight into some universal aspect of a reality external to the text itself. This is the reason that Aristotle can claim that art is more closely allied with philosophy than with history—because like philosophy, art seeks the universal rather than the particular.

---

[10] Donald Keesey, "Mimetic Criticism: Reality as Context," in *Contexts for Criticism* (4th ed.; ed. Donald Keesey; Boston: McGraw Hill, 2003), 205.

Mimetic critics claim that the mimetic relationship between reality, defined as the infinite flux of changing experience, and a text is the complexity of both. While the text may be formal in design and does not replicate reality, it does mirror it in the complexity of the design. The experience of reading a complex text is similar to our experience of life. We attempt to make sense of both by imposing an interpretive grid, in terms of a system of thought, upon them.

Mimetic critics also claim that characterization, setting, plot, and action in literature invite a comparison with life as we experience it outside the text. So, says the mimetic critic, if artistic representations invite comparison with non-artistic experience, literature forces us to ask important questions about life.

Mimetic criticism seems to correspond well to the way that many readers and critics approach the biblical texts and to the way that the Bible as literature courses in higher education approach the texts. When readers of the book of Job ask questions about the relationship between piety and divine blessing, they are assuming that Job suggests something theologically significant. When a biblical scholar suggests that the Gospel of Mark is redefining the concept of messiahship, he or she is assuming that the gospel employs literary strategies, form, and content to suggest something about the way we should view an aspect of life, or when a reader seeks to find guidance in the Psalms or Proverbs, he or she is reading mimetically.

Resources

Keesey, Donald, ed. *Contexts for Criticism.* 4th ed.; Boston: McGraw-Hill, 2003.

Tate, W. Randolph. *Interpreting the Bible: A Handbook of Terms and Methods.* Peabody, Mass.: Hendrickson, 2006.

Narrative Criticism

Narrative criticism is the study of narratives, focusing not only on traditional narrative elements such as plot, setting, and characterization, but also the role of the reader. Like reader-response criticism, narrative criticism assumes that the story does not exist autonomously within the text, but comes into being through the interaction between the text and the reader. Narrative critics treat the narrative itself as the signifier and the story (produced through the interaction between the narrative and reader) as the signified. Narrative criticism is the analysis of the narrative content within the context of relationships between authors, texts, and readers (see diagram on p. 96).

Narrative critics identify a literary entity who is found only within the text. This entity is not the real author, but only an incomplete reflection of the real author. For example, when I read the Gospel of Mark, the only author I encounter is that one which I may be able to construct from the text alone. Even more revealing is the reading of several Pauline epistles. When I read 1 Corinthians, I encounter one entity; when I read Galatians, I encounter another. These two implied authors are not the same because each text yields different information. Consequently, it is possible for a real-world person to author several texts, each one having a different implied author. Another way to put it is that the implied author is a composite of discernible ideologies underlying a particular text.

The implied reader, like the implied author, is defined by the text. The implied author may consciously or unconsciously construct the text in such a manner as to provide guidance to a reader. This means that a text contains unspoken assumptions about the reader. It is obvious that the implied author (the real author for that matter) of Mark's Gospel did not have a twentieth-century reader in mind when he or she wrote. Even though the text provides direction for the reader by giving definition to the implied reader, the implied reader is not entirely defined by the text. The implied author may assume on the part of the implied reader a set of values, literary competence, and background. But there is simply no way to assure that every reader will satisfy this role. On the one hand, even if we assume that the role of the implied reader may be completely defined, no single reader can perfectly and completely conform to the role the text provides for the implied reader. On the other hand, to the degree that the reader fulfills the role of the implied reader provided for by the text, the reader becomes captive to the text and its ideology. But the opposite may also occur, i.e., a reader may discover that the role demanded of the implied reader is so foreign or ideologically distasteful that the reader simply refuses to read, thus rejecting the role of the implied reader.

Since all narratives are told through the voice of a narrator, the person and activity of the narrator occupy a place of special importance in the determination of meaning. A narrative may be told in the first or third person, and the narrator may be outside the action or a character within the story. Further, a narrator may vary in degree of knowledge, from very limited knowledge to virtual omniscience.

Furthermore, the narrator is not identical to the implied author. The implied author creates the fictive narrator who is dependent upon the implied author for any characteristics and abilities which may be discernible from the text. The view of the narrator may or may not reflect the ideology of the implied author. This is true of the third person omniscient narrator or of the narrator who is also a character within the story.

The counterpart of the narrator is the narratee, the entity to whom the narrator tells the story. While the narratee receives the story as it unfolds moment by moment, the implied reader reads what the narrator tells the narratee. The implied reader is an entity with a set of values that enables him or her to complete the work. The narratee, however, has total definition only by the work. Like the narrator, the narratee may be a character within the story, but is usually a person who has no place within the story. The identity of the narratee will determine to a large degree the style and complexity of the narrator's language. If the narratee is uninformed about the subject matter, the narrator may become very detailed, offering extensive explanation.

In narrative criticism the narrative world is not identical to the real world. The real world of both author and reader alike is infinite, but observable and present, with all events working together in an interconnected system. The narrative world is both limited and bounded, the only access to which is the secondary medium of the text. The objects, persons, and events in the narrative may not correspond to anything in the real world. In order for the implied reader to reconstruct the narrative world, determinations as to relative importance of events must be made. The implied author highlights some events, subordinates others, and leaves gaps while moving from one narrative segment to another. The responsibility of bridging these gaps belongs to the implied reader.

According to the narrative critic, meaning begins with the narrative world, not the real world. The meaning of the Gospel of Mark is not to be found in considering Mark an objective, historically accurate portrayal of the life and times of Jesus. What Jesus (or any character for that matter) says or does in the narrative must find its significance within the world of the narrative alone. The implied author shapes the story world by selecting some events and excluding others. This process of selectivity immediately excludes the possibility of the narrative world being a complete replica of the real one. All meaning, therefore, must be constructed in conversation with the narrative world, which is a construct of the text. Meaning must be a function of the relationships, experiences, and connections which the implied reader is called upon to create.

Resources

Powell, Mark Allen. *What is Narrative Criticism?* Minneapolis: Fortress, 1990.

Tate, W. Randolph. *Interpreting the Bible: A Handbook of Terms and Methods.* Peabody, Mass.: Hendrickson, 2006.

Socio-Rhetorical Criticism

Socio-rhetorical criticism is an interpretive method defined by Vernon Robbins as "a textually-based method that uses programmatic strategies to invite social, cultural, historical, psychological, aesthetic, ideological and theological information into a context of minute exegetical activity."[11] For the socio-rhetorical critic, the focus of interpretation is the text as a cultural, social, ideological, historical, and theological discourse, and the data from these various areas have an intertextual relation with respect to the textual signs.[12] The socio-rhetorical critic, then, understands the term "rhetorical" to refer to the text as a literary object, i.e., a story that must be read, and the term "socio" as referring to the text as a cultural artifact that must be opened "to the past, present, and future."[13] From this posture, Robbins has articulated a fourfold framework within which socio-rhetorical criticism works: (1) rhetorical-literary aspects of the text; (2) the intertextuality of the text; (3) the social and cultural dynamics operating in the text; and (4) ideology. Later, however, Robbins restates the fourfold framework of the criticism based upon the various textures of the text and claims that readers of texts will focus on one texture at the expense of the others. The four textures are (1) inner texture, (2) intertexture, (3) social and cultural texture, and (4) ideological texture. In a later publication, *Exploring the Texture of Texts*, Robbins adds a fifth texture—sacred texture.

Inner texture is the entry level of analysis and focuses on the features of the text's language, including such things as word patterns (e.g., repetition of words and the sequencing of terms); textual units; form of argument; voices; literary and rhetorical devices; and the mixing of

---

[11] Vernon K. Robbins "Socio-Rhetorical Criticism: Mary, Elizabeth, and the Magnificat as a Test Case," in *The New Literary Criticism and the New Testament* (ed. Edgar V. McKnight and Elizabeth Struthers Malbon; Valley Forge: Trinity Press International, 1994), 165.

[12] Ibid., 166.

[13] Robbins, *Jesus the Teacher,* xxiii.

speech and narrative.[14] Robbins identifies six types of inner texture: (1) repetitive, in which a word or phrase occurs multiple times in a single unit; (2) progressive, in terms of the sequencing of words or phrases in a unit, such as the alternation of words (e.g., the language of kingship in Mark 15:1–16:8) and word chains; (3) narrational, which encompasses the various voices in the text (narratorial voice, reported speech, written texts, characters' voices); (4) opening, middle and closing of the unit; (5) argumentative, the argument of the text in terms of both modern and ancient rhetorical theory; and (6) sensory-aesthetic, which is concerned with the ways in which the language of the text evokes the senses, emotion, and thought patterns of readers (issues of genre on the level of text and subtexts become important in this texture).[15]

Intertexture is concerned with the manner in which the author interprets and presents material outside the text within the text itself. Two important questions guide this type of analysis: "From where has this passage adopted its language? With what texts does this text stand in dialogue?"[16] Robbins describes five dimensions of intertexture analysis: analysis of reference, recitation, recontextualization, reconfiguration, and echo.[17]

The first dimension of intertexture is reference to persons, objects, places, traditions, and texts. In other words, analysis of reference is concerned with the things with which the text is in dialogue and with the ways that interpreters decide what traditions and texts are referenced and the significance that those determinations have.

The second dimension is recitation, for instance, the manner in which a speech is reported—exact language, modified language, or different language altogether from the original. Recitation also deals with whether an account is summarized, expanded, or just what episode or event is referenced. Robbins argues that the uncertainty of references leaves the interpreter a certain amount of freedom to determine the reference, a determination that may be ideologically motivated. Consequently, the interpreter may foreground one possibility while negating others.

Recontextualization refers to the practice of the placement of narratives, speeches, etc., in new contexts without announcing the fact.

---

[14] Vernon Robbins, *Exploring the Texture of Texts: A Guide to Sociorhetorical Interpretation* (Harrisburg: Trinity Press International, 1996), 3–7.
[15] Ibid., 8–30.
[16] Ibid., 179.
[17] Ibid., 179–85; see also 40–50.

For example, Robbins refers to Raymond E. Brown's *Birth of the Messiah*, in which he points out a significant number of recontextualized speeches from the LXX in Luke 1:26–56.

With respect to reconfiguration, Robbins argues that authors reconfigure both texts and well-known traditions. For example, in the Magnificat, Luke may have reconfigured the Israelite tradition of the barren woman who conceives a child at an advanced age. However, given both the Judaic and Hellenistic influence on Luke's gospel, the reconfigurations may have multiple souces, e.g., the stories of virgins in the LXX and the Greco-Roman stories of women imprenated by gods.[18]

The final dimension is intertextual echo, which goes beyond recontextualization and reconfiguration to include soundings from tradition and culture. Given that the New Testament texts were written within a Mediterranean culture that was multifaceted, socio-rhetorical critics demand that all cultural traditions be brought to bear on the analysis of texts. For example, on the one hand, scholars have compared the Magnificat with the praise hymns in the Psalms. On the other hand, however, Robbins asks about the frequency with which scholars are willing to compare the Magnificat with hymns of praise in Roman-Hellenistic literature as well as other Mediterranean literature.

Social and cultural texture involves theories of both anthropology and sociology. The primary focus here is upon "the social and culture nature of the text."[19] While the text is an artifact of a particular culture and social location, it is also a response to that culture and social location. Robbins delineates the parameters of this texture in terms of "specific social topics, common social and cultural topics, and final cultural categories."[20]

Common social and cultural topics are those that persons in a particular culture are familiar with instinctively. When an interpreter can access these topics, the extent of interpretive anachronism is diminished. In first-century Mediterranean texts, the interpreter will be faced with social structures of honor/shame, clean/unclean, purity/impurity, codes of argumentation, systems of legality, economic exchange systems based upon a variety of subsystems (e.g., agriculture, business), and hierarchical social structures.

The ideological texture is based upon the assumption that every text inscribes an ideology, a body of political, economic, religious, or

---

[18] Vernon Robbins, "Socio-Rhetorical Criticism," 180.
[19] Robbins, *Exploring the Texture of Texts,* 71.
[20] Ibid.

social ideas upon which a culture's values, thoughts, judgments, etc., are based. Within ideological criticism, ideology may refer to three contexts: (1) the ideological context in which an author produces a text, (2) the ideology reproduced within the text itself, and (3) the ideology of a text's readers or "customers." Socio-rhetorical criticism examines all three ideological contexts but tends to focus on the first two. By examining the artifacts (including textual ones), scholars can partially reconstruct the ideology of a culture.

Much of the work of anthropologists and sociologists focuses on this reconstruction. To reconstruct the ideology represented by the text or, perhaps better, to reconstruct the ideology underlying the text, socio-rhetorical critics must analyze the rhetorical structures of language. Robbins suggests that certain questions should be asked: "What and whose self-interests are being negotiated in this text? If the dominant voices in the text persuade people to act according to their premises, who will gain and who will lose? What will be gained and what will be lost? . . . Whose ideology is being advanced, for whose benefit?"[21] From the perspective of the socio-rhetorical critic, then, every text is ideological and to at least some degree propagandistic. If we assume, therefore, that early Christianity had its politics or ideological positions, then we may also assume that its texts are ideological.

By the "sacred texture" of texts Robbins means not only what the text says about the divine but also the ways that readers explore the sacred nature of texts. He recommends that since the sacred texture is embedded within the other four, a more plausible understanding of the text develops as the interpreter allows the sacred nature to emerge from a detailed examination of the first four textures. This idea of the sacred is located in those references in the text to deity, holy persons, spirit beings, divine history, human redemption, human commitment, religious community, and ethics.[22] Again these elements emerge from a multi-textured analysis of the text.

Socio-rhetorical critics recognize that written and oral communication and their interpretations are social acts in which authors, speakers, and readers all stand squarely within meaning-making ideologies and communities. Consequently, texts and their interpreters comprise a multi-contextual location with multiple boundaries. Socio-rhetorical criticism responds to this complex labyrinth by drawing from a variety of interpretive approaches in order to configure readings that account

---

[21] Robbins, "Socio-rhetorical Criticism," 194–95.
[22] Ibid., 120–30.

for the greatest number of meanings and meaning effects that may not be configured by more narrowly circumscribed methods.

Resources

Brown, Raymond E. *The Birth of the Messiah: A Commentary on the Infancy Narratives in Matthew and Luke.* Garden City, N.Y.: Doubleday, 1977.

Malina, Bruce. *The New Testament World: Insights from Cultural Anthropology.* Atlanta: John Knox, 1981.

Meeks, Wayne. *The First Urban Christians: The Social World of the Apostle Paul.* 2d ed. New Haven: Yale University Press, 2003.

Neyrey, Jerome, ed. *The Social World of Luke-Acts: Models of Interpretation.* Peabody, Mass.: Hendrickson, 1991.

Robbins, Vernon K. *Exploring the Texture of Texts: A Guide to Socio-Rhetorical Interpretation.* Harrisburg: Trinity Press International, 1996.

———. *Jesus the Teacher: A Socio-Rhetorical Interpretation of Mark.* Minneapolis: Fortress, 1992.

———. "Socio-Rhetorical Criticism." Pages 164–209 in *The New Literary Criticism and the New Testament.* Edited by Elizabeth Struthers Malbon and Edgar V. McKnight. Valley Forge: Trinity Press International, 1994.

Soulen, Richard N., and R. Kendall Soulen. *Handbook of Biblical Criticism.* 3d ed. Louisville: Westminster John Knox, 2001.

Select Bibliography

Abrams, M. H. *A Glossary of Literary Terms.* New York: Holt, Rinehart & Winston, 1981.

Adam, A. K. M., ed. *Handbook of Postmodern Biblical Interpretation.* St. Louis: Chalice, 2000.

———. *What Is Postmodern Biblical Criticism?* Minneapolis: Augsburg Fortress, 1995.

Adamo, David Tuesday. *Biblical Interpretation in African Perspective.* Lanham, Md.: University Press of America, 2006.

Aichele, G., and G. A. Phillips, eds. *Intertextuality and the Bible. Semeia* 69–70 (1995).

Aichele, George. *The Limits of Story.* Philadelphia: Fortress, 1985.

Aichele, George et al. *The Postmodern Bible.* New Haven: Yale University Press, 1995.

Alter, Robert. *The Art of Biblical Narrative.* New York: Basic, 1981.

———. *The Art of Biblical Poetry.* New York: Basic, 1985.

Alter, Robert, and Frank Kermode, eds. *The Literary Guide to the Bible.* Cambridge, Mass.: Harvard University Press, 1987.

Althaus-Ried, M. "The Hermeneutics of Transgression." Pages 251–72 in *Liberation Theologies on Shifting Grounds: A Clash of Socioeconomic and Cultural Paradigms.* Edited by G. de Schrijver. Leuven: Leuven University Press, 1998.

Anderson, Janice Capel, and Stephen D. Moore, eds. *Mark and Method: New Approaches in Biblical Studies.* Minneapolis: Fortress, 1992.

Armour, E. T. *Deconstruction, Feminist Theology, and the Problem of Difference: Subverting the Race/Gender Divide.* Chicago: University of Chicago Press, 1999.

Arp, Thomas, and Greg Johnson. *Perrine's Literature: Sound, Structure, and Sense.* 8th ed. Boston: Heimle & Heimle, 2002.

Aune, David. *The New Testament in Its Literary Environment.* Philadelphia: Westminster, 1989.

Bailey, Cyril. *Phases in the Religion of Ancient Rome.* Westport: Greenwood, 1972.

Bailey, J. L., and L. D. Vander Broek, eds. *Literary Forms in the New Testament: A Handbook.* Louisville: Westminster John Knox, 1992.

Bailey, R. C., and T. Pippin, eds. *Race, Class, and the Politics of Biblical Translation. Semeia* 76 (1998).

Bailey, Randall C., ed. *Yet With a Steady Beat: Contemporary U.S. Afrocentric Biblical Interpretation.* SBL Semeia Studies. Missoula, Mont.: Society of Biblical Literature, 2003.

Barr, James. *The Bible in the Modern World.* New York: Harper & Row, 1973.

————. *The Semantics of Biblical Language.* Oxford: Oxford University Press, 1961.

Barrett, C. K. *The New Testament Background: Selected Documents.* 2d rev. ed. San Francisco: Harper & Row, 1987.

Bartholomew, Craig, Scott Hahn, Robin Parry, Christopher Seitz, and Al Wolters, eds. *Canon and Biblical Interpretation.* Scripture and Hermeneutics. Grand Rapids: Zondervan, 2006.

Barton, J. "Reading the Bible as Literature." *Literature and Theology* 1 (1987): 135–53.

Barton, John, ed. *The Cambridge Companion to Biblical Interpretation.* London: Cambridge University Press, 1998.

Beardslee, William A. *Literary Criticism of the New Testament.* Philadelphia: Fortress, 1970.

Beasley-Murray, George R. *Jesus and the Last Days: The Interpretation of the Olivet Discourse.* Peabody, Mass.: Hendrickson, 1993.

Bellinger, W. H. *Psalms: Reading and Studying the Book of Praises.* Peabody, Mass.: Hendrickson, 1990.

Berlin, Adele. *Poetics and Interpretation of Biblical Narrative.* Sheffield: Almond, 1983.

Bertens, Hans. *Literary Theory: The Basics.* London: Routledge, 2001.

Bevan, E. "Hellenistic Popular Philosophy." Pages 79–107 in *The Hellenistic Age: Aspects of Hellenistic Civilization.* Edited by J. B. Bury et al. Cambridge: The University Press, 1923.

Biallas, Leonard J. *Myths, Gods, Heroes and Saviors.* Mystic, Conn.: Twenty-third Publications, 1986.

Bird, P. A. *Missing Persons and Mistaken Identities: Women and Gender in Ancient Israel.* Overtures to Biblical Theology. Minneapolis: Fortress, 1997.

Black, F. C., R. Boer, and E. Renions, eds. *The Labour of Reading: Desire, Alienation, and Biblical Interpretation.* Atlanta: Scholars Press, 1999.

Blackshire-Belay, Carol Aisha, ed. *Language and Literature in the African American Imagination.* Westport, Conn.: Greenwood, 1992.

Blancy, Alain. "Structuralism and Hermeneutics." Pages 75–104 in *Structural and Biblical Hermeneutics*. Translated and edited by Alfred M. Johnson. Pittsburgh: Pickwick, 1979.

Bleich, David. *The Double Perspective: Language, Literacy, and Social Regulations*. New York: Oxford University Press, 1988.

———. *Readings and Feelings: An Introduction to Subjective Criticism*. Urbana, Ill.: National Council of Teachers of English, 1975.

———. *Subjective Criticism*. Baltimore: Johns Hopkins University Press, 1978.

Bleicher, Josef. *Contemporary Hermeneutics: Hermeneutics as Method, Philosophy and Critique*. London: Routledge, 1980.

Blomberg, Craig L. *Interpreting the Parables*. Downers Grove: InterVarsity, 1990.

Bloom, Harold et al. *Deconstruction and Criticism*. New York: Seabury, 1979.

Bonz, Marianne P. *The Past as Legacy: Luke-Acts and Ancient Epic*. Minneapolis: Fortress, 2000.

Bornkamm, Günther. "The Theology of Rudolf Bultmann." In *The Theology of Rudolf Bultmann*. Edited by Charles W. Kegley. London: SCM, 1966.

Boyarin, D. *Intertextuality and the Reading of Midrash*. Bloomington: Indiana University Press, 1990.

Braaten, Carl. *History and Hermeneutics*. Philadelphia: Fortress, 1966.

Bradley, David G. "The *Topos* as a Form in the Pauline Paraenesis." *JBL* 72 (1953): 238–46.

Bray, Gerald. *Biblical Interpretation: Past & Present*. Downers Grove: InterVarsity, 2000.

Brenner, A. *Ruth and Esther: A Feminist Companion to the Bible*. Sheffield: Sheffield Academic Press, 1999.

Brenner, A., and F. van Dijk-Hemmes. *On Gendering Texts: Female and Male Voices in the Hebrew Bible*. Biblical Interpretation Series 1. Leiden: Brill, 1993.

Bressler, Charles E. *Literary Criticism: An Introduction to Theory and Practice*. 2d ed. Englewood Cliffs, N.J.: Prentice Hall, 1994.

Brett, M. *Biblical Criticism in Crisis?* Cambridge: Cambridge University Press, 1991.

Brichto, H. C. *Toward a Grammar of Biblical Poetics*. New York: Oxford University Press, 1992.

Briggs, Richard S. *Speech Act Theory and Biblical Interpretation: Toward a Theory of Self-Involvement*. New York: T&T Clark, 2001.

Brooks, Cleanth. "Literary Criticism: Poet, Poem, and Reader." Pages 392–405 in *Literary Criticism*. Edited by Lionel Trilling. New York: Holt, Rhinehart & Winston, 1970.

———. *The Well Wrought Urn*. New York: Reynal & Hitchcock, 1947.

Brown, Raymond E. *The Birth of the Messiah: A Commentary on the Infancy Narratives in Matthew and Luke*. Garden City, N.Y.: Doubleday, 1977.

———. "The Qumran Scrolls and the Johannine Gospel and Epistles." In *The Scrolls and the New Testament*. Edited by Krister Stendahl. Westport: Greenwood, 1975.

Brown, Raymond E. and John P. Meier. *Antioch and Rome: New Testament Cradles of Catholic Christianity*. New York: Paulist, 1983.

Bruns, G. *Hermeneutics Ancient and Modern*. New Haven: Yale University Press, 1992.

Budick, Sanford, and Wolfgang Iser, eds. *Languages of the Unsayable: The Play of Negativity in Literature and Literary Theory*. New York: Columbia University Press, 1989.

Bultmann, Rudolf. *Existence and Faith*. Edited and translated by Schubert Ogden. London: Hodder & Stoughton, 1961.

———. *The History of the Synoptic Tradition*. Oxford: Basil Blackwell, 1963. Repr., Peabody, Mass.: Hendrickson, 1993.

Burnett, F. W. "Postmodern Biblical Exegesis: The Eve of Historical Criticism." *Semeia* 51 (1990): 51–80.

Burns, Gerald L. "Midrash and Allegory: The Beginnings of Scriptural Interpretation." In *The Literary Guide to the Bible*. Edited by Robert Alter and Frank Kermode. Cambridge, Mass.: Harvard University Press, 1987.

Cady, L. E. "Hermeneutics and Tradition." *Harvard Theological Review* 79 (1986): 439–63.

Caird, G. B. *The Language and Imagery of the Bible*. Philadelphia: Westminster, 1980.

Camden, Vera J. "Psychoanalytic Theory," Pages 163–70 in *Encyclopedia of Contemporary Literary Theory: Approaches, Scholars, Terms*. Edited by Irena R. Makaryk. Buffalo: University of Toronto Press, 1993.

Caputo, John D. *Radical Hermeneutics: Repetition, Deconstruction, and the Hermeneutic Project*. Bloomington: Indiana University Press, 1987.

Carson, D. A. *Biblical Interpretation and the Church*. Nashville: Thomas Nelson, 1984.

Carter, Angela. *The Infernal Desire Machines of Doctor Hoffman*. London: Penguin, 1994.

Cartwright, M. G. "Ideology and the Interpretation of the Bible in the African-American Christian Tradition." *Modern Theology* 9, no. 2 (1993): 141–58.

Childs, Brevard S. *Biblical Theology in Crisis.* Philadelphia: Westminster, 1970.

———. *Introduction to the Old Testament as Scripture.* Philadelphia: Fortress, 1979.

———. *The New Testament as Canon: An Introduction.* Philadelphia: Fortress, 1985.

Clarke, Simon. *The Foundations of Structuralism: A Critique of Lévi-Strauss and the Structuralist Movement.* Totowa, N.J.: Barnes & Noble, 1981.

Classen, Carl Joachim. *Rhetorical Criticism of the New Testament.* Leiden: Brill, 2002.

Clements, R. E. *Prophecy and Tradition.* Atlanta: John Knox, 1975.

Clines, D. J. A. *Interested Parties: The Ideology of Writers and Readers of the Hebrew Bible.* JSOTSup 205. Sheffield: Sheffield Academic Press, 1995.

Coggins, R. J., and J. L. Houlden, eds. *A Dictionary of Biblical Interpretation.* Philadelphia: Trinity, 1990.

Collins, Adela Yarbro. *The Beginning of the Gospel: Probings of Mark in Context.* Minneapolis: Fortress Press, 1992.

Collins, Adela Yarbro, ed. *Feminist Perspectives on Biblical Scholarship.* Chico, Calif.: Scholars Press, 1985.

Cone, James H. *Black Theology and Black Power.* New York: Seabury, 1969.

Conzelmann, Hans, and Andreas Lindemann. *Interpreting the New Testament.* Translated by Siegfried S. Schatzmann. Peabody, Mass.: Hendrickson, 1988.

Cotterell, Peter, and Max Turner. *Linguistics and Biblical Interpretation.* Downers Grove: InterVarsity, 1989.

Crim, Keith, gen. ed. *The Interpreter's Dictionary of the Bible.* 2d rev. ed. Nashville: Abingdon, 1980.

Croatto, Severino. *Biblical Hermeneutics: Toward a Theory of Reading as the Production of Meaning.* Maryknoll: Orbis Books, 1987.

Crossan, John Dominic. *The Dark Interval: Towards a Theology of Story.* Niles, Ill.: Argus, 1975. Repr., Sonoma, Calif.: Polebridge, 1991.

Culler, Jonathan. *On Deconstruction: Theory and Criticism after Structuralism.* Ithaca, N.Y.: Cornell University Press, 1982.

———. *The Pursuit of Signs: Semiotics, Literature, Deconstruction.* Ithaca, N.Y.: Cornell University Press, 1986.

————. *Structuralist Poetics: Structuralism, Linguistics and the Study of Literature.* Ithaca, N.Y.: Cornell University Press, 1986.

Culley, R. *Themes and Variations: A Study of Action in Biblical Narrative.* Atlanta: Scholars Press, 1992.

Damrosch, David. *The Narrative Covenant: Transformations of Genre in the Growth of Biblical Literature.* San Francisco: Harper & Row, 1987.

Darr, J. *On Character Building: The Reader and the Rhetoric of Characterization.* Louisville: Westminster John Knox, 1992.

Derrida, Jacques. *Margins of Philosophy.* Translated by Alan Bass. Chicago: University of Chicago Press, 1982.

————. *Of Grammatology.* Translated by Gayatri Chakravorty Spivak. Baltimore: Johns Hopkins University Press, 1977.

————. *Writing and Difference.* Translated by Alan Bass. Chicago: University of Chicago Press, 1978.

Dibelius, Martin. *From Tradition to Gospel.* Translated by Betram Lee Woolf. New York: Scribner, 1965.

Dillon, J. *The Middle Platonists, 80 B.C. to A.D. 220.* Ithaca, N.Y.: Cornell University Press, 1977.

Dockery, D. S. *Biblical Interpretation Then and Now: Contemporary Hermeneutics in the Light of the Early Church.* Grand Rapids: Baker, 1992.

Donaldson, Laura, ed. *Postcolonialism and Scriptural Reading. Semeia* 75 (1998).

Doty, William G. *Letters in Primitive Christianity.* Philadelphia: Fortress, 1973.

Dyck, E., ed. *The Act of Bible Reading.* Downers Grove: InterVarsity, 1996.

Eagleton, Terry. *Literary Theory: An Introduction.* Minneapolis: University of Minnesota Press, 1983.

————. *Marxism and Literary Criticism.* 2d ed. London: Routledge, 2002.

Eco, Umberto. *The Role of the Reader: Explorations in the Semiotics of Texts.* Bloomington: Indiana University Press, 1984.

Efird, James M. *The Old Testament Writings: History, Literature, Interpretation.* Atlanta: John Knox, 1982.

Elliott, John. *What Is Social-Scientific Criticism?* Minneapolis: Fortress, 1993.

Erikson, M. J. *Evangelical Interpretation: Perspectives on Hermeneutical Issues.* Grand Rapids: Baker, 1993.

Ervin, Hazel Arnett, ed. *African American Literary Criticism, 1773–2000.* New York: Twayne, 1999.

Esler, Philip F. *The First Christians in Their Social World: Social-Scientific Approaches to New Testament Interpretation.* New York: Routledge, 1994.

Esler, Philip F., ed. *Modeling Early Christianity: Social-Scientific Studies of the New Testament in Its Context.* New York: Routledge, 1995.

Eslinger, L. M. "Inner-biblical Exegesis and Inner-biblical Allusion: The Question of Category." *VT* 42 (1992): 47–58.

Exum, J. C. *Fragmented Women: Feminist (Sub)Versions of Biblical Narratives.* Valley Forge: Trinity Press International, 1993.

———. *Tragedy and Biblical Narrative.* Cambridge: Cambridge University Press, 1992.

Exum, J. C., ed. "Tragedy and Comedy in the Bible." *Semeia* 32 (1984).

Exum, J. C., and S. Moore, eds. *Biblical Studies/Cultural Studies: The Third Sheffield Colloquium.* JSOTSup 266. Gender, Culture, Theory 7. Sheffield: Sheffield Academic Press, 1998.

Farley, Margaret A. "Feminist Consciousness and Scripture." In *Feminist Interpretation of the Bible.* Edited by Letty M. Russell. Philadelphia: Westminster, 1985.

Farmer, R. L. *Beyond the Impasse: The Promise of a Process Hermeneutic.* Studies in American Biblical Hermeneutics. Macon, Ga.: Mercer University Press, 1997.

Fee, Gordon D. *New Testament Exegesis: A Handbook for Students and Pastors.* 3d ed. Philadelphia: Westminster, 2002.

Fee, Gordon D., and Douglas Stuart. *How to Read the Bible for All Its Worth: A Guide to Understanding the Bible.* 2d ed. Grand Rapids: Zondervan, 1993.

Felperin, Howard. *Beyond Deconstruction: The Uses and Abuses of Literary Theory.* Oxford: Clarendon, 1985.

Ferguson, Duncan. *Biblical Hermeneutics: An Introduction.* Atlanta: John Knox, 1986.

Ferguson, Everett. *Backgrounds of Early Christianity.* 2d ed. Grand Rapids: Eerdmans, 1993.

Ferguson, John. *Greek and Roman Religion: A Source Book.* Park Ridge, N.J.: Noyes, 1980.

Fewell, Danna Nolan, ed. *Reading between Texts: Intertextuality and the Hebrew Bible.* Louisville: Westminster John Knox, 1992.

Fisch, Harold. *Poetry with a Purpose: Biblical Poetics and Interpretation.* Bloomington: Indiana University Press, 1988.

Fowl, S. E. *Engaging Scripture: A Model for Theological Interpretation.* New York: Blackwell, 1998.

Fowler, Alistair. *Kinds of Literature: An Introduction to the Theory of Genres and Mode.* Cambridge, Mass.: Harvard University Press, 1982.

Fowler, Robert. *Let the Reader Understand: Reader-Response and the Gospel of Mark.* Minneapolis: Fortress, 1991.

————. "The Rhetoric of Direction and Indirection in the Gospel of Mark." *Semeia* 48 (1989): 115–34.

Freedman, Diane P., Olivia Frey, and Frances Murphy Zauhar, eds. *The Intimate Critique: Autobiographical Literary Criticism.* Durham: Duke University Press, 1993.

Freyne, Sean. *Galilee, Jesus, and the Gospels: Literary Approaches and Historical Investigation.* Philadelphia: Fortress, 1988.

Frye, Northrop. *The Great Code: The Bible and Literature.* New York: Harcourt, Brace & Jovanovich, 1982.

Funk, R. W. *Language, Hermeneutic, and Word of God.* New York: Harper, 1996.

Furnish, Victor P. *Theology and Ethics of Paul.* Nashville: Abingdon, 1968.

Gabel, John, and Charles Wheeler. *The Bible as Literature: An Introduction.* New York: Oxford University Press, 1986.

Gadamer, H. G. *Truth and Method.* New York: Seabury, 1975.

Gager, John G. *Kingdom and Community: The Social World of Early Christianity.* Englewood Cliffs: Prentice Hall, 1975.

Garry, Ann, and Marilyn Pearsall, eds. *Women, Knowledge and Reality: Explorations in Feminist Philosophy.* Boston: Unwin Hyman, 1989.

Gates, Henry Louis Jr. *The Signifying Monkey: A Theory of Afro-American Literary Criticism.* New York: Oxford University Press, 1988.

Genette, Gérard. *Narrative Discourse.* Oxford: Oxford University Press, 1980.

Gilbert, Sandra, and Susan Gubar. *The Mad Woman in the Attic: The Woman Writer and the Nineteenth-Century Literary Imagination.* New Haven: Yale University Press, 1979.

Goldsworthy, Graeme. *Gospel-Centered Hermeneutics: Foundations and Principles of Evangelical Biblical Interpretation.* Downers Grove: IVP Academic, 2007.

Goodwin, David. "Rhetorical Criticism," Pages 174–78 in *Encyclopedia of Contemporary Literary Theory: Approaches, Scholars, Terms.* Edited by Irena R. Makaryk. Buffalo: University of Toronto Press, 1993.

Gottcent, John. *The Bible: A Literary Study.* Boston: Thayne, 1986.

Gottwald, Norman K. *The Bible and Liberation: Political and Social Hermeneutics.* Maryknoll: Orbis Books, 1993.

———. *The Hebrew Bible: A Socio-Literary Introduction.* Philadelphia: Fortress, 1985.

Gottwald, Norman K., and R. A. Horsley, eds. *The Bible and Liberation: Political and Social Hermeneutics.* Maryknoll: Orbis, 1993.

Greenfield, Jonas C. "The Hebrew Bible and Canaanite Literature." In *The Literary Guide to the Bible.* Edited by Robert Alter and Frank Kermode. Cambridge, Mass.: Harvard University Press, 1987.

Greenwood, David C. *Structuralism and the Biblical Text.* Berlin: Mounton, 1985.

Guerin, Wilfred et al., eds. *A Handbook of Critical Approaches to Literature.* 4th ed. New York: Harper Collins, 1999.

Gunkel, Hermann. *The Legends of Genesis: The Biblical Saga and History.* Translated by W. H. Carruth. New York: Schocken, 1964.

Gunn, D., and D. N. Fewell. *Narrative in the Hebrew Bible.* New York: Oxford University Press, 1993.

Habel, Norman. *Literary Criticism of the Old Testament.* Philadelphia: Fortress, 1971.

Haight, Elizabeth. *Essays on the Greek Romances.* Port Washington, N.Y.: Kennikat, 1943.

Hall, Donald. *Literary and Cultural Theory: From Basic Principles to Advanced Applications.* Boston: Houghton Mifflin, 2001.

Hassan, Ihab. *The Postmodern Turn: Essays in Postmodern Theory and Culture.* Columbus: Ohio State University Press, 1987.

Hauser, Alan J., and Duane F. Watson, eds. *A History of Biblical Interpretation: The Ancient Period.* History of Biblical Interpretation Series. Grand Rapids: Eerdmans, 2003.

Hayes, John H., ed. *The Dictionary of Biblical Interpretation.* Nashville: Abingdon, 1999.

———, ed. *Methods of Biblical Interpretation.* Nashville: Abingdon Press, 2005.

Hayes, John, and Carl R. Holladay. *Biblical Exegesis: A Beginner's Handbook.* Atlanta: John Knox, 1987.

Haynes, S., and S. McKenzie. *To Each Its Own: An Introduction to Biblical Interpretations and Their Applications.* Louisville: Westminster John Knox, 1993.

Hedrick, Charles W. *Many Things in Parables: Jesus and His Modern Critics.* Louisville: Westminster John Knox, 2004.

Heidegger, Martin. *Being and Time.* Translated by John Macquarrie and Edward Robinson. New York: Harper & Row, 1962.

Heil, John Paul. *The Gospel of Mark as a Model for Action: A Reader-Response Commentary.* New York: Paulist, 1992.

Hemer, C. J. *The Letters to the Seven Churches of Asia in Their Local Settings.* JSOTSup 11. Sheffield: JSOT, 1986.

Henn, T. R. *The Bible as Literature.* New York: Oxford University Press, 1970.

Hicks, R. D. *Stoic and Epicurean.* New York: Russell & Russell, 1962.

Hirsch, E. D., Jr. *Validity in Interpretation.* New Haven: Yale University Press, 1973.

Holland, Norman. *5 Readers Reading.* New Haven: Yale University Press, 1975.

Holmberg, Bengt. *Sociology and the New Testament: An Appraisal.* Minneapolis: Fortress, 1990.

Howard, R. J. *Three Faces of Hermeneutics.* Los Angeles: University of California Press, 1982.

Hutcheon, Linda. *A Poetics of Postmodernism: History, Theory, Fiction.* New York: Routledge, 1988.

Iersel, Bas M. F. van. "The Reader of Mark as Operator of a System of Connotations." *Semeia* 48 (1989): 83–114.

Inch, Morris A., and Hassell C. Bulloch. *The Literature and Meaning of Scripture.* Grand Rapids: Baker, 1984.

Iser, Wolfgang. *The Act of Reading: A Theory of Aesthetic Response.* Baltimore: Johns Hopkins University Press, 1978.

———. *The Implied Reader: Patterns of Communication in Prose Fiction from Bunyan to Beckett.* Baltimore: Johns Hopkins University Press, 1974.

———. *Prospecting: From Reader Response to Literary Anthropology.* Baltimore: Johns Hopkins University Press, 1989.

———. "The Reading Process: A Phenomenological Approach." In *Reader-Response Criticism: From Formalism to Post-Structuralism.* Edited by Jane Tompkins. Baltimore: Johns Hopkins University Press, 1980.

Japp, U. *Hermeneutik: Der theoretische Diskurs, die Literatur, und die Konstruktion ihres Zusammenhanges in den philologischen Wissenschaften.* Munich: Fink, 1977.

Jauss, Hans Robert. *The Aesthetic Experience and Literary Hermeneutics.* Translated by Michael Shaw. Vol. 3 of Theory and History of Literature. Minneapolis: University of Minnesota Press, 1982.

———. "Literary History as a Challenge to Literary Theory," Pages 164–83 in *Critical Theory since 1965.* Edited by Hazard Adams and Leroy Searle. Tallahassee: University of Florida Press, 1986.

————. *Toward an Aesthetic of Reception.* Translated by Timothy Bahti. Vol. 2 of Theory and History of Literature. Minneapolis: University of Minnesota Press, 1982.

Jobling, D., and T. Pippin, eds. *Ideological Criticism of Biblical Texts. Semeia* 59 (1993).

————. *The Sense of Biblical Narrative.* JSOTSup 39. Sheffield, JSOT, 1978.

Johnson, E. E. *Expository Hermeneutics.* Grand Rapids: Zondervan, 1990.

Johnson, Luke Timothy. *The Writings of the New Testament: An Interpretation.* Philadelphia: Fortress, 1986.

Johnson, Patricia-Anne. "Womanist Theology as a Counter-Narrative." Pages 197–214 in *Gender, Ethnicity, and Religion: Views from the Other Side.* Edited by Rosemary Radford Ruether. Minneapolis: Fortress, 2002.

Jouve, Nicole. *White Woman Speaks with Forked Tongue: Criticism as Autobiography.* London: Routledge, 1991.

Jülicher, Adolf. *Die Gleichnisreden Jesu.* Vol. 1. Tübingen: Mohr, 1910.

Kaiser, Walter C., and Moisés Silva. *An Introduction to Biblical Hermeneutics: The Search for Meaning.* Grand Rapids: Zondervan, 1994.

Kee, Howard Clark, Franklin W. Young, and Karlfried Froelich. *Understanding the New Testament.* 4th ed. Englewood Cliffs: Prentice-Hall, 1983.

Keegan, Terrance J. *Interpreting the Bible: A Popular Introduction to Biblical Hermeneutics.* New York: Paulist, 1986.

Keesey, Donald. *Contexts for Criticism*, 4th ed. Boston.: McGraw Hill, 2003.

Kendall, Diana, ed. *Race, Class, and Gender in a Diverse Society.* Boston: Allyn & Bacon, 1997.

Kennedy, George A. *Classical Rhetoric and Its Christian and Secular Tradition from Ancient to Modern Times.* Chapel Hill: University of North Carolina Press, 1980.

————. *New Testament Interpretation through Rhetorical Criticism.* Chapel Hill: University of North Carolina Press, 1984.

Kermode, Frank. *The Genesis of Secrecy.* Cambridge, Mass.: Harvard University Press, 1979.

Kille, Andrew. *Psychological Biblical Criticism.* Minneapolis: Fortress, 2001.

Kingsbury, Jack Dean. *The Christology of Mark's Gospel.* Minneapolis: Fortress, 1983.

Kitzberger, Ingrid R., ed. *Autobiographical Biblical Criticism*. Leiden: Deo, 2002.

Klassen, William. "Coals of Fire: Sign of Repentance or Revenge?" *NTS* 9 (1962–63): 337–50.

Klein, William W., Craig L. Blomberg, and Robert L. Hubbard. *Introduction to Biblical Interpretation*. Dallas: Word, 1993. Rev. & exp. ed. Nashville: Thomas Nelson, 2004.

Koester, Helmut. *Introduction to the New Testament*. New York: Walter De Gruyter, 1982.

Kögler, Hans-Herbert. *The Power of Dialogue: Critical Hermeneutics after Gadamer and Foucault*. Cambridge, Mass.: MIT Press, 1996.

Kort, Wesley A. *Modern Fiction and Human Time: An Essay in Narrative and Belief*. Gainesville: University Presses of Florida, 1986.

———. *Story, Text, and Scripture: Literary Interests in Biblical Narrative*. University Park, Penn.: Pennsylvania State University Press, 1987.

———. *Take, Read: Scripture, Textuality, and Cultural Practice.* University Park: Pennsylvania State University Press, 1996.

Kraemer, Ross Shepard. *Her Share of the Blessings: Women's Religions among Pagans, Jews, and Christians in the Greco-Roman World*. Oxford: Oxford University Press, 1992.

Krentz, E. *The Historical Critical Method*. Philadelphia: Fortress, 1975.

Kugel, J. *The Idea of Biblical Poetry: Parallelism and Its History*. New Haven: Yale University Press, 1981.

Ladd, George E. *A Theology of the New Testament.* Grand Rapids: Eerdmans, 1974.

LaSor, William, David Hubbard, and Frederic Bush. *Old Testament Survey.* Grand Rapids: Eerdmans, 1982.

Lategan, Bernard C., and Willem S. Vorster. *Text and Reality: Aspects of Reference in Biblical Texts.* Philadelphia: Fortress, 1985.

Leitch, Vincent B., ed. *The Norton Anthology of Theory and Criticism*. New York: Norton, 2001.

Lesky, Albin. *History of Greek Literature*. New York: Thomas Y. Crowell, 1966.

Lévi-Strauss, Claude. *Myth and Meaning.* New York: Routledge, 2001.

Lightfoot, J. B. *St. Paul's Epistle to the Philippians*. Reprint. Peabody, Mass.: Hendrickson, 1993.

Linnemann, E. *Historical Criticism of the Bible*. Grand Rapids: Baker, 1990.

Lohfink, Gerhard. *The Bible, Now I Get It: A Form Critical Handbook*. New York: Doubleday, 1976.

Long, Burke O. "The Social World of Ancient Israel." *Int* 37 (1982): 243–55.

Longman, Tremper, III. *Literary Approaches to Biblical Interpretation.* Grand Rapids: Zondervan, 1987.

López, Alfred J. *Posts and Pasts: A Theory of Post-colonialism.* New York: State University of New York Press, 2001.

Louis, Kenneth R. R. Gros, with James Ackerman and Thayer S. Warshaw. *Literary Interpretations of Biblical Narratives.* Nashville: Abingdon, 1974.

Lundin, Roger. *The Culture of Interpretation: Christian Faith and the Postmodern World.* Grand Rapids: Eerdmans, 1993.

Lundin, Roger, ed. *Disciplining Hermeneutics: Interpretation in Christian Perspective.* Grand Rapids: Eerdmans, 1997.

Lundin, Roger, Anthony C. Thiselton, and Clarence Walhout. *The Responsibility of Hermeneutics.* Grand Rapids: Eerdmans, 1985.

Lyotard, Jean-François. *The Postmodern Condition: A Report on Knowledge.* Translated by Geoof Bennington and Brian Massumi. Minneapolis: University of Minnesota Press, 1993.

Macey, David. "Freud, Sigmund." Pages 207–10 in *A Dictionary of Cultural and Critical Theory.* Edited by Michael Payne. Cambridge, Mass.: Blackwell, 1996.

Mack, Burton. *A Myth of Innocence: Mark and Christian Origins.* Philadelphia: Fortress, 1988.

———. *Rhetoric and the New Testament.* Guides to Biblical Scholarship. Minneapolis: Fortress, 1990.

Mahan, Brian, and L. Dale Richesin, eds. *The Challenge of Liberation Theology: A First-World Response.* Maryknoll: Orbis, 1981.

Malamat, Abraham. *The History of Biblical Israel: Major Problems and Minor Issues.* Leiden: Brill, 2004.

Malbon, Elizabeth Struthers, and Edgar V. McKnight, eds. *The New Literary Criticism and the New Testament.* Valley Forge: Trinity Press International, 1994.

Malherbe, Abraham J., ed. *The Cynic Epistles.* Missoula: Scholars Press, 1977.

———. *Social Aspects of Early Christianity.* 2d ed. Philadelphia: Fortress, 1983.

Malina, Bruce J. *The New Testament World: Insights from Cultural Anthropology.* Atlanta: John Knox, 1981.

———. *The Social World of Jesus and the Gospels.* New York: Routledge, 1996.

Mann, Thomas W. *The Book of the Torah: The Narrative Integrity of the Pentateuch.* Philadelphia: John Knox, 1988.

Martin, Dale B. *Sex and the Single Savior: Gender and Sexuality in Biblical Interpretation.* Louisville: Westminster John Knox, 2006.

Martin, Luther. *Hellenistic Religions.* New York: Oxford University Press, 1987.

Martin, Ralph P. *New Testament Foundations.* 2 vols. Grand Rapids: Eerdmans, 1978.

Martin, Wallace. *Recent Theories of Narrative.* Ithaca, N.Y.: Cornell University Press, 1986.

May, David A. *Social-Scientific Criticism of the New Testament: A Bibliography.* 4 vols. Macon, Ga.: Mercer University Press, 1991.

McDonald, Dennis R. *The Homeric Epics and the Gospel of Mark.* New Haven: Yale University Press, 2000.

McKnight, Edgar V. *The Bible and the Reader.* Philadelphia: Fortress, 1985.

———. *Meaning in Texts.* Philadelphia: Fortress, 1978.

———. *Postmodern Use of the Bible: The Emergence of Reader-Oriented Criticism.* Nashville: Abingdon, 1988. Repr., Eugene, Ore.: Wipf & Stock, 2005.

Meeks, Wayne. *The First Urban Christians: The Social World of the Apostle Paul.* 2d ed. New Haven: Yale University Press, 2003.

———. *The Moral World of the First Christians.* Philadelphia: Westminster, 1986.

Merlan, P. *From Platonism to Neoplatonism.* 2d ed. Hague: Nijhoff, 1960.

Merleau-Ponty, Maurice. *Consciousness and the Acquisition of Language.* Translated by Hugh J. Silverman. Evanston: Northwestern University Press, 1973.

Mickelsen, A. Berkeley. *Interpreting the Bible.* Grand Rapids: Eerdmans, 1963.

Mills, K. *Justifying Language: Paul and Contemporary Literary Theory.* New York: St. Martin's, 1995.

Moi, T. *Sexual Textual Politics: Feminist Literary Theory.* New York: Routledge, 1994.

Montague, George T. *Understanding the Bible: A Basic Introduction to Biblical Interpretation.* Rev. & exp. ed. New York: Paulist, 2007.

Moore, Stephen D., ed. "Biblical Studies and the New Historicism." *Biblical Interpretation* 5 (1997): 289–99.

———. "Deconstructive Criticism: The Gospel of Mark." Pages 110–45 in *Mark and Method: New Approaches in Biblical Studies.* Edited by Janice Capel Anderson and Stephen D. Moore. Minneapolis: Fortress, 1992.

Morgan, Robert with John Barton. *Biblical Interpretation.* New York: Oxford University Press, 1988.

Murray, Gilbert. *Five Stages of Greek Religion.* Garden City: Doubleday, 1955.

Neusner, Jacob. *Handbook of Rabbinic Theology: Language, System, Structure.* Leiden: Brill, 2002.

———. *Invitation to Midrash: A Teaching Book.* San Francisco: Harper & Row, 1989.

———. *Midrash in Context: Exegesis in Formative Judaism.* Philadelphia: Fortress, 1983.

———. *What Is Midrash?* Philadelphia: Fortress, 1987.

Newsom, C. A., and S. H. Ringe, eds. *The Women's Bible Commentary.* Louisville: Westminster John Knox, 1992.

Neyrey, Jerome. "The Idea of Purity in Mark's Gospel." *Semeia* 35 (1986): 91–128.

Neyrey, Jerome, ed. *The Social World of Luke-Acts: Models of Interpretation.* Peabody, Mass.: Hendrickson, 1991.

Norris, Christopher. *The Truth About Postmodernism.* Oxford: Blackwell, 1993.

Ogden, C. K., and I. A. Richard. *The Meaning of Meaning: A Study of the Influence of Language on Thought, with Supplementary Essays by B. Milinowski and F. C. Crookshank.* New York: Harcourt Brace, 1923.

Osborne, Grant R. *The Hermeneutical Spiral: A Comprehensive Introduction to Biblical Interpretation.* Rev. & exp. ed. Downers Grove: IVP Academic, 2006.

Osiek, Carolyn. *What Are They Saying about the Social Setting of the New Testament?* New York: Paulist, 1984.

Pardes, I. *Countertraditions in the Bible: A Feminist Approach.* Cambridge, Mass.: Harvard University Press, 1992.

Parsons, Mikeal C. "Hand in Hand: Autobiographical Reflections on Luke 15." *Semeia* 72 (1995): 125–52.

Patrick, D., and A. Scult. *Rhetoric and Biblical Interpretation.* Sheffield: Almond, 1990.

Patte, Daniel. *What Is Structural Exegesis?* Philadelphia: Fortress, 1976.

Payne, Michael, ed. *A Dictionary of Cultural and Critical Theory.* Cambridge, Mass.: Blackwell, 1996.

Perrin, Norman. *What Is Redaction Criticism?* Philadelphia: Fortress, 1969.

Peterson, D. L., and K. H. Richards. *Interpreting Hebrew Poetry.* Minneapolis: Fortress, 1992.

Petersen, Norman. *Literary Criticism for New Testament Critics.* Philadelphia: Fortress, 1978.

Phillips, G. A., and D. N. Fewell, eds. *The Bible and Ethics of Reading. Semeia* 77 (1998).

Pippin, T. "Ideology, Ideological Criticism, and the Bible." *Currents in Research: Biblical Studies* 4 (1996): 51–78.

Porter, Stanley. *Dictionary of Biblical Criticism and Interpretation.* London: Routledge, 2007.

Porter, Stanley E., ed. *A Handbook to the Exegesis of the New Testament.* Leiden: Brill, 2002.

Powell, Mark Allen. *What is Narrative Criticism?* Minneapolis: Fortress, 1990.

Pritchard, J. B., ed. *Ancient Near Eastern Texts Relating to the Old Testament.* Princeton: Princeton University Press, 1969.

Pryke, John. "'Spirit' and 'Flesh' in the Qumran Documents and Some New Testament Texts." *Römische Quartalschrift für christliche Altertumskunde und Kirchengeschichte* 5 (1965): 345–60.

Ramm, Bernard. *Hermeneutics.* Grand Rapids: Baker, 1961.

Ray, William. *Literary Meaning: From Phenomenology to Deconstruction.* New York: Basil Blackwell, 1984.

Resseguie, James L. "Reader-Response Criticism and the Synoptic Gospels." *JAAR* 52 (1984): 307–24.

Richards, I. A. *Practical Criticism.* New York: Harcourt Brace, 1952.

———. *Principles of Literary Criticism.* New York: Harcourt Brace, 1925.

Ricoeur, Paul. "Biblical Hermeneutics." *Semeia* 4 (1975): 81.

———. *The Conflict of Interpretation.* Evanston: Northwestern University Press, 1974.

———. *Essays on Biblical Interpretation.* Philadelphia: Fortress, 1980.

———. *Interpretation Theory: Discourse and the Surplus of Meaning.* Fort Worth: Texas Christian University Press, 1976.

Riffaterre, Michael. "Compulsory Reader-Response: The Intertextual Drive." Pages 56–78 in *Intertextuality: Theories and Practices.* Edited by Michael Worton and Judith Still. Manchester, Eng.: Manchester University Press, 1990.

———. *Text Production.* Translated by Terese Lyons. New York: Columbia University Press, 1983.

Rhoads, David. "Social Criticism: Crossing Boundaries." In *Mark and Method.* Edited by Janice Chapel Anderson and Stephen D. Moore. Minneapolis: Fortress, 1992.

Robbins, Vernon K. *Exploring the Texture of Texts: A Guide to Socio-Rhetorical Interpretation.* Harrisburg: Trinity Press International, 1996.

———. *Jesus the Teacher: A Socio-Rhetorical Interpretation of Mark.* Minneapolis: Fortress, 1992.

———. "Socio-Rhetorical Criticism: Mary, Elizabeth, and the Magnificat as a Test Case." Pages 164–209 in *The New Literary Criticism and the New Testament.* Edited by Elizabeth Struthers Malbon and Edgar V. McKnight. Valley Forge: Trinity Press International, 1994.

Robertson, David. *The Old Testament and the Literary Critic.* Philadelphia: Fortress, 1977.

Robinson, James M. "The Historicality of Biblical Language." In *The Old Testament and Christian Faith.* Edited by Bernhard W. Anderson. New York: Harper & Row, 1963.

Rodd, Cyril S. "On Applying a Sociological Theory to Biblical Studies." *JSOT* 19 (1981): 95–106.

Roetzel, Calvin J. *The Letters of Paul: Conversations in Context.* Atlanta: John Knox, 1982.

Rohrbaugh, Richard, ed. *The Social Sciences and New Testament Interpretation.* Peabody, Mass.: Hendrickson, 1996.

Rollins, W. G. *Soul and Psyche: The Bible in Psychological Perspective.* Minneapolis: Fortress, 1999.

Rosen, S. *Hermeneutics as Politics.* New York: Oxford University Press, 1987.

Rosenberg, Joel. *King and Kin: Political Allegory in the Hebrew Bible.* Bloomington: Indiana University Press, 1986.

Rudolph, Kurt. "Mystery Religions." In *ER.* Vol. 7. Edited by Mircea Eliade. New York: Macmillan, 1987.

Rudwick, M. J. S., and E. M. B. Green, "The Laodicean Lukewarmness." *ExpT* 69 (1957–58): 176–78.

Ruether, Rosemary Radford. "Feminist Interpretation: A Method of Correlation." In *Feminist Interpretation of the Bible.* Edited by Letty M. Russell. Philadelphia: Westminster, 1985.

———. *Sexism and God Talk: Toward a Feminist Theology.* Boston: Beacon, 1983.

Russell, Letty M., ed. *Feminist Interpretation of the Bible.* Philadelphia: Westminster, 1985.

Ryken, Leland. *The Literature of the Bible.* Grand Rapids: Baker, 1987.

———. *Words of Delight: A Literary Introduction to the Bible.* Grand Rapids: Baker, 1987.

———. *Words of Life: A Literary Introduction to the New Testament.* Grand Rapids: Baker, 1986.

Said, Edward W. *Orientalism.* New York: Pantheon, 1978. Repr., New York: Vintage, 2003

Sakenfeld, Katharine Doob. *Faithfulness in Action: Loyalty in Biblical Perspective.* Philadelphia: Fortress, 1985.

———. "Feminist Uses of Biblical Materials." In *Feminist Interpretation of the Bible.* Edited by Letty M. Russell. Philadelphia: Westminster, 1985.

Sanders, Jack. "The Transition from Opening Epistolary Thanksgiving to Body in the Pauline Corpus." *JBL* 81 (1962): 352–62.

Sanders, James A. *Canon and Community.* Philadelphia: Fortress, 1984.

Sands, P. C. *Literary Genius of the New Testament.* New York: Oxford University Press, 1932.

Saussure, Ferdinand de. *A Course in General Linguistics.* Edited by Charles Bally, Albert Sechehaye, and Albert Riedlinger. Translated by Wade Baskin. New York: Philosophical Library, 1959. Repr., New York: McGraw-Hill, 1966.

Savran, George W. *Telling and Retelling: Quotation in Biblical Narrative.* Bloomington: Indiana University Press, 1988.

Schneiders, S. M. "Feminist Ideology Criticism and Biblical Hermeneutics." *BTB* 19 (1989): 3–10.

Schubert, Paul. *Form and Function of the Pauline Thanksgivings.* Berlin: Alfred Töpelmann, 1939.

Schüssler Fiorenza, Elisabeth. *Bread Not Stone: Introduction to a Feminist Interpretation of Scripture.* Boston: Beacon, 1985.

———. "The Ethics of Biblical Interpretation." *JBL* 107 (1988): 3–17.

———. "A Feminist Biblical Hermeneutics: Biblical Interpretation and Liberation Theology." In *The Challenge of Liberation Theology: A First-World Response.* Edited by Brian Mahan and L. Dale Richesin. Maryknoll: Orbis Books, 1981.

———. *Jesus: Miriam's Child, Sophia's Prophet.* New York: Continuum, 1994.

———. *Rhetoric and Ethic: The Politics of Biblical Studies.* Minneapolis: Fortress, 1999.

———. "The Will to Choose or to Reject: Continuing Our Critical Work." In *Feminist Interpretation of the Bible.* Edited by Letty M. Russell. Philadelphia: Westminster, 1985.

———. *Wisdom Ways: Introducing Feminist Biblical Interpretation.* Maryknoll: Orbis Books, 2001.

Schüssler Fiorenza, Elisabeth, ed. *Searching the Scriptures: A Feminist Introduction.* New York: Crossroad, 1993.

Schwartz, R. *The Book and the Text: The Bible and Literary Theory.* Cambridge, Mass.: Basil Blackwell, 1990.

Segovia, Fernando. *Decolonizing Biblical Studies: A View from the Margins.* Maryknoll: Orbis, 2000.

Shuler, Philip. I. *A Genre for the Gospels: The Biographical Character of Matthew.* Philadelphia: Fortress, 1982.

Silverman, H. J., ed. *Gadamer and Hermeneutics.* New York: Routledge, 1991.

Soskice, Janet Martin. *Metaphor and Religious Language.* Oxford: Oxford University Press, 1985.

Soulen, Richard N., and R. Kendall Soulen. *Handbook of Biblical Criticism.* 3d ed. Louisville: Westminster John Knox, 2001.

Staley, Jeffery L. "Autobiography." Pages 14–19 in *Handbook of Postmodern Biblical Interpretation.* Edited by A. K. M. Adam. St. Louis: Chalice, 2000.

Stambaugh, John, and David Balch. *The New Testament in Its Social Environment.* Philadelphia: Westminster, 1986.

Stegner, William R. *Narrative Theology in Early Jewish Christianity.* Louisville: Westminster John Knox, 1989.

Stein, R. H. *Playing by the Rules: A Basic Guide to Interpreting the Bible.* Grand Rapids: Baker, 1994.

Sternberg, Meir. *The Poetics of Biblical Narrative.* Bloomington: Indiana University Press, 1985.

Stevens, Bonnie Klomp, and Larry L. Stewart. *A Guide to Literary Criticism and Research.* 3d ed. Fort Worth: Harcourt, 1996.

Stone, K. "The Hermeneutics of Abomination: On Gay Men, Canaanites, and Biblical Interpretation." *BTB* 27 (1997): 36–41.

Stuart, Douglas. *Old Testament Exegesis.* Philadelphia: Westminster, 1980.

Sugirtharajah, Rasiah S. *Asian Biblical Hermeneutics and Postcolonialism: Contesting the Interpretations.* Maryknoll: Orbis, 1998.

———. *The Bible and the Third World: Precolonial, Colonial and Postcolonial Encounters.* New York: Cambridge University Press, 2001.

———. *Postcolonial Criticism and Biblical Interpretation.* Oxford: Oxford University Press, 2002.

Sugirtharajah, Rasiah S., ed. *The Postcolonial Bible.* Sheffield: Sheffield Academic Press, 1998.

Talbert, Charles. *Literary Patterns, Theological Themes and the Genre of Luke-Acts.* Society of Biblical Literature Monograph Series 20. Missoula: Society of Biblical Literature and Scholars Press, 1974.

Tate, W. Randolph. *Interpreting the Bible: A Handbook of Terms and Methods.* Peabody, Mass.: Hendrickson, 2006.

Taylor, Vincent. *The Formation of the Gospel Tradition.* London: Macmillan, 1960.

Tenney, Merrill C. *New Testament Times.* Grand Rapids: Eerdmans, 1975.

Thiselton, Anthony C. "Authority and Hermeneutics: Some Proposals for a New Agenda." Pages 107–41 in *A Pathway into the Holy Scripture.* Edited by P. E. Satterthwaite and D. F. Wright. Grand Rapids: Eerdmans, 1994.

———. *Interpreting God and the Postmodern Self: On Meaning, Manipulation, and Promise.* Grand Rapids: Eerdmans, 1995.

———. *New Horizons in Hermeneutics: The Theory and Practice of Transforming Biblical Reading.* Grand Rapids: Zondervan, 1992.

Tillich, Paul. *A History of Christian Thought.* New York: Simon & Schuster, 1968.

Todorov, Tzvetan. *Symbolism and Interpretation.* Ithaca, N.Y.: Cornell University Press, 1986.

Tompkins, Jane P., ed. *Reader-Response Criticism: From Formalism to Post Structuralism.* Baltimore: Johns Hopkins University Press, 1980.

Trible, Phyllis. "Depatriarchalizing in Biblical Interpretation." *JAAR* 41 (1973): 30–48.

———. *Rhetorical Criticism: Context, Method, and the Book of Jonah.* Minneapolis: Fortress, 1994.

Tucker, Gene. *Form Criticism of the Old Testament.* Philadelphia: Fortress, 1971.

Tuckett, Christopher. *Reading the New Testament: Methods of Interpretation.* Philadelphia: Fortress, 1987.

Tull, Patricia K. "Rhetorical Criticism and Intertextuality." Pages 156–80 in *To Each Its Own Meaning: An Introduction to Biblical Criticisms and Their Application.* Edited by Steven L. McKenzie and Stephen R. Hayes. Louisville: Westminster John Knox, 1999.

Van Til, Cornelius. *The New Hermeneutic.* Nutley, N.J.: Presbyterian and Reformed, 1977.

Vattimo, G. *Beyond Interpretation: The Meaning of Hermeneutics for Philosophy.* Translated by D. Webb. Cambridge, Eng.: Polity, 1997.

Virkler, Henry A., and Karelynne Gerber Ayayo. *Hermeneutics: Principles and Processes of Biblical Interpretation.* Grand Rapids: Baker Academic, 2007.

Waetjen, Herman C. *A Reordering of Power: A Socio-Political Reading of Mark's Gospel.* Minneapolis: Fortress, 1989.

Walhout, Clarence, and Leland Ryken, eds. *Contemporary Literary Theory: A Christian Appraisal.* Grand Rapids: Eerdmans, 1991.

Walker, Alice. *In Search of Our Mother's Gardens: Womanist Prose.* San Diego: Harcourt Brace Jovanovich, 1983.

Warner, M., ed. *The Bible as Rhetoric.* London: Routledge, 1990.

Watson, E. G. E. *Classical Hebrew Poetry.* JSOTSup 26. Sheffield: JSOT, 1984.

Weeden, Theodore. "The Heresy that Necessitated Mark's Gospel." In *The Interpretation of Mark.* Edited by William Telford. Minneapolis: Fortress, 1985.

Weinfeld, Moshe. "Ancient Near Eastern Patterns in Prophetic Literature." *VT* 27 (April, 1977).

————. *Deuteronomy and the Deuteronomic School.* Oxford: Oxford University Press, 1972.

Weinsheimer, J. *Philosophical Hermeneutics and Literary Theory.* New Haven: Yale University Press, 1991.

West, G. *Biblical Hermeneutics of Liberation: Modes of Reading the Bible in the South African Context.* 2d ed. Maryknoll: Orbis, 1995.

White, H. C. *Speech Act Theory and Biblical Criticism. Semeia* 41 (1987).

Whitman, Jon. *Interpretation and Allegory: Antiquity to the Modern Period.* Leiden: Brill, 2003.

Wilder, A. *The Bible and the Literary Critic.* Minneapolis: Augsburg Fortress, 1991.

William, James G. *Gospel Against Parable: Mark's Language of Mystery.* Sheffield: Almond, 1985.

Williams, Delores S. *Sisters in the Wilderness: Womanist God-Talk.* Maryknoll: Orbis, 1993.

Wilson, Robert R. *Sociological Approaches to the Old Testament.* Philadelphia: Fortress, 1984.

Wimsatt, William K., Jr. *Hateful Contraries.* Lexington: University of Kentucky Press, 1965.

Wimsatt, Warren K., and Monroe C. Beardsley. *The Verbal Icon: Studies in the Meaning of Poetry.* Lexington: University of Kentucky Press, 1954.

Worton, Michael, and Judith Still, eds. *Intertextuality: Theories and Practices.* Manchester, Eng.: Manchester University Press, 1990.

Woude, A. S. van der, ed. *The World of the Old Testament.* Grand Rapids: Eerdmans, 1989.

Wright, Addison G. *The Literary Genre Midrash.* Staten Island, N.Y.: Alba House, 1967.

Yarbro, D., ed. *Feminist Perspectives on Biblical Scholarship.* Chico, Calif.: Scholars Press, 1985.

Yarchin, William. *History of Biblical Interpretation: A Reader.* Peabody, Mass.: Hendrickson, 2004.

Yee, Gale A., ed. *Judges and Method: New Approaches in Biblical Studies.* Minneapolis: Fortress, 1995.

Index of Modern Authors

Index of Subjects

absence, 4, 58, 100, 165, 204, 216, 261, 263
actant, 295–96
aesthetic object, 205, 206, 209, 216
aesthetic pole, 192, 196, 216, 229
aesthetics of reception, 318
African-American criticism, 298, 300
Afrocentric aesthetics, 299
allegory, 4, 95, 96, 100–101, 104, 137, 149, 150, 156, 173, 333
allusion, 124, 136, 246–51, 263
ambiguity, 110, 117, 118, 153, 197, 198, 216, 225, 226, 274, 284, 305, 306
anticipation, 43, 108
antithetical parallelism, 129
apocalypse, 100, 138, 171–76, 184, 185
apocalyptic cosmology, 172
apocrypha, 67, 69–71, 226
apophthegm, 147
apostolic pronouncement, 164
apostrophe, 96, 97, 100, 131
archaeology, 80
archetype, 93, 99, 100, 104, 125, 174, 284
aretology, 141, 142
artistic pole, 192, 196, 216, 229
artistic work, 229
author-centered criticism, 73, 74
authorial intent, 13, 274, 294
authorial intention, 3, 20, 185, 295
authorial meaning, 13, 19
autobiographical criticism, 230–32, 234
autobiographical notes, 163
autobiography, 236
autonomous object, 13, 229

background studies, 6, 11, 18, 19, 20, 38, 40, 46, 267, 280
base, 203, 307, 331
basic dictionary, 213, 217

benediction, 160, 164
binary opposition, 293, 296, 315
biography, 141, 142, 143, 177, 185
boundaries, 5, 80, 82, 255–57, 260, 263, 286, 321, 323, 341

canonical criticism, 82–84, 293
captatio benevolentiae, 169, 177
Catholic Letters, 165, 177
cause to effect, 130
characterization, 91, 102, 104, 106, 108, 110, 112, 113, 116, 117, 126, 135–37, 139, 151, 157, 178, 183, 332, 335
chronistic history, 184
climax, 183
closing, 158–60, 164, 177, 339
codes, 4, 6, 89, 91–93, 176, 177, 195, 293, 294, 300, 340
common frames of reference, 214, 215, 217
comparative study, 46, 47, 49, 50, 51, 71, 266
complexity, 117, 201, 284, 313, 335, 337
complication, 104, 110, 136, 139
conceptual inspiration, 225, 226
conceptualization, 192, 193, 217
concordance, 28, 29, 36
concretization, 15, 113, 193, 217
confessional statement, 168, 177
configuration, 231, 262, 263, 327, 341
conflict, 38, 104, 110, 112, 133, 136, 139, 172, 254
congruence, 284
connotative meaning, 295
consistency-building, 206
content, 60, 70, 89, 91, 92, 100, 101, 126, 166, 167, 186, 195, 214, 223, 325, 335, 336
contextual and circumstantial selections, 213, 214, 217
contrast, 92, 98, 112, 116, 300

Index of Scriptures and Other Ancient Sources